DIALOGUES WITH A TRICKSTER

DIALOGUES WITH A TRICKSTER

*On the Margins of Myth
and Ethnography in the Marshall Islands*

Phillip H. McArthur

University of Hawai'i Press

Honolulu

Library of Congress Cataloging-in-Publication Data

Names: McArthur, Phillip H., author.
Title: Dialogues with a trickster : on the margins of myth and ethnography
 in the Marshall Islands / Phillip H. McArthur.
Description: Honolulu : University of Hawaiʻi Press, [2024] | Includes
 bibliographical references and index.
Identifiers: LCCN 2024002852 (print) | LCCN 2024002853 (ebook) | ISBN
 9780824897611 (hardback) | ISBN 9780824898892 (trade paperback) | ISBN
 9780824898779 (epub) | ISBN 9780824898786 (kindle edition) | ISBN
 9780824898762 (pdf)
Subjects: LCSH: Ethnology—Marshall Islands. | Folklore—Marshall Islands.
 | Marshallese—Intellectual life.
Classification: LCC GN671.M33 M34 2024 (print) | LCC GN671.M33 (ebook) |
 DDC 305.8009968/3—dc23/eng/20240514
LC record available at https://lccn.loc.gov/2024002852
LC ebook record available at https://lccn.loc.gov/2024002853

Cover photograph: Kometo Albōt, 1993. Photograph courtesy of the author.
Cover design: Melissa Olaivar Wong.

CONTENTS

Acknowledgments — vii

Orthography, Spelling, Pronunciation, Translation — xi

Transcription Conventions — xv

Prologue: Ethnographic Sorrow — 1

Chapter 1
In the Grip of a Trickster: Mythic (W)Holes
and Ethnographic Entanglements — 8

Chapter 2
Narrative Tricks: The Poetics of "Truthiness"
and Ambivalent Analogies — 41

Chapter 3
Dialogic Riddling: Cosmological Musings and the Kinship of Power — 78

Chapter 4
Hide-and-Seek: The Social Ideologies of Deception and Revelation — 115

Chapter 5
A Trickster's Tropes: Magic on the Margins of Political Power
and Christianity — 151

Chapter 6
Dirty and Dangerous Tricks: Taking Dialogic Risks — 187

Chapter 7
Portending Death: Life-Affirming Laughter
and the Telltale Sign of the Trickster — 222

Epilogue: Ethnographic Exit — 249

Notes   255

References   267

Index   279

ACKNOWLEDGMENTS

This book has been long in the making. It needed time to incubate, and I needed time to manage a range of accountabilities, and time to find a satisfactory method of representation to do justice to a remarkable trickster storyteller, the late Kometo Albōt, and his riM̧ajeļ (Marshall Islander) culture. He is the focus of this book. My deepest thanks and affection go to him. He was not only among my primary teachers in the language (Kajin M̧ajeļ) and culture (*m̧anit in* M̧ajeļ), but also proved to be a patient tutor, brilliant storyteller, insightful cultural philosopher, delightfully funny conversationalist, and, most poignantly, a dear friend. He long ago passed away, but I pay tribute to his memory and to the legacy he leaves for his descendants.

I wish to give my sincerest thanks to the numerous riM̧ajeļ who welcomed me into their homes, offered their food to me and my family, and opened their minds and hearts so I could gain a glimpse into the profundity of their culture and integrity of their lives. I was privileged to be included in their conversations, stories, celebrations, fishing adventures, and social lives. They have been collaborators with whom I have engaged in the most rewarding dialogues. To name everyone would break the trust many of them placed in me. But among those who so openly and graciously offered their time to instruct me include M̧ake, Kijdik George, Anidep Abija, Iban Edwin, Kiat Benjamin, Marie Kabua Madison, Carmen Bigler, Jormeto Moreañ, Piñōl, Aniloñ Aelon, William Swain, Turlañ Jaik, Kaminaga Kaminaga, Anless Mark, Roman Mark, Julitha Alik, Ezekiah Taraua, Mimi Mame, Carson Ainja, Almi David, Kewam Aine, Modern Rignino, Kom Aoimake, Yobi Ueno, Terry Mote, Obit Mote, Amima Alik, Wōjlā Brand, Yashio Kajela, Laibwōjtok Lane, Neibōj Lane, Neilani Ackley, David Ackley, and Forrest Heine. I need to more fully recognize two riM̧ajeļ in particular, both of whom have also passed away. Neito Lane, who adopted me years ago into her matrilineage, became my older sister (*jeiū*) who fed me, nursed me when sick, and counseled me in all things riM̧ajeļ. She represented the strength, dignity, composure, brilliance, and elegance of the most distinguished riM̧ajeļ women. Her husband, Lani Lane, both a grandson of a paramount chief (*ļajjibjib*) and a lineage head (*aļab*), fastidiously schooled me in the depth and richness of cultural meanings and social protocols. Over thirty years, they served as my instructors and tutors in the Kajin Ṃajeḷ language and riṂajeḷ culture, my mentors in how to culturally behave, and unfailingly offered the warmth and affection of their home and family. Their consistent hospitality and care for my wife and children will never be forgotten. I sincerely thank them and all the riṂajeḷ who so freely and openly shared their lives, culture, and friendship. *Ilo kautiej, ij kaṃṃoolol komuij wōtōmjej kōn ami jouj im jibañ. Iban meḷokḷok kom.*

I wish to express gratitude to my mother, Esther, and late father, Vaun, for their consistency (and so often financial support), for having taught me to treat others with dignity, and for encouraging me to seek understanding of the world and people, and report what I thought worth reporting. My oldest children, Brook and Ajri, spent two years of their young lives in the Marshall Islands, adapting to all situations and forming deeply impactful friendships. Along with their younger sibling, Maia (born in the Marshall Islands), followed by their youngest sibling, Elijah (born in Hawai'i), they were all raised within a context of rich cultural engagement and a constant flow of riṂajeḷ visitors to their home, many of whom came to stay for years. Their thoughtful consideration of our riṂajeḷ family and friends was always satisfying and inspiring. And now, as adults, it is clear that many of their intercultural sensibilities and competencies come from a deep association with the riṂajeḷ and their culture. To express gratitude to my wife, Elaine, will fall short of any thanks I may offer. In addition to being my best friend and partner, her temperance, poise, and vision have inspired not only this work but also my life. I am most thankful for her patience, encouragement, motivation, and insight on everything from riṂajeḷ ethnography to how to live life with compassion and grace. She fully embraced the riṂajeḷ, learned their language, and entered into lifelong relationships of reciprocity and friendship. I am also grateful for her countless discussions about this work, seemingly endless reads and edits of the manuscript, and unfailing encouragement to carry on. She more than anyone recognized the value of bringing Kometo's voice forward and reminding the world of the quality and character of riṂajeḷ lives.

I am grateful for the financial support from the Wenner-Gren Foundation for Anthropological Research, the John D. and Katherine T. MacArthur Foundation, the Indiana Center for Global Change and World Peace, the Indiana University Graduate School, and the generosity of Gregory Schrempp in the initial stages of my research. I have received generous support from Brigham Young University Hawai'i with release time and faculty development/travel grants over the years to return to the Marshall Islands on shorter research trips, and to share my work with colleagues at professional conferences. Several peers and administrators at BYU Hawaiʻi offered encouragement, stimulating conversations, or both, including Jeffrey Burroughs, Jeff Belnap, Keith Roberts, Tēvita Kaʻili, Kali Fermantez, Yifen Beus, David Beus, Alohalani Housman, Paul Spickard, Matt Kester, Hiagi Wesley, Rose Ram, Dale Robertson, and Jill Terry Rudy at the BYU Provo campus. Valued colleagues also greatly informed this work through their prodigious scholarship, constructive feedback, and encouragement, including Beverly Stoeltje, Richard Bauman, Gregory Schrempp, Patricia Sawin, Rory Turner, Katie Borland, Ilana Harlow, Donald Brenneis, and Laurence Carucci.

I am also grateful to the helpful staff at the University of Hawaiʻi Press, including Emma Ching for her professionalism, thorough feedback, and ushering this project through to publication, Annalisa Zox-Weaver for her exceptionally careful read and detailed copy editing, Gianna Marsella for her competent managing editing, and Christi Stanforth for her proofreading. The technical support of Ajri McArthur with the cosmogonic genealogy charts and map creation, and Elaine's assistance with preparing the image of Kometo proved immensely helpful.

Lastly, in keeping with my commitment to Kometo, to avoid taking him or myself too seriously, this work, as we once playfully concluded, represents the "knowledge of fools." But as with all good tricksters, such a disclaimer may also come with a power to see, understand, act, and penetrate into the deepest reaches of culture and the human experience.

Orthography, Spelling, Pronunciation, Translation

An orthography and spelling for the Marshall Islander language (Kajin M̧ajeļ) was first developed by missionaries from the American Board of Commissioners for Foreign Missions after their arrival in 1857. With the translation of the Bible, the riM̧ajeļ (Marshallese) converts quickly took to literacy, so that by the end of the nineteenth century the majority of the population was literate, and are to this day.

Mutually intelligible language dialects correspond to the two island chains: the Ratak (sunrise or eastern) and the Rālik (sunset or western). Because the Christian mission first took root in the Rālik chain, its dialect was used for the earliest Bible translations, which subsequently privileged its orthographic spellings in most written communications and the development of the earliest education materials (see Walsh and Heine 2012).

In 2010, the Republic of the Marshall Islands Government adopted and standardized the Kajin M̧ajeļ orthography and spelling found in the *Marshallese-English Dictionary* (Abo, Bender, Capelle, and Debrum 1976). Since then, it has been taught in the public schools, although much of the population continues to use the old biblical orthography and spellings. I use this official orthography and spelling for all of the Kajin M̧ajeļ terms and sentences that I present. The first time I identify a proper place-name, I use both the new and former common spellings, and thereafter only the new spelling.

Kajin M̧ajeļ Pronunciation Guide

Orthography	International Phonetic Alphabet	Description (only approximations in English)
a	[ɑ]	a low back unrounded vowel ("lot")
ā	[æ]	a low front vowel ("get")
b	[bᵚ]	a heavy bilateral voiced stop ("big")

d	[ɹ]	a light retroflex trill—on alveolar ridge ("go*tt*a")
e	[e] or [ɛ]	a mid front vowel ("g*a*te")
i	[i]	a high front vowel ("f*ee*t")
j	[tʸ] or [c]	a light dental stop or affricate ("cra*z*e"; "ju*dg*e"; "mat*ch*")
k	[k] or [kʷ]	a velar voiceless and voiced stop, unrounded or rounded ("*c*ap"; or "*g*ourd")
l	[lʸ]	a light lateral ("*l*ight")
ḷ	[lɯ]	a heavy lateral ("*l*ove")
m	[mʸ]	a light bilabial nasal ("*m*elt")
ṃ	[mɯ]	a heavy bilabial nasal, unrounded or rounded ("*m*arch")
n	[nʸ]	a light dental nasal ("*n*eat")
ṇ	[nɯ] or [nʷ]	a heavy dental nasal, unrounded or rounded ("*n*oon")
ñ	[ŋ] or [ŋʷ]	a velar nasal, unrounded or rounded ("si*ng*")
o	[o] or [ɔ]	a mid back rounded vowel ("t*o*ne")
ọ	[ɒ]	a low back rounded vowel ("c*oa*t")
ō	[ə] or [ʌ]	a mid back unrounded vowel ("r*u*n")
p	[pʸ]	a light voiceless bilabial stop ("*p*en")
r	[rɯ] or [rʷ]	a heavy retroflex trill, unrounded and rounded; Spanish ("*r*ío")
t	[tɯ]	a heavy voiceless and voiced dental stop ("*t*ip")
u	[u]	a high back rounded vowel ("d*ue*")
ū	[ɯ]	a high back unrounded vowel ("t*oo*k")
w	[w]	a rounded velar glide ("*w*ave")
y	[y]	a rounded palatal glide ("*y*ard")

Linguistic translation requires assuming accountability to render the words of another in a manner consistent with the denotative and connotative meanings as well as the grammatical patterns of the language. And such a rendering needs to be accomplished without overwhelming the reader with an excessively literal translation that may come across as stilted, cumbersome, or confusing. Even so, I prioritize transcriptions and translations that retain a feel for the formal features of tense, aspect, voice, possessives, and deictics that form an important part of riM̧ajeļ discourse and storytelling. With such fidelity to language subtleties and sensibilities, however, I have also sought to avoid making Indigenous speakers appear exotic, limited in vocabulary, without grammar, or lacking poetry. The current length of the book prohibits providing interlineal texts for all translations. Nonetheless, when a Kajin M̧ajeļ term or phrase is indispensable to the cultural and Indigenous understanding I seek to address, I will include it to clarify its meaning or grammatical function.

Working with the Kajin M̧ajeļ language for over forty years (total of four years' residence in the islands; hosting many riM̧ajeļ abroad in our home for over six years total; continued engagement with the community on Oʻahu for nearly three decades), I am sensitive to the politics of translation and transcription. In representing another's words and mediating them for a readership, I have sought to responsibly secure the integrity of my subject's speech in a manner that retains the character of his voice and the Indigenous language he used to express himself.

TRANSCRIPTION CONVENTIONS

Initials on the left margin mark the change of speaker. For example, [K] for Kometo, [P] for Phillip, etc.

Narrative renderings, dialogues, interrogatives (questions), and metanarration (a comment or explanation about the narrative, the action, characters, and scene as well as breakaway explanations about its meaning) are indented once from left margin.

Narration is *italicized*.

Narrative lines are determined by clear pauses at the end of sentences and transitional adverbs.

Breaks in narrative action receive an additional return space.

<Text> in arrow brackets provides contextual explanations and paralinguistic and nonverbal communication features.

(Words) in parentheses identify meanings implied in translation as well as my vocalization during the performance of a narrative.

[Words] in square brackets identify clarifications made to the text.

UPPERCASE type indicates significant increase in volume.

{Words and phrases} in brackets indicate a significant increase in tempo.

<u>Words or phrases</u> underlined indicate a stretching out and slow slurring of speech.

/ / Forward slashes signal the overlapping voices of speakers.

~ Tilde symbols bracketing text in *~ALL CAPS AND ITALICS ~* indicate a significant rise in pitch used with song and chant.

An em dash—identifies an incomplete statement or immediate transition into another without completing the thought.

The ellipses . . . signals a key break or short pause.

Several nonlexical sounds not part of the vocabulary are retained such as *mmm, eee,* and *ooo* to capture the speech dynamic. The colloquial "Eh" presents a low front vowel [æ] sound that drops into a short aspiration, and could be translated as "yes" or "that's right." Since the storyteller uses it so often, the expression is captured without translation.

In transcribing all the dialogues and narrative texts, I retain the contour of the interactions, including occasional ungrammatical and broken speech, rephrasing in sometimes redundant ways, and midsentence jumps to another topic, even when it breaks up the narrative flow, to show the dynamic interplay between interlocutors and to reveal how the performance and meaning of the text is emergent in context.

I am responsible for all transcriptions and translations, with some assistance from Indigenous riM̧ajeḷ: Julitha Alik, Kaminaga Kaminaga, Anless Mark, and Romon Mark.

PROLOGUE
Ethnographic Sorrow

With the afternoon stubbornly moving toward sunset, the stillness and oppressive humidity of the equatorial air weighed heavily upon me. This was one of those stagnant moments when not even the lightest palm stirs. It had just rained the hour before, but now the late afternoon sun had once again emerged steadily to accentuate the saturated air, so thick and moist that both lungs and skin feel burdened by the teeming droplets. I had learned from the riM̧ajeļ that there is no value in complaint, but much to be understood through the monotony of endurance.[1] But this time my motivation for perseverance was accentuated, because I knew a piece of my life was slipping away and I wanted to absorb all before me. I sat on a woven pandanus-leaf mat facing my beloved seventy-nine-year-old friend Kometo Albōt (pronounced kɔmɛtɔ albət), with whom I had sat countless hours over the years listening to his playful storytelling, sly communications, and philosophizing. It had been two years since I left the islands with my young family in 1993. I was able to return the following year (1994) for three months to serve as a mediator in a development project, but unfortunately, I could only visit with him briefly while passing through his island on the way to other remote destinations. Now he lived with one of his daughters on the capital atoll, Mājro (Majuro), in a plywood and corrugated tin house with a cement floor. Only the strewn mats on the floor offered any semblance of a traditional riM̧ajeļ home. When I inquired at the door with his relatives whether he was home, his daughter smiled and said, "Io̧kwe Ļakūbwe" (or "Hello, Ļakūbwe," my nickname in the Kajin M̧ajeļ language is a term of endearment for the youngest male sibling, but also literally means "male excrement").[2] "I'm pleased you came to see him this last time." The words "last time" made me shudder.

It's peculiar what kinds of thoughts creep in when emotions run high, but as I looked through the doorway at his old, half-naked body lying almost lifeless on the mat, I thought, "What a place for Kometo to die," and my mind rushed back to the time he and I had wandered the trails of his home atoll Mile (Mili) (pronounced milɛ), where he told me stories of his childhood, about World War II when he served as a scout for the US military, swimming over the reef after dark, sneaking through the Japanese encampments, swimming back out to inform the soldiers of strategic locations they would then bomb the following day; about how he had lost most of the fingers on his right hand in a fishing accident; and about the stories of Letao,[3] the riM̧ajeḷ trickster. He most often told me about this trickster, who, according to riM̧ajeḷ storytellers, traveled on to America in the mythological past. We joked often—laughed to the point of crying (that deep, visceral laughter), not just about the subversive antics of Letao, but about all the allusions to how he, my friend, and I were tricksters in our own right, moving between our cultural worlds, illuminating ambiguities, and celebrating them.

And now, as I looked down at his dying body, I recalled how he had often explained that Letao brought death, but we could also trust he would return it with life. He had asked me once if I could return his body for burial on his home atoll. But all I could think of in that moment was how I could not deliver; I would be leaving the islands the next day, unable to load his body on the boat to take him there. When notification came that he had died three months later, I could only send money to his family hoping it would pay the transportation cost. I learned later they buried him just ocean-side from where he died.

When I crawled into the room in which he slept, his daughter told me he could only lie down and was too weak to sit up. She then encouraged me to wake him and called, "Father, wake up, your companion is here." When he opened his eyes, he grinned, struggled, but managed to sit up after all, faced me, and then offered his trademark toothless smile (all gums).

In his high-pitched raspy voice, he declared, "Ah, my friend, you have returned again, like Letao the trickster," and then he laughed. We talked. I wanted to savor each of his words, his smile (a persistent gleam), his cadence, his deliberateness. I wanted to hold on, not to some ethnographic ideal, but to my friend, my experiences, this effort to peel away the layers of culture, to this intersubjective experience that was deeply meaningful to me. We reviewed our times together, made references to some of our old jokes, the stories he had told, but sometimes, we just sat in silence, both of us groping for the right last words. High humid heat and sorrow make a poor combination. You feel (and sometimes wish) you could just melt away. The sun began to set, and I knew I needed to go. "Letao brings both laughter and sorrow," he quietly said, "We have known both." "Kometo," I offered, voice cracking, "you will forever be my friend and teacher." He reached out and grabbed my hand softly. Through tears he smiled, and nodded his head. "Goodbye my friend." I left. I had held my composure to watery eyes during our conversation, but as I walked away from his house, it seemed like a scripted tale, the sun setting in brilliant colors across the lagoon, the air still and quiet, and all I could hear were my sobs and the crunch of gravel under my sandals.

Kometo Albōt

But much of my sorrow as I walked away was mixed with a dis-ease that comes with my waning postmodern sensibilities. Instead of feeling a confirmation that I had achieved entrée and security with my own ethnographic tale of acceptance, deep personal feelings made my academic project seem cold and dishonest. Cold because my approach to myth and social life has been an interpretive exercise into cultural semantics, and dishonest because of the great leap I had made from personal experience to writing ethnography. I had also come to doubt whether my research with an Indigenous people was "respectful, ethical, sympathetic, and useful" (Tuhiwai Smith 2012, 9). The challenge, however, is not simply critical self-reflexivity, but to not forget that dialogues and conversation produce what we "know," and that we must critically engage how "they" also position "us."

I possess copious tapes that record my interviews with Kometo and many others, conversations full of stories, notes, and journal accounts about him, some that go back over forty years when I first lived on the islands long before pursuing a career in folklore and anthropology. It was as a young volunteer missionary (1982–1984) with The Church of Jesus Christ of Latter-day Saints (Mormons) that I first met Kometo. I was attracted to his lighthearted wit and we became good friends. As we were becoming friends, each Sunday morning I would stand on the lagoon shore next to an old deteriorating edifice that had once served as a bar, but was now used as the church building for the fledgling Mormon congregation. I would look out across the lagoon to see if I could detect his old, battered eight-foot aluminum (World War II surplus) boat breaking through the waves ferrying his grandchildren from a small islet about five miles away. As he would come onto shore, I would take the rope he would toss me and help pull the boat onto the sand and coral rocks. He would comb over his wet wind-blown gray hair then disappear into a small back room of the building to change his clothes from shorts and a T-shirt to a pair of black zipperless string-tied dress pants and a white shirt, yellowed over the years. He was usually the first congregant to arrive even before those within walking distance or who could travel by car. As we waited for people to gather, we would sit and "just talk-story" (*bwebwenato bajjek*), and he would gently correct my pronunciation and grammar, and expose me to more of the Kajin Ṃajeḷ vocabulary. Once during a very low tide, I walked with my Samoan missionary companion and others along the reef to visit him on his small isolated islet (where he and only his grandchildren resided) and spent the night. With faces illuminated by a kerosene wick lamp, it was perhaps the first time for me to hear traditional riṂajeḷ narratives. I only caught a little about the stories he told, but I do vividly remember the joy in his teasing voice and laughter. Over time and under the tutelage of many other islanders who were gracious enough to teach me, my language skills were enhanced, so that by the end of my initial nineteen-month stay in the islands, the topics of my weekly conversations with Kometo ranged from Judeo-Christian and Indigenous cosmologies, to discussions on Western and Indigenous religious practices, from explanations of matrilineal kinship and chiefly authority to the local flora, marine life, fishing techniques, traditional foods, and sailing. It was with Kometo and my adoptive riṂajeḷ family that my nascent interest in riṂajeḷ mythology and ceremonial practices began to take shape.

When I returned to conduct ethnographic fieldwork some years later (1991–1993) on the role of oral traditions and cultural performances in contemporary social life,[4] I found that Kometo had moved from the isolated islet across the lagoon to Teḷap islet, linked by road to the populated city center of Ṃajro atoll. I never assumed that Kometo would become a primary source. I wanted to renew our friendship, and only after several months working with many others did our unique relationship emerge. I discovered, contrary to his disclaimers, that he epitomized one of those individuals who knew and thought much about myth, culture, history, and social power. I had planned to stay away from church connections to maintain some sense of objectivity and to secure perspectives from the broader population of Indigenous riM̧ajeļ. But as our renewed relationship developed, I added him to my pool of ethnographic interlocutors, and I came to admit that every ethnographer finds points of entrée due to a variety of socially motivated locations that will shape their particular gaze (Rosaldo 1989). And now our conversations had changed. As an ethnographer, my engagement with all my "kin" (*nukwi*) and several other associations over a two-year period led to new levels of language competence, especially to a fuller vocabulary no longer circumscribed by my previous ecclesiastical role. I had also returned with a family, which allowed me to assume a different position in the community and participate in a wider range of social events and conversations. So, when I began to work more closely with Kometo and ask more systematically crafted research questions, he became even more deliberate and nuanced in his instructions about language, cultural meanings, social life, and mythology. And he became more playfully sly within our dialogues, and less guarded about the trickster stories he would tell me.

While I did not anticipate that Kometo would be among my key interlocutors and teachers, I most certainly did not foresee how he would become so enmeshed in my family's life. My wife, Elaine, and Kometo became fast friends. Besides her closest riM̧ajeļ women friends, Kometo was one of the few men who would often joke with her, as their sociological positioning (almost a grandfather/granddaughter pattern) allowed such familiarity and levity; although out of propriety within intergender relations he still refrained from rehearsing some of the "profane" trickster stories in her presence. And our children (a six-to-eight-year-old son and four-to-six-year-old daughter at the time) grew quite attached to Kometo, playing in and around his home as their father spent innumerable hours visiting with him. They also came to expect him to frequently join us for meals or travel with us to the cultural and political events I wished to document, or to attend the broader community ceremonies and celebrations among families, villages, schools, and churches. We also all traveled with him to his home atoll, Mile, and stayed on his inheritance land. The children enjoyed his contagious laughter and would often listen in even when they could not follow most of the conversations in Kajin Ṃajeļ, just to watch him laugh. Like Elaine, they also responded to his gentleness; Kometo possessed the gift of interpersonal warmth and friendliness that drew all people to him, most assuredly my family. Because he was so dear to us, we had decided to give the name Kometo to our third child, if a boy, who would be born in the Marshall Islands. But when our anticipated baby was a girl, we gave her a middle name after the woman (Neito) who had adopted me into her family and matrilineage many years before and who was Elaine's cherished friend.

I have returned to the Marshall Islands on numerous occasions, never more than a three-month stay, to aid a variety of education, development, and research projects. And our home in Hawai'i over the past twenty-nine years has become a weigh station for many riṂajeḷ in transit to the US mainland. Some of those with whom we share "classificatory" kinship ties have come to stay longer, to obtain medical attention—the result of exposure to radiation from the nuclear bomb testing and other health conditions. Several of our younger riṂajeḷ relatives have lived with us from several months to five to six years to complete high school or attend college. Our participation with the riṂajeḷ community on O'ahu continues to involve us in occasional church services, and broader social gatherings and celebrations from traditional ceremonies to weddings and funerals. At many of these events, I am called upon to deliver speeches (*jibij*), and oratory (*kwaḷok naan*) on behalf of our kin group, and more frequently, as a person who holds seniority. So, my relationships to the riṂajeḷ are personal, which engenders reflection on my methods of representation, to explore ways to more candidly write an ethnography that is accountable and responsible to those I write about within the ignominious context of colonial and imperial abuses. I seek to allow this ethnography to ethically breathe, to account for my positioning, how I came to know what I know as I unpacked with Kometo a range of riṂajeḷ mythologies and epistemologies, and to not allow Kometo's voice to become masked by generalities and descriptions of an anonymous other.

Colonial religions represent just one of the influences on Kometo's storytelling and philosophizing as he sometimes placed them into dialogue with Indigenous cosmologies and mythologies. Their influence on him is certainly not the only one, and not always the dominant one. More often our dialogues entertained issues of American imperial abuses and riṂajeḷ epistemologies and conceptions of power. Nonetheless, through our conversations, he brought to view some of the less-than-transparent "messy entanglements" (Diaz 2010, 18) of colonial religions with an Indigenous culture. I came to recognize how Kometo represents a complex, mediated subject responding to both deep cultural sensibilities and a recent imperial history in his islands. And, most tellingly, he taught me how the trickster offers a decolonizing alternative that presses back against American imperialism and Western ideologies, including religion, to form historically specific and unanticipated "articulations" (Diaz 2010, 22) of his Indigenous agency and subjectivity. Through his trickster stories and sly commentary, he blurred, twisted, subverted, and rendered ambiguous insider and outsider categories along the margins of myth and the ethnographic method.

By nature, or by habit, I am not sure, Kometo always had a joyous gleam in his eyes. His toothless smile was contagious (even when serious, his permanent grin made it seem like he was always on the verge of laughter), his gray, nearly always ruffled hair was charming, his high-pitched voice was joyful and endearing, and his laughter was consuming and electric. I cannot, in writing, convey the tone of his voice or the flavor of his chuckles and laughter, which were both mesmerizing and comforting. Even now, as I listen again to our conversations many years later, I am as drawn to his cadence, dynamics, and timbre as I am to the content of his words. I cannot but smile again as I know he was smiling, and I cannot but laugh again as he laughs, a laughter that turns to tears.

CHAPTER 1

In the Grip of a Trickster

Mythic (W)Holes and Ethnographic Entanglements

Ethnographic writing is typically an inductive exercise. We move from the multiplicity of specific utterances, observations, and experiences, and then write about singular wholes. But I am interested in holes: holes in cultural boundaries, holes in historical imaginations, even holes in the self. Holes provide openings; things pass in and out of them, creating dynamic reconfigurations. Writing about "a culture" can present a subtle sleight of hand between the general and the specific; a critical ethnography seeks representational accountability to diversity, nonetheless translation and demonstration force us to use words as etic labels, creating the appearance of wholes circumscribing variety and difference into categories of similarity. We generalize from individual utterances to cultural and social patterns, systems, and epistemologies. I am not taking on the limits or vicissitudes of language here; others have productively spilled ample poststructuralist ink toward this purpose. Rather, I am more interested in how we get "from here to there"; from individual moments and individual people, to adjectival statements about the "cultural," or even the more dubious objective statements about "The Culture."

When much of the ethnographic intent is to provide general cultural statements and contextual information about "a tradition," all too often individual personalities such as Kometo's and the stories they tell sometimes blur and disappear. Scientific respectability encourages us to seek breadth, and even though we know we cannot be exhaustive, we must at least try to be proficiently representative. But we also know that the overwhelming number of our descriptions, stories, and conclusions tend to come from but a few key individuals who are both knowledgeable and amenable to satisfying our requests. And though biography, life history, and the relationship between repertoire and the individual represent profitable folkloristic ethnographic projects (Narayan 1989; Lawless 1993; Sawin 2004; Cashman 2016), more often, either the search for "authentic" traditions (Bendix 1997; Otero and Martinez-Rivera 2021) or socially systemic models retain a degree of methodological currency, especially in an age wherein national, transnational, and global considerations of flows, connections, and associations (Marcus 1998) have heightened our attention to the larger processes over the intimacy of lives lived and local interactions. But I propose here that the holes in intimate ethnographic conversations and performances themselves may open us up to a more nuanced understanding of the whole, the "cultural," and the "global."

My personal confession must not be confused as an attempt to absolve any accountability for articulating riM̧ajeḷ mythology, cosmology, storytelling, poetics, social relations, epistemologies, or Indigenous cultural meanings. These matters remain central to this folklore project, as I unpack Kometo's individual uses of the stories and the meanings he generated in ways that resonate with the Indigenous frameworks and paradigms offered by other riM̧ajeḷ. Indeed, my deepest sensibilities of riM̧ajeḷ culture basically came from him and a handful of others, despite my effort to learn from as wide a range of people as was practicable. The ethnographic details I weave around our dialogues and Kometo's performance of Indigenous narratives represent a general understanding of the culture developed through interviews, observations, and deep immersion with numerous riM̧ajeḷ from a broad cross section of society including women and men, the old and the young, titled individuals as well as commoners, and from a range of atolls, clans, religious affiliations, and political parties.

Kometo's repertoire, opinions, and meanings are both unique to him as a situated subject and personality, and relatively common and shared by others. He helps to make manifest a version of the riM̧ajeḷ cultural world, but certainly not a conclusive one or the only one. I merely seek to clarify my point of departure, one in which I attempt to honestly reposition myself vis-à-vis my empirical data, my cross-cultural interlocutor, and what I write about him. I wish to make overt my own leap and that of the "other," from the personal to the large-scale. This leap requires following Kometo into the holes he created through his own discursive strategies and my engagement with those schemes. Within the primary corpus of stories he told me, and what became a running theme between us, were often repeated references to myths about the trickster figure, Letao. I collected more than twenty versions of Letao narratives from other storytellers, but none of them matched the range, poetics, clever plot development, and hilarity of Kometo's. So, mythological stories about Letao do form part of the riM̧ajeḷ body of cultural texts;[1] they are not simply a product of Kometo's idiosyncrasies and our peculiar relationship. But his performances and our discussions about them, and the intertextual links we made to other stories, foreground how ethnographic meaning takes shape in intimate settings. They provide the holes through which Kometo and I first entered into an ambiguous ethnographic friendship, and allowed us to explore riM̧ajeḷ myth along the margins of meaning and power.

For this reason, I will fill this folkloristic ethnography with copious intercultural talk, and in many ways inter-ethnographic talk (sometimes Kometo was as much the ethnographer as I), to show how narrative and conversational exegesis explored cultural meanings and facilitated a "sociology of folklore," or the ways in which traditional myths and vernacular strategies constitute and inform, in part, social relationships and the meaning of social power from the most intimate and local (including that between ethnographer and cross-cultural interlocutor) to the most far-reaching national and global relations in the context of imperialism. The first of these forms of discourse, mythic narrative, is familiar territory, but the second, intercultural dialogues generated through questions and answers—albeit the standard method of the ethnographic interview, will be considered a performance genre in its own right. In this way, my discussions do not obscure Kometo's voice or the conversations from which it emerged, and I will foreground those mythological, historical, cultural, and imperial voices that he engaged through his discourses. I seek to be ethnographically responsible and render as sensitively as possible the integrity of this extraordinary life. A single islander trickster in conversation with an ambiguously situated ethnographer will "collaboratively imagine a space" (Otero and Martinez-Rivera 2021, 21) to unpack much about Indigenous riM̧ajeļ mythic discourse and cultural epistemologies, and the experience of a late twentieth-century islander as colonial, imperial, and global powers increasingly intersected with his modern life.

In global terms, Kometo seems to occupy a marginal geographical, historical, political, and economic location. Yet this atoll dweller in the Marshall Islands, with his trickster discourses, decenters our top-down gaze so that we see how an Indigenous person may comprehend "the order of existence in the modern world in (his) own terms" (Stoeltje and Bauman 1989, 169), to create and re-create the meaning of his life. People, like Kometo, with "fewer resources" by virtue of their "social position are often some of the most talented at asserting agency . . . through the creative recycling of available and inherited expressive culture" (Cashman 2016, 231). Drawing upon a trickster mythology and ethos, the holes he opened in our dialogues allowed us to ascertain new possibilities about a riM̧ajeļ deep past and mythology.[2] It also demonstrates how he employed these cultural resources to offer commentary on imperial and Indigenous social power. By probing such holes, we groped toward a discovery of that elusive whole by way of a range of narrative resources and mythic allusions. Through our interactions, our differences were, paradoxically, at once accentuated and obfuscated. Some of our intercultural differences will become uncomfortably apparent; but even more so, I hope the deep interpersonal empathy and friendship that found liberation and mediation through entering discursive holes also come into view.

Peering into Holes

Kometo once taught me about how holes may prove deceptive and lead to important consequences. The following excerpt from one of our earliest dialogues in 1992 at his home on Mājro divulges much about the nature of riM̧ajeļ epistemological holes. His age mate M̧ake (pronounced m̧akɛ) also participated, while his adult daughter and four of his grandchildren listened in. M̧ake, a distant patrilineal relative and boyhood friend of Kometo, lived in the same compound of houses on Teļap islet of Mājro atoll, but participated with a different Christian religion and would most often join socially with his wife's matrilineal kin. I often found them playing a riM̧ajeļ style of checkers with coral pebbles when I went to visit with Kometo, as was the case on this particular day. During this conversation, Kometo was explaining the trouble Letao creates through deception and how he gives shape to the current state of affairs. He then broke through into a performance (Hymes 1975) of a Letao narrative. The initial [K] identifies Kometo; [P] identifies myself, as Phillip; and [M] identifies M̧ake. A guide to the transcription conventions is provided in the front matter.

This performance of a story from the deep past will acquaint us with a consequence of peering into holes.[3] The hole Letao uses in the subversive act is his anus.

P   Is the story of Letao a true story or just an *inoñ* [tale]?
K   It is also an *inoñ*.
P   But does it teach about true things?
M   Yes! They make stories about the way people will live from that time forward.
P   So Letao was a person? A real human?
K   A person—we don't know whether Letao is a human or not.
P   When I was on M̧aļoeļap [atoll] they said that Letao was really true, that he taught people how to make fire at Likiep [atoll].[4]
K   Eh.
P   So some stories of Letao are only *inoñ?*
K   No. You see stories of Letao—he can make fire, he can make all—
M   Every kind of thing.
K   He can become a papaya tree. He can become—what's the word? . . . *M̧m̧ak* [water-hole-in-tree]. It's the kind of thing on the side of those coconut trees up by the palms, which has water in a hole on the side. It is called "water-hole-in-tree." He can become like a person you see? It is hard to think about Letao. Letao is hard.
P   It is hard to what?

K   To think what, is he a human or not? <everyone laughs>
P   In any case, the stories about Letao do make people happy.
K   <laughing> Yes. <laughs>
P   Do you two know stories of Letao?
M   Oh. Kometo knows.
K   I have a few . . . Okay, do you two think the stories of Letao are true?

Letao is coming . . . coming-from-the-west of this atoll.
He comes on and on and on. Now—

There was a way of life, they say, "*kūttiliekek*" [hide-and-seek]."
P   Hide-and-seek?
K   Hide-and-seek. Like if the two of us just play and I go hide over there and
say, "YOU CAN'T SEE ME."
P   Oh! yes, yes.

K   *Okay, they were coming from over there.*

M   <to children trying to get closer to listen> Don't crowd too close here they
are telling stories!

K   *He comes and comes and then . . .*
He escaped from over there—escaped to here in the east. (uh huh)
Another man . . . he goes and hides.
He becomes a pandanus cluster. (mmm)
He hangs from on top of the tree.
The man says, <high pitched> "READY!"
Letao looks around, he says, {"AH HA THERE YOU ARE MAN."} <laughs>
Okay, his power is great.
Letao says, {"My turn."}
"Okay man, wait right there."
He goes and hides.
He goes and becomes a coconut tree—and makes a water-hole-in-tree.
<points to rear end>
<high pitched>*"READY!"*
Ah the other man looks around much, and then he is thirsty—

PEOPLE DO NOT HAVE NECKS YET. <laughing> When have humans
not had necks? <laughs hard>

The other man, he looks and looks, and then he is thirsty.
Then, he sees the water-hole-in-tree—the hole in the coconut tree.
He says, "Mmm."
Now, he goes to drink. <stretches neck as if putting his head into a hole>
It looks good—but it sinks down—the water sinks down. <laughs>
It just subsides, the water just sinks down. <all laugh hard>
He puts his head further in.
He tries again, it sinks away from him—
{Letao GRABS HOLD of his neck} <laughs loud, all laugh, inaudible words>

Is it true?

AND GRABS HOLD OF THE MAN.
HE {FLOPS AROUND, FLOPS AROUND, FLOPS AROUND.}
<much laughter by all>

By this we have necks. <laughing> Thus, the ancestors say. <laughs>[5]

P   Before that there were no necks?

K   <laughs> There were none. <everyone laughs hard> Okay, the stories of
      Letao will be what? <pause> Like those stories in those movies.

P   Those movies? What movies?

K   The murder movies. <laughs>

P   OH! The American movies? <much laughter by all>

I will discuss at length the themes of hiding, revealing, and deception in this book. But a few things stand out about holes in this first dialogue and narrative performance. First, this conversation presents much about the ambiguity of certain kinds of discourse. Instead of rigid generic categories, stories about the trickster present a slippery kind of discourse, indeed. In my attempt to create some clarity on riM̧ajeḷ genre classifications as they relate to Letao, Kometo pokes holes in any possible schema I seek to pin down. *Ino̧ñ* in Kajin M̧ajeḷ can be tentatively translated as "fantasy," "a story not believed to be true," or "a tale." I also found that, in some circumstances, the islanders will also use *ino̧ñ* interchangeably with *riab,* to "lie" or tell a falsehood. And then, in other contexts, they will employ it to describe folklore generally, and even myth, especially for stories that incorporate deception in their plots. I will return to lying later, but at present this dialogue reveals just how complex Letao narratives are: they sometimes represent "lies" in terms of history, but not always. And they do teach "true" (*m̧ool*) principles, but do so through deception (*m̧oṇ*).

Instead of trying to explain Letao's place within genre classifications, Kometo chooses to address the trickster by describing his shape-shifting capacity—he can move between that which is seen (Letao as person) and that which is unrecognized (Letao as *M̧m̧ak*), which is thus something seen but not what it appears to be (it is not a water-hole-in-tree but Letao's anus). By virtue of his ambiguity, Letao's truth and falsehood become mirror images. With his lies and tricks, he at times functions as a culture hero—he provided fire[6]—while at the same time he blurs the boundaries between what is real and what is not: Is this a water-hole-in-tree or is it Letao's anus? Stories about Letao accentuate the ambiguity in discourse because we are never quite sure which uncertainty he (as well as the storyteller who represents him) will exploit: whether the story is a lie in terms of its history but true in terms of its message (portraying cultural truths), or whether the story is "true" (*m̧ool*) historically but the action depicts a "lie" (*riab*) either because it does not represent accurately riM̧ajȩl culture, or because the behavior described is deceitful. For this reason, Kometo describes thinking about Letao as hard.

When I ask Kometo and M̧ake if they know Letao stories, M̧ake quickly identifies Kometo as the one capable of assuming responsibility to tell them even though they are age mates. After his short disclaimer, I ignorantly press for the truth status of Letao stories. Instead of commentary, he launches into a narrative he had previously referenced when describing Letao's shape-shifting capacity. He just gets started when he breaks away into metanarration for my benefit in order to discuss the principle of hide-and-seek (*kūttiliekek*). "YOU CAN'T SEE ME," a social challenge, foregrounds the interplay between deception and who has power in this narrative.

The individual Letao challenges has the ability to shape-shift as well and becomes a pandanus fruit cluster (*ajjen*). But his deception proves unsuccessful; Letao easily discovers him—the lie is cast into light and thus no social power is obtained. Letao, on the other hand, turns himself into a coconut tree and makes his anus appear as a water-hole-in-tree (*m̧m̧ak*). At this point, Kometo boldly declares an etiological meaning of the story, but then breaks away into metanarration to put this meaning into doubt. He seems to say, "Don't take this narrative literally; it's absurd." The way he concludes this section of our dialogue suggests that we look for another kind of truth within Letao's lies. What cultural truth have we found looking into the trickster's a-hole?

The distraction of Letao's opponent from his task at hand in order to satisfy his desire (thirst) gets him into trouble—Letao constantly exploits desires. What the other man perceives to be reality (water), something that can satisfy him, sinks away, out of reach. Then with the man's head plunged fully within the hole,

Letao clamps down, snaring the man in his pursuit of the illusion.[7] What he thinks is pure, clear water turns out to be a "grotesque" fluid from the "lower bodily stratum" (Bakhtin 1986, 103). Letao symbolically lowers him as far as possible. Also, the substitution of waste fluid for water reminds us how categories overlap and that the boundaries between them are sometimes ambiguous. Nonetheless, as a result of this grotesque trick, people become fully human as their heads become separated from their bodies through the formation of necks. The intense laughter of all those involved is laughter at the subversive grossness, at the deception, and at a contingent world of lying signs. They laugh at our perplexing predicament, so richly revealed through Letao's lies. In this way, Letao, the deceiver, reveals both a truth about social power and an existential one.

The short piece of conversation that follows the conclusion of the narrative reveals further uncertainty in the dialogue. Kometo first distances himself from making claims about the truth status of the myth by asserting, "Thus the ancestors say," which may seem to legitimize the story but actually leaves any conclusion wide open, as it could be taken that what "they" say may or may not be true, that "what they have given us is a conundrum of ambiguities. They didn't solve them. So, do you think we can?" I then try to rehearse the literal meaning of the narrative, and laughing, he concurs, as everyone else erupts into laughter. The intense laughter at this point is partially at my expense; it reveals the cross-cultural slippage resulting from my misunderstanding. The point of the story is about much more than the manifest origin of necks; it establishes the principle of deception and dramatizes profane subversion. The laughter may also reveal their own nervous uncertainty about how I, the outsider, would respond to a story they thought did not fit my Western worldview, a perspective they had become very familiar with from years of Christianity and American occupation. Then Kometo reaches out to include me within this ambiguity, to connect himself and the riṂajeļ people to another kind of perplexity in their lives: the Americans. He asks the rhetorical question of how we can make sense of Letao stories, and then answers his own question: They are like American "murder" movies,[8] something you see, but what you see is not real. People are not really killed in the movies, it just looks that way; Letao's anus is not really a water-hole-in-tree, it just appears that way. Both movies and Letao stories are deceptions. And those movies belong to the Americans, who, like Letao, present many kinds of ambiguities. But Kometo also manipulates this uncertainty to suggest that by being deceivers, the "others" are like Letao, so in this way they are like us (the riṂajeļ). He suggests that my world differs little from his, that what appears to be a strange riṂajeļ story is fundamentally like "my" American stories—they are not what they appear to represent but something much deeper, the deep truth that we all live with deception, ambiguity, and social power.

Their laughter at my "getting it" establishes that through ambiguity and satire social life can be extended, not by a principle of difference but by an analogy. The true brilliance of how Kometo recontextualizes this narrative lies not in the way he negotiates the truth status of the myth, but in how he situates the narrative so that it mirrors the emerging relations within the narrative event (or the setting in which the story is told) and the larger context of his modern world dominated by Americans.[9] This myth is "adjusted from time to time to accommodate the culturally expanded world in which the [riM̧ajeļ] continue to live" (Toelken 2002, 2). And, as an American ethnographer, I must ascertain what is revealed and what is hidden from me in the telling of the story. But herein lies the point. The ambiguity and paradox of Letao stories become a metacommentary on all social relations, including our own. What I perceive as cultural holes may be the pursuit of the illusion. And by writing this book I may have got myself caught tightly in the grip of a trickster. But I do hope that now with a head, thankfully at the end of my neck, I can reflect on experience to illuminate it, even with "humble theory," or that which keeps us "closer to the ground" (Noyes 2016, 11–12), and along the margins where the practice of ethnography and real lives meet.

A Dialogic Ethnography

This book offers a dialogic ethnography. I take courage from Patricia Sawin's effort to "listen for a life" in a single subject, recognizing the "means whereby the subject interactively produces herself" (2004, 4). Sawin's work liberates because it simultaneously remains ethically positioned and honest about the constructedness of the ethnographic project without shutting the window on a rich description of a culturally mediated subject. In her account, she humanely shows how the subject "constitutes herself as a subject by means of various communicative resources available to her and how the ethnographer constructs her as a subject of ethnography" (2004, 2). In this way, her ethnography unapologetically sustains the assertion by Mannheim and Tedlock that "ethnography itself is an emergent cultural phenomenon, produced and reproduced and revised in dialogues between the field-workers and natives" (1995, 2). Drawing upon the insights of Mikhail Bakhtin, Sawin highlights multiple forms of dialogue; within every utterance there is not only an interaction with "one's present interlocutor but also with all the previous speakers who have given meaning to the words one uses" (2004, 7).

I am equally interested in the dialogues that ensued between Kometo and me, as well as his dialogues with the ancestral and contemporary voices of his society, including imperial ones. In all these dialogues, there is a form of appropriation and with it an inevitable modification of the words of others. Bakhtin's seminal statement that "our speech . . . is filled with others' words" (1986, 89) not only admits to this pilfering of words/texts, but also identifies the intertextuality, or interrelationship, of all utterances. Because every utterance in context "alludes to past contexts" and utterances, the privileging of any one as more "authentic" slips away; it is "pointless to regard the ethnographer's presence as contamination" (Sawin 2004, 12). Approaching ethnography in this fashion surely suppresses "a multiplicity of other voices" (Sawin 2004, 10), but also allows us to follow a complex metonymic chain to all the other discourses in which our conversations and Kometo's stories were embedded. As I suggested previously, let us admit our limited sources, then follow the conversational trail as texts and contexts interweave. The theoretical collaborative, interpretive work (cf. Otero and Martinez-Rivera 2021) is then seen as an integral part of the dialogic whole.

This ethnography presents Kometo and me engaging in dialogues as he engaged in a dialogue with a variety of mythological, cultural, and imperial voices and texts. Accordingly, both our relationship and the meanings of these voices and stories were dialogically emergent. Perhaps cultural understanding, and certainly intercultural understanding, cannot be otherwise.[10] Objectivist ethnography stages a circuitous game of smoke and mirrors. "Trying to erase the ethnographer is mystifying and dishonest. Attempting to disentangle the subject's and the ethnographer's purposes is impossible and counterproductive" (Sawin 2004, 13). Recognizing this entanglement illuminates much about the sociocultural and ethnographic process. It also helps us avoid forever chasing after the idealized trope of authenticity. From Bakhtin's dialogic perspective, a stable authentic cultural self is a fiction (cf. Sawin 2004, 20; Cashman 2016, 42), and culture is full of deferred selves in contesting conversations. I want neither to deny the value of ethnography nor to dismiss its problems as a mode of representation (cf. Bakhtin 1986, 6–7) and the language ideologies that control representations of the "other," especially in the colonial/imperial context (cf. Bauman and Briggs 2003).

I cannot overlook, however, a critical issue about power: my privileged position as a non-Indigenous scholar to represent Kometo and the stories he selected to perform from his culture. Several Indigenous scholars in Oceania have poignantly and unapologetically worked to decolonize the Western methodologies and "regimes of truth" with all their notorious histories of minimization, peripheralization, and violence to Indigenous people, land, and epistemologies.[11]

The Maori scholar Linda Tuhiwai Smith (2012) has challenged colonizer methodologies and frameworks for knowing, to offer Indigenous alternatives to the exploitive, racist, sexist, and hegemonic research, education, and publication. Anthropologists themselves have been charged as intrusive pilferers of cultural property without authority to speak on behalf of natives, and who now grow anxious as they are repudiated as cultural experts (Trask 2000). When Epeli Hauʻofa (1993) relocated thinking about Oceania away from a region of peripheral far-flung islands, to place it at the center of an inclusive "Our Sea of Islands," it became requisite for scholars who focus on Oceania to relinquish outdated and unethical Western frameworks and reenvision the region in terms of islander experience and knowledge (cf. Kaʻili 2017) within its own interconnected cultural histories (Hauʻofa 2008) that predate colonial and imperial incursions.[12]

I am keenly aware that I occupy a precarious position, buttressed through colonization and my religious affiliation, with the potential to assert authority or attach other motivations to the representation and analysis of Kometo and his stories. Through the dialogic method, I undertake to decenter my influence, or at the very least tip the representation toward how Kometo chose to represent himself, his culture, history, Indigenous mythology, and the outside forces of domination and control. By employing this method, I endeavor to avoid standing outside riM̧ajeḷ culture with any pretense of objective authority. And by "reconceptualizing the very notions of history, power, and cultures from the locations of [his] vernacular creation[s]" (Otero and Martinez-Rivera 2021, 7), I aim to illuminate and translate the ways Kometo framed for me the meaning and significance of a range of stories situated within his culture and the imperial/colonial context. Kometo offered his own decolonizing method by how he assumed accountability to represent his culture, and by how he repositioned me vis-à-vis riM̧ajeḷ cultural knowledge in a kind of "bicultural research" (Tuhiwai Smith 2012, 17) that demonstrates an "epistemic resistance based on histories (myths) of alternative practices" (Scanlon and Wilson 2018, 578). And I followed him into riM̧ajeḷ cosmologies, ontologies, epistemologies, and ideologies explicated through the mythic stories he told. We should not imagine Kometo on the periphery of power within his sea of islands, because from this position the trickster does his best work to expose, deconstruct, and reimagine power. We will see Kometo ingeniously narrate his culture to the center of power and relevance and, after a fashion, offer a kind of subtle yet tricky decolonizing work. Taking cues and correction from Indigenous scholars in Oceania (Meyer 1998, 2013; Māhina 1999, 2010; Helu 1999a; Teaiwa 1999, 2008; Tengan 2001; Hauʻofa 1993, 2008, Diaz 2010; Tengan, Kaʻili, and Fonoti 2010; Tuhiwai Smith 2012; Kaʻili, Māhina, and Addo 2017; Kaʻili 2017; Vaai and Casimira, 2017), I hazard, as a non-Indigenous scholar, to feature some riM̧ajeḷ categories of meaning, ideology, and epistemology as they emerged through Kometo's storytelling and dialogue, and as he placed them in conversation with Western frameworks as he understood them. This juxtaposition is not just an attempt to be ethically responsible by leveling the relationship to "privilege the indigenous presence" (Tuhiwai Smith 2012, 6), but this was Kometo's way, and I would argue a riM̧ajeḷ way, of engaging with power and generating meaning.

To write as if representing riM̧ajeḷ culture, mythology, and epistemologies in an objectivist way without acknowledging how I obtained much of my knowledge about islander conceptualizations and sensibilities would prove disingenuous, and obscure this brilliant and astute riM̧ajeḷ storyteller, to make him invisible. Blurring him into a mass of cultural others would re-invoke a colonial method and perpetuate a kind of epistemic violence upon the man and the lives of the riM̧ajeḷ. It is in conversation that knowledge is realized and made useful in a riM̧ajeḷ worldview. Such dialogues (with all their strains and ambivalence) are often best accomplished through creative rather than analytical exegesis, and Kometo himself moved between these two poles. Similar to the poetic accomplishments of Kometo's storytelling and dialogues, the Indigenous riM̧ajeḷ eco-poet Kathy Jetñil-Kijiner provocatively takes on the degradation of the environment and culture change, and explores the social injustices of colonialism, imposed migration, and racist dismissal of the islanders. Many of her most poignant works merge her contemporary voice with those that come forth from riM̧ajeḷ mythologies (2017).[13] Similarly, Kometo drew from his mythic repertoire to confront his modern imperial world with all its contradictions, loss, and abuses of power. Together, we explored the multiple forms knowledge and social power can take, and in which our relationship was embedded. Kometo leveled our relative positions of power by how he constructed me into the teller, translator, and analytical reader of his tales. The dialogic method I employ seeks to push back against colonial privilege, to account for my presence, and to offer a view of Kometo, his culture, and the trickster ethos, in all their depth, richness, and subversive power.

The issue is not simply a matter of presence—my presence—and the negotiated meanings, texts, and representations generated in the ethnographic encounter, but also how I became inscribed into Kometo's narratives. "Ethnography is always an ethnography of self who happens to be an other to the others with who s/he engages in mutual scrutiny" (Goldsmith 2000, 52). I am not the only one creating a textual representation; Kometo was too, for me and about me, which creates a double play on semiotic accountability. I reflect on my representation of him representing himself to me, but I also stood, as an ambiguous sign, for something to him. And that something is made manifest, as will become evident, in how he read me and our relationship into mythic narratives. This reading is not just a leisurely exercise in hermeneutics, but generates social relations and actions (cf. Vaai and Casimira 2017). These social relationships and shared actions often become deeply personal, and in an ethnographic context they are not simply outside looking in (yearning) or inside looking out (protecting), but wavering "betwixt and between" (Turner 1967). Humanity is holding on despite the chasm of difference. Consequently, I aspire to present not simply another take on methodological reflexivity or the poetics and politics of cultural representation (Clifford and Marcus 1986), but an ethnography that engages us directly in an individual's life, his culture, Indigenous epistemologies, social ideologies, and mythic traditions in the context of imperialism and colonialism. In acknowledging the "moral entanglements of anthropologist and native," it would be amiss to also dismiss the "range of contexts" in which "we enjoy intersubjectivity and participation in community life" (Rohatynsky and Jaarsma 2000, 11). Obviously, we conduct ethnographies in a context of power, propped by the legacy of classism and colonialism, and now the new global political economy that privileges most who conduct this kind of research (cf. White and Tengan 2001). But it would be naive and demeaning to assume that ethnographers have all power over their subjects. The control of representation is certainly a form of power, and there have been productive methodologies to level this relationship (e.g., Lawless 1993; Evers and Toelken 2001; Glassie 2010; Cashman 2016; Ka'ili 2017; White and Tengan 2001; Otero and Martinez-Rivera 2021). Nonetheless, within the context of the field encounter, the ethnographer occupies the subordinate position of neophyte, and as Johannes Fabian (1994) contends, a deeply intersubjective relationship may form to achieve a degree of equality.

Attending to the dialogic emergence of cultural understanding and meaning through the performance of mythic narratives offers an agent-centered approach to engage with Indigenous understanding within the imperial context of the ethnography. Part of a decolonial intent is to foreground the nuanced ways Kometo employed Kajin M̧ajel̦ vernacular forms as a means of appropriation and crafty resistance. This approach also grants a way to conjoin intimate conversational communication and performances with large-scale social formations in the context of unequal power and foreign representations of the islanders (cf. Tuhiwai Smith 2012; Arvin 2019). The riM̧ajel̦ epistemologies, ideologies, and cultural meanings in our dialogic discourse were not always fully present in Kometo's storytelling, but anchored into culture and social life in a multiplicity of ways. These connections were fleshed out through our dialogues. My careful attention to the situated event may seem far removed from the colonial and imperial entanglements of Kometo and his culture.[14] But I hope to show that this kind of discursive action has the "potential to rearrange" (Bauman 1989, 4) not just meanings, but perhaps social relationships and understanding of Indigenous responses to historical incursions and imperial abuses. The ethnographically situated conversations of two intercultural interlocutors reach back to engage the past traditions and islander voices, and sometimes forward to the immediate surrounding to "envision alternatives to the totality imputed to global modernity" (Heim 2017, 922). As Kometo brought these texts and voices forward, they carried bits of their previous contexts of meaning and use, and when resituated in new discourses, they interacted with other texts and contexts, and in the process exhibited resilience as they generated new meanings that "make a home within intrusive, foreign systems" (Diaz 1993, 334).

While Kometo was in a conversation with me, he was also in a dialogue with other riM̧ajeḷ voices. Some of these voices are internal to the stories he told, dialogues between characters in a narrative plot. Some of these voices reside in the moment of performance, not just with me, but also with others listening in and occasionally commenting. Still, some voices come forth from the past, prior speakers of antecedent iterations of the story. Furthermore, some voices belong to other stories in the riM̧ajeḷ repertoire that intersect with all this cacophony of voices, all those who have previously spoken, all those who are speaking and even, we may anticipate, all those who will yet speak as the islanders seek redress and decolonial emancipation.

A recognition of this kind of "intertextuality" can seem formally erudite, but the process is nonetheless very familiar to Indigenous people such as Kometo (cf. Helu 1999b; Māhina 1999). He implicitly understood the continuity among stories and their dynamic quality in performance. This term may seem nothing more than a posh substitute for old workhorse terms such as tradition and innovation; or, it imposes literary jargon onto a field more clearly plowed by others.[15] While academics may quibble over terminology to capture the process, the idea is not complicated for Indigenous people who have always recognized the multiple and even "contested versions" of any story as they are used in different communities and in the "politics of everyday life" (Tuhiwai Smith 2012, 34). But equal to the importance of the interrelationship among stories is the way in which the mythological stories Kometo would tell point to a variety of contexts, past and present, in which he situated the narratives. This inter-contextual approach to stories recognizes how human agents such as Kometo are active participants in the constitution of social life and meaning and contribute to the production of anthropological discourse (Tengan 2001). It also allows us to witness how this same actor can interpret his contemporary life in the context of the

Indigenous mythology. Kometo's "ability to adjust and reconstruct mythic con-stellations is a feature" (Toelken 2002, 93) of his dialogically produced storytell-ing. There is no question that Kometo possessed a keen understanding of the nature of social power and its relationship to mythic narrative. He used stories of Letao to proffer alternatives to the meaning of modern changes and the relation-ships of power that inform those changes.

Even if the modern nation-state and capitalism are being reconfigured, they nonetheless represent a "continuation and extension of long-standing trends" (Knauft 2002, 16). The time and space compression and global flows of capital and culture that characterize postmodernity do not in themselves necessarily reconfigure social and ideological power. The centers of power under modernity remain in force and local communities must continue to respond to them. Postmodern thought has tended to "sideline the economic and political histories of non-Western peoples" (Knauft 2002, 14) as they variably reply to modernism. We cannot ignore the "modernity at large" (Appadurai 1996), or the "pluraliza-tion of modernity" (Knauft 2002, 19) and the "intricacies of local subjectivity and disposition" (Knauft 2002, 24). Most critical here is that Indigenous responses to these forces by Kometo and the riM̧ajȩl are better viewed as alterna-tive modernities (Knauft 2002), and not necessarily a postmodern conundrum.

Kometo's and my relationship was embedded in modernist social structures of power, and his narratives chronicle and often critique modernity. He made sense of the centralizing forces through Indigenous mythologies about social power and the narration of his life story (cf. Stoeltje and Bauman 1989). And most diagnostic about his sense-making is that even though he profoundly rec-ognized cultural differences and historical changes, there was no underlying rupture between modernity and tradition; he made sense of the modern through the traditional (cf. Hezel 2013), especially the mythological. His sense-making was done within his own island world with its social arrangements, and within the historical interstices of Indigenous polity, colonialism, and imperialism.

An Island Setting, Kinship, Land, and Polity

The Marshall Islands lie in the eastern most region of Micronesia, ranging from two to fourteen degrees north latitude. The archipelago consists of twenty-nine low-lying coral atolls and five coral islands. Never more than twenty feet (or six meters) in elevation at high tide, the nearly twelve hundred islands and islets form two distinct chains, the Ratak (sunrise or eastern) and the Rālik (sunset or western).[16] These chains are separated by approximately 125 miles of open ocean and extend nearly eight hundred miles northwest to southeast.

The climate is tropical, and the atolls consist of irregular oval-shaped coral reefs surrounding a lagoon with the islets distributed along the reef. These atolls are scattered over two million square kilometers of ocean yet comprise only 180 square miles of land. The earliest islander settlement to this minimalist landscape extends back nearly two thousand years (Kirch 2000; Rainbird 2004) by Austronesian speakers from the southeast, likely originating in the Solomon Islands or Vanuatu in Melanesia (Rainbird 2004). In 1862, just after the beginning of missionization, the population was estimated at ten thousand, increasing to about twelve thousand not long after World War II. The precontact population and just how many islanders fell victim to introduced diseases or visitor violence are unknown (although the riṂajeḷ usually got the better of the uninvited in the early skirmishes). The 2017 census identified the current in-country population at just over fifty-eight thousand, while a 2018 estimate identifies over thirty thousand in the diaspora, mostly in the United States.

The riṂajeḷ settlers maintained, developed, and refined their renowned, sleek outrigger sailing canoes (*waḷap*, *tipñōl*, and *kōrkōr*) and navigational practices (*meto*), including the sophisticated stick maps (e.g., *wapepe*). These technologies facilitated inter-island and long-distance voyaging for exchange to offset the limited land resources. The watercraft and technologies also enabled exploitation of immediate marine resources and offered abundant ocean opportunities for migration and maintaining links to neighboring archipelagos.

riṂajeḷ society represents an ambilineal arrangement that tips toward a flexible matrilineally oriented organization where the primary ranks (*laajrak*), titles (chiefs, *irooj*; lineage heads, *aḷab*), and land inheritance (*kapijukunen*) pass through women. Land and rank may temporarily follow through a male line (*bōtōktōk*) if the matrilineage (*bwij*) goes extinct (*ḷot*), or if it is granted by a chief to a man for worthy deeds (*jinōkjeej*). But historically, the assumed paradigm was that it would ultimately resort back to a matriline after a few generations. The *irooj* exercised nominal control over land tracts (*wāto*) occupied by matrilines (*imōn bwij*) and ensured the productivity of the land through his sacred authority (*uo*). In turn, the commoners (*kajoor*) who worked and harvested the produce from the land offered tribute (*ekkan* or *eoj̧ek*) to the chiefs who reciprocated through redistribution (*ajej*) of the resources. The matriclan (*jowi* or *jou*) consists of multiple matrilineages (*bwij*) that trace descent through a common ancestress. Most islanders can recall only three to four generations back in their matrilineal genealogies. Nonetheless, strong affection, identity, and reciprocity adhere among those who recognize they share a matriclan. The names of these exogamous matriclans come exclusively through the *bwij* line, and it was through the matriline that the rank of lineage head (*aḷab*) was principally obtained.[17] The *aḷab* coordinated

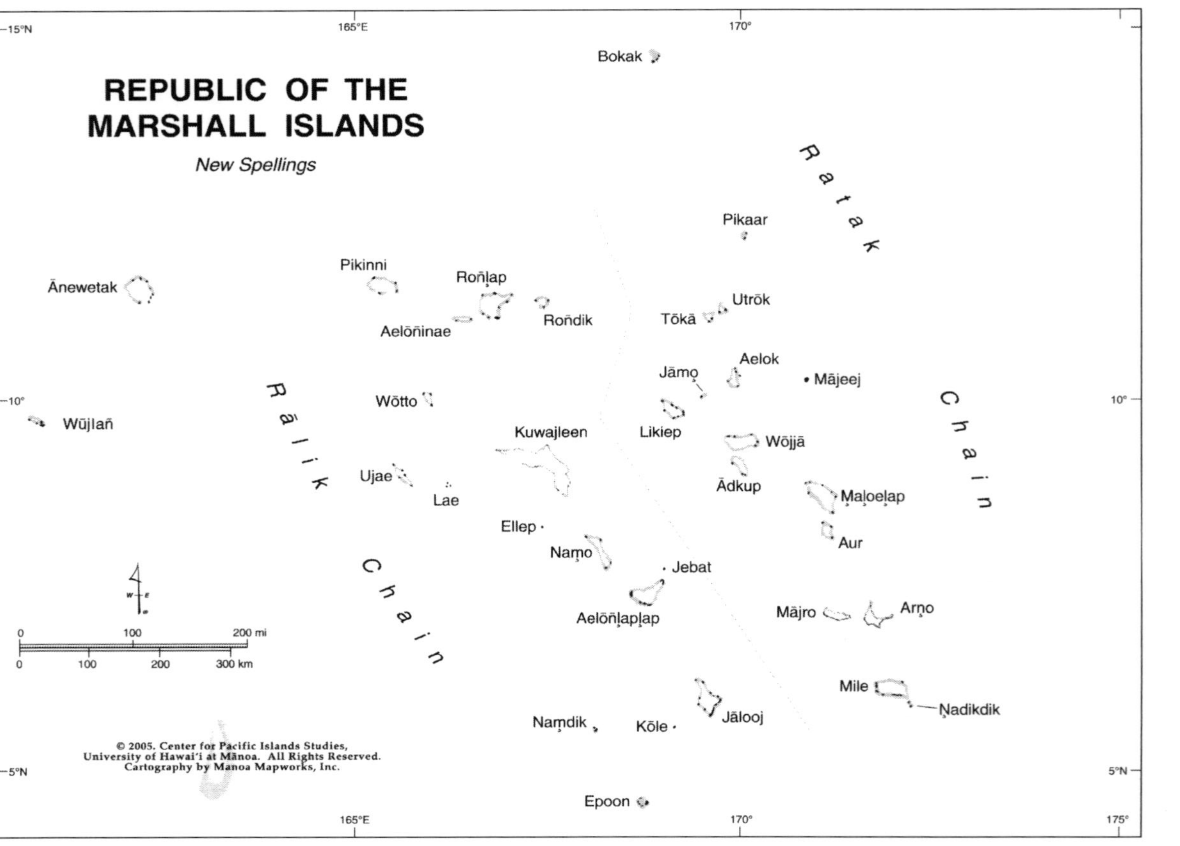

Republic of the Marshall Islands

labor by assigning crop rotations, organizing tribute for the chief, and distributing earnings from copra production. This system adumbrates historical titles and practices overlaid with colonially induced patterns and meanings (see Carucci 1988; Walsh and Heine 2012) when the new plantation economy was imposed in the early twentieth century. The nuances of riM̧ajeḷ matriliny and the ideologies of kinship, land, and polity will become essential to understanding the Indigenous mythology, and I will unpack them further in subsequent chapters.

Both the matrilines and patrilines involve an adaptable system of land inheritance and usufruct rights. Historically, control of these lands by chiefs fluctuated with a range of alliances and successes at warfare. As in much of Oceania, the riM̧ajeḷ chief embodied a dualistic image (Marcus 1989); at once, he was feared and respected for his fierce warrior prowess (*lāj*), while he also maintained his influence as a populist leader by how he took care of his people through the distribution (*ajej*) of land and resources, and through his sacred authority (*ao*) that blessed the land. The perceived sacred power of the chief derived from his divine genealogy (cf. Carucci 1997b) reinforced both the populist and warrior images.[18] Since pacification and Christianity, however, control of land has, for the most part, become routinized, resulting in acquisition primarily through ascription. The control of land may still change, however, but the strategies for its acquisition have altered to fit the new systems of purchase, courts, and government. Many riM̧ajeḷ claim that the new form of warfare (*tariṇae*) takes place through words, including sorcery (*anijnij*) and magic (*kkōpāl*) in the courts rather than through spears and clubs on a battlefield. Even so, these courts constrain chiefs' ability to allocate lands at will.[19] This historical paradigm seeps into modern life to varying degrees. There is much contemporary commentary about how some chiefs can either maintain the dualistic ideal or become self-serving despots who exploit people and the land for their own purposes. With any effort to advocate for decolonization, we must also recognize the existing inequalities within the cultures of Oceania and the "hegemonic aspects of indigenous hierarchies" that form close identification to the interests and values of colonial and imperial officials (Lawson 2010, 301). While this description of kinship, land, and polity represents a relatively consistent pattern, there are many strategic variations in it as individuals and groups manipulate and rework this historically pliable pattern, especially in the context of colonization and imperialism.

A History of Imperial Violence

To understand how riM̧ajeḷ storytellers, such as Kometo, drew upon and situate Letao narratives within their late twentieth-century lives necessitates recognition of their history on the margins of global power. The Marshall Islands have received much attention in recent decades, because they, perhaps more than any other location, became the site of some of the most surreptitious and devious American exploitation. After the US military invasion of the islands in 1943 during World War II and subsequent occupation, the United Nations mandated the Marshall Islands as part of the United States Trust Territory in 1947. In 1983, the Republic of the Marshall Islands entered into a "Compact of Free Association" with the United States; and in 1987, they were granted complete independence, although they remain subject to US imperial and economic controls. The American presence on the islands actually represents the culmination of a long sequence of contact and colonial rule. Western exchanges began in 1529 with the Spanish Captain Álvaro de Saavedra in his attempt to re-cross the Pacific from the Moluccas. Sporadic encounters between Spanish ships and the riṂajeḷ lasted through the sixteenth century, followed by a long break until 1788, when Captains Marshall and Gilbert charted some of the islands en route to Canton. From the first of these British captains, the archipelago actually obtains its modern name. The early nineteenth century witnessed several visits from the Russian explorer Otto Von Kotzebue (1816, 1817, and 1821),[20] followed by American whaleships. The relationship between the islanders and the outsiders was sometimes hospitable, but more often violence led to the destruction of many vessels (Hezel 1983), mutinous castaways, and the death of their crews (Heffernan 2002).

The first Christian missionaries arrived at Epoon (Ebon) atoll in 1857. These were Protestant missionaries from the American Board of Commissioners for Foreign Missions. They came by invitation from Kaibuke, a Rālik chief whose family members had been rescued by missionaries on Kosrae island after an accidental drift voyage, and when the local islanders intended to kill the riṂajeḷ castaways (cf. Walsh and Heine 2012; LaBriola 2019). The Marshalls were among the last islands in Micronesia to receive missionaries due to their fierce reputation for attacking and destroying visiting ships. The mission branched out to Naṃdik and Mile atolls, and subsequently to all the other atolls over several decades. In the early mission, Hawaiian Protestants provided the majority of the missionary labor until the mission was staffed almost entirely by riṂajeḷ converts by 1883 (Walsh and Heine 2012). The riṂajeḷ quickly took to literacy when a Kajin Ṃajeḷ orthography was created and the Bible translated (Hezel 1983, 1995; Walsh and Heine 2012).

Mostly motivated by economic interests, Germany annexed the islands in 1885 to facilitate administration of the new copra plantations, and in small part to protect Christian interests as they complemented their colonial project. The German administration significantly affected the Indigenous land tenure system and solidified power and wealth among a more limited set of chiefs, especially in the Rālik chain (see Walsh and Heine 2012). At the outset of World War I in 1914, Japan seized the islands and was granted control by the League of Nations in 1921. In the early years of occupation, Japan sought to colonize and develop copra plantations and the trade potential of the islands. Later the strategy shifted to military fortifications to use the Marshalls as a point of departure for offensive efforts on the eastern front of the empire (see Walsh and Heine 2012). The US military invasion in 1943 left an indelible mark on the riṂajeḷ due to the rapidity and power with which they extricated the Japanese, and then moved on in their western advance back toward the Philippines. These colonial entanglements with Christianity and imperial powers may be characterized as a history of connivance in which the majority of the islanders visibly embraced these foreign impositions. Indeed, today Christian practices and identities are intimately linked to traditional titles, ranks, identities, and Indigenous religious practices, and the modern state has assimilated models of Western governments with the chiefly system. In addition to the economic and political contradictions of an independent state that is still fundamentally dependent and constrained by the imperial power as well as efforts to merge traditional chiefly authority with democratically elected officials, there are "coexisting" narratives about culture and religion. One is a story of an "idyllic" or deep cultural past embraced for the purposes of identity in a colonial setting; a second story provides a "conversion" narrative about the "coming of light" and the casting off of a dark and heathen pre-Christian culture (Rudiak-Gould 2010). Both narratives are employed equally by the islanders in different settings. Such paradoxical beliefs and seeming contradictions must be seen, however, as responses to Christian colonialism and US imperialism, and there are Indigenous frameworks such as trickster discourses and veiled resistance not only to address the ambiguities, but also to exploit them.

The riṂajeḷ have not slackened their efforts to "tack" between the Indigenous and colonial (cf. Diaz 2010, 19) with concerted efforts to achieve independence and to seek reparations for the atomic bomb testing. But more often, modern chiefly authority has been enhanced through complicated relationships with the vestiges of colonialism (cf. White and Lindstrom 2009; Lawson 2010), and advantages that have come through both control over government, investments, rent payments, and complicity with missionization. Overt resistance to the outsiders' religion is nearly absent in a nation that identifies as strongly Christian, but nonetheless is manifest in the cracks of institutionalized religion in the form of "passive weapons" (Scott 1985), most notably the continued practice of Indigenous magic, sorcery, divination, and narrating stories about Letao. This history represents only a bare-bones chronology of contact. Although the colonial and war histories attract some interest, the events since American occupation have drawn the most intense scrutiny.

On July 1, 1946, the United States Navy initiated Operation Crossroads by detonating an atomic bomb at Pikinni (Bikini) atoll in the northern Marshall Islands. By April 15, 1948, the Navy Department had expanded its operations to Ānewetak (Enewetak) atoll with three additional atomic blasts over a one-month period. These tests were the first in a series of experiments that would last until August 1958. Over twelve years, sixty-six announced atomic and hydrogen bombs were tested—twenty-three at Pikinni and forty-three at Ānewetak. The most infamous of these tests was the March 1, 1954, BRAVO blast at Pikinni atoll. At fifteen megatons, it was the largest hydrogen bomb ever tested by the United States.[21] The violent blasts not only severely contaminated these atolls and altered the landscape, in many cases incinerating entire islets, but the measures taken to exploit the riM̧ajeļ typify a story of deception, duplicity, and abuse (Barker 2004; Smith-Norris 2016; Jetñil-Kijiner 2017; Keown 2017, 2018; Keju-Johnson 1987). While many opponents to testing may be aware of the weapons experiments, fewer are aware of the forced relocation of the Pikinni (Kiste 1974) and Ānewetak (Carucci 1997a) Islanders, who were told by the American military governor that it would be "for the good of mankind and to end all world wars" (Weisgall 1994; Niedenthal 2001, 2).

These islanders were not only forced to leave their homelands, where myth, history, genealogy, and identity are inscribed into the landscape,[22] but also abandoned on uninhabited islands where they faced near starvation due to limited subsistence resources. Even more incredulous was the apparent "human experiment" (despite denials by the US government) that the islanders of Roñeļap (Rongelap) and other northern atolls experienced with the Bravo Blast in 1954 (Barker 2004; Smith-Norris 2016; Keown 2017). Within hours of the first blast, a "gritty white ash" (Niedenthal 2001, 7) began to fall downwind from Pikinni. None of the islanders were warned, nor were any instructions given for their evacuation and relocation. In consequence, for over sixty years these people have experienced severe outcomes from the fallout on their atolls including thyroid, uterine, and other cancers, stillbirths, "jellyfish" babies, deformations, and mental retardation. The history of legal reprisals, monetary compensation, and attempts at restoration represents a convoluted story of intrigue, cover-ups, international pressure, and the emergence of the consolidated, independent Republic of the Marshall Islands. Although weapons testing concluded in the 1950s, the United States Army continues to occupy Kuwajleen (Kwajalein) atoll as an impact area through controversial rent payments. Intercontinental ballistic missiles shot from Vandenberg Air Force Base in California use the lagoon at Kuwajleen for target practice. The Kwajalein Missile Range assumed even greater importance in the 1980s with Ronald Reagan's "Star Wars" agenda.[23] The former secretary of state, Henry Kissinger, most plainly typified the callous imperial attitude of the US government toward the islanders when he said, "When there are only 90,000 people out there who gives a damn?" (Dowell 1988, 26).

These matters typically represent the concerns of lawyers, politicians, and historians, who, looking from without, situate the "Marshallese issue" within the context of an imperial global power imposing upon an Indigenous population, or as the riM̧ajeļ Indigenous scholar and politician Carl Heine described it, as a legacy of, if not serious exploitive abuse, then "paternalistic neglect" (Heine 1974). Some of the details of this history will emerge as they intersect with Kometo's mythic narratives and our dialogues. But my interest here lies less in the "official history" from the top down (even though it is critically important to view it from this vantage point in order to challenge the abuses manifest in that history) and more in the experience of the islanders from below (cf. Dvorak 2018; Jetñil-Kijiner 2017; Keown 2017), and particularly rests with a single islander who lived through these troubling violent historical events. This approach does not ignore the political, environmental, and human tragedy of this history, or the continual struggle by the riM̧ajeļ to seek reparations. Even so, these imperial political and economic forces intersect with Indigenous experience and meanings to generate alternative narratives that make history much less transparent.[24] I wish to explore the meaning of this history for such an individual as Kometo, and follow him as he probed the holes that dramatize an ambivalent history with the Americans, and by extension, all the cunning ways the riM̧ajeļ trickster provides a link between the mythic past and the present. It is Letao who supplies an Indigenous resource for addressing the ambiguities of a modern life characterized by imperialism, Christian missionization, modern state formation, economic dependency, and imposed colonial epistemologies.

Letao the Trickster

To overly define Letao the trickster seems antithetical to his purposes. Like the postmodern maxim, he opens us to "multiple meanings, disguised meanings, contextual meanings and ambiguity" (Hyde 1998, 51). Letao represents a dualistic character who both creates and destroys, gives and negates, dupes and is duped. He also possesses a voracious appetite, a need to wander, and an unbridled sexual drive (cf. Radin 1956; Hyde 1998; Scheub 2013).

Like all the riM̧ajȩl I know, Kometo and those who listened to him enjoy the narratives about the antics, subversion, and insolence of Letao more than any other story cycle. Letao's most notable qualities include his ability to shape-shift, enormous libido, power over nature, cunning intelligence that enables him to outwit an opponent, and penchant for subverting social authority. As much as Letao the trickster is destructive, he also serves a regenerative role in riM̧ajȩl conceptualization. He offers "a margin of mess, a category of inverted beings both to define and to question the order by which we live" (Babcock 1978, 28). Kometo's performance of trickster stories and his playful trickster-like talk undermined, to a degree, the cultural boundaries and power relationships in which our dialogues were embedded. Like other Indigenous storytellers, he demonstrated the "ability to build connections where rifts might otherwise appear . . . and use narratives to dismantle boundaries rather than erect them" (Cruikshank 1998, 3).

During our dialogues, Kometo used the narrated events (or the events recounted in the stories) about Letao and other mythological characters to explore possible analogies between his culture's history and traditions and imperial powers and modern social forces. Within the storytelling setting, we appropriated Letao's image and voice into our voices, and in these liminal spaces and entanglements generated a sense of *communitas* (Turner 1967) between ourselves while we joked, creating the intersubjective equality I suggested previously. Letao is a leveler of power. He is a boundary crosser, and so was I as ethnographer, and so was Kometo as narrator, and so were we as intercultural friends. Letao's ability to find the holes in boundaries and exploit them, his wanderlust and mobility, and his desires to satiate an "empty stomach" and satisfy his libido (cf. Hyde 1998) will paradoxically unpack and reconstitute imaginations about the riM̧ajȩl mythological past, elicit other germane narratives, and create the context for our ethnographic search on the meaning of islander cosmologies, ideologies, and epistemologies.

Among the possibilities, Kometo told stories of the trickster to provide a satire on the sociology of power within riM̧ajȩl culture and history, and on the formidable outside American and Christian presence. I am also interested in the trickster's actions in Indigenous settings, not just the stories about him, and "especially at the manner in which a trickster's action" is "enacted and transacted" (Basso 1987, 6). With Kometo, this enactment and transaction took place often in our conversations as we drew upon the Letao persona in our own speech. Through stories and conversations, a dialogue ensued among former tellings of Letao, which established a "relationship between" the "mythological character and day-to-day understanding and patterning of experience of the people who

[told] them" (Basso 1987, 6). Letao is "not merely a symbol"; islanders like Kometo use him to "interpret, manipulate, and create meanings as a practical activity of strategic social interaction" (Hill 2002, 73). Letao provided more than a meta-social commentary; he mediated our ambivalent ethnographic encounter as presented with the water-hole-in-tree story, a relationship full of conceptual indeterminacy, which could not be otherwise with our intercultural differences and how our engagement was deeply enmeshed in colonial and imperial contexts of power.

In this ethnography, I will keep track of two tricksters: Letao, the mythological character, and Kometo, the modern storyteller. Kometo is more than simply a product of the riM̧ajeḷ trickster tradition; he is a personage that "sets tradition in relief as much as tradition sets in relief" him as an individual (Cashman 2016, 6). Kometo used Letao stories to address his personal reflections on myth and tradition. Even though myths seem "fixed and stable" and "impervious to the incidental and personal," Kometo would still "customize" the Letao myths "vicariously" by identifying with the trickster protagonist, and also "virtually" in how he would insert himself into the story (McDowell 2011, 324–326). His vicarious identification was forged in how he aligned himself with the trickster's ethos and methods of deception, and his virtual identification was in how he, by virtue of riM̧ajeḷ storytelling in the present tense and its abundance of reported speech, created a sense of direct participation in the trickster's actions.

Honest Duplicity

Letao, whose name identifies "the sly one," represents more than a narrative artifact; he remains an active force in contemporary riM̧ajeḷ thought and society. Through inversion and deception, Letao narratives can be used to explore collective ambiguities rooted in their social polity and Indigenous traditions, and in the history of contact, missionization, imperialism, decolonization, and the modern nation-state. Lies paradoxically reveal the truth; we cannot see our options without opposites. Lies are not simply defined as something ontologically false. Instead, they belong to "the moral domain of intention" (Barnes 1994, 12). We can recognize the social efficacy and perhaps morality of altruistic or benevolent lies ("You can do it!" or "You will get better"). All the same, malicious lies, intended to benefit the liar at the expense of a dupe, may upend social relationships to create a socially irreparable breach. Letao creates disjuncture and inverts relationships. Yet contained within a Letao story lies the "seed of transformation" as the "trickster pretends to be something he is not in order to fulfill his appetites" (Scheub 2012, 24). Kometo's stories about Letao's lies reveal powerful, sometimes tragic truths in riM̧ajeļ history, and simultaneously cast a light on the emergence of our relationship.

The Kajin M̧ajeļ word for "a lie" or "to be dishonest" (*riab*) not only serves as commentary on the veracity or ontological status of something, but also suggests a kind of denial and veiling (*ņņooj*) of the truth (*m̧ool*). The capacity to redirect and mask the truth does not necessarily identify something immoral, as it becomes socially efficacious in riM̧ajeļ social practice to disguise one's intentions and actions. All the moral platitudes about lying that come with Christianity overlay Indigenous conceptualizations about speaking or living a lie, but the colonial religion did not create the culturally nuanced sense of veiling and pretext, nor did it generate the ubiquity of Letao narratives in deep history and their cosmologically salient role in society. Another Indigenous term for "deception" or "to deceive," *m̧oņ*, captures both the manner in which Letao works his tricks and a social strategy to confuse another's understanding or perception. But also clearly understood by the riM̧ajeļ is that behind a deceptive act a truth may be revealed, as demonstrated through the water-hole-in-tree story above. What is more, the trickster's name, *etao*, conveys not only that he is "sly," but also that he outwits and outsmarts others through deception (*m̧oņ*). Such deceits become ambivalent because they at once represent something dishonest and socially adverse, but also provide a social strategy when dealing with power in the community or in resistance to foreign powers.

Such deception and ambivalence raise a problem of representation, not just in how I choose to characterize Kometo and his culture, but in how he used trickster discourses to represent himself. If anything, critical reflexivity in folkloristic and anthropological research has brought awareness to the limits and slippage in ethnographic understanding and the implications of power in representing the other. At our best, we seek to be conscientious and trustworthy cross-cultural translators. Literal translations are hard enough, but how do I cross culturally translate lies and deceptions? They may even prove more difficult to decipher than metaphor and irony. How do I situate deception in riM̧ajeļ epistemology, social life, and storytelling when the intent is to confuse or disguise? How do I situate a verbal ruse in the perplexity of intercultural dialogues? Perhaps I was always the dupe in our conversations, fooled by deception and lies, or at the very least, clever redirection and veiling. Did we come to a consensual understanding of our veiled intents and the practice of deception? Can the reader trust that I have captured the nuance of the lies and deception, and the Indigenous framework of the trickster ethos, or did I just not get it? What are my limits to "getting it"? It is not just a matter of admitting that ethnographic writing is in part a fiction, but that all social theater involves a degree of pretext, concealment, and perhaps deliberately intended mendacities. This is the trick of this ethnography, and I hope I learned well from Kometo. Notwithstanding all the possibilities for duplicity and misunderstanding, I believe he honestly sought to help me understand ambiguous discourses and how the riM̧ajeḷ employ narratives of deception, veiling, and uncertainty to reveal relations of power. So, I will try to be as honest about duplicity as possible. I hope to show my own journey through riM̧ajeḷ trickster discourse.

The Social Trickster

The liminal in rites of passage (Van Gennep 1960) describes the ambiguous state of social transition and, by extension, socially "betwixt and between" (Turner 1967) characters who lie on the margins of society, who are neither this nor that, unable to be squarely placed in any category. These people are found within the cracks of their own society, and sometimes in marginal spaces between societies. These anti-structural types (neither in nor out of society, or both in and out at the same time) may seem dangerous as they present subjunctive "what if" considerations, and open us to new thoughts and novel configurations of relationships as they freely move in and out, and back and forth along the margins. Social trickster figures, like their narrative counterparts, are characteristically liminal; they are of their society, but as rule breakers and border crossers, they move outside it, around it, and sometimes smash directly into it. Whatever the case, we just cannot pin them down as they mess with any attempt at strict categorization. Nonetheless, in their wake they may leave something to enliven the social structure and the mind.

Kometo appreciated the subtleties of jokes and their nuanced meanings, and recognized how jesting articulated the "jokes" in the social structures of his life (Douglas 1975), those of his riM̧ajeḷ world, the history of outside imperial and colonial forces in his islands, and the peculiar relationship that we forged. As a competent trickster, he knew how to draw analogies between mythic stories and social power, and he knew how to create a "reversible world" (Babcock 1978), turning even seemingly mundane conversations and topics upside down to evoke a "realm of pure possibility" and "free recombination" (Turner 1967, 97) of ideas and relationships. He honed his craft by living a life situated socially and historically in some curious marginal spaces. Like all the riM̧ajeḷ of his fading generation, he straddled the crevasse between the Japanese and American times. Born in 1917 during the Japanese occupation (1914–1943), he attended a Japanese school, and later worked for the colonial government. He not only witnessed the American invasion (1943) but also participated with the US military in a most dangerous role as a scout, sneaking between these two imperial worlds. Life during the Japanese times certainly proved different from life before it; but with the American military occupation, transformations in everyday experience were hastened and the transition from tradition to modernity accelerated. Among Kometo's primary conversational topics was his commentary on these social changes. But Kometo's reflection on these changes came with a twist, as for him modernity, even plays on power, offered just another take on something very old and recurring. He would position himself between the mythological times of origins, textualized in both riM̧ajeļ mythologies and the Bible, and contemporary times, that is, since the American arrival. By collapsing the space between these periods of time, Kometo worked much of his best trickery.

Kometo viewed his life as not only historically transitional, but also residing in liminal social spaces. Kometo's matriclan, the most significant marker of social rank and identity, was, in his own words, "the lowest of the low." His clan name, Ripit, literally means "the people of Kiribati," the island chain south of the Marshalls with its own language and culture. Kometo explained that sometime in the eighteenth century, people from Kiribati had drifted in their canoes and landed at his home in Mile, the southernmost atoll in the Ratak (eastern) island chain. The riM̧ajeļ killed the Kiribati men but preserved the women. The paramount chief allocated to these women usufruct land rights and thus a new and insignificant matriclan arose, passing on its rights and the Ripit name to its descendants.[25] Notwithstanding his father's relatively elevated matriclan (M̧ōkauleej), Kometo's rank was nominal because the patriline only marginally contributes to status in riM̧ajeļ society.

Despite the lack of traditional rank, Kometo's life history placed him in an opportune position to become knowledgeable about riM̧ajeļ culture. His father had been adopted by the paramount chief of Mile, and Kometo was subsequently taken into the chief's home as well. In this context, regardless of his disclaimers to know nothing, he attentively heard and absorbed much about how power becomes manifest in mythologies, cosmogonies, genealogies, social protocols, divination, magic, and sorcery. When he was only nine, a woman (who had saved his life as an infant through Indigenous medicine and counter-magic) took him to Epoon atoll in the southern Rālik (western) chain. This atoll is historically important, both as a key residence of the chiefs from that chain and the location for the arrival of the first Christian missionaries (1857). He lived on Epoon until the paramount chief died during his teen years, whereupon he returned to Mile for the funerary rites and remained there. In Epoon, however, he participated in another part of the islander world, learned their stories, their Rālik dialect, and became deeply associated with people in the southern islands of the western chain, including his friend M̧ake, who participated in many dialogues with us. Even into his old age, Kometo would sometimes shift between the two dialects in midsentence. His birth on and return to Mile was also on transitional ground. After establishing a mission on Epoon and the southern Rālik atolls, the missionaries went to Mile to open the Ratak chain of islands (Walsh and Heine 2012). Mile also marks the southern boundary between the Marshall Islands and their closest neighbor, Kiribati, from where his matriclan name derives. What's more, Mile became a historically significant space between the new outsiders and the islanders, because on this atoll the first sustained contact between Westerners and the riM̧ajeļ took place. This encounter resulted in the massacre of the majority of the whaleship *Globe* mutineers (1824) and the detainment of two young Americans, who remained over two years before their rescue (Hefferman 2002). Mile sits at the crossroads of the historical changes precipitous of a notoriously volatile contact history.

After returning to Mile, Kometo participated in World War II and gained a certain degree of prestige and notoriety as a brave risk-taking scout. Following the war, he wandered about the islands participating in an assortment of jobs linked to American development. For much of the time, he resided on Mājro atoll, which was quickly transitioning under American occupation into the new political and economic center of the islands. After years of "mischief and drunkenness" (his description), he sought to change his life through religion and was in training to become a deacon and scribe in a Protestant church when he left, disappointed with the perceived hypocrisy of some of its leaders. He then married a high-ranking female chief. As her companion, he again inhabited the margins of social power and closely listened to its machinations. After his wife's death, Kometo once more placed himself in a marginal social world by converting to Mormonism during its fledgling beginnings in the islands.

The Church of Jesus Christ of Latter-day Saints arrived in the islands relatively late among the Christian denominations. The first missionaries came from Hawai'i in February of 1977, and by 1981 Kometo had joined the church. When I arrived in 1982, the islands had become in 1980 part of a newly formed Micronesian mission headquartered in Guam.[26] Like all outside religions introduced into the islands, the Mormon church's missionaries and its American leadership were initially confused by the matrilineal principle that informs kinship, intergender relations, Indigenous social authority, and land tenure practices. These cultural patterns were something Kometo adamantly wanted me to understand from the beginning of our friendship. Through time, but not always seamlessly, the Mormon church adjusted so that today all local leadership positions, both men and women (high ranking and commoners alike), are filled by riM̧ajȩl or those who have married in. Several permanent church buildings now dot the landscapes of Mājro and Kuwajleen atolls after negotiations with matrilineal landholders. All the church's canonical texts and much additional literature have been translated into Kajin M̧ajȩl, and its members continue to seek, as Kometo did, a nexus between Indigenous sensibilities and the religion's formulation of embodied deities and eternal kinship (McArthur 2023). Currently, approximately forty-five hundred members reside in the islands, representing 7.5 percent of the population. The diasporic movement of other church members to Hawai'i and the US mainland that has, over time, created pockets of riM̧ajȩl Mormons mostly comes subsequent to Kometo's passing. When Kometo was alive, the congregations were much smaller, and as it remains to this day, the new religion was viewed by other denominations as a curious departure from mainstream Christianity. This curiosity is due to its theological distinctiveness (especially about the nature of deity, agency and the purpose of life, and the potential for human apotheosis); numinous stories by its founder, Joseph Smith; ongoing apostolic prophecy and an open canon; dietary prohibitions; and a lay clergy with its broadly distributed authority. In the latter years of his life, Kometo served as a kind of bricoleur between Mormon theology and Indigenous mythologies, while performing a colorful role among its congregants until his death.

Kometo presents a conundrum for two disparate perspectives, both disposed to be a bit cautious about him as an ethnographic source. A critical posture toward change may overly risk romanticizing essentialist ideals about tradition and authenticity. Such a romantic position may not only disparage (understandably) the consequential impositions and disruptions to riM̧ajȩl culture occasioned by contact, colonialism, missionization, exploitation, and modernization, but also raise searching questions about Kometo's conversion to his new religion. From such a perspective, this proselytizing religion quintessentially represents a disruption to culture that encourages a dismissal of Kometo as a powerless and colonized individual who gained a measure of social capital through a seemingly conservative transnational religion. Or that, like so many drawn to outside religions, he sought some form of refuge from psychological, social, and economic alienation. The caution with this position is that, one, it often misses coherence to any local manifestations of conversion,[27] and two, it can diminish the agency of Indigenous people, viewing them as passive subjects ignorant of their own motivations and choices as they respond to imperial forces and the culture change of subsequent colonial incursions (cf. Hezel 2001). Even though he was an imperialized subject, Kometo may surprise us and provide unexpected twists to the contours of decolonization. A degree of circumspection is needed to avoid a kind of critical thinking that inadvertently minimizes his agency when it does not speak to certain expectations. With Kometo, his religious and cultural perspectives represent an exceptionally creative synthesis. He resisted any great divide to historical ruptures, cultures, and religious thinking, and maneuvered among them all as a trickster in an apparently seamless fashion. From our dialogues, it will become clear that it was I who lamented the loss of traditional categorical boundaries and epistemologies, whereas he exploited the contradictions to offer evocative possibilities.

On the other hand, those from his new religion may struggle with Kometo's lack of inhibition to address issues often outside the moderation of the standard membership, and the unapologetic links he made between the riM̧ajeḷ mythology and his new faith. The riM̧ajeḷ clown or trickster figure is a recognized social persona in the islands and delivers a significant role in many kinds of events and cultural performances (Carucci 1986). Even so, their role in contemporary religion is ambivalent at best and more often than not discouraged. Such figures are just "bad" (*nana*) and "mischievous" (*kakūtōtō*), and distracting to religious piety and decorum. And although Kometo's fellow church members would often roll their eyes at his antics and startling comments, they recognized his personal aptitude, his deeply informed insights about all things cultural and religious, and his clever wit, which helped everyone avoid taking themselves too seriously. Nonetheless, he may startle even those with the most open sense of play among the congregants.

Kometo occupied the margins of traditional social power. He lacked rank but knew social authority intimately. He lived all his life on transitional atolls, both historically and spatially in terms of regional and global contact. He was keenly aware of their relationship to local and large-scale power. He operated on the margins of mainstream riM̧ajeḷ Christianity through his affiliation with Mormonism, but even there he presented a puzzling figure due to his unabashed willingness to merge pre-Christian riM̧ajeḷ cosmologies with the new religion. By being betwixt and between socially, historically, geographically, and religiously, Kometo assumed the role of a trickster on the margins of riM̧ajeḷ society. By occupying a place on its borders, he often took me to the edge, to peer inside mythological, cosmological, cultural, and epistemological holes. Paradoxically, by making Kometo the focus of this exploration of riM̧ajeḷ mythology, we will see this social trickster narrate his culture and himself to the center of global power.

What follows in this book embodies my textual weaving of those texts Kometo knitted into our conversations that resulted in a curious tapestry of our dialogic encounter. Kometo knew little about my theoretical weaving during our encounters or how I would choose to write about them. Nor was I always aware of how he worked his own threads with me. Only now, as I re-listen to our conversations, do I hear more clearly the careful plaiting together of his own voice with riM̧ajeļ cultural resources to structure my instruction, all the while I thought I was shaping our agenda through my questions. He not only crafted a representation of himself and his culture (cf. Sawin 2004; Cashman 2016), but also fashioned our relationship and responded to my voice as a teacher. He took me down unexpected revelatory paths while also withholding for his own purposes. He characterized a patient and perceptive teacher. Still, he did not know all my motivations as a student. He would often call me "doctor" (*taktō*) or "scientist" (*jaintiij*). In doing so, I think he signaled his recognition that I had my own obscure esoteric purposes and threads.

A Liminal Ethnographer

Ethnographers become liminal characters in their own right, and consequently my relationship to Kometo lay in an ambiguous gap. I realize, as in many ethnographic cases, that I may have served as a dupe to Kometo's antics as he managed our peculiar relationship. Our conversations about Letao and "dirty" matters was something we grew into, as they emerged along the margins of our different cultures, a shared religion, a mythological past, and the context of imperial power in which we were deeply enmeshed. In time, we both found in each other trickster reflections that allowed a certain degree of risk and responsibility. In contrast to my previous stay in the islands as a single young-adult missionary, my sociological status had changed; I was now married and a father, which lent an added degree of access to certain kinds of stories and jokes about the trickster. Kometo could have been "just performing" for me as a kind of veiled or mocking resistance. This is actually a salient possibility because, as previously indicated, it is a great asset in riM̧ajeļ social discourse to veil one's thoughts and intents through indirect speech and tropes of inversion (cf. Carucci 1986; Berman 2019). If this is why he performed trickster stories for me, then these narratives must certainly provide ready-made resources to apply to all similar occasions since the riM̧ajeļ so widely know them, even those about Letao and America. But I actually think another quality of Letao motivated Kometo: he wished to blur the boundaries between us. I was both the "other" and "not the other." I represented American power (I had enough economic resources to wander with my family in the Marshall Islands for over two years just to learn), but I also deferred to his culture and the traditional ranks and statuses, spoke only in the Kajin M̧ajeļ language, and lived among them in reciprocal kin relations. If this relationship appeared fuzzy, it is because I was, like Letao, categorically ambiguous and slippery. This actually became a running theme for Kometo, and he brought it home when once I asked about Letao's location today among several other elderly islanders, and he, in a matter-of-fact way, simply said,

K   He is with you. <everyone laughs hard>
P   Oh, you mean the Americans? So, is he in America? <all laughing>
K   No, he has returned again.
P   By canoe or plane? [I was trying to be funny]
K   In your trunk! <intense laughter by all>

Kometo teasingly proposes that the trickster has not only returned with me personally, but he is also hidden away in my trunk, an object that contained all my shrouded ethnographic opacities. Now this joking relationship between us did not remain only grounded in stories about Letao, but it began to spread, so that his family, the compound, church members, acquaintances, and even at times strangers would playfully comment, "There's Ḷakūbwe, Letao's friend." This public label carried a double referent; it read me into the stories of Letao, while also connecting me to Kometo, whom many considered a Letao figure because of his combination of immense knowledge, much of it sacred, with a joking demeanor. So, others saw our relationship as a bit ambiguous as well, and it was only too appropriate, from their point of view, that he would be among my primary teachers. People loved Kometo and respected him as one who was both wise and funny, and therefore truly wise because, somehow, he seemed to recognize the complexities and ambiguities in everything.

Through the years my transition from youthful missionary to academic and ethnographer, and one tutored by an Indigenous trickster, begs many questions about my positioning within the multifaceted entanglements of religion, scholarship, and cultural advocacy. I have sought to critically reflect on this personal history, to recognize how I was disposed to see certain things. But then again, this same lens may have granted me an alternative route into riM̧ajeḷ mythologies, in perhaps ways missed by others, as I was taught by an ambiguously situated trickster who could not be clearly or categorically placed. In many ways, my particular vantage point, and how I go about unpacking Kometo's illusory trickster discourses, is more informed by interdisciplinary academic training, professional associations, and political alignments than by religion. But still, religion, and particularly the one Kometo and I shared, did provide some of the backdrop to our dialogues, no matter how much we found ourselves on the margins. Instead of retreating from this puzzle, I prefer to employ one of Kometo's satirical tactics, to challenge what may appear obvious by making unanticipated connections, and, in the subversive spirit of Vincente Diaz, engage in a little repositioning (2010, 30–31). This book is not about an official position from "above." Indeed, we eschewed the official narratives (historical, political, religious) in our dialogues and Kometo's stories to offer narratives from "below," or ones that counter and/or play in the margins of colonial and imperial histories, and on the margins of both Christian and Mormon cultural narratives. By doing so, we proffer a nuanced rethinking of riM̧ajeļ trickster mythologies, cultural ideologies and epistemologies, and social life. Ultimately, because of the sly and subversive methods of Kometo the storyteller, and because at the heart of his narrative performances was the riM̧ajeļ trickster figure, our respective positionings sometimes offer a view from "behind" that transgress the boundaries of religions, cultures, and imperial/colonial powers.

If our relationship proved tricky for both us and others, and if I am, in some way, a trickster figure, too, I hope any subversive effects will be seen as part of a renewal as I peer into the holes created by the trickster. As Kometo did for me, I desire to give abundantly, and hopefully through the consideration of this one man's life and dialogues with him, new possibilities for understanding the interrelationship of riM̧ajeļ mythology with social life and power will emerge, riM̧ajeļ cultural ideologies and epistemologies will come better into focus, the role of narrative and performance in constituting ethnographic knowledge will be reconsidered, and that ethnographic friendships, with all their ambiguity and messiness, can be seen to mediate between difference and enrich our lives and understanding. And I seek to follow how Indigenous sensibilities in the context of imperial violence and abuse open a hole through which to move between the poles of the local and global—between the seemingly weak and the markedly powerful. I hope to avoid another "absolutely worthless" (Tuhiwai Smith 2012, 3) outsider research project, and instead offer a useful record of riM̧ajeļ mythology as a decolonizing form of resistance, albeit an unexpected one in the hands of Kometo, the social trickster.

CHAPTER 2

Narrative Tricks

The Poetics of "Truthiness" and Ambivalent Analogies

Mythic narratives about Letao, the riṂajeḷ trickster, and especially those narrated by Kometo, present how he outwits and subverts his opponents who have ascribed status and social authority. His cleverness directs his mischievous actions and permits him to turn power on its head. He never stays around, however, to witness the destruction he leaves in his wake. He moves on to other adventures, to other subversive behavior, taking his knowledge and cunning deceptions with him, and acquiring more acumen as he goes. As Lewis Hyde submits, "Intelligence belongs to the wanderer" (1998, 234). Letao's mobility is boundless; always moving across space and time, he traverses and violates cultural and social boundaries. As a boundary crosser (Babcock 1975; Hyde 1998), he is not rooted in geography, but continually moves about, to the point that Kometo and other riṂajeḷ storytellers narrate him right out of the Marshall Islands on to America. Unrestricted to deep history he continually shows up at important historical junctures. Flowing through spaces and times that divide groups of people, he reveals and blurs cultural differences.

With riṂajeḷ trickster narratives, the past is not complete but filled with dynamism, mobility (Shami 2001), and connections with other lands and people. To understand how the past continues to inform the decolonizing present, we must return to mythic time, before European contact—to deep histories. This will take us back to early episodes of the trickster and his destructive/creative work. Only then can we see how he becomes resituated into modern historical events, and how the present is linked to the past despite historical disruptions through colonization, imperial war, occupation, atomic bombs, and nation building.

In this chapter, I will present narrative episodes performed by Kometo that rehearse a series of deceptions by Letao the trickster. As an Indigenous trickster storyteller himself, Kometo made unexpected connections between the mythological antics of Letao and a contemporary history and experience with America. He used the stories of Letao to "narratively claim the world into which" the riṂajeḷ "moved, and to adjust that claim as the world has subsequently moved in on them" (Toelken 2002, 92). To illustrate this claim, I wish to first present an ethnopoetically rendered trickster narrative performed within an intercultural dialogue,[1] and then ascertain several playful narrative tricks: one, the means by which Kometo the storyteller situates the narrative into the context of a dialogue through riMajel storytelling poetic devices and blurred genres; two, how, through these devices and genres, he probes the uncertain truth status, or "truthiness" of narrated events; three, how we may unpack riMajel sensibilities regarding an evocative set of equivocations and ambivalent analogies about American power. While the following performance of a myth may seem far removed from the violent and ambivalent history of the riMajel with the United States, the contextualization, or situating this story (narrated event) into a performance setting (narrative event), will eventually illustrate how it offers a setting to explore analogies between the trickster's wiles and a history of American behavior.

Kometo's rendering of the ensuing Letao narrative echoes numerous versions by other tellers. Nearly all of the following dialogic performance at his home on Telap islet was rendered with a smile, and his adult daughter, grandchildren, and a few visitors from the compound listened in through the windows, frequently giggling or laughing quietly until moments of great outbursts of punctuated laughter.[2] Kometo performed this version from his small, one-room-kneeling-only house, which was on the southeast corner of Mājro atoll (Telap islet). His use of locatives and directional morphemes were made from that point of reference.

The initial trick in the story takes place on the far western side of Mājro atoll on Mājro islet, thirty miles across the lagoon from where the performance took place. The episodes that follow present an atypical sequence because, as will become clear, during his performance I returned Kometo to an episode I knew he had skipped over. Because he had performed this myth for me nine months previous, I was familiar with the sequence. I had heard other storytellers relate it as well. These episodes follow the geographical course Letao took as he departed the Marshall Islands.

Episode I

P   I heard a story that Letao took his power—the Americans got their intelligence from Letao. <all laugh> You know this story?

K   Well, Letao deceived them . . .

A story is told that the two of them hewed—hew outrigger canoes.

MĀJRO ATOLL
0 1 2 3 4 5
NAUTICAL MILES
Roñroñ
Ocean
Kōḷaḷ-en
Kōḷaḷ-en Pass
Inner Lagoon
Irooj
Jarōj
Mājro Islet
Wūlka
Lagoon
Telap
Ocean

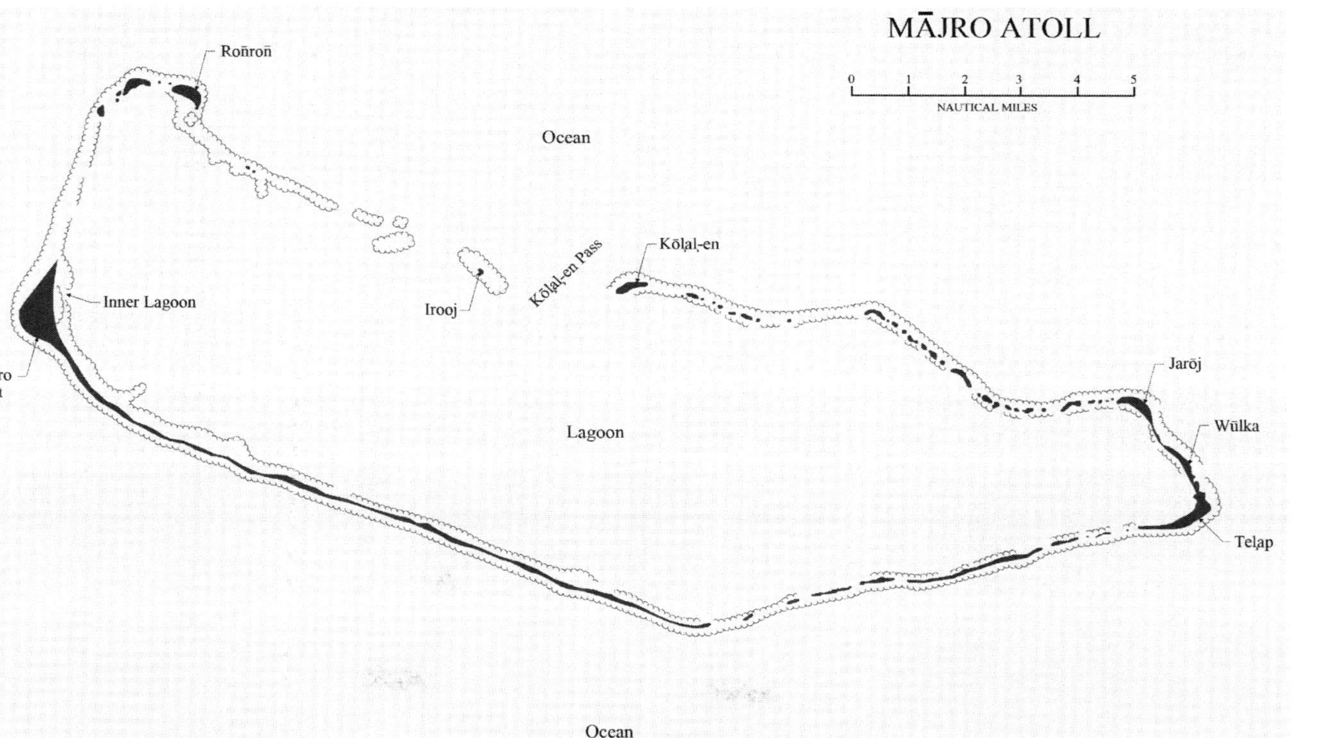

Mājro Atoll

P   Where? Mājro?/
K   /Mājro.

Then, his high chief brother Jemāluut makes a canoe, a real canoe.
He makes it from a breadfruit tree [mā]. (uh huh)
But Letao is really a mischiveous person.
He makes his canoe from ironwood [kōñe].[3]

P   Ironwood?
K   An ironwood canoe does not know how to float.

He takes his canoe and places it on the coral head inside that inner-lagoon of Mājro.
Etao does this. (uh huh)

Now you see the food there? There is a food called *jāākun*. They make it from breadfruit and pandanus. If there is no breadfruit, then they use pandanus.

And he prepares a pandanus leaf around it and ties it. (uh huh)
So that it does not have—

What's it called?

So that insects cannot enter there—
He has <patting hands> tightened it so that an insect can't enter. (uh huh)
So that ants and flies can't enter and—/(uh huh)/
Well, he makes one of them, Etao makes it.
He makes jāānkun and places it there on Jemāluut's canoe.
He makes pandanus paste and ties it and wraps it in pandanus leaves.
And places it there in the canoe.
{Jemāluut then sees Etao's canoe.
He says, "MMMMNN THERE IS NO BETTER THAN THAT CANOE OF YOURS."}

It's like when you prepare that kind of wood, you sandpaper it, and it really shines.

Then, he says, {"OKAY, THE TWO OF US SHOULD EXCHANGE."} <laughs>
Then, Jemāluut, he says, "Yes, good."

Now . . . Jemāluut goes to sail Letao's canoe, he goes to sail it. (uh huh)
But Etao just sails his, the canoe of Jemāluut.
There is much food, jāākun is on it, real food. <we chuckle>
Then, after casting off from—shoving off from that coral head—
Jemāluut carries along his wife. <we laugh>

Was it not long ago that women were very important? <laughs>

And carries his mother also.
Then, after releasing the canoe from off the coral head, {the canoe sinks downward.}
<we all laugh>

P   It sinks?

K   *It sinks and stays there at the bottom and the women float—*
     <laughing> And the other people too.
     And they swim toward the island.

It sinks—<we all laugh> because of the ironwood.
P   Letao deceived him?
K   <laughing> The man Letao really lies. <we all laugh>
P   And where is Letao?
K   He is with you. <pause, everyone laughs>
P   No, at that time. <we laugh hard>
K   Oh! At that time?

Launches the canoe from the coral head and the canoe sails.
Just sails and takes off quickly from over there.
He goes, goes on and on . . .
All the people say, "Well, chase after him!"
He sails the canoe from Mājro islet . . . they chase after him.
They sail and seek to kill him.
He goes toward the north, to the northside over there. <points north>
He tacks and comes through from the north of the atoll.
Sails from there coming into the lagoon-side.
The others have to tack, and they also strive to arrive over there.
<points to northern islets of Mājro atoll>

See? There is a long coral horn, it's lagoon-side of that Kōḷaḷ-en channel way over there. A long coral head. (uh huh)

He has gone and made a coral horn.
Stands on it, so that it grows longer.
Now, the canoes are coming onto the coral horn.
They turn to miss it.
They go on and on, they are really far out to sea.
They must sail back westward out to sea.
That coral horn there, they say he made it so that there are now great waves.
So the canoes, they just have to stop and go around it . . .

The canoes of long ago had no covers, if that much water was inside <mea-sures about one and half feet with hands> it's finished . . . If there is water that enters inside.

P   Uh huh. And they would bail it out?
K   And they would just bail out that water.

Now, Letao just sails east, northeast by those islands.
Then, he comes south to here. <pause>
Letao sails to that islet over there (close by) and takes his canoe to ocean-side.
In the space there between Teḷap and Wūlka [islets]—

You see that gas station over there? He is there. (uh huh)

He takes his canoe over there to ocean-side, it is a very high tide.
Exits his canoe ocean-side through the opening-there-between-the-islets.
Takes it over on to the ocean-side. <long pause>
Then, by the time the other canoes appear, he has made it low tide over there
so they can't pass over the reef.

Episode III

{He goes, goes, and then arrives at Kiribati—} (uh huh)
When he arrives there is no food; they are having a famine.
Then, he goes to the chief.
He says, "My friend, why don't we have food?"
The chief says, "Man, there is really no food on this island."
"Mmmm, well, you tell those women to make that earth-oven."[4]
Then, the women go to make the fire.
They place firewood inside, and then, when finished, they put stones in.
And then, when that is complete, they spread the coals.

They spread stones around inside. (uh huh)
Then, when complete—

See?

He jumps inside and lies down. <I chuckle>
He lies down and says, "WELL, COVER IT WITH LEAVES AND DIRT."
Then, {they come quickly to cover him, cover him}.
And when finished, they go away from him.
But the chief's house—it is there on the lagoon-side—

See?

Next to the lagoon.
Then, they are surprised as Letao comes inland from the sea.
He cleans his hands and <claps hands> claps.

Long ago we did not dry our hands with a towel and those things, but we wash our hands and then, when done, we say, "<claps hands>." (mmm) So that they dry.

P   Letao had been inside?
K   He was inside and they cooked him.
P   So, he came out from the earth-oven?
K   He came out from the earth-oven. Well, is this man human? <pauses, then we all laugh>
P   I don't know.
K   Since they say, "Human." Me? I don't believe he's human; it's just like talking-story. <baby crying in background; he goes on>

<chuckles> *Well, he washes and dries his hands. <claps>*
Comes inland.
"Women go uncover it!"
The women go and uncover the earth-oven.
They uncover many kinds of food.
There is fish, there is chicken, there is preserved breadfruit, taro, (uh huh)
turtle, roasted breadfruit, preserved pandanus.
All kinds of food—there is much inside the earth-oven.
They bring it all here and everyone eats.
He stays another day and does it again.
Two times he does it.

*On another day he says, "HEY MAN, MY FRIEND, I'M READY TO GO
TOMORROW."*

But you see the women? They really hate him.

P   They hate who, Letao?/

K   /Etao.

When he lays down in the house he just lays over there on one side.
But the chief and the women they lay down here.
<points to two sides of the room>
There are two women. (uh huh)
Then, after a while he says, {"Well me, my friend, I am leaving}."

The word "friend" is big. It can be true; it can be false. <laughs hard>

P   The word "friend"?

K   Yes. <we all laugh>

*The chief says, {"WHAT MAN, YOU'RE LEAVING? BUT WON'T YOU
TEACH ME?"}*
"OH! YOU WANT TO LEARN?" <short laugh>
The chief says, "<u>Yes</u>." <short laugh by both of us>
"Well, tomorrow.
You just get up, and both you and the women start that earth-oven.
Bring the firewood."
Then, the next day they bring the firewood.
{Goes on and on} and then afterwards it's done.
It's afternoon, after making the earth-oven fire.
And after it's done, he says, "Well . . . come."
He spreads the coals of the earth-oven, and he spreads the stones inside.
It is just the length of the chief. (uh huh)
Letao says—he is to jump inside the fire.
He says, "JUMP NOW."
The chief jumps.
He says, {"UKKŌK IT'S HOT!"} <everyone laughs>
Then, Letao says, "OOOH I KNOW THAT"—

<laughing> Is this not a lie? <laughs harder>

He says, "Ukkōk It's Hot!"
"AH I KNOW THAT"

{"So, now the two of you just cover him and hold it down"—} <chuckles>
Now, the two women jump up and sit on the oven and {pack it, pack it, pack it tight}.
After they have covered it and packed it tight . . . <we chuckle>
Letao goes away . . .

P   Then what?

K   <clears throat >*Towards evening ooo the women say,*
"Hey man, hasn't it been a long time since the chief should have come?
Like, it was not this long with you."
He says, "Hey there is no problem, how else can it be?
He is making a lot of food." <laughs hard>
"You will see ah, what?
If it's not true that he is making those kinds of food that just take time to make."

It goes on and on, it is night.
Then, he says,
"OH YOU TWO GO AND JUST UNCOVER THAT EARTH-OVEN.
AND SEE WHAT KINDS OF FOODS HE MAKES.
SEE IF THEY ARE NOT MANY." <laughs>

After the two of them go and uncover the earth-oven, and see him, the chief,
he says, <opens mouth wide and stares blankly, eyes wide>
<we all laugh hard>
THEN, THEY RUN, "UKKŌK."
SO, THEY ESCAPE. <we laugh hard, K tries to get composure>

He takes off and goes and lays down in the room.
It's <u>over there</u>, his place is <u>over there on</u> his half [away from them].
But he stays for a while, and then goes outside and it is dark.
He goes outside and brings the chief.
Brings him, and then, he places him next to the women where they lay.
{The women, they then turn to look, "OH MY, the man!"} <laughs hard>
He is cooked! Well done! They run.
They just go and lie down with Letao. <pauses, bursts out with laughter>
The two of them are afraid because the chief is dead. (ah)
Well, now, they just go and lie down with Etao. <we all laugh> *(mmm)*
In the morning they announce that the chief is dead.

The people of Kiribati get up to look for Letao.
They come to kill him.
Then, he escapes.
Because they want to kill him.

P   So, once Letao killed the chief he escapes?
K   He killed him by deceiving him. <all laugh> The women had refused to lay
      with him. But then, in the end, they lay with him. <laughs>

Then, he escapes.

Episode II

P   Letao was at Mile?
K   He was there. He deceived other people at Mile.
P   How did he deceive them?
K   Also, in that same kind of way, he goes and . . . makes mischief.
P   After he had escaped from Jemāluut?
K   Yes.
P   And do you know a story about him deceiving the chief or people in Mile?

K   *He went and then . . .*
      He arrives at Ṇaallo [islet]. (uh huh)
      He stays there . . . and then goes to Mile [islet].
      And . . . says . . . to the chief of Mile . . . that they should prepare food.
      Then, the two of them go fishing.

P   Ocean-side?
K   Lagoon-side. Lagoon-side of Mile.

      Then, they make a hut and fish-with-coconut-leaf-chain [aḷeḷe].[5]
      But they go on and on along the shore.
      And then, over there, they again fish-with-a-coconut-leaf-chain.

See? (uh huh)

The chief chases fish with the coconut-leaf-chain—

And it folds up. That coconut-leaf-chain is a kind of fishing instrument.

And then, everyone gathers together over there.
It's bad to spear the fish too soon, it's bad to throw the spear. (uh huh)
And, it's just not quite ready, but Letao goes and spears too soon.
And all the fish escape.
They, they are angry. <I, then he chuckles>
They are angry with him, but he escapes.
They again chase him quickly, {he goes on and on to Jelbōn islet.}

It's part of Lukwōnwōd [district].

He goes and places his canoe lagoon-side of the island.
And he proceeds inland and makes his food.
Then, he unveils his knee and stabs it down into the ground over there.
And now, there is fresh water at that islet—

It is a small islet, not very big, only the size of maybe from here to what,
Mako? (building we can see at distance outside his open doorway) <point-
ing to locations out the door> Go to Mako and <u>come</u> <u>back</u> <u>over here</u> to <u>that</u>
house, and <u>back</u> to <u>here</u>. (uh huh) And it has fresh water there even though
it is small.
P   Fresh water?
K   Eh.

Well, they say, "He lifts up his knee, extends out his knee, and pokes it into the
ground and water appears." (hmm)
All the canoes they go to find him.
{Then, they say, "There he is."}
{Then, they lower the sails.}
It is low tide over there, he has made it low tide.
Then, the canoes come back around and arrive on the ocean-side.
Then, over there, oceanward, they go and remain there.
Then, as they are still oceanward Letao becomes a coral stone.
And just lifts his knee, he stands it up like so. <lifts up knee>
Then, the canoes come and see the knee, they think it is coral stone.

See?

They say, "There is a place to anchor."
They come and tie up.
A canoe comes and anchors.
Anchors <u>there</u> at the only place to anchor.

The other canoes tie up beside it.
Goes ooo, and those men disembark to find him.
They are gone away, but he pulls in the canoes.
And . . . <coughs> loosens the canoes and sets them adrift.
But he sails his canoe and shouts, "THE CANOES DRIFT AWAY OOOO."
<laughs>
They then turn and run but there are no canoes; they have drifted away.
<we laugh>
They can't swim for them. They can't swim because they are too far away.
(mmm)
They will go again to Lukwōnwōd [islet] to find a canoe and go look after their
canoes. <long pause>

He goes and again makes his food at Ṇadikdik, at that small islet called Luklap.
It's not really Ṇadikdik, but Luklap, the small islet next to it.
And sails to Kiribati.

Episode IV

Well, thus is this story. The end of the riṂajeḷ knowing about him in the
islands is at Kiribati. But,

They say, he went south and just went to those southern islands.
And then, he just goes on and stays in America.
They say, "The reason the Americans are smart, it's because Letao remains in
America."

P   The ancestors say this?
K   Yes, the ancestors say this. Well, is it true what all these people think?
P   I don't know. Why do the riṂajeḷ really enjoy telling this story about Letao?
K   Because of the many things he does, he is really bad. <all laugh lightly>
P   He really is entertaining. He makes everything a joke.
K   Yes, he is a joke.
P   How many generations ago was he in Mājro and Mile, the last time?
K   Ooo—/
P   /Before Germany?
K   Before that, long, long ago.
P   Long, long ago?
K   This is a portion of the stories of long, long, long ago, like all those that pres-
     ent something about the life of the riṂajeḷ.

In this dialogic performance, Kometo recontextualizes the myth in two interesting ways. First, the narrated events, those actions of Letao that predate Euro-American encounters, when resituated into historical time after World War II and nuclear tests, provide a seamless narrative thread between the past and present. The deep mythological past flows into contemporary history to give it shape and meaning. Second, these mythological events, when resituated into a dialogic event, become enmeshed in the contexts of recent history and an immediate intercultural relationship. Kometo achieves this textual recentering, which I contribute to, through distinct formal poetic and linguistic devices of the two discourse genres: narrative and interrogative dialogue. Before unpacking the multiple meanings of this suggestive myth, a clarification of the plot as it emerges in a dialogue, and then a careful consideration of riM̧ajeļ storytelling poetics and blurred genres, will shed light on the contextualization of the story into an ethnographic dialogue and how he sets up the fluid ontological (cf. Goldman and Ballard 1998) truth status of the narrated events.

The plot of this multi-episodic narrative may seem disjointed, but in fact it is clearly rooted in the Marshall Islands landscapes and seascapes, and captures several deceptions of Letao.[6] In Episode I, the story begins on Mājro islet of Mājro atoll, where Letao has carved a shiny fake canoe (*wa*) from ironwood (*kōñe*) that cannot float, in contrast to the high chief brother Jemāluut's real canoe, carved from the buoyant breadfruit (*mā*). Letao places his canoe on the reef of the inner-lagoon so that it appears to float. Anticipating that Jemāluut will desire the attractive canoe, Letao sets up a seemingly amiable exchange, the fake one for the real one. We also see that Letao anticipates his theft of the canoe and escape when he provisions Jemāluut's canoe with the pandanus food (*jāākun*). They launch the canoes, but Letao's canoe (which Jemāluut has obtained) sinks with the women on board. Letao takes off in Jemāluut's canoe and a great chase ensues. Letao is able to escape his pursuers by transforming a reef and extending a coral horn, which forces the others to tack back or be swamped by the waves. He furthers his escape by passing from lagoon to ocean over the reef at high tide, and then making it low tide so those trailing him cannot follow.

In Episode III, Letao sails on to Kiribati, the island chain south of the Marshalls with its own language and culture. When he arrives, they are experiencing a famine and he takes up residence with the chief. He devises a plan to alleviate the famine through the earth-oven trick. He instructs the chief's wives to prepare an earth-oven (*um̧*), and then he jumps inside, commanding them to cover him with leaves and dirt. As they leave, Letao suddenly appears, clapping his hands as if just having washed them. He then charges them to open the earth-oven, where they find copious amounts of food, enough to relieve the hunger of all on the island. Letao performs this trick twice, then informs the chief that he will be leaving. The chief asks Letao to teach him the trick so that he can, we may assume, perform it on behalf of his people. Letao again advises the women to prepare the earth-oven, and then orders the chief to jump inside. Despite the chief's painful protests, Letao directs the women to quickly cover the chief and pack it tight. Unlike Letao, the chief does not appear quickly, and Letao explains that the chief is simply taking time to produce an abundance. Eventually, Letao allows them to open the earth-oven, where they find a well-done and thoroughly cooked chief. Frightened by the sight, they rush off. That night, Letao takes the body of the cooked chief and places it next to the women. Startled and afraid, they rush over to Letao on the other side of the hut, and "lay" (*babu*) with him.[7] The next day, word gets out about the murdered chief and the people chase after Letao to kill him. He again escapes.

Because I remind him, Kometo retraces back to Episode II to narrate Letao's mischief at Mile atoll. Here he joins a fishing party, but instead of waiting for the right time to cast his spear, he launches it too early (on purpose), which allows the fish to escape. Another great chase ensues. Letao travels to an islet where, by pressing his knee into the ground, he creates a freshwater source. He then shape-shifts into a coral stone and lifts his knee to make it look like a good place for canoes to tie up.[8] Those chasing him land their canoes, tie up at the fake anchor, and go inland. Letao then releases the other canoes so they drift off, and finally he escapes in his canoe, taunting them as he sails away. They will have to go to another islet to obtain canoes to retrieve those set adrift. Letao then visits some other islands to obtain food before sailing on to Kiribati.

Episode IV only briefly narrates that Letao departed Kiribati, sailed south, and eventually traveled to America, where his imparted knowledge makes the Americans "smart." Kometo provides very little narration about Letao going on to America and simply uses it to supply closure to the narrated event. The event unfolds mostly through dialogue. It could be argued that this hardly represents an episode at all, but as I will advance in the next chapter, the dialogic interaction of the interrogative genre itself serves to extend this episode of the narrative.

Kometo's confidence with Episodes I and III, often elaborated and developed by other storytellers as well, reflects their popularity: they are the most widely circulating pieces of the Letao corpus. These episodes also embody key images about the trickster that he wants to foreground in the creation of an analogy between Letao and the Americans. Kometo skips over Episode II, though chronologically and geographically situated between leaving Mājro and arriving at Kiribati, and only narrates it because I bring him back to it after he has recounted Episode III. When I do bring him back to Episode II, Kometo elaborates a great deal on the narrative action in Mile, and recounts Letao's localized exploits at his home atoll. As soon as he completes this episode, he returns to the concluding Episode IV with its briefly framed narrated action and follow-up metanarration.

The interrogative frame within the dialogue obviously contributed to the emerging structure of the narrative plot. My questions reflect my intentions to elicit stories from Kometo, and then follow up with questions of clarification, both about the narrated event (so that I would understand the story) and the cultural information necessary to situate the myth in its cultural context. Kometo demanded my reciprocal engagement while he told me stories, as evident in the transcription above. This is not unlike other riMajeḷ storytelling sessions I observed that represent a give and take between the teller and audience, with multiple voices simultaneously breaking the narrative flow and contributing to the emergence of the plot by offering questions, clarifications, corrections, and encouragement.

In the attempt to close "intertextual gaps" (Briggs and Bauman 1992; Bauman 2004), our conversations forced a dialogue between the ethnographically situated narrative event in which the story is told and the mythologically situated narrated event. Sometimes I would interrupt him during the flow of his telling for clarification, and often he would actually interrupt himself with metanarration to clarify the narrative action, location, relations of the characters, to explain the meaning of terms, or to question the events and meaning of the myth. Kometo's perpetual movement from telling the story to metanarration was not just a result of my occasional questions, but a dialogic device employed to develop the meaning of the myth and to ensure understanding (e.g., Episode I, when talking about pandanus food and the shiny ironwood). All the back and forth in the dialogue may seem sloppy, yet this makes transparent the simultaneous and multiple ways we sought to situate the myth in an ethnographic dialogue, generate cross-cultural understanding, and entertain the truth status of the story.

Kometo came to expect our interrogative conversations and adjusted his performance of the stories accordingly, becoming quite competent in managing this setting. Most of his commentaries were developed metanarration, but one of his primary methods was to disengage from the narrative, even in midsentence, to check my linguistic and cultural competence to follow the story with the question, "See?" In Kajin Majeḷ, this phatic communication is actually registered with the use of a question particle "*ke*" and not the actual word "see" (*llo*). Because Kometo inserted the particle into the narrative flow to "see" if I understood, I have translated it in this fashion. His use of this interrogative ensured our intercultural conversation as he moved the story along.

Storytelling Poetics and a Sense of "Truthiness"

Now how does Kometo so competently ground this story into a situated narrative event, or the event of its telling? Because emic paradigms and epistemologies are embedded in the forms and poetics of storytelling, ascertaining some of the riM̧ajeļ poetic/linguistic devices and generic forms available to Kometo will demonstrate how this telling becomes a communicative accomplishment wherein he irresolutely wavers as he plays with a sense of "truthiness" in the narrated event. The formal poetic devices he uses evoke a narrated event that emerges in the context of the situated narrative event, wherein the truth status is entertained. The issue here is less one of commitment to the fidelity of the events recounted, and more how Kometo uses the mythic narrative for "obscuring, hedging, confusing, exploring, or questioning what went on" and keeping the "narrated events open to question" (Bauman 1986, 5–6). Not unlike the modern trickster comedian who coined the term "truthiness,"[9] Kometo playfully draws attention to the appearances of truth, always working in the cracks between the narrative performance and the narrated event's ontology. While such indefinite portrayals of the mythic past may complicate the verity of events, it will ultimately offer a forceful analogy of American power and abuse.

Time and Tense

The boundary between the narrative genre of myth and the interrogative dialogue is porous and places the two genres in a constant conversation with each other. Nonetheless, each is framed differently with respect to tense.[10] One overt poetic device that frames riM̧ajeļ narrative discourse, and which Kometo clearly uses, includes the present tense. In riM̧ajeļ storytelling, a shift into the present tense clearly sets off a narrative telling from simple indirect discourse or descriptions of the past rendered in the past tense. Typically, the two of us used the Kajin Ṃajeļ past tense forms in our conversations and metanarration. For instance, at the beginning of Episode I, Kometo uses the past tense ("deceived") to describe Letao's actions. But then he immediately shifts to the present tense when fully launching into the narrative: "Then, his high chief brother Jemāluut makes a canoe . . ." Throughout the dialogue, this shift is clearly evident. Occasionally, during the questions and commentary we maintain the present tense, especially to establish the ongoing reality of the myth. For example, "The man Letao really lies" establishes that the trickster and his habits continue from the past into the present. However, occasionally Kometo will slide into the past tense during narration, and then quickly reposition the action back into the present. Note the effort to reframe the narrative through the abrupt alterations and correction of tense in the beginning of the narration.

Attention to this linguistic feature may seem superfluous to the meaning of the story. Nevertheless, the performance of the narrated event (the story and event recounted) in the narrative event, by using the present tense, provides a salient poetic device used by riM̧ajeļ storytellers to bring the past into the present. In this way, an important conversation ensues between both time frames, creating a historical present (cf. Ochs and Capps 2001), and in the process permitting the present to be read through a past lens. And within the dialogue, narration in the present tense is just more engaging; performance is "affecting" (Bauman 2004, 10). Use of the present tense allows the action to move as we come to feel part of it. It borders on mimesis, a participation in the past, and provides an alternative to the diegetic telling, or simply looking "back at" the past. To ignore the tense aspect would obscure one of the ways the riM̧ajeļ meaningfully explore the mythic past. Kometo also indicates the passage of time through additional narrative devices. His multiplication of verbs such as "He goes, goes, and then arrives at Kiribati," or "{ . . . pack it, pack it, pack it tight.}", or "They come quickly to cover him, cover him", is a device to describe an action that took some time to do. The most common multiplication involves the verb "go" (*etal*). When rendered in the Kajin M̧ajeļ, it will be multiplied three to four times to communicate duration. To capture this nuance, I translate it as "goes on and on."

Reported Speech

The most obvious form of recontextualizing the voices of the past consists of the manner in which Kometo often employs reported or quoted speech. Like tense, this poetic device is critical to the kinds of dialogue that ensue between the past and present, and between the two of us. Speaking in the voice of another typifies the most overt textual appropriation; it contextualizes voices vis-à-vis each other and brings them directly into the narrative event, closing the "intertextual gap" (Briggs and Bauman 1992; Bauman 2004). Reported speech also facilitates the action and reveals the intentions of the characters. riM̧ajeļ storytellers do not develop descriptions of character motivations in the narrative frame except through quoted speech; otherwise it is achieved through breakaway metanarration. In the earth-oven (*um̧*) trick (Episode III), the action unfolds through the dialogic exchange between the characters and reveals their motivations by means of what they say (e.g., Letao's lust, the chief's coveting, the women's concern and anxiety). Reported speech repeats "what was done in the original past event of which the narrative is an account" (Bauman 1986, 65), and again inclines the discourse away from diegesis and toward mimesis—telling to enacting.

Kometo uses a variety of linguistic devices to establish the quotative frame. Frequently he does this by means of attribution; for example, "he says," "the women say," "they say." Much less often he sets apart reported speech through a command to the addressee; for example, "Women go uncover it" (Episode III), or through the use of particles, connected to whoever performs the most immediate action: "The women, they then turn to look over, 'OH MY,[11] the Man!'" (Episode III). He also uses recognizable conversation routines where obvious turn taking identifies one speaker's response to another, such as in the following example: "The chief says, {'WHAT MAN, YOU'RE LEAVING? BUT WON'T YOU TEACH ME?'} 'OH! YOU WANT TO LEARN? The chief says, "Yes. Well, tomorrow. . . ." (Episode III). In Kometo's performances, the increase in volume nearly exclusively identifies reported speech, and he characteristically renders the voice in a higher pitch and sometimes increases the tempo (for example, {"OKAY, THE TWO OF US SHOULD EXCHANGE."}). While these latter devices serve to register reported speech in their own right, the way Kometo uses them should be seen to actually doubly mark the narrative frame as they always accompany the other devices.

Kometo also effectively used nonverbal gestures as a form of quotative action. Instead of reported speech, he "reenacts" the behavior of the narrated event by substituting a gesture for spoken discourse. He does this on two occasions in Episode III. When they open the earth-oven to reveal the cooked chief, Kometo <opens mouth wide and stares blankly, eyes wide>, a gestural quote that "tells" us that the chief is cooked. Kometo's use of this gesture draws abundant laughter as he imitates a "well-done" chief. On another occasion, when Letao comes out from the earth-oven, he claps. The clapping replaces the verbal discourse once in the narrated event, <claps his hands and clapping hands>; and then in the meta-narration, he even claps as if the gesture itself is the quote, "when done, we say, '<claps hands>.'"

Deictics

Locatives and other spatial deictics establish an exacting linguistic quality in Kajin M̦ajeḷ and are often lost in translation in an effort to avoid seemingly stilted talk.[12] Kajin M̦ajeḷ, like other languages of Oceania (Blust 2009), is very specific about the location of objects and actions in space in relation to the speaker. These deictic resources designate either "by the speaker but not the listener" (e.g., *ije*), "by both the speaker and listener" (e.g., *ijin*), "there by you" (e.g., *ijene*), "away from both the speaker and listener but within sight" (e.g., *ijen*), and "away from both speaker and listener but conceived of" (e.g. *ijo*). Although at times it may seem somewhat awkward in English, I have tried to retain some of the locative nuances in Kometo's narrations and our conversation because it is through these devices that we accomplish much of the work of contextualization as well as create a sense of participating in the narrated events. For instance, in Episode II, Kometo narrates, "Anchors <u>there</u> at the only place to anchor." This specific locative in Kajin Ṃajeḷ designates the location as "away from both the speaker and listener but conceived of," in this case by those participating in the narrative event. This again blurs the boundary between the narrated and narrative events. Action in the story is referenced in relation to the location of the narrative event. But if situated within the reported speech in the narrated event, the deictics used reference the speaking character, not the narrator, as in, " . . . well, you tell those women to make that earth-oven" (Episode III), where "those" and "<u>that</u>" mean "away from both speaker and listener but within sight of the two (characters)." Most utterances are full of multiple and duplicate locatives such as this example in Episode III: "It's <u>over there</u>, his place is <u>over there on</u> his half" (away from them). Similarly, in Episode II, the metanarration exemplifies the distances in the past narrated action through comparative locations in the storytelling setting: "Go to Mako and <u>come</u> <u>back</u> <u>over here</u> to <u>that</u> house, and <u>back</u> to <u>here</u>."

Kajin Ṃajeḷ is also exacting about the direction in which action proceeds, and numerous deictic devices are also affixed to most verbs. Action either proceeds "to the speaker" (-*tok*, e.g., *kātok*, fly-to-here), "to the listener" (-*wōj*, e.g., *kōnonowōj*, speak-toward-you), or "away from both speaker and listener" (-*ḷọk*, e.g., *peḷọk*, drift away). Other directional morphemes indicate to and from. For instance, if one is standing on land, the movement of a canoe toward the land is *ānetak*. In contrast, the same movement, if one is positioned on the canoe, is *ānelak*. This is the same for "in" or "out" to sea. These directional verbs are essential to a maritime culture in which the activities of sailing, tacking, and launching are served by specificity. A more literal translation would render the following (from Episode I) as "Just sails and takes off quickly from over there (out of sight)," and "comes south to here (by both of us)"; or "He tacks and comes through (over there away from both of us) from the north of the atoll"; or "Launches (away out to sea) the canoe from the coral head and the canoe sails (away from that place)." These grammatical forms facilitate the recontextualization of the mythic past into the immediacy of the dialogue.

riṂajeḷ speakers are very aware of their cardinal directions at all times and specify these locations vis-à-vis the speaker or action easily and often, not just for major sailing methods, but even with mundane activities, for example, "move the pole a little toward the northeast." In the narrative episodes presented here, Kometo most obviously employs the four points in Episode I, when the chief's people chase after Letao: "They must sail back westward out to sea," and "He tacks and comes through to the north of the atoll," or, "Now, Letao just sails east, north east by those islands. Then, he comes south to here." Not only are sailing directions designated by the cardinal points, but also Kajin M̧ajeļ has specific terms for sailing into (*taḷọk*) or away from (*toḷọk*) the wind, which is essentially toward the east or toward the west, respectively, due to the prevailing winds, or wind at the starboard, going north (*niñaḷọk*), or port, going south (*rōñaḷọk*). In these cases, I use cardinal directions to translate them into English, but they nonetheless convey culturally appropriate and nuanced references in Kajin M̧ajeļ. Kometo also employs very specific spatial reference terms, such as "ocean-side" (*lik*) and "lagoon-side" (*iar*), referring to the islets and atolls (the middle, *iooj* or *ioḷap,* and ends of an islet, *ajoklā* or *jabōn,* are also specified). These terms form an essential part of everyday speech since these locations are ever present on the low-lying narrow coral atolls. Like all riM̧ajeļ storytellers, Kometo applies these locations frequently to position the action or location of important sites in the narrated event, for instance: "But the chief's house—it is there on the lagoon-side" (Episode III); "takes his canoe over there to the ocean-side" (Episode I); "arrive on the ocean-side" (Episode II). I would also ask questions in the narrative event to get my bearings in the narrated action (e.g., at the beginning of Episode II).

As is evident even from just this version, place-names (e.g., Mājro, Arņo, Mile, Ņadikdik) clearly specify the location of action. Atoll boundaries are plainly demarcated by ocean borders. Within an atoll (*aelōñ*), each individual islet (*āne*) is also named and placed within a district (*bukwōn*) typically composed of several islets or section of a large islet. The riM̧ajeļ know the names of every islet (" . . . {he goes on and on to Jelbōn islet}," or "exits his canoe ocean-side in the *space there between Teḷap and Wūlka [islets]*—"), and districts ("It's part of Lukwōnwōd"), and boundary identifiers for the land tracts (*wāto*) that cross lagoon to ocean.[13] Everyday conversations and stories will ascertain residences, objects, and actions within these territorial references. In the dialogic performances here, Kometo not only follows Letao from one atoll to another, but also steps out of the narrated event through metanarration to clearly locate the past action in relation to present references at the same location, such as (in Episode I), "You see that gas station over there? He is there." Note the collapse of the two events again when he places Letao "there" at the gas station (located in the narrative event) by maintaining the present tense framing device for the narrated event. He does not say Letao "was" there.

The spatial deictics in Kajin M̧ajeļ prove difficult to translate, but they simultaneously connect the narrator and audience as well as the characters in the story to the actions on the landscape or seascape. My simplified rehearsal of these poetic devices is not meant to get lost in the minutiae of linguistic details of an Oceanic language, but rather to briefly illustrate how Kometo contextualizes the narrated event, situates me (as audience) in relationship to these events, positions me in relation to him as storyteller, and informs the myth with a sense of truthiness. This sense is most fully communicated through a nonlinguistic poetic device: laughter.

Laughter

At first glance, laughter may not seem to contribute to the poetics of storytelling. But fundamentally, poetic devices function to draw attention to the message itself (Jakobson 1960), facilitate situating the story within the event of its telling, and register an attitude about the truth status of the narrated event. Laughter at a Letao story arises from both the deception and farce within the narrated event, and how the story is performed by the storyteller in the narrative event. Kometo as storyteller draws from the comedic actions within the story, and then through his own laughter and that he generates in his audience, he points back to the story's message; he holds it up for scrutiny. Laughter, and Kometo's humorous performances that elicit it, serves many functions, but three of them clearly communicate something about the sense of truthiness in the story: first, there is laughter at deception and the "cognitive mayhem" (Stoeltje 2014, 106) brought about by the subversion and inversion of the social order; second, laughter marks the content of the story as deception within the narrated event, to highlight the continual ambiguity between what is true (*ṃool*) and what is false (*riab*); third, laughter raises the question about the truth status of the story within the narrative event, communicating ambiguity about the performer's position and intentions. Letao's power derives from his deceptions and ambiguity, and thus the laughter at his antics registers a degree of uncertainty, and some catharsis, about both the doings in the narrated event and our respective roles in the narrative event.

The laughter that punctuates each telling of a Letao narrative foregrounds that we are experiencing a deception. With other forms of narrative performance, there may be occasional moments of laughter, but with Letao stories laughter contributes an essential part of the unfolding structure of both the narrated and narrative events. The presence of laughter, as part of the stylized qualities of this form, is what the listening audience primarily contributes to the emergence of the telling. The narrator may often laugh with amusement at the trickster antics, or may laugh in collusion with the audience, or may even pause after a singular telling moment of deception in the narrative to cue the audience to laugh, but the audience contributes the bulk of the laughter. A Letao narrative of deception not only anticipates laughter as a key part of its framing, but also in fact, insists upon it, otherwise both the teller and audience have not met the cultural expectation to assume accountability for the realization of the form. No laughter at all with a Letao narrative would prove a failed performance.

Kometo's voice, when performing stories about Letao, consistently teeters on the brink of laughter, and at multiple points during narration, he erupts into high-pitched laughter that shakes his whole frame. Those listening smile for nearly the duration of the performance. His own responses represent a continuum from a pervasive slight chuckle to a strong hard laugh, and even long intense laughter that makes him gasp for air. The ludic in the stories leads to moments of great mirth, and since Kometo and those listening anticipate the most hilarious points in the narratives, we are poised to laugh (cf. Toelken 2003). As a result, the whole storytelling environment with Letao narratives is one of genial levity.

Little cultural competence is necessary to understand what is funny in these stories. Letao's subversive, lustful, tricky, self-serving actions are not couched in speech play with multiple meanings; they border on physical comedy, even though they are verbally rendered. Much of Kometo's laughter precedes or follows reported speech, which accentuates the physicality of the comedic behavior in the narrated event. On several occasions, the laughter becomes so intense, with uncontrollable squeaks and gasps, that the discourse is unintelligible in some recordings. I recall that in the moment we would laugh as much in response to his laughter as we would to what he was saying—because sometimes we did not know what he was saying. At times the laughter follows overt rule breaking (cf. Toelken 2003) and subversions, but equally, the laughter results from the behavioral farce of the narrative characters, and most importantly, the stylistic manner in which Kometo renders action and reported speech.

With Kometo's vocal modulation, cracking voice, and prankster tone, all of us present are prepared at any moment to erupt into laughter. I have listened to other riM̧ajeḷ storytellers perform Letao narratives, but none of them elicit the sheer quantity of laughter through the course of a performance as Kometo. riM̧ajeḷ know how to laugh as viscerally and cathartically as any people I know; their outbursts can be shrill, shocking, and accompanied with slaps and hits. Such laughter stands out all the more from the staid, dignified, and veiled demeanor that accompanies deferential conversations and formal discourses, such as oratory, chant, and prayers, especially as they are informed by a Judeo-Christian stoicism that marks a performance as sacred. In Kometo's performances of narratives, the audience is always prepared, but nonetheless sometimes surprised, by his unexpected insertions of humor. Such punctuated moments are multiplied in his performance of the Letao stories. Again, the physical antics of

Letao generate much of the hilarity, in contrast to puns or wordplay. Letao's ambiguity would seem to lend itself to this kind of humor, but most of his deceptive work comes more from his categorical liminality and how he conceals the truth. When described in narrative, his comedic behavior is obvious to us, even though those he dupes in the narrated event remain unaware. We, the audience, are made privy to how he is setting up his trick, while the characters in the narrated event only come to realize it after the damage is done.

While Kometo and his audience laugh often during his performances, we laugh just as much in our interrogative dialogues and at his metanarrations. Laughter during the performance slides the discourse out from the narrated event and relocates it back into the narrative event. Accordingly, laughter belongs to the dialogue between participants in the narrative event. It comments on the narrated event and indexes the position participants take toward it. It also indexes the relationships between participants in the narrative event. To laugh jointly (laugh with, not at) points to a shared understanding of the "joke" and a fusion of identities. In these non-narrative dialogues, our laughter shifted from the physical comedy of the story to humor as wordplay, ambiguous narrative references, and analysis of our social relationship. I will illustrate each one of these dimensions of laughter.

In Episode III, Kometo steps back into the narrative event to explore how Letao unpacks the ambiguity of a word in the narrated event: "The word friend is big. It can be true; it can be false" <laughs hard>. For another example, Kometo narrates, "—Jemāluut carries along his wife" <we laugh>. This is simple laughter, acknowledging that I understand the basic narrative content. In Episode III, he breaks away from the narrative after Letao obtains the wives of the Kiribati chief: "They just go and lie down with Etao." <all laugh> Again, the laughter signals that I understand the sexual implications of the story. Later, I assume the narrative has ended, and I ask, "So, once Letao killed the chief he escapes?" Kometo answers: "He killed him by deceiving him." <all laugh> "The women had refused to lay with him. But then, in the end, they lay with him." <laughs> In this example, Kometo laughs about death, then he laughs about the deception and the trick to get sex. This presents an example of dialogic laughter at Kometo's word play as I seek and he explains the meaning of the narrated actions.

Kometo also laughs (and we often laugh with him) when he highlights deceptions within the narrated event by stepping out from it with metanarration. For instance, P: "Letao deceived him?" K: <laughing> "The man Letao really lies." <we all laugh> (Episode II). When I seek to understand the narrated event, Kometo makes us laugh as we recognize that the event is unfolding through Letao's creation of lies. Even more telling is when (in Episode III) I break him off from the narrative to ensure I understand what is going on, P: "Letao had been inside?" K: "He was inside and they cooked him?" P: "So, he came out from the earth-oven?" K: "He came out from the earth-oven. Well, is this man human?" <pause, then we all laugh>." Here, as I seek simple understanding of the narrative content, Kometo reads it as a doubt about the possibility of someone coming out from an earth-oven. He then brings the ontological status of the narrated event into question, and we all laugh at how he highlights Letao's general ambiguity through his question.

These moments of dialogic laughter facilitate the creation of social relations in the narrative event. The following example even more profoundly links the narrated event to our ethnographic conversation through analogy. In the first episode, I ask, seeking clarity again about the narrative action, P: "And where is Letao?" K: "He is with you." <pause, we both laugh> P: "No, at that time." <we laugh hard> K: "Oh! At that time?" My question is intended to remain attached to the narrated event, but Kometo pulls back, not just to explain, but to make a joke by creating the ongoing likeness between me, my country, and the Letao character. He knows I know the outcome of this mythological story; it is actually the second time he performed it for me, and we have joked about Letao going to America many times in other conversations.

Recognizing the intertextuality of our dialogues, his answer is not intended to clarify the narrated event but to create the analogy between the story and our intercultural relationship. He pauses for me to get it, since I expected a descriptive answer, and then we laugh. My next comment resituates the action back into the narrative, not our immediate performance context, which only increases our laughter. He then acts sarcastic about which time frame we are really working with, but in doing so throws them both into question.

I rehearse the role of laughter in the two discourse genres in order to show its central role in the constitution of the narrative event, and how it poetically functions to offer commentary on the narrated events. More than any other poetic device, laughter signals how both the storyteller and the audience hedge and equivocate on the "truthiness" of the narrated event. In many ways, laughter serves as the glue holding the narrated and narrative events together. No question, some of Kometo's laughter and of those participating was attributable to the uncertainty my presence created. This also generated some uneasiness, especially for those who did not know Kometo's and my implicit agreement to joke. In such moments, the response was nervous laughter, as the other audience members wondered how I would take the comedy in their narratives and even Kometo's antics as performer. Our mutual laughter created the ground for trust, enabling us to explore the larger implications of the myth in a decolonizing context and to mediate our emerging ethnographic friendship. Laughter provided a form of *communitas* (Turner 1982), a kind of equalizer, especially as our jokes became highly calibrated, something we shared between only each other.

Blurred Genres

The Letao story under consideration here, and Letao narratives generally, raise several questions about how they fit within islander categories of oral expression. The riM̧ajeļ apply a variety of Indigenous genre labels to their forms of narrative discourse. These labels both categorize the discourse, identify an attitude people take toward them (Burke 1941), and "coordinate social attention both to themselves and to the actors who collaborate to realize them" (Noyes 2016, 133). Indigenous categories of narrative expression are not inconsequential; they offer culturally salient alternatives to frame how a story is to be received and suggest an epistemology regarding the truth status of events rendered in the story. Just as the meanings of a story are dynamic as they are resituated in different contexts, so too are the ways riM̧ajeļ storytellers generically frame their discourse. The flexibility of oral genres has been consistently raised by others (e.g., Ben-Amos 1976; Dorst 1983; Briggs and Bauman 1992; Schrempp and Hansen 2002; Thompson and Schrempp 2020) who attend to them not as hard and fast categories but as porous in the way they "leak" into each other when "used in creating intertextual relations with other bodies of discourse" (Briggs and Bauman 1992, 149,163). Consequently, an identifiable story among the Letao corpus, such as the one presented above, could have a "variety of relationships" to other versions located in more than one generic form.[14] Such stories "breach genre classifications" (Harris-Lopez 2003, 115) made either by the insider or outsider. Not only do specific riM̧ajeļ narratives move in and out of different genres depending on island location, matriclan, religious group, or storyteller, thus making any classification unstable, but also the genres themselves blur together in actual social practice across time (cf. Bauman 1992; Harris-Lopez 2003). Different emic genre labels may be applied to the same story by different riM̧ajeļ tellers depending on how they contextualize and perform it, how they provide authenticating details, or the relationship they may have to the narrated event and former storytellers from whom they learned it (cf. Huntsman 1995).

For this reason, applying a genre label to the above Letao story must always be provisional. There is perhaps a serendipitous dimension to this discussion. In his optimistic attempt to define and clarify oral narrative genres, William Bascom (1965) wished to retain the three analytical labels of myth, legend, and folktale,[15] but with a twist; their application would be determined from a "native's" point of view in terms of their belief orientation (fact or fiction, sacred or secular), time (remote past, recent past, anytime) and place (other world, world of today, anywhere).[16] To illustrate his classificatory schema, he drew upon William Davenport's study of "Marshallese Folklore Types" (1953) to inform analytical categories with ethnographically determined terminologies.

Working with riM̧ajȩļ storytellers, Davenport identified what he considered "native" categories, then translated them into analytical genres roughly analogous to the Western tripartite schema. He recognized, however, that the boundaries between the genres are soft because "any classification of cultural data is a strained one, for sharp distinctions are seldom made" (1952a, iii). Still, Davenport would later identify the Kajin M̧ajȩļ terms *bwebwenato* for those narratives comparable to myth because they present "traditional history, genealogies, and explanatory tales" and are "generally accepted as true" (1953, 221); "*bwebwenato in mol*" (literally, "story of truth") as "true stories of today," which he glossed as "modern myths" whose "veracity is undisputed" and "they are always modern in setting" (1953, 223);[17] and *ino̧ñ*, which he glossed as "fairy tale." Narratives in this latter category were identified by the framing device (*kiriwatne*), which he claimed to mean "this is a fairy tale; it may or may not have happened long ago; it is not to be taken seriously; it is not always supposed to be logical," and a concluding formula (*jiribino̧ñ*), which means, "this is the end of the tale; no explanation necessary" (1953, 224).[18] He also suggested that another set of stories, *bwebwenato Edao* (Etao Stories), follows the "general pattern of fairy tales" (1953, 229) but are classified differently. Consequently, stories of Letao represent a specific subcategory of *ino̧ñ* or fairy tale in Davenport's schema.

Through my efforts to elicit creation stories from several storytellers, however, and by reviewing the narratives recorded by the first ethnologists in the Marshall Islands,[19] it is apparent that Letao was once included among the gods (*anij*) and primordial beings, whether he was variably placed among stories entertained as *bwebwenato* (mythic) or *ino̧ñ* ("not to be taken seriously"). Moreover, the term *bwebwenato Edao* fundamentally means "A story about Letao," wherein some storytellers may either freely ascribe it to *ino̧ñ* (a fiction or story about lying), or *bwebwenato in etto*, a story about the ancient mythic past in which the trickster Letao is the main character. It all depends on what the storyteller wants to achieve by telling it in a given context to a particular audience. The word *etto* in Kajin M̧ajȩļ means "ancient times" or a "long time ago," and is often used to designate the times of the gods, creation, and the earliest people. When telling stories about these times, the riM̧ajȩļ will often refer to them as *bwebwenato in etto*, or stories of the ancient times. This reference aligns more closely with the analytical genre of myth.

This malleability in genre terminology reveals genre classifications in the Marshalls as fluid and full of interrelated stories that flow between them. Yet, there is some utility in using such labels so long as we recognize the flexibility, blurring, and intertextuality that permits people, most especially a trickster storyteller, to explore the truthiness of events within and among genres in the actual social practice of telling stories. While riM̧ajeļ attitudes toward a mythic narrative may vary from one context to the next, the genre still provides an interpretive and ideological frame about time, ontology, meaning, and its use.[20]

If "myths are recurrently characterized as foundational, primordial, sacred, and theomorphic," Letao stories both fit and do not fit, as there is a "difficulty, if not futility, of attempting to rigorously uphold distinctions between 'myth' and other oral narrative categories like 'folktale' and 'legend'" (Schrempp 2002, 2). Kometo and others would sometimes refer to Letao stories with the term *bwebwenato in etto* (mythic), and sometimes as *inoñ,* or the fairy tale in Davenport's classification. Their use of this latter label, missed by Davenport, was to identify a story as either, one, a "falsehood" about what transpired in the past, or, two, involving lies and deceptions by the trickster. The former gesture seeks to manage a modern and Christian worldview about the ontology of a mythological past, while the latter emphasizes how the stories carry "perceptual significance" (Scheub 2012, 10) about the utility of pretext in social life and culture.

The reason Letao stories are so hard to pin down in terms of form is that the qualities of the trickster himself blur the generic boundaries between myth received as true and sacred, and tale received as fiction and profane, and between myth set in the primordial beginnings, and tale set in an indeterminant time and place. The trickster character and the teller of trickster stories obscure the boundaries between the sacred and profane, between fiction and truth, and between the primordial past and the present. In the performance of trickster stories, these contrasts fold in on each other to, paradoxically offer a fictional truth, define the sacred through the profane, and envisage a mythological past that is profoundly present. Both the trickster and the trickster storyteller challenge any literal reading of the story. Those who take things literally, both characters in the story and those listening, will ultimately find themselves in the position of dupe. Instead of any literal conclusions, Letao exploits the "serious playfulness … of myth" (Wheelwright 1965,167) symbolically laden with cultural truths,[21] to consider "the ideological, cultural, and cognitive categories necessary for discussing what is, and what is not, true" (Thompson and Schrempp, 2020, 2).

Kometo flexibly applied a range of the riM̧ajeļ genre labels to the story of Letao stealing his brother's canoe, tricking the chief at Kiribati, and then moving on to America. His application of a genre label depended on the point he wished to make and the meaning of the story he wished to foreground in our dialogues. Sometimes he applied the term *inọñ* when he wished to emphasize the deception involved or question the truth status of the events. But when he wanted to identify it as part of the great repertoire of riM̧ajel̦ mythology and highlight Letao's cosmological origins, he referred to it as *bwebwenato in etto.* Usually, he simply called it a *bwebwenato in Letao,* to key those who would listen to be prepared to laugh at the antics of the trickster and to test our acumen at unpacking its tricky sociological meaning. Being able to move across genre categories allowed him, as a trickster storyteller, to exploit a variety of intertextual references and meanings, and leave open the truth status of the event, as he placed stories and voices from the mythic past into conversation with a modern present. Whether Letao stories are referred to as *inọñ* or *bwebwenato in etto,* they nonetheless retain striking continuity with the genealogies, events, and characters of other mythic stories. This episodic story performed by Kometo, even though he placed it in diverse generic contexts, resides on the margins of myth, not because we can demarcate fact from fiction, or the sacred from the secular,[22] but because it draws upon two riM̧ajel̦ epistemologies and senses of mythological time: (1) the ancient past (*etto*) distinguished from the present (*raan kein*) after Christianity, colonialism, and imperialism;[23] and (2) a deep past typified by the primordial actions of foundational nonhumans and divine characters with all their powers, capacities, cosmogonic genealogies, and relationships to each other. Using the etic term *myth* resonates with the flexible use of an Indigenous genre and narrated settings that I heard Kometo and many others tell about the deep past of the gods, including the origin and exploits of Letao.

Sensibilities and Ambivalent Analogies

Now what of this plot, composed of several episodes of the trickster usurping others through deception, and ultimately ending up in America? The account of Letao traveling to America and bestowing his power has become a well-formed and popular episode in the repertoire of riM̧ajel̦ storytellers. In addition to my recordings from a range of different individuals across the islands where I studied (five in the Ratak Chain and two in the Rālik Chain), several others have recorded this episode (Carucci 1989, 1997a; Tobin 2002; Kelin 2003; Hess 2004; Tanner 2008). Both the recent generation and the elders who lived during the war know this motif and view it as a crucial part of the total narrative. This episode clearly developed after World War II and American occupation in the 1950s, yet the narrated event it presents is set in a time prior to the war. This temporal context of the myth exploits ambiguity and creates a symbolic analogy between the devious trickster and the Americans. To illuminate how Letao serves this meta-phoric role for the Americans necessitates exploring the qualities they share. The mythic text does not simply narrate a well-worn episode; it offers additional insights into the trickster's capacities and qualities that the Americans replicate.

Learning from many islanders over decades, I piece together below what I ascertain to be the sensibility of riM̧ajeļ culture regarding social life and power, and its historical manifestations. By sense (or sensibility), I do not mean a fixed or stable underlying logic, but rather a flexible form of consciousness, respon-siveness, or susceptibility to cultural meanings, distinctions, epistemologies, ide-ologies, or historical patterns of behavior.[24] Some of this sensibility, however, emerges with the imposition of colonizing institutions that accompany American imperialism and new state politics, and yet such things are talked about as if a continuation of a deep history. Much of it does belong to a deep history that car-ries over into the contemporary narrative of Letao traveling to America. Having pieced together this sensibility with many islanders and storytellers, and using Kometo's narrative performance as a point of departure, I wish to reflect on how the riM̧ajeļ, within the margins of myth and history, draw upon the ambiguity Letao offers to reimagine their ambivalent history of exploitation and abuse by the Americans.

In the opening episode, Letao creates a beautiful shiny canoe from wood that will not float. This is the first deception. In making it appear what it is not, Letao exploits the greed of his brother to trick him. Part of the effectiveness of his tricks comes from his astute awareness of human weaknesses. His high chief brother has dominion over all in his atoll. In effect, he has access to everything and it is at his discretion whether to use it or not. But Letao sets up an exchange that makes it seem as if he is getting the worst part of the bargain. Letao trades some-thing fake (a sinking canoe that appears to float) for what is real (a floating canoe); he obtains the "true" (*m̧ool*) canoe and is empowered through his lie (*riab*). He makes his brother look like a fool by outwitting him in this exchange, and in doing so he steals a prominent cultural symbol for chiefly authority. By desiring it enough to give up the "real thing" for the fake, the riM̧ajeļ chief becomes a dupe.

Establishing these qualities of Letao (cleverness, deception, thievery, subver-sion of power) in the opening episode begins to set up analogies with the Americans. They are not only a subverting force (upending Japanese control and status), but what seems a fair exchange (an atoll for world peace, occupation for significant amounts of remuneration) is not what it appears to be, and the out-come may make riM̧ajeļ look like fools. Letao escapes in his brother's canoe, and we can assume that it is in this vessel that he sails on to America. By doing this, he transports more than his destructive power to the Americans; he takes along with him one of the key symbols of chiefly power, albeit a stolen symbol.

A few seemingly insignificant incidents associate Letao with food: loading the pandanus food in Episode I, disrupting the acquisition of it in Episode II, and performing the earth-oven trick in Episode III. Making, obtaining, stealing, or disrupting the acquisition of food lies at the heart of each episode. Food is a symbol that condenses much about riM̧ajeļ kinship. Sharing food characterizes the most fundamental obligation between relatives (*nukwi*). Offering food is also the ultimate gesture of sociability and good will. This symbolic gesture is both cosmologically substantiated and socially rooted in everyday actions. The god constellation Jebro (Pleiades) is praised as both legitimate (*m̧ool*) and kind (*jouj*) because when he is in the sky he feeds people (brings fertility to the earth),[25] while his angry older brother Tūm̧ur (Antares), who was usurped because of his selfishness, brings famine and distress as he courses the heavens. Food is also socially constitutive; through sharing food, social relations are generated and maintained, and it is the means whereby a chief confirms his power, by receiving tribute (*ekkan* or *eojek*),[26] and by distributing (*ajej*) food. Historically, the riM̧ajeļ chief literally fed the people through redistribution of the tribute and by granting usufruct rights to the land. In return for the tribute, the chief redistributed the "wealth" (*m̧weiuk*) to the commoners (*kajoor ro*) and ensured the land's fecundity by blessing it through his divine and sacred genealogy (Carucci (1997b). By providing strength to his commoners, he acquires political power (*kajoor*) because the people (*kajoor ro*) will remain loyal to him. Clearly, the term for power and people derives from the same root word. In one usage, it means "the people" but also denotes "strength" or "cause to stand" (literally, "to impost or implant a pole"). Thus, through military strength a chief acquired people, who in turn gave him more strength, or caused him to be "elevated" or "respected" (*kautiej*).[27] A chief may have attained his power by bravery (*peran*) and fierce prowess (*lāj*) in battle, but he maintains his power by being kind (*jouj*) and distributing food (*m̧ōñā*) or land (*bwidej*). We can assume Letao purloins this primary symbol of power and takes it with him, to eventually become a principal symbol of American power—they possess an abundance of food and distributed it freely after the war.

Shortly after the war, American forces developed a military base and airfield on Mājro atoll. This project shifted the economic and administrative center from Jālooj (Jaluit) atoll that had been used by the Germans and Japanese. Later, the military built a dock and runway, and the atoll continued to serve as the headquarters for the Navy administrators who assumed responsibility to administrate the islands immediately following the war. Kometo and many islanders view Mājro as Letao's home atoll. For them, it is no coincidence that the Americans selected it to be their administrative center. Several islanders, including Kometo, who lived on Mājro at the time, recall how the American servicemen had so much clothing, equipment (such as flashlights and cooking utensils), and especially food (unopened cans), that they just "dumped it" for the islanders to take, thus both displaying their chiefly wealth and kindness (*jouj*).

The motifs of Letao kicking up a coral horn at Mājro, creating a freshwater islet, shape-shifting into a coral stone at Mile, and changing the tides, demonstrate his power over nature. This supernatural ability to control and change nature permits him to escape. Many riMạjeḷ attribute to the Americans a similar power. In addition to the power demonstrated by the bomb testing and its effects on nature, other technological advances exhibit the same qualities—airplanes, heavy construction equipment, submarines, and rocket ships all seem to defy nature and subdue it. The war and nuclear waste ruins provide a constant reminder of the extreme power the Americans displayed. Those who remember the war do not see this dramatic narrative as complete, even while the environment slowly but steadily erases the material reminders. Even those who were born after the war (that is, the vast majority of the current population) have the remains as a backdrop to their lives or hear the old people recall the past and its meaningfulness in the present.

One evening in 1992, I sat talking with several elders by a small kerosene lamp late into the night, to one side of a bombed-out Japanese building on Tōrwa islet of Mạḷoeḷap atoll. They were tired of my questions and pushed me to explain how the United States military had so convincingly "destroyed" (*ko̧kkure*) Iraq during the Gulf War the previous year (1991). They wanted to know about "smart bombs" and airplanes that avoid radar and with computers that lead missiles to their targets in the middle of the night. Their curiosity was intense and they grilled me for over two hours—just about this topic. When I suggested that some people thought America's conduct was misplaced, they became agitated and said that America is "greatly good like Jebro" (the god of fecundity and shared abundance) and must "take care of other countries." They said also that the Americans are "kind" (*jouj*), the same descriptor for a benevolent chief. And like so many other islanders, they inquired about the Kennedy family, claiming that JFK was the greatest president because he stood up to the Russians and sent out the Peace Corps. For the riMạjeḷ, Kennedy represents the combination of warrior prowess (*lāj*) and populist kindness (*jouj*), the dualistic qualities of a good chief (cf. Marcus 1989). In these seemingly remote atolls, the islanders' memory of world events is acute as they intersect with their own history. Reading the Americans through the lens of chiefly power (a warrior, knowledgeable, and kind), the riMạjeḷ, such as Kometo, ostensibly cast America in an estimable light, combining military strength and kindness into one image.

The memory of World War II, atomic bomb testing, and continued missile testing at Kuwajleen provides an indelible memory of the Americans (cf. Dvorak 2018). Often, I was annoyed by the seemingly pro-American sentiments offered to me, and by their praise of the US military that appeared to justify American global actions. I often reflexively viewed this as their negotiation of intercultural space with me as an American ethnographer. Nonetheless, anytime I tried to reposition myself vis-à-vis this problematic history, they would remind me of my own genealogy and maintained that it was my responsibility to represent it well. Kometo underscored this point often. On another occasion with Kometo and several older friends, including women and men, I must have come across as absurdly romantic when I protested the benefits of American military power and suggested that the wisdom of the riM̧ajeļ provided a much more profound way to live. Kometo quickly and sternly questioned me: "Who invented the bomb? The riM̧ajeļ? Who makes guns? The riM̧ajeļ? Who puts food in cans? The riM̧ajeļ? Who makes shirts and pants? The riM̧ajeļ? Who flew to the moon and just walked around up there? The riM̧ajeļ? No! The Americans. They really know. They are the most powerful chiefs on earth and they feed everyone." If, as many riM̧ajeļ claim, the Americans were both great warriors and took care of people, thus satisfying the dualistic image, then they are the presumptive world rulers. In this way, riM̧ajeļ sensibilities about chiefly authority make intelligible the continued extension of American global power and influence through both international welfare assistance and structural violence (cf. Dvorak 2018). The reading of their unresolved history with America combines chiefly kindness and military strength with its destruction into one image. Like chiefs, the assessment of Americans is ambivalent: they are both munificent and dangerous.

While the Americans appear to enact the chiefly image, they also draw upon the powers of the Trickster. As with other great chiefs, Letao's power does not come through his warrior prowess alone. Instead, he is able to escape from his pursuers because he is smarter than his enemies; he outwits them. Likewise, for many islanders, the Americans are good warriors (*rūttarinae*) not simply because they are fierce (*lāj*),[28] but because they are smarter (*mālōtlōt*), as evidenced by their sophisticated technology and how they strategically outmaneuver their enemies. A significant part of Letao's power resides in his mobility, which contrasts with the chiefs, who retain their recognized authority on the land. Letao is always on the move; therefore, his power can be transported to other places. Similarly, the Americans are also always seen to be on the move, subverting global power relations.

The chief is "kind" by definition, but, while Letao is at times kind, it is usually for his own selfish reasons. The American motives for kindness are similarly suspect. The episode of Letao in Kiribati (south of the Marshalls) presents a resonant "lack—lack liquidated" tale structure (Dundes 1975, 74); there is a lack of food and Letao provides it—but at a price. Letao's ability to get into the earth-oven and supply food for the famine-stricken Kiribati appears to be an act of chiefly kindness. But with Letao, everything has a veiled motive; he wants to kill the chief so that he can obtain the sexual favors of his wives. Thus, the trickster makes things again appear to be something they are not; that he is the benevolent chief who brings bounty to the people in a demonstration of kindness. On the basis of the narrated event, he does provide for the people and alleviates their hunger. But there are strings attached. For Kometo and many riMạjeḷ, the Americans' gifts of food also had strings attached; they tested bombs and continue to occupy Kuwajleen for missile testing.

Letao's ability to get into the earth-oven, escape unnoticed, and bring forth bounteous food again displays his power over nature, symbolizing his perpetually regenerative capacity. Then, by manipulating covetousness in the Kiribati chief, Letao appears to offer him power, so that he can perform the ultimate chiefly act: feed the people and thus retain their support and dominion over them. But as is clear, the chief does not really obtain Letao's power and is tricked into cooking himself. This is not only a critical act of subversion, but it inverts the meaning of food, kindness, and the sustaining of life. It is not food or life that is uncovered, but grotesque nonfood (human flesh) and death. A most diagnostic moment in this episode is the reported speech when Letao calls the chief "my friend," followed by the Kometo's metanarration, "The word friend is big. It can be true; it can be false."[29] Here the magnitude of Letao's deceptive capacity and his power becomes epitomized: the blurring of what is true (*mọol*) with the false (*riab*). In it we can see the riMạjeḷ vision of the Americans: they may act as your friend, but in the end, they will "burn you" or "cook you," both figuratively and literally—for those who experienced the nuclear fallout. The root meanings of the word *jeraamṃan*, "luck, good fortune, blessing," is *jerā/jera* (friend) + *mṃan* (good). Good fortune is a good friend. On the other hand, the meaning of the word *jerāta*, for bad luck or misfortune, also derives from "friend." The etymology of *jerata* is *jerā/jera* (friend) + *ta* (what). Thus, misfortune is "what kind of friend?," meaning, "none at all." Accordingly, a true friend is a blessing and good fortune; a false friend is a misfortune and a liar. What kind of friend will Letao be in the end? What kind of friend will the Americans prove?

Letao's trickery was at first renewing; he fed people. Then he became destructive; he brought death to the chief, completely subverting the chief's status and the institutions upon which his social power derives. Nonetheless, from death comes regeneration. Letao went on to engage in sexual relations with the chief's wives (the Americans are also viewed as highly libidinal, tactlessly exhibiting sexuality in public). He got what he wanted—Letao always gets what he wants, and the Americans do too. The Americans brought death and destruction with the war, and continue to do so elsewhere, but they also brought food, regenerating life (*kamour*) and giving strength (*kajoor*), and therefore they accumulate chiefly power. Ultimately, the people of Mājro (Episode I), Kiribati (Episode III) and Mile (Episode II) rejected Letao's subversion and chased him off: they remained loyal to the legitimate chiefly line. If Letao has brought a new modern chief back to the islands, can it be considered legitimate? Kometo's metanarrations and the interactions that conclude these performances clearly connect Letao to the Americans, their "smarts," and their bombs. He is the source of their intelligence and thus the source of their military power.[30] The statement that the "ancestors say" it gives this myth historical saliency, but at the same time throws it into doubt. As in many riM̧ajeḷ performances, this device is not used to establish the legitimacy of a recalled past as might be expected, but to retain ambiguity and avoid committing oneself to the truth status of the narrated event. Kometo is essentially saying, "The ancestors said it, but we don't know." He reveals his position about the ancestors' voices earlier in the dialogue when he proclaims, "Since they say 'human.' Me? I don't believe he's human; it's just like talking-story." Also, at the conclusion of the final episode, he states, "Well, thus is the story," and accordingly, brings the entire mythic conclusion into question, but leaves open its utility to reveal salient cultural understandings.

For the riM̧ajeḷ, Letao is an enjoyable figure because he provides a "mischievous" (*kakūtōtō*) negative; he is a "bad person" (*nana*) and gets away with it. The rules he breaks expose his power. He is a "joke" (*kōjak*), not in the sense that he is not to be taken seriously, but because he is the master of artifice and illusion; he makes things appear to be what they are not. A joke is ambiguity and paradox, and so entertainingly subversive. This is the meaning of joke for the riM̧ajeḷ and a reason they laugh. Similarly, the Americans, with all their power and wealth, also appear ambiguous and elusive, and for this reason they too may seem like a joke, but one that, like Letao, may come with serious consequences.

Letao's powers derive from his ambiguity, destructiveness, regenerative capacity, mobility, inversions of cultural rules, lies, and deceptions. Myths about him offer an interpretative framework to the colonial, economic, political, and social relationships the islanders have been forced to confront. These relationships are ambiguous and implicate social power. The meaning of Letao's power casts into relief the powerful "other." As a between character, he not only links the riM̧ajeḷ to the Americans, but also becomes the source of their dangerous and ambiguous dominance. Through the paradoxical trickster, riM̧ajeḷ storytellers, such as Kometo, explore American power on the margins of myth and history, and in the process playfully dramatize their history with the Americans. In this way, they imagine themselves connected to the great figurative "world chief," not just by history (war and occupation), but cosmologically, from the time of origins and demigods (*anij raṇ*). The ubiquity of this myth and its couched analogies provides a resource for exploring global forces in local, intimate storytelling sessions, even with an American interlocutor. Within this small-scale scene where Kometo situates the myth in performance, large-scale issues (imperial relations) are incorporated into Indigenous sensibilities about social life and power at the local level.

Kometo's performance of the story about Letao and the Americans was genuinely a resource "for conceptualizing the world, resisting some aspects, embracing others" (Cashman 2016, 231). This mythic narrative was among the "vernacular strategies" he and other riM̧ajeḷ used for "belonging, survival, and reinvention in" a "time of trouble" (Otero and Martinez-Rivera 2021, 8). It became the location for addressing issues of social power attendant to significant historical changes, and its images and meanings afforded the riM̧ajeḷ a culturally germane means of confronting American power and abuse. The embedded images of the story were drawn upon in a period of transition (colonialism, expansionism, decolonization, migration, nationalization, and globalization) when "different social interests" led "to ideological conflict" and "struggle over social meaning acted out through the performance" (Stoeltje 1988, 235) of the myth. The discerning historical consciousness of the riM̧ajeḷ lies in how they made sense of the force of American global imperialism through the lens of Indigenous power. Indeed, they come to mirror each other as they narrated and commented on them, creating a veiled form of political resistance through appropriation of the powerful other.

Letao is not a static but an evolving personality (a shape shifter) as he is resituated in different historical periods. As a result, not only do the meanings about Letao's power expressed in myth becomes more focused as he is applied to modern life, but also narratives about him continue to emerge. The appearance of the chiefly Americans has been subverted over time through their unceasing presence, duplicitous behavior with atomic tests, continued neglect of the nuclear waste,[31] and intense interactions from the Trust Territory years (1947–1986) and since the UN recognition of their independence (1991). Through travel and migration, the riM̧ajeḷ have come to know much about America and its people. This familiarity has been accentuated since independence and the Compact of

Free Association agreement that allows the islanders access to US borders, education, and government funding (Barker 2004). The immense amount of travel to and from the United States resulting from the Compact of Free Association (Ogden 1994) has provided the riM̧ajeļ firsthand exposure to the realities of American life, both the good and bad. When coupled with their pervasive exposure to American media and popular culture, this revelation presents the islanders with a rather ambiguous and contradictory image of America.

The generous judgment held by those who experienced the war and immediately after it is not as glorified for later generations. They see just how culpable and common American life proves to be. When I conducted my initial fieldwork (1991–1993), some riM̧ajeļ were puzzled by the challenges to the "rightness" of US imperialism, both by other nations and some Americans themselves (they had heard the critiques). For many riM̧ajeļ, the negotiations concerning nuclear claims and sovereignty have made the Americans appear like fickle, opportunistic, and deceptive chiefs. But then, again, this dissonance finds a degree of resolution in the dualistic chiefly image; the nurturing caretaker counterposed to the arbitrary and dangerous autocrat who continues to inform world violence. Among these contradictions, the narrative of Letao developed, in part, to mediate the dissonance. Because his power comes through his ambiguity, he continues to offer a striking explanation for the behavior and uncertain nature of America.

In this chapter, I have charted some of the ways a playful storyteller employs a range of poetic devices (including laughter) and flexible generic framing to situate a riM̧ajeļ myth in an interrogative dialogue, how he entertains the story's sense of truthiness, and how the episodic plot reflects islander sensibilities and comes to serve as an analogy for the ambivalent history of American presence in the islands. In the following chapter, I will follow additional intertextual links to antecedent and culturally germane mythological texts that Kometo's performance of this myth elicits. Further exploration will extend the meaning of the myth explored above, both back into cosmological time, and forward into the present through continued dialogues about it. As with the previous symbolic analogies, I will observe Kometo moving beyond "the situational contexts of use" to "transcendent . . . ties to other situations" (Bauman 2004, 2) in which he attaches the myth to larger historical and sociological considerations about power (cf. Thompson and Schrempp 2020, 168–177).

I begin this intercontextual study by attending to how a riM̧ajeļ storyteller explored the relationship between deception, ambiguity, and American power. In the late twentieth century, Kometo and other riM̧ajeļ recognized their history of exploitation and domination by the United States. However, through the immediate performance of a trickster myth, they playfully dramatized analogies full of ambivalence toward America at a specific historical juncture. Kometo clearly articulated American ambiguity and their link to the trickster when once he stated, "Letao is the embodiment of all extremes; he is at once good and bad, possesses all knowledge and all stupidity, all love and all hate, all kindness and all meanness, all truth and all lies." After recounting these qualities of the trickster, he observed, "Isn't that just like the Americans?" Then, he laughed deeply.

CHAPTER 3

Dialogic Riddling

Cosmological Musings and the Kinship of Power

In this chapter, I continue to follow the most provocative implication of the mythic episodes about Letao that Kometo and the riM̧ajeļ perform—that is, the deep historical accounting for American global power and imperial forces in the Marshall Islands. I will explore and unpack further the sensibilities and social meanings raised in the previous chapter. As articulated by Kometo and others, the analogies drawn from the story illustrate the malleability of the trickster myth, enabling it to forcefully emerge to account for the modern riM̧ajeļ experience. Through Letao the trickster, deep history and contemporary life, tradition and modernity, cosmological origins and imperial forces all blur in on each other. That riM̧ajeļ storytellers end the narrative episodes of Letao with his travel to America, taking his "intelligence" with him, creates a "prehistory of globalization" that merges "popular memory with mythological time" (Shami 2001, 233). These "prehistories . . . seek pasts characterized by mobility . . . and linkages that displace the notion of the past as stagnant and bound by empire and tradition" (Shami 2001, 234). These narratives do not represent a naive longing; rather, resonant with descriptions of Native Americans (Toelken 2003), we see how Kometo and others dramatized their ambivalent historical relationship with the United States. The episode of Letao traveling to America provided Kometo and the riM̧ajeļ a text with deep cosmological underpinnings for reflecting on American behavior, and repositions the islanders not on the margin or periphery—which is how others envision the riM̧ajeļ—but at the center of global power (McArthur 2000).[1] Kometo enjoyed expanding on the possibilities for how such power works and musing upon its cosmological origins.

As I have contended, it is impracticable and ethnographically misleading to separate the meaning of a narrative about the trickster from the ethnographic dialogue. While the narrated event that recounts Letao moving on to America links cosmology, deep history, and the recent past, the ethnographic dialogue does more than simply hook back into the story; it continues to grow the narrative (cf. Bauman 1986). Enlarging the narrated event by continually recontextualizing the myth into an intercultural dialogue linked a situated encounter to larger cosmological, genealogical, historical, and social contexts transcendent of the immediate setting. Enlarging the narrated event was less achieved through a performance of the myth than through continual references to the story through our speech and questions. Kometo's genius at expanding the final episode of Letao going to America lies in his seamless interpretative jumps between the present and back into the riM̧ajel̦ cosmology and the genealogy of the trickster, and to fashion analogies between American and riM̧ajel̦ forms of social power.

Mythic Enlargement through Dialogic Riddling

In the previous chapter, I addressed dialogism by attending to the contextualization of a story, its meanings, and the flexible generic forms in which a mythic narrative is embedded. In this chapter, I will continue to follow intertextual threads in two directions: one, I will seek to locate the mythological story within a larger textual history that takes us into the riM̧ajel̦ cosmogony, to follow Kometo as he traced the story from its most immediate setting of an intercultural performance to antecedent texts and voices; two, I will chronicle the links he made to larger social and historical considerations about social power, which will occasion a more nuanced ethnographic articulation of riM̧ajel̦ kinship and chiefly authority. Both of these threads expand the myth. The text itself only hints at these larger contexts, but further riddling dialogues directly link the narrative back in time to the riM̧ajel̦ cosmogony and then forward to modern possibilities in a decolonizing present.

The transcripts of the performances alone leave the meaning of the last episode dangling, and certainly wide open for interpretation. I proffered in the previous chapter some nuanced possibilities that I hope will prove salient to Indigenous sensibilities. The ethnographic readings I have applied to these texts (McArthur 2000, 2004, 2008, 2012) represent my piecing together what the riM̧ajel̦ shared with me in one domain (mythic narratives, cultural descriptions, and behaviors) with that of another domain (narrative performances of Letao by Kometo). These interpretations and his performances can be further contextualized by our conversations that either overtly or indirectly referenced Letao traveling to America.

With fieldwork, we often present an ideal image of the ethnographic interview as a serious methodical elicitation of germane cultural knowledge. But ethnography is also often filled with moments of just "hanging out" and "talking-story" (and necessarily so if we hope for any real relationships and meaningful friendships), a movement between the more formally structured interview and loose conversation where talk is more relaxed. The dialogues presented here represent either more casual times of free wandering questions and conversation with the recorder still rolling, or interludes in the formal interview. Taking the Letao myth as a point of departure in our informal conversations, Kometo addressed exceptionally large-scale cosmological, historical, and social issues through riddling dialogues.

To argue that ethnographic dialogue provides a location for mythic enlargement begs many questions about it as a form and how it functions in this interplay of discourses. Minimally, to ask questions provides shape to talk, which demands, or at least expects, an interactive response, an answer. Questions inherently encourage dialogue, requiring the involvement of at least two voices (cf. Briggs 1996). Vernacular forms offer an orienting framework (Bauman 1977, 2004) for discourses to be produced and received in a particular fashion. I have been using the etic label "interrogative dialogue" for the kind of talk in which Kometo and I participated. While Kometo would not apply such an analytical label, he would implicitly recognize its form, a form we became very familiar with through our conversations. This form provided the context to most of our talking time together. The occasional "breakthrough into performance" (Hymes 1975, 11) in which Kometo would perform a narrative was most often contextualized within this genre, and by asking questions, stories were elicited (Sacks 1992; Brenneis 1996).

This genre label is certainly unconventional. Even so, it shares an affinity with a more conventionally recognized genre, the riddle. The interrogative dialogue bleeds into and siphons off many of the formal qualities of the riddle even though the particular content of each question is in no way traditional. Nonetheless, the riddle structure of the interrogative discourse took on a distinct contour and provided links back to the existing traditional myth. Our interrogative dialogues do not characterize the "true riddle," the "enigmatic questions in the form of descriptions whose referent must be guessed" (Abrahams and Dundes 1972, 130). Instead, they are more like "wisdom questions," or "questions that test the knowledge or wisdom of the person to whom they are posed" (Bauman 2004, 41). In this light, much of the thrust of my questions were "tests" of Kometo's knowledge and wisdom—perhaps all ethnography is riddle-like. Now, by no means can I serve as the final judge about the cultural or historical accuracy of this test. Indeed, a few (but only a few) riṂajeḷ told me that Kometo was the wrong person to go to for "true" knowledge (jeḷāḷokjeṇ eṃool) about their culture and history. While some riṂajeḷ questioned my focus on Kometo as not necessarily the best source for obtaining "real knowledge," in part because of his relatively low status and their caution about his recognized role as a social trickster, most respected him greatly and often asked him cultural questions and deferred to him when he would tell stories. Ethnographers often first obtain access to marginal people and then develop networks with others at the cultural center (Noyes 2003). My ongoing education into riM̧ajeļ culture, however, was provided first by many others, both women and men recognized as exceptionally knowledgeable, and then I came to particularly emphasize learning from Kometo when it became clear that his trickster ways and willingness to share trickster stories offered a nuanced lens on riM̧ajeļ cosmology, cultural epistemology, and society. My test, however, was not to compare his answers to some "authentic" or "legitimate" cultural account—all answers from any riM̧ajeļ I engaged with came from distinctly situated and motivated vantage points—but to create a space for Kometo to fill as he would with meaningful discourse. Like riddles, my questions and Kometo's answers exploited ambiguity and a multiplicity of meanings through verbal play, unanticipated references, and intertextual conundrums.

Riddling (*lōn̄n̄a*) for the riM̧ajeļ is viewed as traditional speech play for children to develop their mental acuity, detect subtle comparisons, and recognize the slipperiness in the meanings of words.[2] It also characterizes a mode of speech employed by all ages to use obscure references, redirection, and subtle innuendo. A common islander conversational practice often becomes one of playful banter and teasing among equals, in which interlocutors seek to goad, veil, ridicule, or indirectly mock each other in a game of jest and wordplay. These verbal battles often elicit intense laughter by the participants and those listening in. The template for this kind of riddling game is noticeably informed by the deceptive actions of the Letao image. Stories rehearsing Letao antics are in part riddle-like, and his speech within the narrated event is likewise. When someone cleverly exploits riddling, the islanders will often refer to them as being "etao," or sly in speech. Kometo was considered very good at this kind of furtive talk and sardonic banter. So, our conversations in many ways recast a familiar form of riM̧ajeļ discourse. Kometo was exceptionally competent with this form, and when enacted in an ethnographic dialogue, it took on both a subversive quality (challenging the formality of research talk), as well as providing a leveling quality as he sought to educate me and bond us as friends. Riddling for the riM̧ajeļ can be used to both subvert authority through veiled speech or affirm mutuality between equals.

Thinking about the interrogative genre as riddle-like does more than give clarity to its formal qualities; it sheds light on the means by which we enlarged the mythic narrated event. The affinity between riddles and narratives is a close one: "The question-response sequence itself lends itself to narrativization; the reporting of a question-response sequence can itself constitute a minimal narrative" (Bauman 2004, 46). Our riddling dialogues became narrative-like since its sequence paralleled, accompanied, and facilitated the unfolding story. But more importantly, it generated additional parts of the storyline to expand the narrative text; "interrogative verbal routines" were turned into "narrative action" (Bauman 2004, 48). By situating the myth within the riddling discourse, the narrated event was more fully located in larger cosmological contexts and emerged with all its enigmatic social possibilities.

Riddling speech play is all the more anticipated in a conversation with a social trickster about a trickster myth. Enlarged through riddling dialogue, the myth also served to transform our interactional power relationship, both in terms of our immediate association, and the contextual ground in which we interacted: my powerful culture and his seemingly peripheral one. In this way Kometo took me into a riddle of cultural meanings and ideologies both about an ancient cosmological genealogy and chiefly authority as well as how these become manifest in recent history. This genealogy provides an "anchor" to Indigenous perspectives and conceptualizations (Tengan et al. 2010; Kaʻili 2017). This is especially poignant in how the riM̧ajeļ trace their genealogies back to cosmogonic beings. Stories about Letao present plots that never seem to resolve themselves (cf. Hyde 1998). Instead, they open up to further elaboration, interpretation, and mischievous exploits. The riddle-like dialogues capitalize on this open "endedness" to grow the myth and playfully mediate our ethnographic relationship. The following riddling dialogue took place just between Kometo and me at his home. After the first time he performed the story of Letao moving on to America, this dialogue ensued when I conducted a follow-up interview several months later.[3]

P   You said that Letao is in America, that he has gone to America. <he chuckles> How did he go to America from Kiribati?

K   He sailed by canoe.

P   Sailed by an American boat?

K   No, a canoe of these islands.

P   He sailed to America?

K   Eh.

P   Oh, and how did the Americans take him?

K   They don't take him. They don't know who he is.

P   Oh, because he can conceal himself?

K   He can conceal himself. <he chuckles >

P   So, how did he teach them about all his knowledge?

K   I don't know. Since,

The ancestors say,
"The reason the Americans are so smart, it is because Letao is in America."

P   And he teaches them.
K   He teaches them . . . In the loincloth (*kaḷ*) of the man there is a power. See? This object, the loincloth, it is powerful.
P   In what way does it have power?
K   Because it's his clothing!
P   And, the loincloth covers only the front and back?
K   Eh. The ancestors, they wore that loincloth . . .
P   If people acquire the loincloth of Letao will they be smart?
K   Yes.
P   Letao got the loincloth from where?
K   It is among his clothing. <chuckles>

P   You said that all things happen to America now because Letao is there.
K   Yes.
P   Like what? What is in America?
K   Lies. The greatest liars are Americans. <we both laugh> Is it true?
P   It's true.
K   Etao is an American. He is smart. Eh. <chuckles> There are many people in America who are smart, but some, they are really stupid. There are many people in American who are stupid. <chuckling> Letao deceived them. <laughs> See? They are not doing well because of Letao. He deceived them and they are now stupid. See? Eh. There are many kinds, all kinds of people there.
P   Do good things also come from him?
K   Eh many. All kinds of good things. Letao gives them all.
P   Letao deceives people, but can he also bless people?
K   He blesses people. He deceives people.
P   In this atoll he deceived the chief.
K   He deceived the chief and the chief went to kill him, so,

He escapes.
Then, he stays in America, but they don't know about him.
Then, he goes on, eh, <chuckling> to Chicago.
And they go to kill him in Chicago.
He goes to New York. <laughs hard>
They go to kill him in New York.

He goes to Idaho. <we both laugh hard>
So, he is in Idaho now. <we both laugh>

P   <laughing> Well, I hid him in my bag and he has returned again to these islands.
K   <laughs to the point of choking, I laugh too> Ha, ha, ha, well, I don't know. <more laughter> I don't know about that.
P   <laughing> Where is his loincloth now?
K   It just remains in America.
P   With who?
K   I don't know. <laughing> Perhaps it is with the president. <laughing> He is the smartest of all.
P   <laughing> And the greatest liar.
K   <laughing> And the great liar. You should tell the president that "the loin-cloth of Letao is with you in your house." <we both laugh hard>

P   You said that Letao did not just stop at America but sailed on?
K   Possibly. Do you think he can't just go about anywhere?
P   To where?
K   And he goes to Germany, Russia, and what's it called? Eh, Israel and those places. Who says he's not with him . . . what's his name? That president of Ir—
P   Iraq?
K   Iraq. <laughs>
P   Saddam?
K   Eh, doesn't he go and make Saddam's decision? <laughs into chuckle>
P   But Saddam lost.
K   Well,

he lost . . .
The reason he lost is because of the intelligence that Letao left with the Americans.
They destroyed Saddam.
<laughing> Then, when Saddam is destroyed . . . Letao leaves. <laughs>
He escapes.

Thus, it is. I don't know if this is really true or not, or just a story. <chuckles>

This interrogative riddling dialogue itself represents an emergent product that explores the meanings of the Letao myth and expands its implications. First, as previously suggested, Kometo responds to my query about Letao traveling to

America. His response in part serves as a continuation of Episode IV of the myth he performed for me (see previous chapter). In a variant I heard from another storyteller, Letao strikes a deal with the Americans, that if he will travel to America and teach them all he knows, they will make him rich. And in another recorded version, he is captured by the Americans and released only after he imparts his knowledge, which will empower the US military (Carucci 1989). But for Kometo, Letao sailed on alone to America,[4] taking the stolen symbol of a chief with him, the canoe. With this symbol, he crosses boundaries, cultural and historical. I ask questions and press Kometo to respond. His confident responses suggest a degree of forethought about these implications, or a very competent bluff.

We then discuss how Letao's true identity remains concealed, such that even the Americans do not recognize his powerful presence. One of Letao's essential qualities is his ability to hide his identity and manipulate both concealment and revelation. The story about Letao creating human necks through the game of hide-and-seek in chapter 1 illustrates this hiding principle. Whether incognito or not, Kometo emphasizes that Letao teaches the Americans, giving this conclusion a sense of traditional authority by stating, "They (the ancestors) say, 'the reason the Americans are so smart, it's because Letao remains in America,'" echoing the conclusion to Episode IV. Kometo then shifts into a most interesting explanation for the location and transmission of the trickster's power, his loincloth. I have never heard or read about anything similar to this, but this loincloth subject would become an important part of many future conversations with Kometo. As revealed in other narratives and suggested in early ethnological accounts, a chief was identified by a finely plaited pandanus-leaf loincloth (*kaḷ*). This clothing indexed his power. But Kometo is my only source on any association between the loincloth and the power of the primal gods (*anij*) or demigods (*anij raṇ*). Indeed, he is very adamant that the loincloth not only serves as a symbol of Letao, but it also contains a power that may be exchanged with whoever possesses this article of clothing. Because the Americans obtain Letao's loincloth, they now possess the trickster's power. The loincloth represents Letao's power in the most potent form of contagion, and its contiguity to this highly libidinal character is notable.

Our conversation then shifts; because Letao has also taken his lies to America, they now become the greatest liars. For Kometo, the trickster's power in fact derives from his lies, which give temporary power over others, even those with customary or ascribed rank. Then, imagining Letao as the embodiment of extremes, he explains how the Americans represent opposites: intelligence (smarts) and stupidity. Some Americans the trickster makes smart, but some he deceives, and hence they become stupid. By implication, those who are smart are "sly" (*etao*); those who are stupid are easily deceived. Americans represent the full range of these attributes. I sometimes wondered if he was testing me to see if I could detect his allusions and thus prove myself as one of the smart Americans. We then rearticulate Letao's extremes: he both blesses and deceives, brings good and bad.[5] His power to deceive does not give him legitimate authority however, because once his deception is unveiled, the chiefs seek to destroy him and he must escape. Letao is a traveler, in part because he is frequently chased off; and because he does not stay rooted in one place, he takes his bag of tricks with him.

The next segment of our conversation reveals how quickly Kometo turns narrative exegesis into unexpected commentary on our relationship. We move from dialogue to a breakthrough into narrative, but in this context the myth serves as a kind of metacommentary on the immediate dialogic relationship, the one serving as an analogy for the other. After placing Letao in America, Kometo imagines his continual movement from one great city to the next—Chicago to New York. This does more than reveal his geographical awareness. It intimates that the trickster's movements result from a series of deceptions at each location and attempts to kill him, just as with the chiefs in the Marshall Islands and Kiribati. He stays one step ahead and moves on, however, finally to Idaho, a seemingly obscure reference. This clever connection clearly absorbs me into the myth as Kometo is well aware that I was raised in Idaho. This resituating of the emerging narrative into our immediate relationship receives intense laughter. He is as amused by his adroit performance as I am. Kometo always expected me to enter into such repartee, which made many of our dialogues a bonding jovial banter. After locating me in the comedic narrative, I take up the role and respond that I have brought Letao back in my bag. This response overwhelms Kometo and he laughs uncontrollably.

Our bantering one-upmanship continues when he responds to my question about the location of Letao's loincloth, placing it with the president of the United States. That is why he is "smart." Picking up on this joke and Letao's extremes, I also suggest that by implication then the president is also the greatest liar. Kometo subsequently becomes his most facetious, creating an imagined scenario in which he orders me to inform the president that Letao's loincloth is in his house. Through dialogic humor, we not only use Letao to create a link to the symbol of American authority (the president), but also constitute our relationship through playful language, a shared understanding of Letao's and America's power to deceive, and laughter. We both become neither "in" nor "out" of our respective societies but on the margins; we locate our conversation within the cracks of America and the Marshall Islands.

At the end of this dialogue, I seek to bring us back to the narrative and explore further his suggestion that Letao keeps moving on. He then takes the trickster to other world powers that come to mind (Germany, Russia) and even Israel, where he knew there were many volatile activities. And then he asserts, through a question, that it is even possible that Letao has moved on to Saddam Hussein in Iraq. This conversation took place in early 1992, just a year after the Gulf War, and Kometo demonstrates just how informed he was in his relatively isolated location about current world events, especially those implicated in power and warfare. So now, even Saddam has been deceived by Letao (and thus that is the reason for the war) and when I assert that Hussein lost, he quickly explains how the outcome is due to the intelligence Letao left behind with the Americans. After apparently tricking Saddam into his "destruction" (loss), Letao has escaped again. Kometo then questions this whole imaginative speculation, and even the truth status of the myth itself is tenuous. Nonetheless, it is "just a story," and something fun to explore. This interchange, even though outside the narrative proper, extends Episode IV through metacommentary and newly imagined mythic possibilities. We add to the narrated event, but not through the traditionally framed narrative discourse. Rather, we add to the emerging plot through a riddling dialogue that also generates a friendship that draws from both the myth and the qualities of a trickster. But just what are the salient qualities of the riM̧ajel̦ trickster and from whence do they come? Kometo's philological musings will situate Letao in the riM̧ajel̦ cosmogony and a genealogy, which, according to the myth, the Americans share.

Cosmological Musings
with an Indigenous Philologist

In many ways, this work represents a "philology of the vernacular" (Bauman 2016, 64). While I realized, even when entering the field to conduct research in the Marshall Islands, that my intellectual genealogy could be traced to the philological tradition, it became ever more clear working with Kometo just how profoundly intertextual relationships informed my thinking. Philology represents a line of inquiry that explores and "calibrates the gaps" between languages and texts. Kometo himself represented an Indigenous philologist (cf. Māhina 1999; Helu 1999b), exploring textual histories, hypothesizing about the similarity of root words across languages, and tracing textual linkages by comparing different mythological and cosmological traditions.[6] Such a presentation of cultural variants to the mythological underpinnings of the riM̧ajel̦ cosmology recognizes the cultural achievements and epistemological foundations that may even provide an additional resource for decolonization (cf. Hau'ofa 2008; Tuhiwai Smith 2012).

At times, Kometo was more of a diffusionist, discussing historical links to other places. Contrary to the efforts to rethink intentional versus accidental voyaging that led to island discovery and colonization (Irwin 1992), Kometo would often assert, like other riM̧ajeļ, that his islands were discovered out of sailing misfortune, and once he even noncommittally claimed they came from Hawai'i. This route of settlement, while certainly dubious, identifies a sensitive point for some of the Marshall Islanders. There are oral historical accounts of contact with Hawai'i (Tobin 2002) that predate European visitors. The riM̧ajeļ not only claim the most northern Ratak islands of Bokak and Pikaar, but also report numerous trips to Wake Island (which they call Ānenkio, but this goes unrecognized by international law) and beyond. But nowhere is there evidence of migration from Hawai'i that peopled the islands, which would also run contrary to archaeology that dates the occupation in the Marshall Islands at least four to eight hundred years prior to Hawai'i colonization (Dye 1987). More often, Kometo ascertained Yap (*Ep*) as the point of origin. He, like many other storytellers, would first identify two men, Lewa (sometimes identified as Ļowa) and Ļōm̧tal, who hewed the first paddling canoes at Wōtto (Wotho) atoll, then the goddess Lōñtañūr, who introduced sailing within an atoll, followed by two men from Yap who arrived on a current through Micronesia (*kapilōñ*) to pass on their knowledge of currents and navigation to a daughter named Liben.[7] Tobin (2002) records a version of two men teaching a woman of *kapinmeto* (the northern Rālik atolls) but does not give their point of origin (drift voyages from Yap to the Marshalls have also been recorded by Riesenberg 1965).

Kometo was very aware of these diffusion scenarios and spoke of the role of these key figures often. But he more often entertained the work of the autochthonous gods who imparted knowledge, power, and the social order long before the arrival of other voyagers. His textual reconstructions of Indigenous mythologies through our riddling dialogues challenged alternative versions to the riM̧ajeļ cosmology and genealogy of the trickster. In what follows, I seek to adumbrate Kometo's version of the cosmogony and contrast it to antecedent texts in the riM̧ajeļ tradition, and then witness how a riddling dialogue extends the original myth as he provides the genealogical background to Letao's power and behavior. Kometo's version and our riddling dialogues will reveal a fantastically uncertain cosmogony, genealogy, and deep mythological origins, but even so, it illustrates the subversive qualities of the trickster and provides a cosmological context for Letao's, and by extension, American abusive social power.

Cosmological Variation

Every storyteller is positioned historically, geographically, and sociologically. Occupying a specific place in time, space, and society shapes what stories they will hear and the circumstances of their development as a personality and artist (cf. Dégh 1969). Stories themselves have a history; their realization in any given historical period will vary from what was and may yet be told. Because variation is a factor of place as much as time, a teller's stories will also reflect the interests and histories of people at particular locations: they may become "oikiotypes" (von Sydow 1948), or localized versions. And because stories belong to social life (cf. Siikala and Siikala 2005)—the relationships a teller has to both previous tellers and their immediate audience—they are influenced by what one hears and remembers, and whether one develops a sense of "entitlement" to them (Shuman 2005). All of these stories enter the dialogic process; they interact with narratives in the past, those of a place, and within particular social configurations. Kometo's cosmological narratives reflect all the peculiarities of these factors. Having been born and lived at a particular historical moment (1917–1997), raised in specific places (Mile and Epoon atolls), then living the majority of his adult life at the urban center (Mājro atoll), and maintaining very significant social relationships both to those from whom he learned stories and with those whom he would tell them, made his performances variably different from other repertoires and collections. His view was always in dialogue with these alternatives, and much of this exchange with the past and other contemporary storytellers unfolded in our conversations.

riM̧ajeḷ myths that relate the cosmogony in which Letao emerges do not form a consistent integrated whole. There have been numerous collections of oral narratives in the Marshall Islands over the past century (Erdland 1914; Kramer and Nevermann 1938; Buckingham 1949; Grey 1951; Davenport 1952a, 1953; Chambers 1969, 1972; Mitchell 1973; Pollock 1976; Knight 1980; Carucci 1986, 1989, 1997a; Downing et al. 1992; McArthur 1995; Kowata et al. 1999; Tobin 2002; Kelin 2003; Tanner 2008). Not only do these collections reflect broad and diverse repertoires, but even when similar narratives have been collected, each shows important variations, not just in terms of general motifs and details, but also in terms of the cosmogonic genealogy. Because the riM̧ajeḷ were so widely colonized by Christianity, very few living individuals rehearse the cosmological genealogies or even know them. Those genealogies that have been collected and published by outsiders have taken on "authenticity," even for most riM̧ajeḷ, because they have assumed authority as derivative of older sources that then get repeated by chroniclers (Grey 1951; Downing et al. 1992; Kowata et al. 1999;

Flood 2002; Kelin 2003) and novelists (Barclay 2002; Downing 2003; Kelin 2013). This "traditionalization" of specific narratives and versions privileges some stories and multiforms over others. But even though these sources reflect such a significant degree of variation, it is unwise, even though seemingly obvious with oral tradition, to propose any definitive conclusions about the riM̧ajeḷ cosmogony. Moreover, any attempts to validate certain versions clearly represent motivated political interests (cf. Leach 1964) among different clans and chiefs, and those riM̧ajeḷ who care to remember such things display significant variety in how they construe the past. Despite all the variation in the collections and among modern tellers, as a whole they present a pattern in the cultural memory. Across them all, there is little variability in the basic events described, moderate variability about where these events took place, and significant variability about which characters did what. It is the events themselves that show the greatest continuity, while characters, their genealogy (*kadkad*) and relationships to each other vary from one account to another.[8]

Kometo's mythic narratives about the trickster recount events similar to the other variants, but he diverges notably from these accounts in terms of the characters involved, how these cosmogonic beings are related to each other, and their placement within a chronology. What follows cannot be construed as the "riM̧ajeḷ version" of the mythological past, but narratives performed by a particular man situated in particular contexts. All the collections that preceded my work with Kometo—including those I collected from several other men and women elders (*aḷab ro*), also reflect the particular motivations, interests, backgrounds, and experiences of the collectors. Thus, my contention is that the mythology presented here reflects Kometo's dialogue across time and space with other riM̧ajeḷ as well as our dialogue with each other. My philological work extends his philology, both vertically, back in time to other versions, and horizontally, with me and other immediate social relationships.

Kometo's narrative repertoire generally, and about Letao specifically, is much larger than what this book presents. For one, he did not tell me every story he knew, and furthermore, I have not included all that he did tell me. This would prove too extensive; and in a more focused way, I am fashioning a representation for how our dialogic encounters enlarge the meaning of this particular myth. Consequently, I will be selective, while duly representative. At any rate, the Letao narratives he did perform for me can be situated within a larger corpus of trickster mythology and a cosmology that reveals how he gave shape to and made sense of the riM̧ajeḷ trickster. Kometo possessed definite ideas about Letao's genealogy that illustrate the subversive power he would pass on to the Americans.

Kometo was adamant that Letao and the chief Jemāluut (whose name means the rainbow) were brothers, in contrast to some versions (e.g., Bender 1963), and that they shared a distinct genealogy. Several past accounts either present Letao and Jemāluut as having emerged from a boil on or bursting from a tree grown out of the head of Wullep, the son of the primal god Ḷowa, who spoke all things into existence (Erdland 1914; Kramer and Nevermann 1938). Other primal gods enter the picture in a variety of ways. Ḷewōj and Ḷaneej, the gods who descended from the sky at the decree of either Ḷowa or Wullep to Aelōñḷapḷap (Ailinglaplap) atoll, tattooed all things, fish, birds, and humans, starting with the chiefs on Bouj islet (cf. Tobin 2002). Some accounts offer that Ḷewōj and Ḷaneej were the cross-cousins of Letao and Jemāluut (Erdland 1914), while others suggest that they are siblings, emerging from Wullep at different junctures (Kramer and Nevermann 1938). These accounts also describe how Ḷowa placed four gods at each of the cardinal directions, Iroojrālik in the west to ensure a multiplying and vibrant world, Ḷajbwināmᵤōṇ in the north, who would have power over death, Ḷakōmᵤraan in the east, to ensure the sunrise, and Ḷōrōk in the south, to control the winds and provide the harvest. Iroojrālik resided on the island of Ep, referred to in many accounts as the spirit island or homeland without specific location in the West. Likewise, Kometo identified the centrality of these gods of the cardinal directions, but he also identified several others as generational siblings to these gods whom Ḷewōj and Ḷaneej placed at the various atolls in the archipelago.

Some scholars suggest that Ep (or Eb) is the Kajin Ṃajeḷ pronunciation of "Yap," an island in the western Caroline Islands (Kramer and Nevermann 1938; Downing et al. 1992; Tobin 2002).[9] Yap Islanders retained a substantial exchange relationship with (Petersen 2009) and perhaps control over much of Micronesia due in large part to fear over their presumed powerful magic and sorcery (Hezel 1983; Dobbin 2011), but very little is known about their control ever extending to the Marshall Islands.

Several riṂajeḷ, including Kometo, claim that many generations ago Yapese men (this may actually be other Micronesians under Yap control) came to the Marshall Islands, had children, and imparted to one of their female children the knowledge of navigation by the stars and how to read wave currents and patterns. There are also numerous well-known accounts of two primal females, Liwātuonmour and Lidepdepju, who came from Ep, and subsequently became stone pillars on Namᵤo and Aur atolls, respectively (cf. Erdland 1914; Mason 1947; Spoehr 1949). Whether Yap Island is the source of the name for the place of the mythical gods remains hypothetical, yet the identification of this location recurs in many versions, including Kometo's and of others I spoke with. Some commentators view the god's name "Wullep" to mean "from Ep" and another name for the god of the west, Iroojrālik (meaning chief of the west), while others suggest it merely means "the egg" (*lep*) (Kramer and Nevermann 1938). Epoon atoll in the southern Rālik Chain, where Kometo spent much of his childhood, may have received its name after this primal homeland.

In an alternative account recorded by Jack Tobin, who collected the most elaborate cosmological narrative to date in 1975, the storyteller (Jelibōr Jam) identified how a woman named Jineer ilo Kōbo represented the primal mother of the four posts of heaven that held up the sky.[10] These are the same four deities of the cardinal directions identified by Kometo and others. When these props fall down, the world as we know it begins. Jineer ilo Kōbo is also the one who gave birth to Ļakam, the name of the first coconut in the ancient language.[11] From the coconut, multiple blessings will come, including food and materials for buildings and canoes. She is also important in the development of the social codes of kindness and cooperation. Her son, Iroojrālik is the highest ranking of the four sons, and Tobin indicates that Ep (or Yap) was their homeland. Ļowa (voice of the land), with his companion Ļōmṭal (voice of the sea), simply appear without a progenitor in the Tobin version, as do Ļewōj (who calls things to come forth) and Ļaneej (who colors all those called with the tattoo). They appear after the four cardinal directions who represent the sons of Jineer ilo Kōbo before she gives birth to Ļakam. Neither of these sets of gods is the descendant of any primal being. Ļowa and Ļōmṭal are also credited, including by Kometo, with hewing the first canoe. Letao also just appears without an identifiable progenitor, but he is referenced in conjunction with Ļajbwināmọṇ, the god of the north and death.

To keep this cosmological introduction to a minimum, I will underscore only three additional key female deities that figure in some of the accounts, and especially Kometo's. One is the woman Lōñtañūr, who after descending to earth to Aelōñḷapḷap atoll, rewarded her youngest son, Jebro, with the knowledge of the sail due to his obedience. This led to the title investiture of the first paramount chief (Carucci 1997a; McArthur 1995, 2004). All of her offspring became star constellations and determine the course of the seasons. A second is Lijenenbwe of Namọ atoll, who bestowed upon her twelve sons the power of divination. The third woman is sometimes recorded as Limejọkdād of Mājro atoll, who as a witch and/or ogress, gave birth to all the creatures that afflict and irritate man such as mosquitoes and flies. In one account, she is the "Aunt" or classificatory mother of Jemāluut, and thus Letao (Erdland 1914). The variant relationships among the gods appear in the genealogy charts (figures 1–4).

Rālik Cosmogonic Genealogy

(from Erdland's accounts)

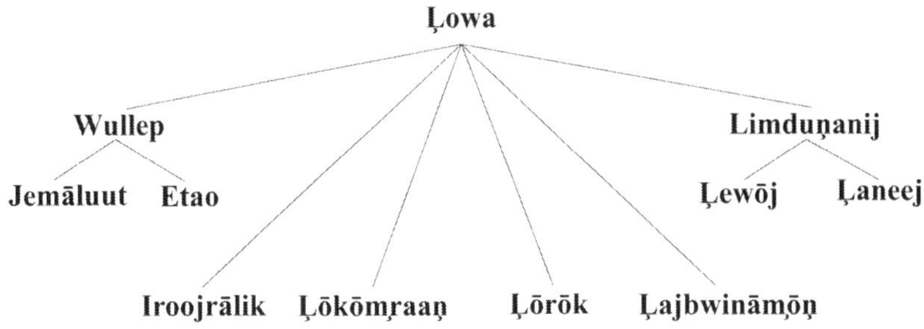

Ratak Cosmogonic Genealogy

(from Kramer's and Nevermann's accounts)

Tobin's Cosmogonic Genealogy

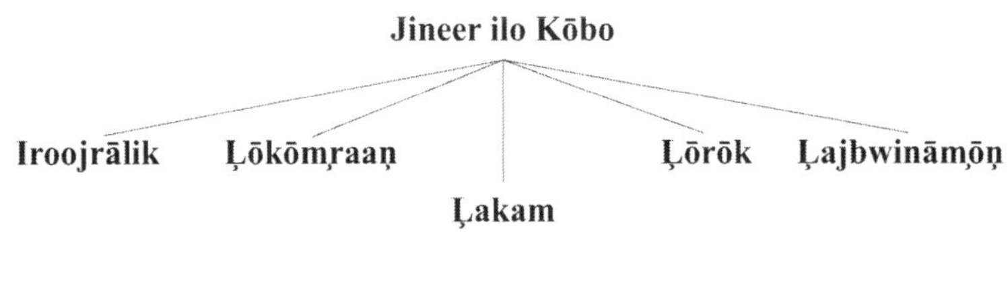

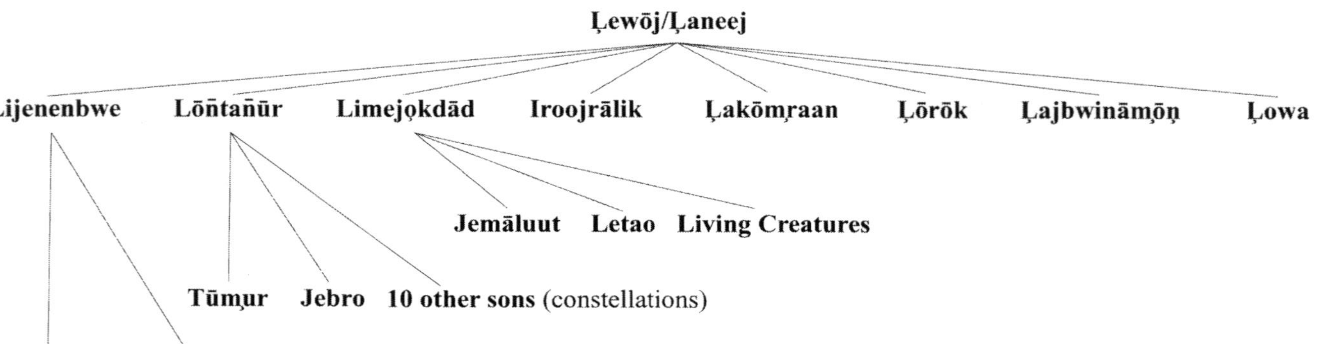

Kometo's Cosmogonic Genealogy

Ļewōj/Ļaneej

Lijenenbwe   Lōñtañūr   Limejọkdād   Iroojrālik   Ļakōmṛaan   Ļōrōk   Ļajbwināmọ̧ọ̧n   Ļowa

Jemāluut   Letao   Living Creatures

Tūmṛur   Jebro   10 other sons (constellations)

Lañinperan   11 other sons

I present this abbreviated outline of the gods and demigods to provide a context for the intertextual links in our dialogues that illustrate the qualities and power of Letao. Kometo did not simply appropriate these myths and genealogies, but out of his own place and time offered alternative relational scenarios. In many ways, his genealogy is more elaborate and complicated than the other recorded versions.

Kometo always wished to foreground Ļewōj and Ļaneej (instead of Ļowa or Jineer ilo Kōbo) as the key god(s) who placed several other gods/demigods in their present cardinal directions or locations throughout the islands and gave to each one a different power.[12] He essentially democratized all the islands so that each possesses a divine empowerment on par with the gods of the four cardinal directions.[13] From these primal deities, human beings came forth resulting in matrilines (*bwij*, literally meaning "navel lines"), matriclans (*jowi* or *jou*), and patrilines (*bōtōktōk*, or "blood lines"). Kometo's version here resonates and contrasts with that of Tobin's storyteller in 1975, who described how the fission of matriclans resulted out of social discord from not obeying Jineer ilo Kōbo (Tobin 2002). Notably, Kometo also turns the sky gods Ļewōj and Ļaneej into a singular being, in contrast to all the other versions that identify them as two (but always connected) beings. In other conversations, he overtly offered that these are two names for one individual god in an effort to calibrate this divinity to his modern Christian beliefs. For him, the names are simply substitutes for God and Jehovah, two appellations for the same god, which actually follows the riM̧ajeļ mythic practice of giving two distinct names for one individual god (e.g., Wullep and Iroojrālik, as indicated above).

On several occasions, he explained how after giving birth to all living land creatures (cf. Spoehr 1949), Limejo̧kdād then brought forth Jemāluut (a human child and chief with legitimate authority) and last Letao, "a mischievous person." In addition to Jemāluut, Letao's older siblings include the animals. The fauna (*menninmour* in Kajin M̧ajeļ) are categorically contrasted to humans (*armej*), or in this context, humanlike gods.

Like Kometo, the female Limejo̧kdād referenced in other narrative collections (e.g., Erdland 1914) is placed at Mājro atoll, but instead of being the ogress/witch-aunt of Letao and Jemāluut, Kometo identified her as their mother. This confusion may be the result of classificatory terms, as a maternal aunt will also be called "mother" (*jine-*).[14] Alexander Spoehr (1949) also identifies her as Jemāluut's mother (but not Letao's) in his study on Mājro atoll just after the war. But of greater import here is Kometo's logic for tracing Letao's descent through this particular female and her two sibling goddesses. While other individuals will also link the three primal matriarchs to their respective atolls Aelōñḷapḷap, Naṃo (Namu) and Mājro, they do not establish their generational kinship bond. The most renowned of these goddesses, Lōñtañūr, can be readily identified by every adult or child in the Marshall Islands as the one who rewarded her obedient youngest son, Jebro, with knowledge of the sail and who instituted the high chief title. All her sons became the constellations that govern the seasons. Her notoriety comes from ubiquitous recitations in intimate settings, from the prominent placement of narratives about her in most published collections of tales (Grey 1951; Mitchell 1973; Knight 1980; Downing et al. 1992; Carucci 1997a; Tobin 2002), through continual intertextual references in popular songs and speech making (McArthur 2004), and in dramatizations at festivals (Carucci 1997a; McArthur 2004). Fewer individuals know the name of Lijenenbwe, but those who do also place her at Naṃo atoll and identify her connection to the veiled practice of divination (*bubu*), the esoteric folding and reading of pandanus-leaf knots. Even fewer know about Limejoḳdād, and if they do, most place her also on Mājro atoll like Kometo. But only Kometo made the overt matrilineal link of Limejoḳdād to Letao and established these sisters as the origin of three culturally salient kinds of power (divination, chiefly authority/seasons, deception). This reflects how he understood the way the riM̧ajeḷ cosmos continues to inform contemporary social relations.

Kometo often referred to Letao's mother as "a dirty thing," which corresponds to other descriptions of her, and foregrounds the etymology of her name Limejoḳdād, which literally means "woman (*li*) who (*me*) is dirty (*joḳdād*)." Her sisters' names also serve as indexes to their influence and power. Lijenenbwe means "woman (*li*) from/of (*jen*) the (*en*) divination knot (*bwe*)," and Lōñtañūr means "from the sky (*lōñ*) striving (*tañūr*),"[15] who descended from skies to provide sailing technology and chiefly titles. Kometo also identified their birth order, with Lijenenbwe as the eldest, Lōñtañūr the second, and Limejoḳdād the youngest.

Kometo rarely elaborated on Lōñtañūr and her celestial sons. He knew I was familiar with her power and that I had heard several stories about her from other storytellers who focused on this particular goddess (McArthur 2004). He more often emphasized the roles of Lijenenbwe and Limejoḳdād. One day at Kometo's house at Teḷap islet, when I pressed him with questions about these two female deities, this next riddling dialogue emerged.[16] It develops the import of Letao's mother and his siblings, and provides some explanation for the trickster's behavior.

K   They say, what's her name? "Limejoḳdād." (oh) His mother, she is a Mājro woman. This woman, she is the mother of Letao and Jemāluut. See? The older sibling is Jemāluut. (oh) And . . . there are also other older siblings, the living things.[17] These men [Jemāluut and Letao] are the younger. The children of the woman are the ant, black ant, fly, mosquito.

P All are Letao's elder siblings?

K <laughs> They are the older siblings of Letao. Do you see the rat, gecko, black lizard, ant, fly, mosquito? They say they first appeared at Mājro.[18] They are the children of this woman.

P And, Letao is the youngest?

K Yes, Jemāluut, then Etao. <I chuckle, he joins> Thus, they say. They say she is the reason for the rat and the things that crawl and fly like mosquitoes and flies and—

P She gave life to all these things?

K Eh.

P Now all the children of this woman, they bother people, correct?

K Yes.

P Now, some of these words I don't know about . . . You said the rat and what else?

K *Mānnueal.*[19]

P What is a *mānnueal*?

K There is an animal, there in the middle of Mājro, like ah, like what? Those big lizards, and it looks like an alligator. (oh) But it is just as long as that. <measures hands about six inches apart> Now, they are on those coconut tree palms, /(mmm)/ it is a green animal that crawls.

P Well, the green lizard and what?

K *Aop.*[20]

P Aop, what is an aop?

K It is that kind creature on those coconut tree palms and it crawls. You will see it on the bark of those coconut trees. They crawl way up there, and again it is about this long. <shows about four-inch length with fingers>

P Oh, black lizard. Then what?

K Just all living things.

P It's not the dog and cat?

K Well, it's not. The dog and cat, those are things of the foreigner. They are brought with the foreigners.

P But all the other living things are from Letao's mother?

K <chuckles> Yes. Letao as the youngest, does those kinds of mischievous things. And he is intelligent, and what else? There is much power with him. See? <pause>

P The spider. Does it come from the woman?

K Also, from the woman. It is also the child of the woman.

P   And the cockroach?

K   Yes. <chuckles> They are all her children.

In this riddling exchange, Kometo again establishes Letao's origin at Mājro atoll, the location upon which we were conducting this particular conversation. He places Letao's mother on Mājro, and then overtly establishes the birth order of Jemāluut and Letao, which is critical in determining social rank in riMạjeḷ society. He also confirms that Limejoḵdād, after giving birth to all the creatures that annoy humankind, gives birth to the two humanlike children, Jemāluut and Letao. We then dialogically create a list of all the creatures that bother human beings, rehearsing numerous possibilities in island fauna.[21] Except for the dog and cat, which he concedes came with the foreigners (Western), land animals, all of which are rather annoying and pesky, represent the offspring of Limejoḵdād, and thus the older siblings of Letao. While Kometo and I did not invent the motif of Limejoḵdād creating bothersome creatures, which I heard also from others, we did dialogically imagine the extent of their possibilities. So again, our riddling dialogue extends the mythological associations.

In this cosmological genealogy, Kometo explains that the trickster is the youngest son of the youngest matriarch, who is "dirty," and is the sibling of all those creatures that bother humankind. In his family of origin, then, Letao is linked to a troublesome set of siblings. He is the culmination of that which will agitate. His endowment is intelligence, and with it he will prove the ultimate trickster. It is this smart youngest member of the annoying set of siblings who will travel to America, taking these qualities with him. Letao's status at the bottom of this notorious family also places him in a marginal position in which he can only resort to subversion to achieve power. The place of the youngest male child in riMạjeḷ society is known as "ḷakūbwe" (likūbwe, if female). Because they are so far away from ever achieving ascribed rank, they do not pose a threat to social authority.

In riMạjeḷ society, for royalty and commoners alike, rank and title in general follow matrilines.[22] To ascend to the title of chief (*irooj* or *lerooj* for a female chief) or the lineage head of commoners (*aḷab*), birth order determines the succession. Age, rather than gender, establishes title, and in Kajin Mạjeḷ, siblingship is similarly marked by identifiers of age, not gender. For example, my older sibling receives the term "*jeiū*" and my younger sibling the term "*jatiū*," regardless of gender. To designate brother or sister, additional terms must be added, *mṃaan eo jeiū* (my older male sibling) or *kōrā eo jetiū* (my younger female sibling). But again, in the determination of rank, these gender identifications are not relevant as title is held by the eldest male or female. The firstborn or oldest sibling is also referred to a *utm̧aan,* and is accorded great respect by the younger siblings. If the oldest sibling is female, she will obtain the appropriate chief or lineage head titles. Even so, in public settings, she may designate a younger male sibling to speak or act on behalf of the matriline (*m̧m̧aan maroñroñ*). Despite this public role, he will consistently consult with and defer to the decisions of his elder sister. Accordingly, when the chief (*irooj/lerooj*) or lineage head (*aļab*) dies, the title will pass to the next oldest sibling, in principle, but there is some variation in actual practice depending on their competence (cf. Petersen 2009). Because the primary inheritance (*jolōt*) and titles belong to a matriline[23]—not a nuclear unit—rank must be determined by attending to the birth order of the previous generation (*epepen*). The result is that the children in the current generation of the oldest sibling in the previous generation will receive titles before the children of the next eldest sibling of the previous generation even if they are in actual age older than their parallel cousins. All parallel cousins from both the matriline and patriline receive the same classificatory terms for siblings (*jei-* or *jati-,* older or younger sibling, respectively). All cross-cousins, mother's brother's children, or father's sister's children, receive a different term (*riliki-*) because they do not belong to either an individual's matriline or patriline. Add to this that all the siblings of the first generation include all classificatory siblings from mother's sisters, one perceives quickly that opportunities for the youngest siblings (current generation) of the youngest siblings (previous generation) to obtain a title are very slim indeed. This is the place of Letao; he is the youngest child of his mother, who is the youngest sibling of the three primal sisters.

The term *ļakūbwe* ("the youngest [male] child") literally means "little male excrement." It is only fitting, then, that Letao occupies the position that lends itself best to the qualities of the trickster—cross-culturally a scatological figure (cf. Hyde 1998). From this sociologically subordinate position, he engages in the most audacious acts of subversion of his superiors. He is the youngest sibling who comes out ahead only through deceptions and reversals. Lurking behind this identification of Letao as the *ļakūbwe* lies Kometo's awareness of my sociological standing, because many years ago the riM̧ajeļ family who "adopted" me (*kaajiriri*) in islander terms—with the concomitant reciprocal obligations—also gave me the nickname Ļakūbwe, because I am also the youngest in my American family (actually the youngest child of the youngest child in my matriline as well). To this day, many riM̧ajeļ will address me with this term. The chiefly husband of my older female sibling explained that this term actually serves as a term of endearment for the younger sibling. Because the ļakūbwe is so far away from ever achieving title for the chief or lineage head, he is never a political threat to be concerned with, and consequently, an affectionate and fun-loving relationship adheres between the elder siblings and the youngest. In this marginal position, however, he is granted a certain degree of liberty to say and behave in ways considered off-limits to others. By being classified as such, I present no threat to sociologically ascribed power and may enjoy the joking privileges that accompany this categorical placement. And by extension, America's association with the trickster may also reflect a kind of siblingship and ranking. The riM̧ajeļ are the source of the deep cosmological power, the older siblings, whereas America is now the younger, but clever sibling. For this reason, Letao continued to serve as a relevant and dramatic analogy of American power. His position in the cosmogonic genealogy highlights ambiguity and a degree of unpredictability and danger. This is only what we should expect of a trickster, especially the Americans.

The Kinship of Power

With their auspicious links to the cosmological genealogy, the Americans as the embodiment of dangerous intelligence has only taken shape in the islanders' conceptualization since their arrival during World War II. Because Letao is the source of their intelligence, this new global power has roots in riM̧ajeļ cosmological origins. But the Americans also represent a range of extremes embedded in the trickster. As Kometo repeated often, "In America there is intelligence and there is stupidity, there is bad, there is good, there are lies, there is truth, there is love, there is hate, there are all kinds." America becomes the modern personification of all of Letao's extremes. Within this ambivalent image, the Americans simultaneously characterize the trickster's subversive qualities and provide the paradoxical image of the powerful high chief who is both benevolent and a formidable warrior.

In the previous chapter, I maintained that the Americans, by analogy, showcase the dualistic image of the chief, his kind generosity and warrior prowess. In order to see how Kometo and islanders generate this correlation, I need to recapitulate some essential dimensions of riM̧ajeļ kinship and chiefly authority,[24] and the sensibilities attached to these underlying features of social power. This will set the ground for understanding the oxymoron of a kind warrior, and the riddling dialogues in the remainder of this chapter that extend the myth with its commentary on social power.

Notwithstanding some important variations (e.g., Likiep and Ānewetak atolls),[25] riM̧ajeļ kinship and power begin with the concept of mother (*jinen*) and her relationship to the land. The term for matrilineage (*bwij*), derives from the root of *bwijen,* which means umbilicus or navel. As a result, while in the womb, a child "eats" (*m̧ōñā*) from its mother, through whom life passes as well as one's spiritual substance (*an*)[26] and physical strength (*kajoor*). The matrilineage is the kinship extension of the mother and her life-giving power. After birth, a child nurses (*ninnin*) from its mother and again eats from her. As a child grows, the mother will continue to feed her child (*naajdik*). Then, when grown to adulthood the child commonly receives land (*bwidej*) through the mother's lineage and again, essentially eats from her. The ultimate act of kindness is sharing food. Concomitantly, the primary symbolic act that binds a matrilineage is the distribution (*ajej*) of food and the land resources from which food derives, where one will always receive *jouj* (kindness as exemplified in food sharing).[27] As a result, the matrilineage (*bwij*), and indeed all kinship ties, is described as being constituted on kindness (*jouj*). All of these social proprieties echo the virtues established by the primal goddess, Jineer ilo Kōbo (as presented in Tobin's cosmogony).

The kinship-ordering principle, founded on a pliant metaphor of the kind and life-giving mother, is analogous to the power of chiefs (*irooj ro*). Their power and prescribed behavior replicate this kinship sensibility. Certainly, chiefs were expected to defend and promote their people through warfare, but they were also to take care of them through kindness, or the distribution of food and allocation of land, similar to mothers and reciprocal obligations within matrilines. Mothers and chiefs become a complementary reflection of one another because it is from them that land, food, and life come. Those who receive the land are described as nursing (*ninnin*) from their chiefs.

Similar to the dualistic image of chiefly power found in much of Oceania (cf. Marcus 1989; Petersen 2009), the riM̧ajeļ chief is simultaneously a feared warrior due to his military prowess (*lāj*), and a populist who cares for (*jouj*) and distributes (*ajej*) food and land resources to his people. His spiritual power (*ao*) derived from a cosmological link back to the gods ensures the fecundity of the land (cf. Carucci 1997b). A chief may achieve power through military success, but he maintains it through the "kind" treatment of his common people (*kajoor ro*), who, in turn, offer tribute (*akkan* or *eojek*) and support in his battles. Recognizing that the centralization and routinization of the social hierarchy and chiefly authority with respect to land comes with German colonization and the development of plantations (Carucci 1988; Walsh and Heine 2012), the riM̧ajeļ sensibilities about chiefly authority I present here nonetheless represent a continuity in deep history.[28] This historical paradigm seeps into modern life to varying degrees. There is much contemporary commentary about how chiefs can either maintain the dualistic ideal or become self-serving despots who exploit people and the land for their own purposes. In practice and in discourse, individuals and groups manipulate and rework this historically pliable sensibility (cf. Meyer 2013), as will become evident in the remainder of the riddling dialogues in this chapter.

A New High Chief

The "chiefly kindness" exhibited by the Americans just after their occupation (1943) coupled with their military prowess, stands out to both Kometo and his friend Ṃake.[29]

K   *We did not have any clothes, but now, the Americans come and bring clothes.*
      The clothes were in a box.
      It had not yet been broken open.
      Then they pulled it open—

P   What were the things they brought in the boxes to these islands?
K   Shirts and trousers and shoes and hats and—
P   When the Americans came to these islands after the war, how were your lives different from the times of the Japanese?
M   Really different from the times of the Japanese. At first, we are afraid of the Americans.

K   *The Japanese say, "If you will go with those Americans, they will take you, tie your legs and carry you, and throw you into the sea.*
      Or take you to Hawaiʻi.
      Tie your legs and say, 'Gone with you.'"
      And you end up in Hawaiʻi.
M   *But then, when the Americans come it is good; they bring many things.*
      We are not afraid since there is much food.
      And there is a lot of clothing too.
      Life is good, we don't worry anymore.
      It's not like during the Japanese times that were hard. A hard life . . .

K   After the Navy people left, see? It is a hard life again.
P   Why is it a hard life?
K   Well, see, there is no food after the companies are raised.
M   Now, we pay with money.
P   Oh, before with the Navy/
M   /We don't pay./
K   /There is no cost for food.

M   *The Micro Fieldtrip Ship goes around the Marshalls and—well, it keeps going*
     around—
K   *They go around with food and take it to the outer islands. See? (uh huh)*
     And they give it away and there is no cost.
     Nonetheless, we make a little (money) with handicrafts. See? (uh huh)
     We make handicrafts and/
M   */and we sell them.*

Because the riM̧ajeļ need to live. In the Japanese time,

the people make handicrafts and place them in a store over there.
Now, with the Americans a boat comes and just takes the handicrafts.
They buy them and take them and . . .

P   What did the Americans do with the handicrafts?
M   Well, some take them to America and we don't know after that. /
K   /We don't know, but some,

they send away, and some they buy and return them . . . to the sea.
They just throw them out. <we all laugh>
They only buy them because they want the riM̧ajeļ to live.

Here in these segments of our dialogues, Kometo and M̧ake collaborate, moving seamlessly between story and explanations through metanarration. This exchange rehearses how the American military provided clothing in abundance for the riM̧ajeļ during military occupation. On another occasion, Kometo told me how this gesture impressed him because it showed that the Americans were kind, and that they had so much abundance they could just give it away, a sign of a powerful chief. If they had been afraid of the Americans at the time of the invasion,[30] and due to the Japanese threats of American torture, their opinion changed with the provisions of clothing and food. Those who satisfy simple survival needs will always be respected, but offering food is doubly meaningful for the riM̧ajeļ; it serves as both a symbol of chiefly kindness (an index to their power) and familial protocol (relatives feed each other).

That the Navy simply supplied food at no cost impresses M̧ake and Kometo and they lament their withdrawal because they then had to enter a cash economy. Expatriate and local businessmen alike emerged to introduce an economy different from Indigenous exchange, and different also from that under the indentured plantation practices of the Germans and Japanese. The riM̧ajeļ quickly sought to enter into an exchange relationship with the Americans, offering traditional handicrafts (*amimọ̄ṇo*).[31] But what stands out for these two is how the Americans took the crafts, more out of a sense of benevolent obligation than from want or need. The riMạjeḷ offered the crafts as reciprocal kindness and tribute to the new "chiefly" power, but the Americans buy them. Kometo concludes that not only did they not use the crafts for economic or personal items (such as with the Japanese), but they likely just discarded them in the sea. But instead of seeing this as an offense, it only reconfirms the American chiefly power—indicative of their strength—because they do not need them. This view of the Americans is compounded by the fact that as Kometo told me, outside a recorded interview, that he and others had been impressed that the Americans did not demand riMạjeḷ labor to build the airstrips as the Japanese had, instead they just moved the islanders out of the way. To this point in the interchange, American qualities in the narrated event parallel good chiefly behavior rather than the subversion of Letao. Instead of seeing the image of America developing sequentially, from trickster to chief, we should view these as paired images ascribed to the same entity. Americans may achieve their power through the cosmological power of the trickster, but they also maintain the paramount chiefly image.

For Kometo's generation, the legitimacy of American chiefly power remains intact, in spite of forced relocation, nuclear bomb tests, and continued occupation of Kuwajleen atoll. In an effort to elicit a cultural perspective and criticism of the nuclear tests, I asked both Kometo and Mạke. This led to an inverted dialogue,[32] me trying to poke holes in their assessment of American conduct, and they seemingly assenting to the American chiefly presence.

K   So we will say—how can it be explained? It belongs to the Americans to decide.
P   Why? It's not theirs. The islands belong to the riMạjeḷ.
K   Yes, they belong to the riMạjeḷ, but the Americans have looked after them. You see we met at a camp? Over there at the place of the riMạjeḷ on Mājro.
P   A camp?
K   Eh, over there, at the docks, all the riMạjeḷ who worked for the Americans were there.

Now, the highest-ranking man, the captain—

See? (uh huh)

asks the riM̧ajȩl, "Who do you want to look after you?"
Then, we say, "Who do you think it should be?"
Now, he says, "If you all say the Russians, well it will be the Russians.
If you all say that the Japanese should look after you again—okay then.
If you all say, England, then it will be England."
Then, after all of his words,

See?

they say, "No we want, <strong accent in English> The United States of America."

Since then, thus it is, they remain today. Permission was given for America to look after the Marshalls.

P   Under the TT (Trust Territory).[33]

K   Eh.

Now, they take this country and take it to eh—

I think perhaps all of Micronesia also wanted it—that America should look after them.

Now, they take the government and place it at Saipan.
Amata the president then says, "Well, I'm taking the Marshalls from Micronesia."
Well, now, he takes the Marshalls from Micronesia.
And now, it's just the riM̧ajȩl by ourselves.

But the riM̧ajȩl still have to live—we just nurse from America. <some chuckling>

P   But not now. Your independence has begun.

M   Yes, now the government is independent.

K   It will be independent, but will still live because of America.

P   Because there is much aid from America?

K   Yes . . . the riM̧ajȩl will still nurse from America.

P   But didn't the Americans bring great suffering?

M   Yes.

K   Nnn, (with sarcastic tone) what suffering?

P   The bomb. It makes people sick.

M   Well, the bomb is huge./

K   /We don't know anything. They know. No matter, anything they do is good!

P   How can you say this? It's not good.
K   It's for the paramount chief to decide.
P   Yes, Letao. <both of them laugh> The Americans have deceived the riM̧ajeļ.
K   Well, because of the loincloth at America.
P   The what?
K   Loincloth, see? <gestures to groin and buttocks>
P   Oh, the loincloth. <all laugh>
M   We are sad that the Americans are gone now.
P   Why are you now sad that America is gone?
M   It's good that America looks after these islands. But now we look after our-
     selves, see? Independence? It's hard. There is no power here in the Marshalls.
     Life is very hard now . . .
P   But is it good that a country like America has power over you?
K   (acting disgusted) Is there another country like America that has such
     power?

Try as I might, I could not dissuade them from applying the concept of chiefly power to American occupation. Certainly, they may have been assuming this position to provide a favorable ground upon which an American and two riM̧ajeļ men could discourse. I nonetheless propose it is representative of an underlying sensibility that informs their perspective. The respect and ambivalence they have for chiefs mirrors their feelings about American power, at least for those who experienced it during World War II. They are the generation who created the episode of Letao traveling to America. This dialogue is striking also in that they seem to be less concerned about feeding me what they thought I desired than seizing the moment to lecture me, and both spend ample time pontificating. Kometo's contextualization through reported speech of the American captain offering the riM̧ajeļ a say in who will govern them (note, they are not to govern themselves) sets up a situation in which he then explains the history of the Trust Territory and eventual independence. They both refuse, at least on the surface, my attempts to assign culpability to America. Their perspective is certainly not shared by contemporary generations who now push back against the United States and its abusive legacy of imperialism on the islands (e.g., Jetñil-Kijiner 2017). And yet, what seems like resignation on their part may actually offer a cunning, and in many ways sardonic, commentary on how the Americans come to imitate the ambivalent nature of chiefly power.

In the beginning of this dialogue, Kometo grants the Americans the right to decide, a parallel to the same kind of everyday gesture accorded chiefs. When I reject any sense of American ownership to the islands, he reframes the past with a narrated event about the American "captain" offering the riM̧ajeļ a choice about their colonial overseers. The current situation is not just a result of American force but of riM̧ajeļ complicity. Whether Kometo attended this event or only heard about it, or if it happened at all I am not sure. I do believe, however, that he was among the crowd before some American official and that his sense of entitlement to the captain's words derives from firsthand experience (cf. Shuman 2004). He worked on Mājro when the US military established its primary base on the atoll. Certainly, his reported speech delivers an authenticating device, giving the story an air of accuracy and mimetic presence. That the riM̧ajeļ chose the United States may be just Kometo casting history into a positive light in the presence of an American. And clearly, what option did the islanders really have (if this offer was ever really extended) after witnessing the destructive power of the United States military, given that the offer was being proposed by the military force currently occupying their islands? Nonetheless, the contextualization of this narrated event shows Kometo rendering a past that explains strategic acquiescence to the modern chief.

The "list" of options provided by the captain, Russia, Japan, England, the United States, is not arbitrary, but reflects Kometo's sense of the geopolitical history that has come to bear on his islands since the war. He was aware of the Cold War intrigues with Russia (he and others report that Russian submarines have entered the Marshalls to spy on Kuwajleen), he had lived under Japanese occupation, and the British had occupied Kiribati to the south until recently. He is listing off the superpowers that he knows. If the so-called captain did make this kind of speech, Kometo at least minimizes the textual gap between the narrative and the event through the reported speech. The shift from quoting the captain to quoting the collective riM̧ajeļ "they," with his slow and droll pronunciation of the United States, caps the narrated event, providing a humorous, explanatory accounting for US occupation—they had been granted "permission . . . to look after the Marshalls." This kind of postured acquiescence to American power mimics the populist sustaining of chiefly authority. Just before this explanation, he claims, "thus it is" (*āindein*), the quintessential riM̧ajeļ way of summation and closing an argument: It is just that way. Are you going to overtly argue with a paramount chief?

We then discuss the Trust Territory period briefly and there is a reference made to Amata Kabua, the paramount chief and first president of the nation who resisted the attempt to unify all the island groups into a single nation. It is he who led the break of the Republic of the Marshalls Islands from the rest of Micronesia in 1979.[34] Kometo's point is that whether part of the regional whole or separate, the islands are still dependent on America; like an infant, they must "nurse" (*ninnin*) from their mother/chief. This metaphor turns riM̧ajel̦ dependence into a mother-child/chief-commoner relationship. In this riddling encounter, Kometo tests me to see if I will "get" the riddle that correlates imperial history with chieftaincy. When I make claims about political independence and then return to the point about the suffering that has resulted from the bomb testing, Kometo seems to challenge any legitimacy to riM̧ajel̦ resistance, and grants America, as both the chief and trickster, the privilege to do what it does. At the time, as shown by the ensuing disagreement I have with him, I express dismay at such fatalism and resignation. But now, many years after this conversation, I detect the sarcasm; he was employing a veiled strategy to uncover my view on the nature of power and its source—just as I was trying to understand his. He was testing me to see if I understood the trickster ethos underlying his play, if I would "get" the riddle. Perhaps I start to perceive this, when exasperated with their response, I shift my disbelief to comic relief by invoking Letao, which signals to Kometo that I understand his analogy between the trickster and the Americans. They both enjoy my abrupt redirection. Then he immediately reinvokes the loincloth idea (symbol of Letao's power), which takes me a moment to catch, and when I do we all erupt into laugher, at one, my recognition of how the immediate conversation intertextually expands antecedent dialogues, and two, at the denouement of the riddle.

M̧ake then claims that the riM̧ajel̦ are sad to see the Americans gone. I think he means the more overt presence during the military occupation so long ago, and perhaps the incremental withdrawal of American interests since the end of the Trust Territory. As one who had experienced direct colonization and the terrible effects of war, he felt more comfortable with the Americans administrating the islands and distrusted islander independence. That "life is very hard now" reveals the economic stresses faced by many. When I ask about the legitimacy of a powerful country having influence over another, Kometo responds in a disgusted fashion with a rhetorical question that suggests: Can we really do anything about such power? Is he responding to what he perceives as an ignorant question, or annoyance at this reality? Perhaps a little of both. These responses, the opposite of what I had hoped, are infused with sensibilities and ambivalence about the nature of chiefly power.

This whole dialogue represents an inversion; as an American, I take a critical stance toward US abuses to advocate for the riM̧ajel̦, while Kometo and M̧ake appear to defend American actions and dismiss their own nation. But for Kometo and M̧ake, current riM̧ajel̦ powerlessness was really not what it appeared to be since American "chiefly" power derives from the riM̧ajel̦ trickster. Modern geopolitical relations grow out of the original usurpation presented in the narrated event about Letao's trickery. From their perspective, it is better to align oneself, or at least demonstrate some deference, to a powerful trickster chief than to be left on the margins, alone, weak, and vulnerable. Now of course, this was all part of the good-humored subtext to our dialogues, but it does help conceptualize the Americans as enacting chiefly power and their ostensible deference to it. Feigned acquiescence has utility as a weapon for the weak (cf. Scott 1985). It offers a historically salient strategy for managing relationships to powerful chiefs, while at the same time retaining some autonomy through the trickster's bluff. Such tactics at least seemed to satisfy immediate needs (e.g., food). Later in this dialogue, I asked: "But is it good that America imposes its land customs, genealogy, and language on the riM̧ajeḷ?" Kometo responded, "Well <long pause> don't bring language, customs, and genealogy. Just bring food!" <I laugh hard and then they laugh> Tricksters are fundamentally motivated by a satiated stomach (Hyde 1998).

The Power of Land

Kometo often emphasized that real power lay in the land. This perspective was informed by both his Indigenous understanding of the interwoven connections among land, commoners, and chiefly authority, and how it becomes entangled with the changes brought about through colonization. During German and Japanese colonization, chiefs assumed a greater sense of "ownership" or possession over the land (Carucci 1997b; Walsh and Heine 2012), with the result that commoner (*kajoor ro*) rights to land, instead of being rooted in deep historical connections through occupation by matrilineal families, became increasingly just usufruct rights.[35] All the plants and foodstuffs produced on the land belong to the commoner who is expected to offer tribute to the chief (*ekkan* or *eọjek*). This entitlement, however, becomes a moot point if a chief decides to remove the commoner from the land—the trees cannot be taken with them. Up until the early colonial period, a chief acquired power over the commoners through military prowess and the acquisition of land. All power for Kometo begins in the land because life itself is rooted ultimately in the earth and who controls it. The minimal landscapes of the Marshall Island atolls, within the immense and ever-present ocean, serve literally and figuratively as a primary symbol of power. The seaways are not something a chief can "possess" or control like land. The open ocean (not the lagoons that are seen to be contained by the land) represent an ever-changing and flexible highway connecting atolls. A chief may cross it to increase his dominion over other lands, but he does not claim the sea and its resources. A chief can control reef resources connected to the land (from which he receives tribute) and authorize major fishing expeditions, but his power is rooted in the land by claims to the territory and his spiritual ties to the land that ensure its productivity. His "right to rule" that comes through women is a "localized [source] of power contained within the perimeter of an atoll" (Carucci 1989, 91).

One day we were talking about the relationship of the land to the commoners and chiefs.[36] As was typical of many of our discussions, he contrasted American ways to the riM̧ajeḷ. The following riddling interchange, comprising singsong questions, expose the significance of land to social power, and the American president as paramount chief. We were casually bantering when I tried to explain that political power today in America is not based in land ownership but through a variety of business dealings or political work. I tried to trip up the trickster:

P   So, President Clinton does not possess any land.

K   But, where is he?

P   He is the president of the government.

K   Yes, where does he sleep?

P   He sleeps in the White House.

K   To whom does the White House belong?

P   It belongs to the government.

K   What did they do, so that they have the White House?

P   A president long ago made the house. He built one for the presidents.

K   Where is it?

P   Washington, DC.

K   Is this not on the land?

P   To whom does the land belong? Does it belong to Clinton?

K   Ah, now it belongs to Clinton.

P   It does not belong to Clinton, it belongs to the government of the people.

K   Well, see please. <chuckles> Now, all the people in America belong to Clinton today. <I laugh with him> And they are on the land. And now, Clinton is the paramount chief of America.

P   So, he is paramount chief as you say, but not because of his land, it is because the people chose him to be chief.

K   Yes, he is similar to a paramount chief. He battled with <wind blows, inaudible>. . . .

P   . . . with Bush.

K   <laughs> With Bush.

P   And now he is chief.

K   He is chief.

P   So where does his power come from? Not by possessing land.

K   It comes from the commoner people, and the people are in the land. The American people, they give him power like a paramount chief. <long pause, chuckles>

P   You are very clever.

K   Ahh. Just debating a little with you. <laughs>

The concept of genealogically ascribed access to land and thus resources is fundamental in riM̧ajeļ society. Resources and power come by ascription, unless one achieves power through warfare, and even that is still contingent upon mobilizing kinship links that are conjoined by mutual land access. The American model of individually achieved status is only possible through kinship and genealogical links. The economic success of certain riM̧ajeļ through business or political positions within the state government is typically only possible by virtue of ascribed titles and family capacity. Kin predictably buy from kin, and kin vote for kin. Indeed, much to the chagrin of American educated commoners who return to the Marshall Islands hoping to succeed in business and politics, find that the economy and democracy line up with kinship ties and chiefly affiliations. Any opportunities for advancement belong to these links, and every link is advantaged or disadvantaged by connections to land.[37]

I try to disentangle political status from the land by invoking President Clinton as a powerful figure without land. In a familiar riM̧ajeļ fashion, Kometo shifts our roles to challenge me with a riddling series of questions about where the president sleeps and who owns the White House. People, even the president of the United States, are situated in the land. Often the land or a land tract (*wāto*) in Kajin M̧ajeļ is referred to as a "house" (*m̧weiō*) of a particular matriclan. It is on this tract that a building (*em̧*) is erected, and a person is identified in terms of the network of social relations and land to which they belong. I want to insist upon democratic privilege to use government property (the house), but Kometo brings the point back to a genealogy on the land. I contend that Clinton is a servant of the people's government, and he only has, in a sense, usufruct rights to the White House. But Kometo argues that because Clinton is now the paramount chief (*irooj ļabļab*), the people belong to him, and they are in the land. He extends this metaphoric conceptualization (US president as paramount chief) by offering how he achieved his title through a battle, not that of spears and stones, but through democracy itself. Clinton democratically battled Bush (senior), who had been "paramount chief," to assume power. Like a riM̧ajeļ chief, his power (*kajoor*) comes from the people, the commoners (*kajoor ro*) who are in the land. Thus, Clinton's power is no different from a riM̧ajeļ paramount chief.

Shortly after this segment of exchange presented here, I claimed that even though my ancestors came from Europe, I am a landless American. Kometo responded with a story about when the chiefs of Arṇo (Arno) atoll battled their "fathers" to gain power over Mājro. The sons were of the Rim̧wejoor matriclan in Arṇo, but their patrilineal kin, who married their mothers, were of the Raarṇo matriclan on Mājro. These Rim̧wejoor chiefs came to battle in Mājro with their patrilineal kin and were victorious, and thus, chiefly authority and possession in this atoll shifted to a new matriline (cf. Tobin version 2002). He maintained that land is acquired by battle, and as a kind of theft—chiefly authority is accomplished through land acquisition. This is not a prescriptive conclusion by Kometo, it is simply a matter of fact. He who has land is the chief, and land is acquired through aggressive battles. The chiefs of Mājro came from somewhere else and achieved power through warfare. The modern American chief came from somewhere else and achieved power through military invasion. That usurping chiefs come from somewhere else across the sea is a prevalent and recurrent motif in the mythology and history of Oceania (Sahlins 1985; Carucci 1989, 1997a; Dening 2004; Kirch 2012). Thinking through the Americans as the warrior chief whose genealogy goes back to Letao is like solving a riddle, a riddle that enlarges the cosmological and social context of the myth again.

Kometo took great interest in the 1992 US presidential campaign between George Bush and Bill Clinton. It was not their specific positions on the issues (he knew few if any of these) that interested him but what he saw as a "battle" between two political warriors vying to become the "great world chief." When I told him that Clinton had won, he boldly articulated, "The person who is president in America is the most powerful paramount chief in the world." This power comes not just by virtue of his personal prowess, but because, like riM̧ajeḷ chiefs of the past, he can gather many around him those who possess great knowledge.[38]

K   *"The chief should know."* [traditional maxim]
P   Like his "pit of knowledge." [*Nitijelā*, or Indigenous royal court]
K   Well, his royal court it's like, what's it called—those who gather to meet in America? In the White House? Well, it's also like a royal court.
P   Like the royal court of long ago with the chiefs?
K   Same as with the chiefs of long ago.

Kometo and others often reminded me of the riM̧ajeḷ maxim "The chief should know" (*Irooj en jelā*); that is, the chief is the one we can go to for knowledge. He is, however, not directly in possession of all knowledge (genealogy, navigation, divination, stories, medicine, etc.); instead, he gathers around himself all those with knowledge into his Nitijelā ("pit of knowledge"),[39] or royal court. With this understanding, we compare the Nitijelā to those who assist the US president, and Kometo makes the connection explicit—that the White House, and perhaps the cabinet, is equivalent to the Nitijelā, revealing his recognition of a similar function for both political structures. Clinton is a link to deep history; he is like a paramount chief of long ago who won through warfare (in this case, battled in an election), and as such may exert his will. For Kometo and his generation, battles for power are part of the chiefly past, now mirrored in the imperial present.

Decolonization may come in the form of overt resistance, but in this case, the riM̧ajeḷ use Indigenous mythologies with deep cosmological underpinnings and epistemologies to appropriate for themselves reflections of power. Some may cynically view this tactic as resignation to imperial forces. But Kometo, like his generational peers, with his storytelling, cosmological musings, and reflections on chiefly power, poses a more nuanced understanding of a trickster-like subversion that blurs boundaries of difference among hierarchical distinctions that those in power (both the local and imperial) seek to maintain. Narrating the Americans as deceptive tricksters who have become a powerful paramount chief presents an unexpected leveling, and offers a subtle riddle-like commentary on their abusive and dominating power. They characterize the contradictory dualism of all chiefs; they are both benevolent and notoriously dangerous. As a social trickster, Kometo contained American power by giving it a genealogy back to Letao the trickster and all his extremes, and by collapsing the imperial force into the image of a powerful paramount chief.

In this chapter, I have presented how riddling dialogues about the kinship of power and musings about the trickster's cosmological power enlarged the myth. I explored how this ever-growing story becomes resituated in an intercultural dialogue that considers the realities of the imperial power intersecting with the Indigenous culture. When performed, this vibrant narrative lends itself to all the formal and poetic means whereby a narrator highlights particular meanings and creates a memorable event. But most of the ways this story is recontextualized in the modern world do not come by its full performance. Rather, through intertextual and indexical referencing, like others who make quick references to Letao and the Americans, we brought the myth over and over into our conversations. And in doing so, we made explicit possible meanings about the Indigenous cosmology, the trickster's genealogy, and social power, connotations not as evident in the narrative. The metacommentary about the meanings of this myth, through dialogic riddling, extended it into ever-increasing cosmological, sociological, and modern implications. Kometo selected certain content, images, ideologies, and meanings from the myth that drew from deep cultural resonances regarding the cosmology of mythological gods, matrilineal kinship, chiefly authority, land, and food, to manage the ambivalence that comes with American violence and generosity. In the process of our dialogues, we jointly participated in imbuing the myth with added meaning and possibility by drawing from Indigenous sensibilities about social life and power. A narrative is never closed just because the story has ended. It continues to be used to speak out from and back into itself. We not only entertained mythic extensions of this old story, but used it to shed light on a modern riM̧ajeḷ experience filled with the ambiguously powerful other, the Americans.

CHAPTER 4

Hide-and-Seek
The Social Ideologies of Deception and Revelation

In the children's game of hide-and-seek, the roles of hider and finder are typically delineated and clear. But with Letao the trickster, just who is doing the concealing and who is doing the revealing is not always so transparent. When a narrative character becomes entangled with Letao, they may find something, and thus celebrate their detection, only to realize that what they have found makes them a dupe. Or they may think they have something to hide when the trickster has known it all along. And those of us listening to the trickster story and witnessing the deception in the narrated event may believe we are getting a privileged vantage point, that we are being let in on what is "really" happening or will happen. But such revelations in a plot may evoke other ambiguities, that possibly Letao is still playing tricks and we may be getting only part of the story. And stories told by cunning storytellers leave us guessing in the context of the narrative event; we may be several steps removed from the significance of their play with signification. Even when a trickster performer casts into doubt what is revealed in the myth, it may simply prove another iteration of concealment. The hidden intents of skillful storytellers can make trickster semiotics messy indeed.

Perhaps all storytelling is a bit of a deception cast as a kind of revelation, since "there is something of a trickster in every narrator" (Briggs 1996, 27). This quality makes dialogues with Kometo doubly complex as I can only guess at the layers of deception and revelation he worked along the margins of the narrative performance and narrated events. All I can attempt is to reveal something of the trickster's deceptive indirection, all the while realizing that there is much more hidden. And then, even I, as an accomplice of a sort to the trickster's wiles, will veil some things, some intentional and some not, as I too have been both the dupe and in collusion with the trickster (Barnes 1994). Notwithstanding these caveats, attention to the forms of deception and revelation will help unpack some riM̧ajeḷ cultural semantics, especially as they relate to underlying ideologies about social power. It also manifests just how opaque a dialogic ethnography can be, but also, how potentially revealing.

Studying Kajin M̧ajeḷ under the tutelage of Kometo and other riM̧ajeḷ enhanced my appreciation for just how complicated signs can be, if for no other reason than because of the slipperiness in translating multivalent words and Indigenous mythic discourse. Linguistic signs both reveal and conceal. "If something cannot be used to tell a lie, conversely it cannot be used to tell the truth; it cannot in fact be used 'to tell' at all" (Eco 1976, 7). This potential of all signs, to lie simply because they are not what they represent, reveals a two-faced Janus dilemma; that lies/falsehood (*riab*) and truth (*m̧ool*), the hidden and the found, the concealed and revealed, are all realized through their opposite. Cultural and moral values, including those from riM̧ajeḷ tradition and Christianity, may be applied to one side or other of these oppositions, but such values remain constituted upon the dialectical relationship. Conversations with Kometo in which he purposefully drew upon narrative contrasts of hiding and seeking, or deception and revelation, demonstrated his awareness for how such oppositions permit a degree of human agency, and make a profound commentary on meaning, ideologies of social power, and conceivably, even consciousness itself (cf. Barnes 1994).

Resisting any attempts to separate form from meaning, in this chapter, I will consider the link between narrative forms and ideological considerations. I will attend specifically to the forms of deception and revelation as they give shape to both riM̧ajeḷ mythic narratives and our ethnographically situated dialogues. By carefully unpacking these forms, both riM̧ajeḷ and interculturally constituted social ideologies will be unmasked—but only partially, due to the trickster teller I worked with and the intricacy of translating his playful manipulation of signs. Translators, not just storytellers, are tricksters in their own right (Hyde 1998), since they too decipher and reveal the hidden meanings in languages and discourses, but at the same time they cannot help but conceal much.

In what follows, I wish to explore several dialogic moments in which the forms of deception and revelation, as two culturally salient forms of Indigenous mythic storytelling, lead to a complex interplay of social ideologies in riM̧ajeḷ culture. Through this interplay, we may also detect something of the "emergent circumstances and agendas . . . (of) these hybrid forms" (Bauman 2004, 7) and their attendant ideologies about social power.

The Trick of Divination

I start with a myth that represents the hybrid forms of deception and revelation. All narratives about Letao the trickster involve a deception that turns someone into a fool. Recall the story in chapter 1, in which, during a game of hide-and-seek, Letao fools the man into sticking his head into the trickster's anus, looking for something that does not prove real in the end. Similarly, Letao's deception of his brother to exchange a real sailing canoe for a fake one, his deception of the chief of Kiribati into cooking himself, and ultimately, we may suspect, tricking the Americans into making him rich in exchange for knowledge, establishes a generic pattern: Letao desires something (food, canoe, sex, power), he sets up a trick through deception and disguise, he outwits his opponent to obtain what he desires, he makes an escape. By tricking others, he gains a measure of social power over them, but only temporarily, as they chase him off or he moves on to other exploits. Those he leaves behind retain their rank. Indeed, his tricks and lies reveal the social structure more than undermine it.

The mere mention of Letao's name frames the narrative form of deception. When storytellers either announce that they will tell a Letao myth, or simply launch into the story identifying the trickster as the key character, they notify the audience to take what is about to be told as a form of deception. Through the remainder of the performance, the audience anticipates that Letao's actions will lead to a series of lies and deceptions that will leave some other character in the position of dupe. The key here is that the form of deception "belongs to the moral domain of intention" (Barnes 1994, 12). That is, Letao's behaviors intend to create a false understanding about what is going on by other characters in the narrated event. With Letao's narratives, the audience is asked to follow the chain of deceptive acts. They are, to a point, aware of the lies while the characters being duped are not. However, even the audience must continually work to decode the lies, not only in the mythic plot, but also in the performance of the narrative.

According to Kometo's cosmological musings, the three primal goddesses (Lijenenbwe, Lōñtañūr, Limejo̧kdād) represent three forms of social power in the Marshall Islands. As described previously, Lijenenbwe, the eldest sister, provides the power of divination (*bubu*), or revealing that which is hidden, including wealth, sorcery, navigation, and lies. The second sister, Lōñtañūr, bestows the power of chiefly rank and the knowledge of sailing that permits interisland travel and social intercourse, warfare, trade, and power relationships between chiefdoms. Finally, Limejo̧kdād (the dirty one) provides, through her trickster son, the power of deception and concealment, which curiously facilitates social life and leads to the creation of life through sexual union. Because Kometo hardly narrated anything directly about Lōñtañūr, she did not form a prominent part of our dialogues. In contrast, besides the myths about Letao, Kometo talked often about the power of divination and how it originated with Lijenenbwe. Perhaps he knew that many other storytellers related and performed the myths of Lōñtañūr to me and thought it would prove redundant (see McArthur 2004). But likely, his personal interest lay less in the chiefly polity (from which he was excluded by birth) and more in the means by which deception through trickery and revelation through divination constitute alternative kinds of social power. For many months, Kometo told me stories only about Letao's exploits, and then one day when visiting with him at his home, he surprised me with a hide-and-seek story that blends the forms of deception with revelation through divination. At the time his grandchildren were coming in and out of the house. A few of them remained to listen to the story.[1]

K   *The men took their mother to Namo. (mmm) Etao—*

and what's his name?

Jemāluut. The two of them said, "Well, we two should take mama and just go visit Namo./

P   /Namo?

K   *Because their mother says she has an older sibling there. (mmm)*
     She's at Namo.

Now there is a custom with the riMajel, you see—you will see it with children. They play hide-and-seek [*kūttiliekek*]. (mmm) Have you seen it with them? With all those children? They like to play hide-and-seek.
P   Oh yes.
K   Well, that thing is a custom. (mmm) It reveals power. The signficance of that game is it reveals power.

Those men, the two of them go and visit with the sons of Lijenenbwe.
The two of them, they come to play hide-and-seek.
They say, "WELL, LET'S GO PLAY HIDE-AND-SEEK"

Like those children see? <quiets some of his grandchildren> (mmm)

Then, the sons of Lijenenbwe say, "WELL, YOU TWO GO FIRST."
Then, Letao and Jemāluut go and hide over there.
And one of them becomes a sergeant major fish [badet].

Those fish on the ocean-side.

The other becomes a banded surgeon fish [kupañ]. (mmm)
<quiets children again>
Now, the two of them come in next to a channel in the reef.
And then, they say, <high pitched> *"FINISHED!"*
Then, the sons of Lijenenbwe just come next to the channel in the reef.
These men [sons of Lijenenbwe] say, "AH, THERE YOU BOTH ARE!"
Then, the two of them again become people—and say,"Well, it's your turn."

Then, the sons of Lijenenbwe go hide.
One man is up under a coconut, under the . . . fronds at the top.
The other man comes and climbs up and becomes a louse [kij].
Like a fly. (uh huh)
And climbs up outside and then there, <points to eyebrow> *he sits on Letao's eyebrow.*
<I chuckle> *(ok)*
He uses the divination knot.

And so if you divine and see that knot Lañinperan, well, it's really good—when seeking to find something as the sons of Lijenenbwe did, see? (uh uh) And if you use another pandanus leaf knot, and you go hide, they won't see you. The name of that knot, they say, "*demenek.*"

P   Ok. <change side of the audio tape>

K   *Now,* <coughs> *Letao and Jemāluut {looked (and) looked.*
They see the one man under the coconut fronds, but the other one they do not see him.}
Then, they say, "WHISTLE A LITTLE."
Then, he that is here <points eyebrow to ear> *whistles.*
He then whistles close to Letao's ear, here. <points to eyebrow>
Letao then turns around, and they look for him.
"What, where is the man?"
They then go to find him over there where it sounds like he whistled.
Go on and on, they don't see him.
They again say, "WHISTLE A LITTLE."
He again whistles.
Then again mmm, <chuckling> *his voice appears from over there.* <points past ear>
But it's not really, since his voice comes from there. <points from eyebrow to ear>

Goes on and on they say, "WELL, WE GIVE UP"." <laughter by all>
He just jumps down, becomes a man, and stands on the ground.

Well that knot, it is the best of all the knots for hiding.

P   So, what does this story mean? It teaches the riM̧ajȩl about what?

K   About this purpose of finding.

P   Finding?

K   Mmm. The brilliance of the riM̧ajȩl is in these knots. Do you see when you sail and don't know where Jebwad [of Jaluuj atoll] is? (uh huh) You can make a knot in the pandanus leaf and you will know where it is. (mmm) If you saw that something is stolen, you can identify with that knot which person is the thief.

P   Uh huh. So, what is the purpose of hide-and-seek? Does it give power to a person?

K   It displays that those men played hide-and-seek, and when they don't see him, he wins. If they see him, he loses. And so, the men of this island, they went and they lost. Since they have many mothers.

P   At Nam̧o they lost?

K   They lost to the men of Nam̧o.

P   So, the diviners won, because of the divination knot?

K   Yes.

P   And Letao and Jemāluut lost?/

K   /Etao loses.

P   Because the men of Nam̧o found them?

K   Eh.

P   And the son of Lijenenbwe hid there. <points to eyebrow>

K   <chuckling> He is there. They call that knot "*demenek*."

P   Demenek?

K   The oldest man, his name is Lañinperan.

P   And he divined to find Letao and also to hide?

K   Eh. Eh. Well, if we divine and it shows Lañinperan, see? Whatever you seek, <pause> you will find it. If I say, "Did Phillip steal? And it says, Ooo, that thing says, "Lañinperan." It is clear, it is Phillip. <long chuckle>

Before attending closely to the specific contextualization process of this narrative performance and dialogue, a brief consideration of the riM̧ajȩl form of revelation will prove helpful. This will illuminate how Kometo calibrated these two forms in this performance as well as the interpenetration of the two genres and their attendent social ideologies (cf. Briggs and Bauman 1992). In contrast to the deception form with its emphasis on the hidden, the form of revelation is fundamentally anti-deception, working to achieve the opposite effect—to reveal what is concealed. This form unveils the truth, whether the ontological existence of things, or the sociological truth that underpins the social order. Its manifest intent is not to deceive but to achieve the inverse effect, to reveal the truth. Very little laughter marks this genre, other than the chuckle at the sometimes strangeness of the events taking place and the wonder at that which is revealed. For this reason, the narrative contextualized in our dialogue is most peculiar as it fuses the two forms, deception and revelation, the latter drawing from the ideological structure of the former. They also paradoxically become fused as each is used to establish an alternative kind of power in riM̧ajeļ social life.

The myth begins in the typical deception form when Letao and his brother engage in a game of hide-and-seek with their parallel matrilineal cousins. And indeed, as with all Letao games, a challenge is proposed to see who is the best. At this point, if we are familar with Letao narratives generally, we expect that he will get the better of his challengers, and our expectations continue to be met as he and his brother engage in shape-shifting. There is an intimation of slippage, however, indicating that the formal expectations may be upended even before the cousins divine Letao and Jemāluut's whereabouts; Limejo̧kdād's sons go first whereas the more powerful position typically goes second, presaging the eventual inversion of the anticipated structure. Kometo will use this hybridized myth to index the birth order in the cosmogonic genealogy and to represent the two forms of social power that still come to bear on human relations.

The merger of the two forms is most pronounced when Letao's competitors, the "diviners" (*ribubu*), also participate in shape-shifting, and although Letao and his brother dectect one of them, the other remains hidden; he bests the trickster and his brother by cleverly deceiving them through the whistle trick. Unexpectedly, the success of this hiding trick is made possible through divination, a form of revelation. Once Lañinperan the diviner reveals himself, and thus becomes the victor in the game of hide-and-seek (*kūttiliekek*), we have completely slid over into the form of revelation. Divining reveals the whereabouts of the deceptive trickster; it unveils the deception. Nonetheless, it has also been used to hide, only for a different purpose, not in order to ursurp or undermine, but to reveal the priority of sociologically ascribed power. Lañinperan has put Letao in his place by unveiling his trick. He has beat the trickster at his own game, and in doing so reinforces his seniority in the cosmological kinship structure by revealing the truth. But there exists a curious tension in the form of revelation, as divination for the riM̧ajeļ, a tool for revealing the truth, is also carefully guarded by its practitioners. It is hidden. Enough is known about its general working—most everyone knows that it involves the folding of pandanus leaves and decoding knots—to receive much admiring discussion and commentary about its efficacy.

An important dimension of this hybridized myth lies in how it is achieved through the dialogue of the two ideologies carried in the respective forms. The power of deception has sociological significance by undermining the social order. But in this hybridized myth form, deception is inverted as the power of revelation exposes it as a lying form, both in terms of communication and sociology—the social order is reconfirmed once the deception has come to light. Social rank for the riMạjeḷ is determined by relative seniority in age among a set of classificatory siblings, including parallel cousins, within the same generation (*epepen*) of a matriline (*bwij*). Letao is Lañinperan's younger parallel cousin in the same matriline of their mothers. The former would actually be referred to as the younger sibling (*jatin*) and the latter the older sibling (*jein*) in the riMạjeḷ classificatory kinship system.

I have never heard this particular myth performed by other storytellers nor have I found it in any collections. It stands out as a telltale moment for how the two narrative forms interact and bleed into each other. The contextualized myth of Letao being bested in a game of hide-and-seek pulls together two narrative genres to achieve a blending of formal and functional capacities, and consequently blends two ideologies about social power into one narrated event. This dialogue of genres served as a means whereby Kometo could reveal his vision of social power to me. The tension along the margin of these genres parallels the strain between the Indigenous social structure and modern iterations as well as a tension embedded in the game we were playing. We were seeking to reveal essential truths about that which is taken for granted in his culture.

In addition to the dialogue of genres within the narrative, the resultant hybridized genre creates a dialogue within the narrative event. Kometo contextualizes the narrative in ways similar to those discussed in previous chapters, including most prominently the management of tense, marked dialogism in reported speech, and metanarration. Because he wanted me and those listening in, especially the children, to understand the meaning of the myth, he broke into metanarration often. This device is critical to the recontextualization process of the story. He uses it to foreground the meanings of the story he wishes to emphasize regarding the respective powers of hiding and divination. In mirroring seniority by age in the myth, the ideologies of social power are also set into a hierarchy: Lijenenbwe's oldest and thus senior son wins over Jemāluut and Letao, the youngest children of the youngest sister, suggesting that his command of divination is more powerful than Latao's power of deception.

In the first lines of the interchange, Kometo sets up the characters, place, and genealogical ties between the mothers. The audience prepares for the encounter between the sons of these primordial sisters who each possess their respective power (deception and divination). But Kometo barely gets going when he shifts back into metanarration to frame how the entire myth should be taken, even before the audience can experience the two narrative forms in dialogue. He explains that hiding and not being found demonstrates more than a game; as he says, it "reveals power." This should not be viewed as merely a game of winners and losers, but one in which relationships become hierarchical. Kometo wants to ensure that we understand this social hierarchy. In everyday riM̧ajeļ practice, people take intense care not to reveal what they are thinking or their personal agendas. The ability to veil (ņņooj) one's intention is of utmost social value. Thus, in a way, everyday discourse itself is a kind of concealment, a less formally structured game of hide-and-seek. A valued social strategy is to avoid offering information unless questioned directly and to the point, and even then, care is taken to sidestep any obligation to provide the whole story. This ability to hide intentions becomes critical in land tenure negotiations and disputes in a high context village life. Hide-and-seek for children then, is not just recreation; it is schooling in a very important interpersonal act—hiding and not unveiling what is on one's mind (cf. Berman 2019). Concomitantly, narratives about Letao, and especially those about hiding and seeking, represent a more formalized genre of a pervasive social value and practice. That is why, among the various reasons, listeners find these narratives so appealing; they resonate profoundly with a lived subjectivity of social power. To veil well, or to detect information another wished to conceal, comprises two forms of empowerment. What's more, I often heard references to individuals with such accomplished discursive skills in everyday life as, "He is so etao."

This quality in riM̧ajeļ discourse assumes an essential role in our conversation as Kometo is at once concealing and revealing. Our ethnographic moment reveals our two discursive strategies with regard to things hidden and revealed. It manifests our respective cultures' expectations. The riM̧ajeļ continually conveyed to me that Americans talk too much and always say what is on their minds. Conversely, in my interactions with numerous expatriates over the years working in the Marshall Islands, they express exasperation with trying to get the riM̧ajeļ to open up to them, or that after thinking they had come to an agreement, the islanders will do something else entirely. Out of this cross-cultural difference in communication practice, some Americans have developed their own stereotypes about a perceived riM̧ajeļ duplicity, when in fact they are merely working within a cultural system of discourse in which to convey too much leads to a social disadvantage. Indeed, this communicative style is empowering not just among the riM̧ajeļ themselves, but provides a means for resisting the hegemony of American power since the war and occupation, and I must assume that Kometo applied it to our conversations as well. By asking all my questions so boldly, I reenact an American pattern of speaking openly. Kometo on the other hand reenacts Letao's pattern by veiling and concealing. And yet, he also assumes the diviner's pattern, revealing what is hidden. He was a trickster in how he assumed accountability to tell narratives about "lies," and to test me to see if I would understand the deceptive mode he was using. He was a diviner in how he pulled the cover off cultural knowledge and the nature of riM̧ajeļ social life and power.

From the first lines of the story, Kometo establishes the meaning of the hybridized myth before really even performing it. He is clearly going to juxtapose the different kinds of social power of the two primal matriarchs' sons. And then the game begins with Letao and Jemāluut hiding first. It should be remembered that most riM̧ajeļ know several stories about Letao's subversive victories over everyone he challenges, and I believe that Kometo assumed that I had this expectation as well. This story was the first time I, and I believe others present, had heard of Letao meeting his match. His ability to deceive, hide, or make things appear to be what they are not establishes his power. Consequently, in this story, we see that he is challenged at his own empowering game.

In the narrated event, Letao and his brother turn themselves into fish but Lijenenbwe's sons find them easily. They are able to do so through the control of divination. This immediately juxtaposes the two forms of power and their social ideologies. While one form of power is to veil or hide the truth, divination offers the ability to unveil that which is hidden: that in the past and what the future will bring. It serves as a counter principle to "hiding," with all its associations, including magic (*kkōpāl*), sorcery (*anijnij*), jealousy (*juunm̧aad*) and lust (*mejkaiie*). Thus, through divination, the sons of Lijenenbwe uncover Letao's and his brother's deception. Knowledge, through divination, is more powerful than deception because it reveals what deception hides. By performing the role of the diviner, Kometo seeks to both reveal a kind of social power in his culture that must be taken seriously, and to constitute our ethnographic relationship as one given to uncovering that which is hidden.

Nonetheless, divination provides the knowledge to also mislead more effectively, as we see in the mythic narrative. After Letao and Jemāluut are discovered, the sons of Lijenenbwe go to hide. Kometo does not give the less well-known names of these men during the performance (he does so in a second performance), except the elder son (Lañinperan), which is also the name for a divination knot. These men hide in a variety of places, and the eldest, and thus the one with seniority, turns himself into a louse, then climbs up onto Letao's eyebrow. This hiding place and Kometo's efforts to clarify it are important as the etymology of Letao's name derives in part from "*āt*" meaning eyebrow (cf. Erdland, 1914).[2] Lañinperan's hiding place amplifies the point that the "eyebrow" trickster himself is the one being tricked.

The same dialogic stretch as the eyebrow explanation contains further clarification of the power of divination and how to interpret this hybridized myth. Without unveiling too much, and thus playing the trickster again, Kometo mentions that divination involves reading signs. Divination (*bubu*) represents the highly respected practice used to uncover that which is hidden, anything from the location of an atoll while sailing, the detection of a liar or sorcerer, and the portending of favorable weather or natural disasters. Historically, paramount chiefs retained at least one diviner (*ribubu*) in their royal court (*nitijeḷā*). The knowledge and power of the diviner typically passed through lineages within matriclans. Most riM̧ajeḷ do not know how divination specifically works, and even those who do veil their abilities (very few ever admit they are a diviner but most people know who they are). Most will usually just indicate that the practice involves the folding of pandanus leaves (*maañ*) or coconut fronds (*kimej*)[3] in various knot patterns from which certain signs (*kakōḷḷe*) can be diagnosed (cf. Erdland 1914; Kramer and Nevermann 1938; Tobin 2002). Kometo here uses the term "*bwe en*" to identify knots that serve as divination signs. Some knots function as signs that permit one to uncover the truth such as the knot Lañinperan, the one used to divine Letao's location. Here in this story we also see the son of Lijenenbwe use the *demenek* knot to conceal himself, but paradoxically, for the ultimate purpose of revealing the sociological truth.

Because Letao and Jemāluut cannot find him they ask for a clue, that he whistle, but they cannot discern its origin. They ask him to whistle again, but because he sits close at his ear, Letao is confused about where the sound comes from. This is the most humorous part of the narrative as Kometo uses reported speech in a high tone when they ask the louse to whistle. Then Letao and his brother give up, admit their loss, and proclaim Lañinperan best at hiding—or in other words, admit that he is more powerful than they. "It reveals power," as Kometo asserts. The genealogical hierarchy replicates the hierarchy of social powers: the power of the children of the senior sister is greater than the power of the children of the youngest sister.

Kometo's interest in divination does not bring into question his Christianity or modern experience (cf. Rudiak-Gould 2010). Most riM̧ajeļ feel that divination is a good thing, something compatible with Christianity for flushing out "Satan's evils" such as dark magic and sorcery, or to provide prophetic declaration. This principle of divination, uncovering some hidden truth, comes to bear in a variety of personal and public contexts that do not necessarily involve manipulation of the pandanus leaves. It was revealed to me on many occasions that new forms of divination have developed: instead of using the pandanus leaves and esoteric knowledge, many perform personal rites of augury with the Christian Bible by opening up to just the right passage to unveil a truth or determine course of action to be taken. I have also witnessed divination applied to land tenure negotiations and in criminal court cases unbeknownst to the American judges. Herein we see the integration of tradition into modern imperial institutions in a seamless fabric of social practice.

I previously suggested that to conceal and reveal in everyday practice highlights forms of power in riM̧ajeļ social life. Those who have the ability to detect or conceal the truth through discourse in public arenas wield significant social influence. Silence for the riM̧ajeļ represents a most powerful personal and public political strategy as well as the ability to use veiled speech as a rhetorical smokescreen to hide one's intentions. To "hide" or conceal is a way to display social power. Indigenous myths of Letao provide the blueprint for deception, but as Kometo's narrative of hide-and-seek demonstrates, it is countered by those who possess the power of revelation—divination. These larger social discursive strategies in riM̧ajeļ society become clearer as Kometo performs a hybrid narrative that integrates both the forms of deception and revelation into one.

That this hybridized and well-calibrated narrative becomes a metaphor of the ethnographic dialogue is most tellingly illustrated at the conclusion of the discourse segment presented here. When Kometo seeks to explain how the sign of Lañinperan, a divination knot named after the key character in the myth, reveals the truth about that which is hidden, he narrates me into the form of revelation. "If I say, 'Did Phillip steal?' And it says, 'Ooo that thing says Lañinperan.' It is clear it is Phillip." He has detected me; he has uncovered my method. For sure, he is in part simply being clever to illustrate his point and to tease a bit. But I also surmise that the myth genre and our dialogue have bled into each other and become closely calibrated. To a degree he is being forthright; I just may prove a thief, taking cultural knowledge. He knows what I am up to as I go about uncovering shrouded cultural knowledge. But now that I know where social power lies, and he is the one who has let me in on it and schooled me on how both deceptive tricks and divination work in riM̧ajeļ epistemology, we are both party to unveiling the truth.

Hidden below the Surface

Kometo's interest in the story of Lañinperan the diviner outwitting Letao in a game of hide-and-seek reflects his conception of social power. His affection for Lañinperan can be attributed partially to his home atoll of Mile, the site of another narrative of hiding and revelation, a recurrent theme in many of his stories. This myth, also recorded elsewhere (Tobin 2002; Chambers 1969, 1972), describes how Mile atoll, hidden below the surface of the sea, is fished up by Lañinperan. Mile then gains the reputation as an atoll of great abundance, which it retains to this day, owing to its plentiful rainfall. In some versions, it is Letao who has hidden the atoll below the sea. Instead of Letao, Kometo identified the god Ororao as the one responsible for submerging the atoll. The significance of this substitution will come clear shortly. This story makes clear how the two forms of deception and revelation occupy an important place in Kometo's repertoire.

One day at Kometo's house on Teḷap islet, I asked him several questions about the genealogy of the gods, especially about those he claimed Ḷewōj and Ḷaneej had placed at each atoll. In what follows, Kometo used a discussion between the two of us about the cosmogonic genealogy to enter into the myth of Lañinperan at Mile.[4]

K   *Now, Ororao see? He has hidden Mile there under the surface of the sea.*
      Then the reason Mile appears . . .

      Do you know the woman I said who is . . . at Namọ?
P   Uh huh, go ahead.
K   The woman's name is Lijenenbwe.
P   Lijenenbwe has twelve sons?
K   Eh, the twelve sons of Lijinenbwe. (ok) <chuckles> There are twelve.

      The sons of Lijenenbwe are those who they say, "divine."

      See? (uh huh) With those divination knots. (uh huh)

      Now, all the time these men go fishing.

      See?

      They go fishing, but there is no food in the atoll.
      There is no food at Namọ.

Then, their mother says, "You go and fish way over there."
They all go and fish.
They go and fish but she goes . . . the woman.
She goes down under the sea.
She goes and falls into the breaking wave.

See?
P   Breaking wave?
K   A wave like—

One, two, three, four, five, six, throws it.
After throwing the net a path appears.
{Now, she comes to the path and goes in.}
Travels to Mile, and brings back food.
Many kinds of food, much breadfruit, and much fish.
Carries it back and leaves the preserved pandanus she has cooked.

P   This is the meaning of Mile?
K   MMM. At Mile there are all kinds of blessings.

Like Lōrōk said, ~MILE! AND MILE OPENS UP~

See? Have you heard what Lōrōk said?/
P   /What did he say?/

K   / ~MILE! AND MILE OPENS~

P   I don't know it.
K   There is an abundance of every variety of food at Mile. Because in the past,
     the people of Mile were blessed and ate much. (uh huh)

So now, Mile is opened and filled with food.
The woman goes there and brings back the food.

See? (uh huh)

Her sons come home, and there is much food at the house.
They say, "Where does this food come from?"
She says, "I don't know, they are just here."

Many times she does it.
The oldest man, his name is Lañinperan.
He peeks, the others go and fish, but he spies on her.

P   *Kōjjaad?*
K   The meaning of *kōjjaad?* When a person is bathing but you go and do this, <acts like peeking around corner> see? He spies on her. (ok) <chuckles>

Now, his mother goes again; he just follows after her.
She goes and goes ooo she arrives at Mile.
Then, Lañinperan appears.
His mother says, "Mmmm, how unfortunate."
She will die.
When she returns to Namo she will die.

Now, when she returns to Namo she dies.
All her sons at Namo then sail away.
They sail southward.
They seek out all those southern islands first and go ooo and arrive at Kiribati.
Then, after they stay at Kiribati, they come back to the Ratak islands.
They come and then arrive above Mile.
Lañinperan says, "Divination knot! Take down the sail and drift."
He knows, he knows that Ororao is over there above Mile.
Then, the canoes simply drift, but the older man remains inside his house on the canoe.

Because long ago a small house (*boktōk*) was on that canoe. And it's small, perhaps the size of this area between us. See? (uh huh). At the time of their sailing they took along this house and placed it on the canoe. When they are at an island, well, they remove it to the land. (mmm) About the size of that house of those birds. <points to chicken pen outside> (uh huh)

Well, now, then they drift away—he remains inside the house.
Some of his younger brothers, they look out and they see the man, Ororao.
He sits on the outrigger and faces east.
He is turned away from them.
They say, "Who could that be since we see all of this place and there is no atoll?
*But who is that person?" <coughs>

They don't know. You see, they don't know him. This means they are weaker than him.

Now, they ask Lañinperan, "LAÑINPERAN, WOULD YOU JUST KINDLY COME AND SEE WHO THIS IS?"
Then, he gets up and looks out and sees him.
He says, "MMMM. GREETINGS TO YOU ORORAO.

This means Lañinperan has a power over Ororao.
P   Oh, because he recognizes him.
K   Because he recognizes him.
P   Ororao is hiding his identity?
K   He is hiding it. <chuckles> When he turns away he hides it.
P   Ororao is the younger sibling of Lañinperan's mother?/
K   /Yes, yes./
P   /He's like his mother's brother?
K   Yes. <slight chuckle> Well, he did not know about him previously, but there was that time he spied on his mother /(mmm)/ and he found out about Ororao. (mmm)

Now he says, "GREETINGS TO YOU, ORORAO."
He turns around, toward him and he says, "Ahahah." <slight laugh>

This means Lañinperan has won against him. (mmm)

Ororao says, "WHAT FOOD DO YOU HAVE IN THIS CANOE?"
They say, "THERE ISN'T ANYTHING.
There is just nothing else left of what we brought from there to here."
Ooo there is a coconut midrib stem.

There is a pandanus tree called *būkien*. (uh huh) That kind of pandanus tree has bumpy skin. (mmm) But its leaves become soft when they want to make a woven mat—by scraping it with a clam shell. And then, when finished, they sun dry it. (uh huh). When it is dry they weave it into a basket and they place food inside and cover it. And take it to those chiefs. That kind of food belongs to the chief. (Ok).

He takes the Būkien. (uh huh)
They say, "There is only one other thing, the pandanus basket"

It's called Būkien.

Then, he says, "WELL, GIVE IT HERE.
Tie it to the kōm̧ñūr" <pause>

The canoes of long ago, they have a middle part that they use when they anchor. See? (uh huh) There is not just one anchor. There is not just one rope they anchor with. (uh huh) They anchor with two. (Ok) One of those ropes (*to*), they call it the "great anchor" (*añkō* or *emjak eo elap*), Then there is a small rope. For that second anchor, they say it ties to the *kōm̧ñūr* (mmm). That rope too is called *kōm̧ñūr.*

Well, he takes the two ropes and goes.
He dives down; he has tied the basket to the Kōm̧ñūr.
And, ties Mile to the great anchor rope. (uh huh)
And, attaches it to Mile
He connects the food in the basket with the kōm̧ñūr.
And, the men pull it. (oh)
Then, they pull on the kōmñūr tied to the large meshed net basket.
A full basket appears.

See? (uh huh)

There is much inside—

Remember they were hungry—

There is much food inside.
There are all kinds of food.
Then, they pull it and lift up the basket and place it there on the canoe.
Now, they come and try to release their canoe.
Pull in the great anchor rope to sail the canoe.
But they are secure, because he has tied them with the great anchor rope.
Hooked with the coconut midrib.
Then, they pull, pull hard eee it's really secure.
Then, Lañinperan comes, the oldest man is the strongest /(mmm)/
/He comes and grabs hold of the great anchor rope and pulls it.
He pulls it and he says,

~LAÑINPERAN IS POISED AND HARD~
~HE DOES NOT HOOK IT IN THE NORTH~
~HE HOOKS IN THE SOUTH~
~SECURED BY JUST THE COCONUT MIDRIB HOOK~
~HE TUGS HARD~
~HERE IS MILE ATOLL!~
~IT STANDS UP AND BREAKS THROUGH~

Then, ooo the atoll appears.
Mile appears above the surface, and he picks up the mast [kaju].[5]

The post which connects to the sail (*wōjḷā*) and those ropes.

Picks it up and stabs it.
After stabbing it, it bleeds, bleeds, ooo and it appears.
Mile appears.

P   Mile appears.
K   Eh.
P   Excuse me a little, I'm fixing the tape. <I fiddle with the tape recorder>

K   *~THE ISLAND OF MILE RISES UP AND APPEARS~*

<chuckles as I fiddle with tape>

Well there are many stories at Mile, but we will say the chief of Mile, his name is this, Ororao.

In the opening of the dialogue we both, but especially Kometo, expend a great deal of effort to locate the kinship ties between these characters and place the action at Mile. To set up and tell this story, he articulates a mosaic of associated ideas: genealogical kinship among the primordial beings, Letao, Lañinperan, and his home atoll, Mile. At another point in this interchange (it lasted over two hours), he wanted to clarify for me that this individual had two names that are often used interchangeably. When Kometo uses the word for chief (*irooj*), it must be understood in this context that Ororao is a god (*anij*), or chiefly ruler of Mile placed there by the god(s) Ḷewōj and Ḷaneej. Gods and chiefs are sometimes interchangeable. To this day, chiefs are believed to possess divine-like sacred potency (cf. Carucci 1989; LaBriola 2019). In a conversation the week previously, he moved back and forth between these two names:

K   The chief of Mile—What's the man's name? They say, "Ororao." He has two
      names. You see in the days past? (uh huh) People (the gods), had two names.
      Now the name of the man, they say, "Lojenmile." Lojenmile means a person
      who is through the middle of Mile. (hmm)
      Lojen, is like, it will be where man? The stomach of Mile?
P   Oh, ok, ok.
K   <sniffs> Now—
P   Ororao was his name before Lojenmile?
K   Uh, no, he always had two names.[6] Lojenmile and Ororao.
P   Why are there two names for the person?
K   Because he is a person of Mile? Lojenmile. (uh huh) And Ororao,
      because he was the one who made Mile and surrounded it with islets.
      And he hides it there below the sea.
P   Ororao was the child of . . . Ļewōj and Ļaneej?
K   Yes. All these people . . . you will hear about in every story are his children.

So Ororao, who is hiding but exposed by Lañinperan's divination, is also
Lojenmile (two names allow a certain kind of veiling), which means "stomach"
(*loje-*) "of" (*-n*) "*mile*" (Mile atoll). His other name means to "encircle" (*oror*) "the
halo" or sign of Letao (*aao*). In this short excerpt, Kometo confirms that Ļewōj
and Ļaneej as the creator god of Ororao, which is consistent with his cosmogonic
genealogy in which he identifies this god (with two names) as the one who placed
other gods at their respective atolls. He employs the riM̧ajeļ practice in mythology to give two names for one god, and in doing so he can remain consistent
with his Christian conceptualization of two names (God and Jehovah) for one
divinity. We can deduce, then, that Ororao is accordingly a male sibling to the
mothers of Lañinperan and Letao. Thus, by outdoing him, Lañinperan has
bested his maternal uncle, a familiar pattern of usurpation in this matrilineally
oriented society.

A second important feature in this excerpt is that Kometo identifies Ororao
as the one who has hidden Mile below the sea, not Letao, a variation from other
accounts (e.g., Tobin 2002). This identification is indicative of a teller who provides a different kind of localized detail from his home atoll. But the continuity
between these two characters is clear. The root of his name, *aao* for "halo" as
well as the sign of death, is the same as with Letao. Kometo understood the
convergence of these two beings as variations of a similar character. Both perform the same narrative function to deceive and hide, in this case to hide the
atoll, the location of which will be revealed through divination. Once he has

elaborated the kinship links, Kometo begins the story by stating that Lijenenbwe's children possess the power of divination, that they are fisherman, and that there is a famine at their home atoll, Naṃo. Their mother instructs them to go fishing, which seems a ploy to just get them out of the way, a trick to divert them so she can exploit that which is hidden at Mile. She submerges and travels to Mile, which is below the sea, by magic, passing through a wave via a throw net. Mile is full of copious foodstuffs. Our dialogic aside reaffirms the abundance of Mile; Kometo gives me a portion of a chant, ~MILE! AND MILE OPENS UP~, and wants to know if I had heard this chant, attributed to the god Ḷōrōk, one of the four gods of the cardinal directions (namely, the god of the south who is linked to the season in which there is great fecundity on the land and in the sea). I have not. He explains that Mile actually means abundance. Rich blessings of food and other kinds of goods lying below the surface is a common motif in many riM̧ajeḷ narratives, especially those relating to the ṇoonniep figures,[7] little people who live under the earth and perform beneficial acts for individuals, and if they don't reveal their assistance, the ṇoonniep will continue to bless them with abundance.

When her sons return to Naṃo they are surprised and ask where she obtained the food. Their mother, Lijenenbwe, tells a lie that leads to the oldest son, Lañinperan, spying on her. I misunderstand a term Kometo uses and we have a funny little exchange in which he explains "peeking" or spying on someone. He returns to the narrative, where Lañinperan follows his mother to find out where she goes through her magical action. This detection is unfortunate, as his mother exclaims, because it will lead to her death. Adverse consequences, even death, are often the result of being detected in an effort to conceal. Why this is so is not always clear, but the loss of social power resulting from the revelation of what one has hidden may provide a hint. In this case, the myth suggests that possessing personal abundance and then hiding it is a social offense that is serious enough to cause death when the deception is uncovered.

The sons of Lijenenbwe then sail to Kiribati, the archipelago south of the Marshalls and where Letao performed his earth-oven trick. They then tack back north to Mile's location at the southernmost end of the Ratak Chain. At this point, Lañinperan conducts divination, and we can assume he employs the knot used by sailors to locate an atoll that cannot be seen, a truly valued ability of navigators. He is familiar with Ororao's location, having followed his mother. The motivation for Ororao to hide his abundance from his maternal nephews perhaps again suggests a social misstep that will lead to his undoing, just as with his sister. That his sister had traveled to his underwater world of bounty reflects their close sibling relationship, and that Lañinperan will expose them both to achieve power may reveal the tension inherent in transferring matrilineal power from mother's brother (*wūllepa-* or *rūkore-*) to sister's son (*mañde-*). In any event, at the location of where Mile atoll should be, they set the canoe adrift.

At this point, Kometo breaks off to explain about the small houses (*bo̧ktōk*) attached to the sailing canoe (*wa̧lap*),[8] in which the chief would rest. This disruption in the narrative brings us immediately back to our intercultural dialogue, one in which he makes a great effort to establish a common vocabulary and understanding about this ancient form of sailing. After this aside, Kometo re-enters the narrative with the brothers detecting Ororao, who has appeared on the outrigger of the canoe. But they cannot determine his identity because he turns away from them. Kometo breaks away again to instruct me that by not recognizing him—having his identity remain hidden—he has power over them and they are the weaker, thus reconfirming the ideological power of deception and hiding. The brothers ask Lañinperan to identify him and he does so, and consequently he obtains power over Ororao because he has exposed or revealed his maternal uncle's identity. Lañinperan can do so because he has divined not only the atoll's location but also, by association, that island's god, who hides his abundance below the sea. Accordingly, the myth outlines again how the revealer is more powerful than the concealer.

After I make sure I understand the kinship relations among these individuals, Kometo returns to the narrative to explain how Lañinperan has won in this game of hide-and-seek. Exposed and detected, Ororao discovers that they do not have any food on their canoe. The only things with them is the coconut midrib he will use as a hook, and a basket about which Kometo provides a metanarration for me to explain making baskets from a species of pandanus leaves. Then he elaborates, both through metanarration and the narrative, how Ororao dives down with the two anchor ropes, one fastened to the basket and the other with the coconut midrib hook. He fills the basket with food attached to the smaller rope, and hooks Mile with the great anchor rope. When the men pull up the basket tied to the first rope, they find a great abundance of food. Seemingly content, they try to release their canoes to sail away, but they cannot because he has also hooked them to Mile. They pull forcefully, but it takes Lañinperan, the oldest and the strongest, to pull up the anchor. As he does so he chants, using rather obscure references, and fishes Mile up from below the surface. "The island appears": it has been literally revealed by the diviner. He then picks up the canoe mast and, using it as a spear, stabs the atoll as one would stab a fish to kill it. The atoll "bleeds," or the water drains out from it, and thus it remains above the surface to this day. Finally, as I work on fixing my tape machine, Kometo recapitulates the conclusion of the myth about how Mile appeared and that he has revealed to me, among many stories, the name of the god of his home atoll.

Three additional dialogic components of the contextualization of this myth suggest important sociological considerations: one, is situated within the ethnographic dialogue; two, emerges internal to the narrative; three, forges an intertextual link far beyond the performance event. The most evident of these formal dialogues is similar to all of our ethnographic conversations, specifically, the dialogue between narrative proper and metanarration. Sometimes I am the one who instigates this dialogic mode through my questions, but just as often, Kometo breaks from the story to explain things to me. This movement between forms demonstrates a shift from the narrated event to the narrative event. Within the narrated event, a story of hiding and revelation unfolds. Within the narrative event, cultural knowledge hidden from me is revealed by Kometo the storyteller. The two generic frames index each other.

The second formal dialogue within the performance is embedded in the narrated event itself. This is a dialogue between narrative prose and chanted verse. These two genres, while both serving as verbal icons for the event recounted, accomplish different outcomes in relation to the past, and their interaction facilitates a dialogue between the past and present. Because the riMạjeḷ deliver their narratives in the present tense coupled with an emphasis on reported speech, the past seems to appear before us in the present of the narrative event. But chant breaks down, even more markedly, the boundary between past and present; the genre expects conservative fidelity to tradition and the ancestral voices it echoes. In this narrative, there is a clearly marked movement between the prose and chant genres as they frame and contextualize each other (cf. Bauman 1992). The prose remains more attached to "what happened" whereas the chanted verse to "what is happening" as the voices are recontextualized into the present. In Kometo's performance of Lañinperan at Mile, both of these genres are clearly rendered in the present tense, but the narrative prose shares a closer affinity with telling, and the chanted verse with enactment. Like other riMạjeḷ storytellers, when Kometo performs in chanted verse he takes on the voice of the mythological character in a highly marked form of reported speech, and in prose he simply narrates the story or recasts what the characters say as if a witness. When chanting, Kometo as storyteller, becomes a more direct participant in the past rather than just a reporting observer.

Reporting history, even in the present tense, makes the past appear complete. In contrast, in an oral performance of the chant, the mythological past is re-presented as it enters into present social relationships. Because enacting heightens a sense of being in the past while in the present, the interaction of time frames may revise the conceptualization of both of them (cf. Bauman 1992). This, I believe, is the effect Kometo hoped to create through this performance. He brought me/us into the Indigenous mythological past to show its relevance in the present, a present in which deception and revelation remain essential to all social relations—including our emerging intercultural one within the context of decolonization. The enduring landscape of Mile, and the lasting chant of the gods that he echoes, replay for Kometo a persistent reality that is not locked in the deep past, but provides resonance to modern social realities.

Kometo's performance of the chants, nonetheless, presents a curious slippage in the calibration of the two genres, as the chants consist of only fragments, never fully realized in the rendering of this story. He gives me only bits and pieces in the chant register and on no account a fully chanted verse. Some of the chants even seem like aborted attempts with the genre, and differ in language significantly from a similar chant recorded by Tobin (2002, 315). These unfinished chants may be because he did not know them and could only render them in a minimized fashion. Or, it may be that he anticipated that the rather esoteric language of chants would be lost on me. Or, that he himself was participating in a game of hiding by not revealing them in their entirety. Or, that he only wanted to partially close the gap between the generic forms and thus retain a marginal degree of ontological distance between the past and the present. All these possibilities may not be exclusive, but represent the multiple functional structuring of the performance in the context of the ethnographic dialogue.

Whatever his motivation, the chanted discourse is clearly marked as he shifts to a higher voice register with a rhythmically paced slide from one word into the next. Not quite song, riM̗ajeḷ chanted verse is delivered in a single tone without breaks, so that words flow in on each other. I ethnopoetically render this by the (~) tilde symbol and all capital letters because the volume also increases. Kometo first inserts a chant segment when he quotes the god Lōrōk of the south, during a metanarration. He wants to know if I have heard ~MILE! AND MILE OPENS UP~. This "opening up," declared by the god of good winds and the harvest, suggests in this context that Mile is full of food. By giving me this abbreviated chant-like saying, perhaps from another myth, he foreshadows what will come in the story. The other chanted insertion comes at the conclusion of the narrative, when Lañinperan chants about himself: ~LAÑINPERAN IS POISED AND HARD . . . HE DOES NOT HOOK IT IN THE NORTH . . . HE HOOKS IN THE SOUTH . . . SECURED BY JUST THE COCONUT MIDRIB HOOK . . . HE TUGS HARD . . . HERE IS MILE ISLAND! IT STANDS UP AND BREAKS THROUGH~. But Kometo seems to exit the chant before completing it, to shift back into the prose style of telling. The content of this chant is, to a degree, straightforward, purely descriptive: Lañinperan is poised to spear the fish/atoll and is "hard" (*pen*), which in riM̧ajeļ imagery represents a firm and strong warrior. That Lañinperan does not hook in the north but in the south is vague in terms of reference; could it mean he does not hook the northern atolls of the Ratak chain but has done so with the southernmost atoll? Or, does it mean he has hooked Mile itself as a fish/atoll in the southern part of the atoll rather than the north? If there is any other embedded symbolism in this it may be that the southern atolls where Lañinperan performs this great feat are recognized for their abundance in food, whereas the northern atolls experience severe hardships with droughts and famines due to significantly less rainfall. Tobin's recording in 1975 and translation of the chant (2002) by a chanter named Jọwej, seems to suggest that there are two hooks, one of the north and one of the south, the latter connected to Kiribati, which may symbolize the discovery of islands when the ancient riM̧ajeļ immigrants moved south to north. Perhaps these hooks also reflect the historical relationship between Kiribati and Mile and the reason that Lañinperan and his brothers first sailed south to Kiribati before returning north to Mile.

The conclusion of this portion of the chant relates that Lañinperan achieved the gigantic task of fishing up the atoll by using the coconut midrib hook; hardly something one would imagine could achieve such a Herculean task. But again, the chant rendered for me seems decontextualized and only partially resituated as a fragment. I question the delivery of these chants by Kometo because of the more fully and richly archaic version collected by Tobin (2002). Narrative and song fragments, however, may or may not represent performance failures, but rather they could possibly signal the performer's narrative management, agency, and diverse motivations and intentions in specific contexts (Goldstein 2021). When Kometo gives me only a fragment, we may conclude that through the dialogue of genres, he only gives me a fragment of that past, and I am still excluded from how those voices may fully come to bear on the present. By giving me only a rudimentary rendering of chant, he also gives me only the skeleton of the past, a minimal portion of it. And perhaps it reveals that his relationship to the past is a story of disruption, and that he and his culture's interactions with the outside imperial world have created a deep fragmentation in cultural and personal selves, mirrored by this uneven dialogue of genres.

The third dialogic component relates to how intertextual links of this myth go far beyond the setting of its performance. The motif of the god fishing up an island represents the most widely distributed and prevalent narrative motif in all of Oceania. A quick glance at the Pacific motif indexes (Kirtley 1955, 1971) discloses more references for this motif (A955.8) than any other, and its geographical distribution the greatest of all. Most renowned is the demigod Maui (see Dixon 1916; Beckwith 1940; Helu 1999b), recognized in Hawai'i, Aotearoa (New Zealand), French Polynesia, Tonga, Samoa, and others. Kometo's knowledge of the localized version of this motif situates him in a larger regional history and culture (cf. Lessa 1961).

All of these Oceanic cultures narrate how the islands came from below the surface of the sea, and how a demigod (often a trickster) pulls them up to provide a place for human habitation. In the riM̧ajel̦ case here, Ororao (or Letao) the trickster is not the one who performs this task; rather he actually hides the atoll below the surface. Instead, it is Lañinperan, the diviner, who reveals the atoll. The riM̧ajel̦ example is quite complex and nuanced by having the trickster represented as the one who conceals and hides, whereas the diviner is the culture hero who reveals and unveils. The two principles (hiding and revelation) are in dialogue once again. The fishing up of the island narrative motif in Oceania seems to recognize that a reality is concealed below the surface, and that things that are hidden will come to light. Kometo's riM̧ajel̦ variant emphasizes that such an action presents how the social powers of deception and revelation become inscribed into the landscape through story.

Some have speculated that the fishing up of the island by the demigod motif represents a metaphorical rendering of the volcanoes breeching the surface of the sea (Nunn 2003). For the riM̧ajel̦ atoll dwellers, relatively unfamiliar with volcanic eruption, coming upon an atoll situated low on the horizon below the curvature of the earth, could be interpreted as emerging from below the sea.[9] My interest here, however, is not to explain the possible origin of a worldview, but to suggest how the practice of divination to locate atolls would certainly have proved a powerful aid in finding elusive, low-lying targets. Consequently, divination as the means by which the protagonist raised Mile atoll is historically resonant. Jack Tobin also records that the storyteller who provided the chant of Mile being fished up was encouraged to do so after he had related how Maui from Hawai'i had visited Mājeej Island in the Marshalls. This version even explains how the riM̧ajel̦ killed the Hawaiian Maui. It could be ventured that this slaying indicates a deep historical connection between Hawai'i and the Marshalls, but it more likely conveys a new sense of the regional map generated by the riM̧ajel̦ after contact and missionization.[10] This is not to question, however, the historical interconnectedness of Oceania (Rainbird 2004; Hau'ofa 2008) as a whole, wherein the fishing up the island motif predominates. But it is to suggest a predilection in riM̧ajel̦ storytellers to explore links in their myths and cosmology to other places. In other words, Kometo is not alone in this practice as a storyteller. And more to the point, attending to this larger mythic context sheds additional light on how the immediate face-to-face dialogue is situated in a deep historical regional setting.[11]

Unmasking Social Difference

Kometo's life was marked by intense social upheaval through war, migration and relocation, urbanization, religious conversion, the modern capitalist nation-state, and dramatic economic shifts from subsistence to wage labor, imported goods, and fiscal dependency (cf. Alexander 1978). Nonetheless, like so many of his generation, he remained guarded and protective of the customary matrilineal social order. He and his cohort recognized the pressures placed on the matrilineal system and how it was weakened by the imposed changes to riM̧ajeḷ society. But they continued to espouse how it informs the whole land tenure system and as a most effective means for reckoning kin relations. While nearly all riM̧ajeḷ, young and old, know their matriclan name and about the strict prohibitions against clan endogamy, very few can recall their clan histories and genealogies— let alone clan histories in general. But one Indigenous myth in particular that formed part of Kometo's repertoire rehearses the origin of a specific matriclan that some islanders consider the first. He performed the same myth to me three times over a ten-month period. Each time, he sought to help me understand the origin and order of the matrilineal system. Kometo's repetition of this story demonstrated his desire to emphasize and connect the forms of hiding and revealing to kinship and social power. It provided him the perfect resource to explore his cultural identity with reference to larger modern social realities, and to expose the fundamental underpinnings of riM̧ajeḷ polity as expressed through matrilineal kinship.

In a dialogue in the company of his family members, I asked Kometo to explain how riM̧ajeḷ kinship differed from other traditions. He offered, "It was the women who made the matrilineages (*bwij*) in these islands; they had the children (*ajri*)." I took this to be a concise statement about women, rendered often by the riM̧ajeḷ, as the conduit of both children and matrilineal descent. But then he inserted a story about the origin of a particular matriclan (*jowi*) that recasts social differences, including our own.[12]

K   You know, there is a story . . . about a chief of Nam̧o.

And, the name of that place there, they say, "Ukāren."
Their chief stays there.
And, a boy is playing lagoon-side with a canoe, a toy canoe. (uh huh)

Do you know about the toy canoe?

P   A little.

K   That kind of toy which looks like a canoe of these islands—they come and play with it, and it's about this long. <shows about eight-inch distance between hands>

Now, he makes the sail, and makes the outrigger, and it runs lagoon-side.
And, the boy goes away with his toy canoe.
Then, his mother Kijdik (rat), she says, "It's bad to sail the canoe toward the north.
Only sail the canoe toward the south."
{The boy sails the canoe southward.}
{It's not a very good wind for his canoe.}
After sailing the canoe southward, he sails it northward, the wind is good.
Then, he releases his canoe and the canoe goes.
And, it goes away fast, along the shore of the islet.

Over there where he is coming from, it's called Ṇabubu over there.

But he says . . . now, he sings,

~THE CANOE IS STEERED TO AND FRO~
~DESTROYS THE WAVES LAGOON-SIDE OF ĀNEPIÑ ISLET ~
~BREAKS UP THE WAVES~
~THE ISLET HIDES~
~THE ISLET AGAIN MOVES~

He takes his canoe to the bush and escapes.
Then, over there, they say,

~HE IS OFF TO THE BUSH AND HE'S GONE~

Off to the bush is like he escapes into those bushes. (uh huh)

Days later, he again goes to sail the canoe.
Some people see him Ooo they notify the chief.
"We just saw a boy coming, he comes sailing his toy canoe toward you.
But then, he takes that canoe and returns and goes away."
The chief goes and sits there; he wants to be way over there where the boy was seen.
The boy again releases his canoe—

~THE HOUSE OF ṆABUBU~
~THE CANOE IS STEERED TO AND FRO~
~DESTROYS THE WAVES LAGOON-SIDE OF ĀNEPIÑ ISLET~
~BREAKS THE WAVES~
~THE ISLET HIDES~
~THE ISLET AGAIN MOVES~
~HE IS OFF TO THE BUSH AND IS GONE~

The boy takes his canoe and runs, but the chief calls,
"OOO HEY BOY, HEY BOY"
The boy stops.
The chief says, "Come here please."
Then, the boy goes to him.
"Where do you come from?"
Then, he says, "Ṇabubu.

Over there, which is his and his mother's place.

"You and who are there?"
"Me and my mother."
"Go and tell her that she should come here."
Then, the boy says, "EEHH THIS IS NOT GOOD, BECAUSE SHE IS A RAT."
"What, a rat?!
No matter if she is a rat, but go and say that she should come here."

Then, the boy goes.
Another power is with the woman.
{He just goes—and he calls, "MOTHER."}
Then, the woman says, "MOTHER!" (mmm)
"They say I should come and say"—
"They say I should come and say!"—
What did I tell you when I said do not go to the places of all those other
people?"

Well, do you think these things are true?

P   I'm just thinking. <he laughs> It's just good for me to listen.

K   *Then . . . the woman, his mother, just wanders thinking about it.*
      And then afterward, she says, "{Well, go and bring} copra to prepare oil."
      He brings a copra [waini].[13]

The boy, he comes carrying a copra to her.
She says, "Come and grate it."
There is no stool grater, but they grate it.
He comes and grates, grates, grates, grates, he has prepared it, and it's complete.
She says, "Well come and anoint me."
Then, he comes to anoint her.
He strains it to make coconut oil [pinneep] and then anoints her.
He anoints her, and she says, "Step on me."
He comes to step on her.
Steps, steps, steps, steps, steps, his mother says, "What kind of skin is there?
After stepping there, the skin of a rat starts to disappear.
Like just a little of the human skin begins to appear.
Then, she says, "What kind of skin is there?"
"Black skin."
"Well, step again."
The boy again steps on her.
{Steps, steps, steps, steps, steps she again asks,} "WHAT KIND OF SKIN IS THERE?"
Then, he says, "White skin, the skin of the foreigner." <laughs>
"Well, step again." <we laugh>

P   Why doesn't she like white? <much laughter>
K   I don't know. She didn't like white. (uh huh) <laughter>

Steps, steps, steps—
Many kinds of skin were shown, white skin and black skin, yellow skin, and then a skin called "real skin."
He says, "Real skin."
She says, "OKAY, THAT THERE."
"OH, MY HEAD NOW."
Now, he comes to anoint her head and step on her.
Steps on her head.
{Steps, steps, steps} his mother says, "What kind of hair is there?"

Rire is like a style of head hair. (uh huh) Whether it's straight or wavy.

Then, he says, "The straight style."

The smooth kind is like there is no curl; it just goes down.

Steps on her again.
{Steps, steps} "What style is there?"
Then, he says, "The curly style."
"Well, step."
Steps, steps, steps, "WHAT KIND OF STYLE IS THERE?"
Then, he says, "ALMOST THE RIGHT STYLE."

There are many head styles of those people. (mmm) <pause> Now, the good style, is the style which is not very . . . what's it called? Straight. But it's not like curly either, like the head of a New Guinea person and people of those places. (mmm) But it's like—it is pleasing to look at. What's it called? Long, but a little wavy.

Then, after stepping and achieving the style she says, "Okay that there."
The woman comes and gets ready, comes and anoints their skin with per-fumed oil.

Their skin in those days, it's like it itched.

Anoints it and then when finished, she puts on her prepared clothes and they go.
The two of them go.
The two of them arrive at the house of the chief.
And, the chief takes her in . . . there inside his house.
And, he throws out the women who were inside the house.
Then, later a child of the woman is born, they say,"Jiddikdik!" [little rat]
Because he is a child of a rat.
This was the beginning of the Ijjidik clan

P   Mmm.
K   <long pause> So, what do you think? <we laugh>
P   It's good.
K   Ahh. <laughs>

When compared to another version of this myth found in a government edu-cation reader (Grey 1951), this performance represents a classic case of Kometo adapting a mythic narrative both to modern social relations broadly, and specifi-cally to our immediate intercultural relationship. The version in the reader locates the narrated event in Aelōñḷapḷap atoll, which actually has a "Ānepiñ" islet, rather than Namo (both of the Rālik chain). It too presents the little boy going out to race his toy sailing canoe with other boys, and his mother scolding him for associating with other people. The version in the reader includes the chants (and others Kometo does not provide), the interrogation of the boy by the chief, and his mother scolding him, amazed that he is not embarrassed about her condition as a rat. The anointing of the coconut oil and stepping on her is also presented, but only represents a very small section in the reader, explaining simply how she changed from a rat to a human (motif D300) and that the changes to her hair and person made her the most beautiful in the entire atoll. The remainder of the education reader version diverges sharply from Kometo's performance; the two do move in with the chief after he expels his former wives, but the written version concludes with a blissful boy now able to play always with his friends. Nothing is mentioned about the series of skin and hair possibilities, and notably absent is how the narrated event culminates in the first matriclan (Ijjidik).[14] Kometo's performance not only presents alternate meanings of the story by foregrounding a history of matrilineal kinship, but also unmasks the cultural means for delineating variation and the natural categories used to register social difference.

In the opening of the dialogue, Kometo places the narrated event at Namo atoll, and although this conflicts with some versions, it amplifies his understanding of clans and their origins, and consequently represents a point of departure for considering social difference. The association of the Ijjidik clan's origin with Namo is documented in early twentieth-century accounts by the German ethnographers August Erdland (1914) and Augustin Kramer and Hans Nevermann (1938). While Kramer and Nevermann claimed that this Namo clan was one of the two most highly ranked, Erdland ranked it third. The anthropologist Nancy Pollock (1976), who conducted research on Namo, notes that the relative numerical status of this clan was quite low on Namo, and that the hierarchy of clans described by the German ethnologists and others (Mason 1947) could not be replicated at the time of her research in 1968. But she also observed that the hierarchy had continually fluctuated in the past due to warfare, so that we lack any surety about an original hierarchy. This additional information may all seem to diverge from understanding how Kometo uses the Indigenous myth to achieve his sociological commentary. Nonetheless, it all links up in his mind in a profound way: by establishing a key thread back into a myth about matrilineal genealogies, where that which is hidden becomes manifest, he can again show the interplay between the forms of deception and revelation. By attending more carefully to antecedent genealogies and texts from other ethnographies and oral narrative collections, we can see how he constitutes his point.

Coupling early ethnological reports of the Germans with her own data, Pollock attends mostly to the genealogy of the Erroja clan (or Iroja).[15] This matriclan went extinct (*ḷot*) only four generations ago, due to the absence of female offspring. This disappearance resulted in the titles and statuses passing through the patriline (*bōtōktōk*) to this day. Pollock suggests that this clan's high rank came from a single woman on Namọ. Her other descendants, due to a schism, divided off and consequently lost their royalty. The early German and Tobin accounts as well as Pollock's data concur that a woman named Liwātuonmour was the most powerful sister of a sibling set which included the woman Lijelālijet, and that the former's descendants emerged as the most powerful. Indeed, from living royalty in the Rālik chain today, we can trace back ten generations to Liwātuonmour. I collected a version of this genealogy from a high chief in 1993 (name withheld for promised confidentiality), which corresponds with that recorded by Mason (1947) and presented by Walsh and Heine (2012, 204), but the one I recorded extends four more generations to Liwātuonmour. In contrast to this primal matriarch, Lijelālijet's line has become obscured. Pollock's account provides further ethnohistorical data about these women. Liwātuonmour, in the form of a basalt rock, was believed to have remained at Namọ until a nineteenth-century missionary had her cast into the sea. Some accounts suggest that she originally came from the Ratak chain in the east and that another of her sisters, Lideprepju, still remains as a basalt rock on Aur atoll.[16] Other versions recount how these sisters came from the ancient homeland of Ep. And there are other proposals about these basalt rocks: one, those found on coral reefs served as totems for specific clans; two, they simply represent washed up remnants of the now sunken volcano; three, they were brought from high islands in the west (possibly Yap or Pohnpei), indicating a migration pattern or once foreign domination.

Liwātuonmour's daughter was called Irooj, from whom the clan of high chiefs descended, and their name subsequently becomes the term used for an individual chief (*irooj*). Because Pollock's subjects declared that the Rālik people at least descended from Liwātuonmour, it may be imagined that through schism and warfare the Irooj line ascended to dominance, while other lines from Liwātuonmour became commoners. But before I seem to diverge too far from the narrative performance, on another occasion Kometo maintained that Liwātuonmour was the child of Lijenenbwe, the matriarchal goddess of divination from Namọ. With this understanding, we begin to see how he conjoins the myth to larger considerations of divination and to Namọ atoll.

Kometo claimed that every clan has its own emergence story. He also claimed that the Ijjidik clan members (descendants of the rat) were the first descendants of Lijenenbwe to emerge as a clan, and that later the Erroja clan, with its own story, became dominant. No matter the order of ascent, Kometo performed this story to point out how clan differentiation served as a significant marker for kinship identity and social authority in the deep past, and to foreground issues of "difference" in modern historical international relations at the same time. Consequently, divination, revealing the concealed, provides the means by which important social differences become manifest.

Kometo's performance of this myth of Kijdik and her son has all the poetic and formal dimensions characteristic of his other performances, including the highly marked chants. This version, like the one presented in the education reader, presents the mother and her son as isolated and unknown to others. In this way, the discovery of the boy by the chief's people highlights the mother's attempt to hide her identity as a rat. We may anticipate that the hidden will be unmasked. At one point, Kometo breaks off from the narrated event to offer a short comment, for my benefit, that identifies how the boy's actions begin at a place referred to as Ṇabubu. His chant, in narrating the action of the toy boat, includes reference to this location as well. Clearly the term for divination (*bubu*) forms the stem of this place-name, and as a whole it means "place of divination." Thus, Kometo not only links the woman Kijdik to Lijenenbwe as a descendant, but also brings into the narrative an association with the power of divination. The twice-repeated chant juxtaposed with the narrated event emphasizes divination: namely, the boat (vessel of discovery) comes out of Ṇabubu (the place of concealment and secret knowing), then the boy with all his secrets, like the boat at risk, is placed in jeopardy (of being undone), so he "hides" and escapes without being found. Then the narrative, however, undoes the chant as the boy is not only discovered, but the identity of his mother as a rat (the purpose of the concealment) is exposed. In a sense, what is hidden at Ṇabubu ("the islet hides") is revealed at Ānepiñ islet.

The interrogative conversations of the chief with the boy and the mother with the boy extend this theme of hiding and finding out the truth. The chief wants to learn about the boy's home and mother; the mother is upset about being discovered. The mother repeating her son's announcement displays her anger at being found out, and even Kometo must pause to directly question me about whether I believe this revelation to be true. The narrated action and narrative event begin to parallel each other; both entertain issues of concealment and revelation.

To understand the next part of the myth, we need to refer to Kometo's earlier claim that "Another power is with the woman." Her power is not that she is a rat, but that she, like her maternal ancestor Lijenenbwe, presents something useful to effect change. The mother instructing her son to retrieve copra, prepare the oil, anoint it, and step on her, divulges the skeleton outline of a magical act. As with all the primal women thus far, we witness again a woman who imparts knowledge to her son (motif D1737.1). This idea of investiture by females (motif P231) runs through Kometo's performances and reiterates his point about the distinctiveness of the riM̧ajel̥ matrilineal social order, and it emphasizes complementary gender relations between sons/mothers and brothers/sisters encoded culturally in a variety of ways. For instance, as intimated by the presence of the toy canoe in this story, the hull (*ānbwin*) of an actual sailing canoe (*wa*), is identified as male (it is firm and strong), while the outrigger (*kubaak*) is identified as female (the part that gives balance to the canoe on the water, facilitates speed, and prevents tipping over). Similarly, the spar (*rojak m̧m̧aan*) of the sail is identified as male while the boom (*rojak kōrā*) is identified as female. The spar makes the sail strong, able to be planted firmly into the boom socket, whereas the boom aides in steering and allows tacking into the winds. Each of these canoe parts become metaphors for gender in social life and the functioning of matrilineages and matriclans.

The transformations of the mother-rat through magical practices demonstrate a range of social identifications. Whereas the version in the reader only presents her as becoming human, Kometo turns this episode into a declaration of the revelation of difference. First, he transforms the animal into a human, something categorically different for the riM̧ajel̥.[17] The selection of skin as the key symbol for marking difference between the rats and humans establishes the natural sign and logic by which he will then differentiate the riM̧ajel̥ from others. By using this epistemology, he draws the narrated event right into the larger international context in which the narrative event is embedded. Now that he has delineated the animal kingdom from the human, he can delineate kinds of humans. He identifies a range of skin colors until they arrive at brown, which our mythological characters call "real skin," or that which belongs to the riM̧ajel̥, in contrast to others. All these "others" come from the outside, as shown by his humorous highlighting of my own difference from him.

The mother-rat and her son then apply the magical act to transform the hair style to get it "just right" as well. A range of possibilities is again the central issue. Whether the hair style is curly, straight, or something between, the differences delineate kinds of "others" in contrast to the riM̧ajel̥. While Kometo clearly recognizes the variation within "other" groups in terms of skin or hair, and even within the riM̧ajel̥ population, he emphasizes a general quality in order to establish boundaries between "us" and "others." The most recent imperial experience of the islanders involves the Americans, with their stereotypically white skin and straight hair. That I am a white American myself in the ethnographic moment (but with curly hair!), allows a degree of levity, and a recognition that we represent larger cultural worlds brought together at this historical juncture. Although not overtly stated, the yellow skin distinguishes the Japanese, who loom large in island history, and with whom he lived and worked during their colonization of the islands. When Kometo identifies black and curly haired people as a significant "other," he includes people closer to home in the Oceania region, specifically Melanesia.

The last geographical designation is obviously home, where the brown skin and in-between hair style not only identifies the riM̧ajeḷ, but also registers a female aesthetic, one that is accentuated in the sensual play of Kūrijmōj festival (Carucci 1997a). Kijdik becomes not only a human, but a beautiful woman who also adorns herself with the perfume oil (this would be on her skin and hair) that stands for a symbol of sexual enticement (cf. Carucci 1997a). The chief expels his other wives and takes her in, presumably because of her beauty. Kometo subtly ensures I understand that this revelation is full of innuendo. He concludes with the beautiful woman serving as the origin of the Ijjidik clan and the beginning of matriclans generally, thus instituting a key way to differentiate people and a means for establishing social identity and authority.

Kometo does not comment about difference in the first-person indicative, rather, he presents the mythic ancestors as the ones who institute difference, not only within the Marshall Islands in the form of matriclans, but between the riM̧ajeḷ and international others. In this way, he holds up the voices of these primordial ancestors against the social realities of recent history. In the recontextualization of this Indigenous myth, Kometo turns it into an index of the islanders' colonial history, the decolonizing present, and modern international relations, including our own. He brings to view, through the voices of the ancestors, those outside "others" who have left their indelible legacy in the islands or by whom the riM̧ajeḷ construct images of difference. In this way, he addresses the most fundamental defining criteria of identity within the islands, namely matrilineal kinship, and highlights at the same time differences with others through the narrative forms of deception and revelation.

The simple natural symbols of skin and hair open up a more complex history of contact and the cultural constructions of social difference. The performance of this story indexes these constructions through a magical story of the origin of matriclans. Kometo's use of the myth allowed him to draw again upon the forms of deception and revelation to contextualize our relationship in this grander scheme of difference. I am being let in on his vision of a relevant social difference in the deep past and within modernity. Because I get a glimpse of how deception and this kind of "divination" works, I become privileged, though still limited, to these two ideologies of riM̧ajeļ social power, and how the social order comes from something hidden being unmasked. Because he wants to see if I understood his revelations regarding all the hidden parallels between matriclans, social differences, and the modern world, and between him and me, he drolly asks, "So, what do you think?" and then we laugh. He has played the role of both trickster and diviner.

CHAPTER 5

A Trickster's Tropes
Magic on the Margins of Political Power and Christianity

Among the more difficult things to translate cross-culturally include the tropes of language such as metaphors and metonyms as both are deeply rooted in cultural connotations that belie any denotative literalism. The intercultural competence necessary to unpack such tropes and figurative language requires deep immersion, not only in lexicons and grammars, but also into culturally germane references and contexts of meaning. In many ways, the trickster's work exploits and manipulates such modes of tropic representation, to redirect cultural and social meanings in novel and unexpected ways.

Deception is in one part achieved by manipulating the inherit equivocation in signs and what they refer to. Consequently, while decoding tropes cross-culturally is hard enough, such semiotic resources in the hands of a trickster tale character or narrator prove even more just how oblique and obscure references may be. As illustrated in the previous chapter, concealment and revelation offer a Janus-like problem; apparent opposites can at times appear to blur in on each other. There is a kind of magic in this interplay, as one sign vehicle is substituted for another. Meaning can seem a bit deferred by a trickster's abstruse analogies and indexical references.

This chapter in many ways represents a continuation of the previous wherein that which is hidden becomes manifest. But I will foreground even more the workings of magic, in both the mythic narratives and our dialogues, that conceal and reveal political power as well as a relationship between Indigenous epistemologies and Christianity. Attending to magic as a play of tropes, both the metaphorical and metonymic, will demonstrate how trickster myths and dialogues present culturally specific riMʼajeḷ sensibilities about political power, and about the entanglement of traditional religious beliefs with Christianity. Both of these forms of speech conceal, or at least redirect, meaning and reveal it in culturally nuanced ways. And when embedded in Indigenous mythological narratives, Kometo fashioned connections between the deep past and our intercultural moment filled with Western forms of political power and a Christian metaphysic. Kometo's recent attachments to Mormonism do not fundamentally vary with a general Christian worldview in this context. His trickster work not only articulated references and analogies within and between the Indigenous and Christian myths, but also allowed these "stories to breathe," to facilitate the way social life and stories may come to index and imitate each other (Frank 2010).

Magical discourse and practice represent a complicated employment of cultural tropes. This is no "false science" as Sir James Frazer (1922) proposed, but a keen appreciation for the complex and illusory relationship of representation to reality. Like figures of speech, magic allows us to see one thing in terms of another; it is a form of substitution, and thus an exchange of signs for signs and what they signify. For this reason, when considering the semiotics of cultural tropes, if signs can be substituted in linguistically and culturally salient ways, then there is a kind of transference, or displacement of qualities, from one sign or code to another, which replicates the practice of magic. Linguistic and cultural tropes, then, present a kind of magic in themselves and, conversely, magical speech and action draw heavily upon them to achieve their affect. The problem with Frazer was not his theory of sympathetic magic, for as I hope to demonstrate, this framework remains useful for ascertaining how Kometo and the riM̧ajeļ relate stories of magic. But in his erudite and condescending treatment of the "other," to force them into a social evolutionary scheme, he missed the point that even scientific and modern cultural discourses are riddled with tropic communications. There is a little magic in all discourse.

Even so, Frazer's formulation of sympathetic magic as either homeopathic or contagious adumbrates an important semiotic that will assist entrance into how Kometo used stories as couriers for magic. Magic was "sympathetic" for Frazer (1922) when it expresses a connection between two things, an "invisible" transmission from one sign to the other. Homeopathic magic functions as imitative or mimetic, or by the "law of similarity." Things that resemble each other sustain a mutual effect, as like produces like. Contagious magic functions on the principle of contiguity, or by the "law of contact." Things once in contact or proximity remain always connected in some way even after separation. Linguistic and cultural tropes of metaphor function similar to homeopathic magic (creating resemblances between signs), and metonyms to contagious magic (one sign comes to stand for or affects another).

Kometo's stories about magic demonstrate riM̧ajeļ sensibilities about political power and religious belief. These stories of magic offer an Indigenous framework for knowing and thinking (see Tuhiwai Smith 2013) about power, which also allowed him to make continued commentary on his modern life and our complex intercultural relationship. The tropes of magic provide the trickster storyteller with resources to seriously play (Turner 1982) with ideas about power in a complicated decolonizing moment that fuses Indigenous social authority with the modern nation-state, and an Indigenous belief and its epistemologies with an imperial religion. While only occasionally drawing overtly upon the images of Letao the trickster in these stories, Kometo nonetheless continued his method to invert, question, and reimagine the character of political power and religious belief on the margins of mythological time and the present, and within our intercultural friendship.

The Magic of Political Power

In the following storytelling dialogue, Kometo continues to draw upon the riM̧ajel̄ cosmogony to perform a myth riddled with references to magic (*kkōpāl*). We had been discussing just between the two of us the current status of political power in the new nation-state. He then abruptly shifted into this story about two primordial chiefs at Aelōñl̄apl̄ap atoll, one in the Ratak or east side (Je islet), and one in the Rālik or west side (Wōja islet).[1] Each possesses a great power over the area ("air space"—*mejatoto*) in which they preside.

K   *Now the child, its mother went and bathed it.*
Bathes it lagoon-side in a wooden tub.
She is bathing lagoon-side and now some rain falls.
Then, she goes to take in something.
She goes and takes in their things—the mats, since they were drying-in-the-sun.
She takes them inside and forgets the child.
<I chuckle, and then he chuckles>

Is it not like a person that they get distracted and then forget some other thing?

Now, the child drifts off.[2]
He goes, drifts a long way to an islet, the islet of the Chief of the Rālik side.
Then, the Chief of the Rālik side, he says to his wife, he says,
"Look, it's like there is a light rain at our bathing place."

In their language, they say it is like a light rain (*wōt dikdik*). This weather identifies a chief at his bathing place (*juwadel*). He says there is a light rain or moisture droplets, like there's just a little rain. It's the sign of a royal person at a bathing place. (oh, yes, yes)

He says, "Just go and look please."
After she goes she sees the boy there, further off.
Then, she says, "It's a boy over there."
He says, "Mmmm bring our child here!"

Do you know the reason there is a light rain at the bathing place?

P   I don't know.

K   Because there is a chiefly power with the boy, see? The light rain is a sign.

After this one child arrives, there is also another child born to the chief.
A girl.
Now, there is a power with the boy, a power that comes from the air and sur-
rounds him.
It reveals the child.

P   It reveals the child?

K   Yes. <breaks as we greet someone and talk about their kin relations>

Then, he looks after the boy, looks after him . . . he is grown.
Then, he says, "Do you want to go to papa?"
He (the boy) says, "Why, where is papa?
But you are papa." <laughs>
The chief says, "He is in the east."

See this please, he knows. Because this chief has a power with him also. He
has knowledge of all things and the movements in the air. He knows (oh)
about the other chief [the biological father].

Now, the boy says, "Well, it's like I do want to know."
Then, the man says, "Well, you can go."
Then, he makes his preparations and departs.

P   He sails?

K   No

He walks along the islets.

Because way over there at Aelōñḷapḷap atoll, see? Before, there was <point-
ing, moving across horizon> one islet over there, one over there, one over
there, one after another to that islet farthest east. (oh)

Now, he travels from over there in the west to those places in the east.

See?
P   He went along the islets at the time of low tide?
K   Eh.

And, he goes and then it is high tide.

<interrupted by someone calling for instructions. We stop and restart after he returns.>

Okay.

He goes along the islets.
Now, the girl, his younger sibling, who is the child of the chief of the Rālik side,
she goes away with him.
They travel on and on, it becomes high tide.

Now, between the islets, there was a break over there to the south. Now Aelōñḷapḷap, see? from one islet it goes, (signaling a break between islets with hands) goes over there to another islet. (mmm) Just like Mājro now.

Then . . . the boy he <u>jumps</u>, and stands on the one islet.
He <u>floats off</u> and lands on the other islet. (ha)
The girl says, "My older sibling, my older sibling how will it be for me to go to you?"
Then, he says, "You should bite that empty copra [moṇ], and spread the basket of sand."

Moṇ is like that copra which has no fluid inside. See? The name of that thing is *moṇ*.

Well, he says, "You should bite that empty copra, spread the basket of sand."
After the girl does it, bites the copra and spreads it, she joins the islets.
Then, she just runs across.
Because the sand fills in and the islets are joined.
She comes running oooo and then she is on the islet with him.
They both go on.
They both go, go, and at another islet they do it again.

She says, "My older sibling how will I go to you?"
He says, "Bite that empty copra, spread the basket of sand."
She does it again, goes again, and runs to him.
They go, go to the furthest islet in the east.
Now, at that islet furthest east—

Now listen, there is a channel between the lagoon and ocean. There was a place to enter the lagoon there; there is none now. There is none. We could say, the reef went along and then just stops. (yes)

Well, they both stop at the islet by the channel.
Then, later, after they play with a stick—
They push the stick into the ground like a post (ah) and they vault way over there.
Well now, some boys there on the islet are playing with their fast toy canoes [riwut].
They are there on the islet.
One has a fast canoe [to race a toy canoe kariwutut].
They say, "Ooo that guy is the winner" . . .

Since back long ago a man's canoe . . . it is his power when he wins. (uh huh)

Now, the boy goes and asks from the other boys, he says,
"My friends, just give me that toy boat of you two."
"AAAAH."
Well, he asks if he can hold it.
After that, one boy, he says, "What are you, the son of Etao?"
"Etao?" <laughs>
He asks for the canoe, and the other boy gives it.
Then, the boy comes . . . he takes the canoe, and comes, and does sorcery.
He does his sorcery on that canoe, he says,

~KWAALŌN, KWAALŌN, KWAALŌN~

And he repeats it again.

~KWAALŌN, KWAALŌN, KWAALŌN~

Then—
He says, "Bring my canoe and stay here behind the chief's house on the south end."

It is low tide, and then he pushes off the canoe, the canoe flies away fast.
Flies away and goes, <on and on then hits the post.>
"Cast the stick at the thatch hut!"
It goes and hits the post of the hut.
The woman is leaning there, his mother.
His mother sits and talks story with the other women.
BAM, it hits the post.
She says, "MMMM, strikes the eye of the chief."

Because he is doing it toward the houses of the chief, and this is prohibited. (oh) It's prohibited to throw anything towards his house. It's prohibited to yell towards it . . . the customs of long ago.

P   Oh, yes, yes.

K   We should say, to throw towards or yell next to his house, or to make noise, it is all prohibited. They call that thing, they say, "*koḷapḷap.*" It was a custom long ago.

P   A custom of long ago, yes.

K   These days there are none, because it is filled with foreign customs. <laughs>

P   Unfortunate. <K chuckles>

K   *Now, they say, "Well, who holds the eye of the female chief?" [who threatens her]*
The wife of the chief, "Who holds her?"
They say, "That boy."
The chief says, "<unintelligible> . . . bring him here!"
They go to kill them.
Carry them over there and put them above in the house, up over there in the place for food and for important tools.

They call that place, *nikāi kan.*

P   *Nikāi kan?*

K   Like a tall house . . .

P   I don't know *nikāi kan.*

K   Do you see this house? It does not have another place up above.

P   Oh, yes, yes.

K   Well up over there the chiefs liked to sleep there. Because people can't as easily kill them there, and . . . They say, "Don't walk by, if the chief should lay in that direction." See?

P   Yes.

K   *Well, they place the children up over in there.*
     And thus, they are prepared to kill them.
     Now, the chief of the Rālik side has his power.

Among the powers of the chief of the Rālik side is that of a bird. *<pause>*

The bird comes and sings.
The boy's name is Kikiao.
The chief's name is . . . Ḷōrōkiewa.
His mother's name is Letuajowa.
And the bird sings, she says,

~KIKI E KIKIAO, KIKIAO, WHAT IS YOUR MOTHER'S NAME?~

Now, she alone calls,

~LETUAJOWA~
~WHAT IS THE NAME OF YOUR FATHER?~
~ḶŌRŌKIEWA~
~KIKI E KIKIAO~ <laughs>

They haven't heard. She sings again,

~KIKI E, KIKIAO~ <laughs>

The songs of long ago are bad.
P   The songs of long ago are really good.
K   Is that true?
P   They are good with me.

K   *~WHAT IS YOUR MOTHER'S NAME?~*
     ~LETUAJOWA~
     ~WHAT IS YOUR FATHER'S NAME?~
     ~ḶŌRŌKIEWA~
     ~KIKI E, KIKIAO~

They haven't heard. She sings again, ~KIKI E— ~ but just increases her song,

<with strong, low guttural voice>

~KIKIAO~ <laughs>
~WHAT IS YOUR MOTHER'S NAME?~
~LETUAJOWA~
~WHAT IS YOUR FATHER'S NAME?~
~ḶŌRŌKIEWA~
~KIKI E KIKIAO~

Then, all the women they say, "Mmm, it's just like a voice is singing."
<we chuckle>
As if it says, "Your mother is Letuajowa, your father is Ḷōrōkiewa?"
"Ooo, well let's listen."
Now, they all listen.
Then, they listen, the bird sings,

~KIKI E KIKIAO~
~WHAT IS YOUR MOTHER'S NAME?~
~LETUAJOWA~
~WHAT IS YOUR FATHER'S NAME?~
~ḶŌRŌKIEWA~
~KIKI E KIKIAO~

"Oh my!"
But the woman she says,
"It's like the name for this my son . . . who is missing, who I forgot." <laughs>
He was the size of a baby when I bathed him, and now he is grown up.
(uh huh)
He is a young man now.

Possibly an Elder [missionary]. <we laugh>

Yes, the size of an adult.
Then, now they say, "Ah, get that chief.
It's as if there is singing."
The chief comes and listens. (uh huh)
Ooo listens, listens,
"Oh My! Well, let down the child from the upper story."
He asks, "Hey boy, what's your mother's name?"
Then, he says, "Letuajowa."
"What's your father's name?"

He says, "Ḷōrōkiewa."
But where do you come from?"
"From the house of the chief of the Rālik side." (uh huh)
The man holds close his son and cries over him.
He takes the thing, the axe, he has just sharpened it.
Takes it and chops a turd. <laughs> [meaning he was about to kill the children with it]

Well, that story is about the kinds of people that go and what? Forget their children, see? And now, it reveals something about how the powers of the chief in the west and the chief in the east are combined in the boy.

P   There are powers from two places with that boy?

K   Yes, he has received two powers now. Because he is the son of both the chief of the east and the chief of the west, who adopted him . . . and now he has received two powers. He is very powerful. Like Amata today. He possesses the most power of all.

As with the other dialogues and narratives, here, again, we see a clear dialogism between the narrative frames, generic forms, and intercultural voices. The plot structure that takes some time to emerge due to my interrogative insertions, disruptions by others, and his metanarration, presents the well-known "tests of identity" motif pattern that is familiar on a global scale, and particularly in status conscious Oceania (H12—Recognition by song or chant). What stands out here, and will need some attention to unpack, is how Kometo will recapitulate the principles of concealing and revealing to imply an important parallel of this story to current politics. A summary of how this narrative unfolds through the tropes of magic will set the ground for Kometo's decisive trick, to fashion an analogy between the mythological past and contemporary political power within the nation-state.

Before he enters into the narrative proper, Kometo establishes the associative power of godlike chiefs (*anij raŋ*) who inhabit different cardinal directions. Being linked to the "air space" indexes a power that comes with the territory. This kind of metonymic relationship will inform the outcome of the narrative, and even the ideas about contemporary power with which he will conclude. The mythic plot unfolds with the child drifting off in the wooden tub (*jāpe*) from what we may infer is the Ratak side (sunrise, east) of the atoll. Once it arrives in the Rālik side (sunset side, west), he is identified with the "light rain." Kometo uses the Kajin M̧ajeḷ word for sign (*kakōḷḷe*) as an index for the chiefly child. This sign that identifies royalty characterizes a pervasive motif in Oceania

(F960.11.1–5; see Cummins 1984). It illustrates a kind of contagious magic that indexes the true, but hidden identity of a royal child. After being raised by his "adoptive" parents in the west, the chief asks the boy if he wishes to go to his real father. Surprised, the boy inquires further and is told about his biological father in the east. The "power" with this chief allows him to know about the other paternal chief.

The boy, whom we will later come to know by the name Kikiao, then embarks on a journey to locate his biological parents with his adoptive sister. A son seeking his unknown father or parent represents another pan-Oceanic motif (H1381.2.2.1),[3] a quest that will ultimately reveal the true identity and legitimate authority. The accompanying sibling sister denotes a complex sign. Siblings are in one part homeopathic, connected through resemblance (if biologically related), and also contagious, linked through literal proximity to each other. For the riM̧ajeļ, this connection is particularly salient as matrilineal siblings share an umbilicus (*bwijen*).[4] As this sibling set journeys to the east, Kikiao will engage in two magical practices. With the first, when they travel along the reef, they come to a break between two islets at high tide that prevents them from walking over. Kikiao, somehow magically flies and floats across the break (motif F 1071, prodigious jump). While we do not know why Kikiao possesses such a power, we come to find out later in the story that a magical bird will sing the song of identification, who is metonymically connected to the power of the west from which Kikiao journeys. But his sister, unable to perform the same feat, calls out to her brother. He instructs her to "bite that empty copra and spread the basket of sand," thus joining the islets so she can run across the break. This gesture, to imitate the action desired, magically produces a land bridge between two sides. The siblings are creating a passage between the two sides of the atoll and its respective powers. This magical act has deep mythological resonance. In a version collected by Knight (1980), the narrator's chant is similar to Kometo's recitation of the boy's instruction to his sister, but it is not the spreading of just any sand, but that from "Ep," the primordial homeland. So, the movement that links the west to the east in the story retraces the movement from the mythological homeland in the west to the Marshalls in the east. In Kometo's narration, the boy and girl perform this magic trick twice. The second act of magic comprises the use of a stick to jump across a channel, almost like pole vaulting. This extraordinary action offers an oblique metaphor of social power. In Kajin Ṃajeļ, a post (*joor*) driven into the ground often serves as a metaphor for strength and social authority. This term is the root to *kajoor* (or power) which is also the same term for commoners or the people. A post firmly planted in the ground corresponds to this power and clearly roots people and power in the land (cf. LaBriola 2019).

This act of "imposting," which links two sides, alludes to a consolidation of power via this magical metaphor.

The myth continues when the siblings encounter the boys playing with the toy canoe, who are seeking victorious "power" over each other. Kikiao requests the toy canoe and there is some resistance. They purport that perhaps he is the offspring of Letao. So, while this story is not performed as one with levity and jest, we are reminded that the trickster ethos lurks behind this story of magic. The immediate release of the canoe to Kikiao intimates that our primary character is sly and potentially dangerous. There is more than just an allusion here as the boy's name possesses the same root as Letao (*ao*), meaning "halo," or "spiritual power," plus *kiki,* which means "to sleep." Thus, he could be viewed as the sleeping or "unaware" trickster, who through a series of tricks of magic, will eventually unmask an unsuspecting true and powerful identity. The storyteller's magic chant by the bird in Knight's collection (1980, 26) is more developed than Kometo's, and makes an overt reference to Letao. Perhaps this archaic chant informs Kometo's gesture to insert the trickster into the story. Now, once in possession of the toy canoe, Kikiao performs sorcery (*anijnij*) on it. Just how this works is not exactly clear. Kometo recites in chant form some archaic terms. *Kwaalōn* represents a form of *kkọọḷ,* which means to put a spell or curse on someone or something. This incantation turns the toy canoe into a dangerous fast-flying projectile. This act of sorcery, through metaphorical transference from one sign onto another, transfers the qualities of a sharp spear to that of a toy sailing canoe. The toy canoe flies off and hits with force the post near his chiefly mother. Kometo calls out in quoted speech Kikiao's intentions for the toy canoe. He also uses reported speech to register a metaphorical saying with regard to "strikes the eye of the chief," which is a figurative way to identify a serious threat to the ruler. Kometo breaks away into metanarration to explain that such an action, and similar gestures, is strictly prohibited (*mọ*). Breaking such a taboo is life-threatening due to the risk it presents to the chief. He uses another metaphor that draws the similarity between a life-threatening danger to "hold(s) the eye of the female chief (his mother)." In this sense, it would mean targeting her head, both as the seat of her spiritual power or soul (*an*) and symbol of her life. This action will receive a swift response. They capture the children and place them in the upper story of a thatch hut.

As the chief and Ratak side islanders prepare to execute Kikiao and his sister, the bird from the Rālik side comes to perform a song of revelation. At this point, as Kometo prepares to offer the song, he remembers the names of Kikiao and his parents. We have a short diversion as Kometo will disclaim the quality of the riM̧ajeḷ songs. He nonetheless enjoys rendering this bird's voice four times until the others recognize that the song identifies the boy's true identity and their mutual kinship. The bird's repetition exemplifies an iconic duplication of this magical scene in which the messenger bird asks the questions and gives the answers. This bird, which comes from the chief of the west (in Knight's version, the bird is the sister's mother or Kikiao's adoptive mother), brings with it the powers from whence Kikiao came to be reunited with the powers of his chiefly origins. By contact at birth, Kikiao draws power from his birth parents, and by adoption, he absorbs power through contiguity with his western parents. The metonymic chain draws together the dual powers contained in Kikiao. This magical moment of revealing what was hidden through the law of contact, unveils upon whom true social and political power lies. Curiously, the sharpened axe (*ūlūl*) that was to be used in the execution of Kikiao ultimately is used to chop a turd. The turd, or excrement, now stands in for the dispatching of the children. Something foul is substituted for a son with all his magical and divine powers. The most abased takes the place of the most elevated. This mythic story of reversal, from lost and unknown to found and known, is completed through a series of magical acts.

But this myth is not just another illustration of the principle of concealment and revelation; Kometo draws it into our dialogue to register a profound political reality in his modern life. The conversation about contemporary political power that elicited the mythic narrative sets up the frame for how he wishes the story to be understood. And then, through this narrative of hiding and revealing, the true identity of the royal boy comes to light. And it also unveils links to the cosmological genealogy. Because Kikiao was raised by chiefly parents in the west, and then rediscovered by his chiefly parents in the east, it represents the consolidation of his political power. This merging of power in the story mirrored the current political environment in the Marshall Islands when Kometo and I were dialoguing, and he overtly draws the parallel to Amata. At that time, Amata Kabua was the president of the Republic of the Marshall Islands.[5] He epitomized a man of unified power (*irooj pweio,* a child of both a chiefly father and chiefly mother); he held high chiefly status both from the Rālik (west, on his father's side) and the Ratak (east, on his mother's side) chains to make him the most politically powerful individual in all the Marshall Islands imbued with sacred authority. This was a topic about the current social polity of the islands, which we both talked about together often. Indeed, it was a topic most riMạjeḷ talked about often. Laurence Carucci (1997b) identifies how the commoners (*kajoor ro*) offer contemporary critiques of the chiefs (*irooj ro*) as they compromise their sacred image by participating in and empowering themselves through state politics and gaining wealth through the new economy. So, here, a myth of concealing and revealing through magic provides an important commentary on current political power achieved through the play of metaphorical and metonymic tropes. This, then, is a very clever dialogue, indeed, veiling a subtle appraisal while exposing an implicit contemporary political order.

Very little laughter is created by this performance, partly due to the interruptions and Kometo continually reentering the narrative to get his bearings and to keep me on track. Only his joking in metanarration about the age of Mormon missionaries and his disclaiming question about the songs of long ago provide any comic relief. But there is also nothing really funny about the story with its chants and obscure language of sorcery. Perhaps, because that which is revealed through metaphor and metonym is not an inconsequential imagining, but identifies a real social hierarchy by which Indigenous tradition and modernity are integrated. This was a serious kind of magic. The calibration between the past reflected in the myth and the present of the narrative event is minimized. But I sense Kometo also intimates another possibility here. Although he was not a royal person himself, he was, as my mentor, alluding to his own identity as a man from both the east and the west, and thus knowledgeable and informed by both. He was testing me to see if I could unpack the hidden message and recognize the intrigue between us. Seeking to reveal oneself comes with some danger and risk, not unlike in the narrative. Just at the moment before the children are to be killed, their true hidden identity is made manifest. By using the hybridized forms of deception and revelation, he was unveiling the political import of the story while also seeing if I would detect the hidden messages about himself. We were playing our own game of hide-and-seek through the magic of metaphors and metonyms.

Death Magic and the End of Telling a Tale

Christianity in the Marshalls, similar to much of the Oceania as a whole, presents a complex interrelationship of tradition and modernity, imposition and agency. riM̧ajeļ adoption of Christianity is neither singular nor transparent; it takes on distinct localized dimensions and continues to be riddled with ambiguities and seeming contradictions (see Rudiak-Gould 2010). Kometo the trickster storyteller mediated a range of oppositions by employing islander tropes along the margins of the Indigenous mythological past and a modernity informed by Christianity and his new attachments to Mormonism. He regularly foregrounded how the "new" religion characterized less a rupture than a blurring and flow across the boundaries of a mythological past and the present.

Effectively, in the assimilation of Christianity with riM̧ajeļ sensibilities, Jesus Christ now occupies a sociological positioning of the paramount chief. *Irooj*, the Kajin M̧ajeļ term for chief with their traditional sacred authority, is used to express Christ as Lord. But as God, he moves between heaven and earth. He is, then, in a fashion, a mediator like a trickster, and in Kometo's mind, he ties not only the vertical axis of the earth to the cosmos, but horizontally through time; he makes a leap back to the beginning of time and then reappears, much like Letao, at a different historical juncture. For many riM̧ajeļ, including Kometo, cosmological beliefs about the Indigenous gods do not represent an independent tradition precedent to Christianity, rather, the Christian god corresponds to what the original ancestors knew. For some, the story of Christianity's arrival to the Marshalls (see Hezel 1983; Walsh and Heine 2012) characterizes less a new narrative, and more a kind of intertextual housekeeping—a textual calibration linking the distant mythological past to the present in a seamless fabric of time. Now, certainly, for the riM̧ajeļ, Christ does not assume the attributes of a deceptive, lying, sly one. But just like all good tricksters, he does mediate and work on the margins of life and death. So it is no contradiction when Kometo continues to use signs of life and death embedded in mythological narratives (that to some seem wholly non-Christian) and remain planted in the Christian metaphysic.

When the Christian missionaries arrived in the Marshall Islands (1857),[6] they made a concerted effort to replace polytheism with monotheism. Through time, the belief system adjusted and created a hybrid and complex entanglement. Many of the islanders have found a confirming nexus between Christian and Indigenous conceptualizations of divinity. And while the liturgical worship of deity has assumed a very public role within Christian denominations, private religious rehearsals continue unabated, and undergird many riM̧ajeļ cultural sensitivities and religious practice. This includes numerous forms of magic (*kkōpāl*), divination (*bubu*), sorcery (*anijnij*), belief in demons (*tim̧oņ* and *mejenkwaad*) and spirit possession (*tuwe*), idols (*ekjab*), healing powers through native medicines and practice (*wūno* & *kōbbōkakkak*),[7] negative/dark medicine and practice (*m̧admōd*), humanlike beings under the earth (*ņoonniep*) and the water (*riikijet*), and numerous spirits (*jetōb*), including evil spirits (*anjinmar*) that cast spells, and the ancestors (*rūtto*). These beliefs and practices carry over from the distant past into the present to mix with Christian metaphysical conceptualizations or remain salient alternatives (cf. Dobbin 2012). Working within the interstices of organized religion, these practices have their origin in deep history and offer a form of decolonial resistance even as the islanders appropriate the colonizing religion.

In the following dialogue, Kometo performs a mythic narrative full of several tropes of Indigenous medicine and sign reading to reveal a blurring rather than a break between an Indigenous belief structure and that of a modern Christian trickster storyteller. This was the second time Kometo rehearsed this story for me. This performance tenders an intertextual reference to his own prior performance,[8] and I will draw a little from that dialogue as well to contextualize Kometo's second rendering. Because of a heavy rain that day, we simply sat on the mats of his house and talked for a long time. When he began to tell this story, many family members began to listen in from the side. He seemed to relish the detail of this myth about death magic he knew very well. This performance also exhibits several links to antecedent texts as it merges different mythic episodes and makes implicit ties to the canonical texts of Christianity. The first two episodes represent separate stories in other collections, whereas Kometo combines them into a larger mythological whole. The third episode is unique to Kometo's mythological repertoire. Because in two separate performances of this amalgamated myth he attaches it to the total story, I designate it as the third episode.

Episode I

K   Well,

The man's name is Joṛukwōd.

See?
P   Where is he?
K   He is a person of Nam̗dik [atoll], they like to talk-story about him there. (uh huh)

There is—a boil swells on him.
And, then it breaks open.
After it's pinched, two girls appear.

Now, to make this story, we must say he has a power, see? He is a riM̗ajeḷ being from long ago.

The girls appear and remain with him.
The older girl is Lino.
They stay and just make food, live with him, and they become young women.
And go on and on . . . then he dies.
Their father dies.

Now, their father makes a promise with them before he dies.
He says, "When I die you two should bury me over there.
Just next to the window.
And, wait for something to appear.
And, when there is fruit, you two take it and go to your [classificatory]
mothers."
He says, "way over there is where they live."

In Naṃdik they thus tell this story, but in Arṇo there is another version of
this story. Because the same riM̧ajeḷ stories are in the east, or in the Ratak
chain also.

Then, oooo the thing appears where they buried him.

See?

The Banana tree.
The two of them chop it and take it to their mothers, their old mothers.
Then, the old women see them coming, they say, "Mmm our food."
When they see the young sisters one says,"Our food."
Then, the one old woman says,"No, they're our children."
Ooo the two of them argue.
"They should be our food."
"No, they are our children."
They argue, they really argue a long time.
"Our food, our food."
"Our children, our children."
"Our food, our food."
"Our children, our children." <we laugh>
They decide to go eat the girls.
Oooo, one says, "Well, first put them in the upper story" [of the hut].
And they wait, the two of them light the fire to cook their food.

Like preparing a fire to cook those pigs. <laughs>

Then, the two of them make the fire, but the two young women sing.
Their song says,

~OUR FATHER FROM AH— ~

The songs of long ago were often slow. I think those kinds of songs with the Americans are good—I like to sing them also. <laughs> And also the Japanese singing is good.

~HE IS JO̩RUKWŌD~
~HE SENT THE TWO OF YOU TO THE SPELL OF THE BUSH~
~TWO OF THEM AT THE HOUSE~
~THEY WILL EAT HIM~
~OUR FATHER, OUR FATHER, JO̩RUKWŌD~

The two old women don't hear.
The two young women sing, go on and on many times, the two of them sing.
Iooo the two old women hear.
"Ah, it's like a voice."
Then, the two of them hear, and really listen for where the voices come from.
"Ooo from that house over there."
The two of them say, "There from that house, really listen please."

~OUR FATHER, OUR FATHER, JO̩RUKWŌD~
~WHY DID YOU SEND THE TWO OF US TO THE SPELL OF THE BUSH?~
~TWO OF THEM AT THE HOUSE~
~THEY WILL EAT HIM, OUR FATHER~
~OUR FATHER, JO̩RUKWŌD, JO̩RUKWŌD~

"Mmmm."
"They say their father is Jo̩rukwōd."
Eoo the two of them open it over there—(uh huh) the lower window of the hut.[9]
And call into the two young women, "Aaah, where do you two come from?"
They say from the house [reference to a land tract] way over there.
"And you two and who were there?"
"Our father."
"Who is your father?"
"Jo̩rukwōd."
"Then, where is he?"
"He is dead."
"Mmm. And he told us to find our mothers on this islet."
The two of them say, "OH MY."
The two of them hold the two sisters close and cry.
They all cry together.
Cry, cry, just cry ooo and after they cry, they stay together and have peace.

Now, with those islanders this is the end of their knowing. The story you will hear takes it to the end.

Episode II

Now, they are good together.
But one day people appear, children—many, many children.
They come to find the young sisters.
They have been sent to get the young women.
To take them to the chief to be his wives. (oh it's clear)
The eel man. <I laugh, he joins>

Eh, it's not only now, but also long ago its was like this. It comes from long ago.

Now, they come and sing,

~LINO OO LINO~
~ḶAMAWŪNO SENT US FOR THE WOMAN LINO~

Then, the old women respond,

~WHAT ARE THESE THINGS AMONG LINO'S FOOD?~

Then, they (the children) count,

~A COCONUT TREE HERE~
~A BREADFRUIT TREE HERE~
~A PANDANUS TREE HERE~

All kinds of food.
The women say, "Aaaah, just all our fruits of this house [leen m̩we] already."

The meaning of *leen m̩we* is like many kinds of fruit at this house. Do you know the saying "fruits of the house?" (uh huh)

Ooo the children return.
Then, that kind of person who is more grown up comes.
They say the youth and older.
They come, come singing,

~LINO OO LINO~
~ḶAMAWŪNO SENT US FOR THE WOMAN LINO~

The old women respond,

~WHAT ARE THE THINGS AMONG LINO'S FOOD?~

Well, they count,

~A COCONUT TREE HERE~
~A BREADFRUIT TREE HERE~
~A PANDANUS TREE HERE~
~TARO PLANTS HERE~
~A BANANA TREE HERE~

<laughing> All kinds of food. Then, the old women say,

~AAAAH, JUST THE SAME FRUITS OF OUR HOUSE~

The young adults are embarrassed and return.
Then, like this it continues.
Then, the elders, who are the kind which come crawling or using a cane.
He sends them also.
The crowd persists.

And you will see with that younger kind of person, if you tease him, he is embarrassed, embarrassed and returns. But if it is an adult, the kind who uses a cane, and if you tease him, he won't be embarrassed.

~LINO OO LINO~
~ḶAMAWŪNO SENT US FOR THE WOMAN LINO~

The old women respond,

~WHAT ARE THE THINGS AMONG LINO'S FOOD?~

They answer, "Each and every kind of food," and say the names of the food trees.
The women say,

~AAAH, JUST THE FRUITS OF OUR HOUSE~

The crowd doesn't stop, but they just press on, just get closer to the house.
They press on and on, many arrive outside the house.
Then, the old women say, "Ikuk [expletive] we will be destroyed by that crowd.
Let's go."

Yes, the people of long ago were like cannibal demons, see? (uh huh)

Ooo the two young women go and get the bananas and escape.
The crowd presses on to eat the two young sisters.
Then, they [young women] peel the skin of many bananas and toss them.
Many demons jump in and fight over them.
Eee the smell of a human. (hmm)
They eat the bananas and grab all they can.
When they throw the peels out there is a smell of a human.
Then, they smell the human and say, "Smells good." <laughing>
"Like what kind of fish? Where are they?"
They hunger for it ooo they all fight and fight, fight over it ooo—
The young women escape.

They (the crowd) say, "Mmm. They escape!"
{The young women escape, they again run.}
The crowd tries to catch them.
They almost catch them to grab them and hold them to eat them.
But the two of them again throw out the banana and skins.
The demons again fight and fight over them.
They go, go, go ooo they arrive outside the house of Ḷamawūno in the sky.
And, he brings them in.
The man shouts to stop the crowd. <chuckles>
He brings the two of them in and they stay with him.

Episode III

They stay on and on for a while.
Then, one day the youngest sister, she says she wants to return home.
Now, then the oldest sister comes and promises her,
She says, "When you return, if you see two coconuts, if they fall together, you
should say, 'Mmm, the coconuts appear from my older sibling.'"

This means her older sister has a large stomach. (uh huh)

And, you will carry on and on and just go about things.
And, if you are just working, and if you see a coconut seed fall and face you,
you should say, "Mmm, the coconut appears from my older sibling'"
When this appears—then it is born. (uh huh)
She has a child.
"And yes, if you stay and carry on and then when you see under your sleeping
mat a dead lizard there, you should say, 'My older sibling has died'"

Well these things are signs for the riṂajeḷ. (uh huh) Also for me, today, I do it. (hmm) When I saw a dead lizard there under my sleeping mat, (mmm) it was the time my older sister died. I saw a dead lizard there under my sleeping mat. And this thing is not a lie, the riṂajeḷ have confirmed it. (uh huh) And those who know these stories, they have confirmed it. I was walking and coconuts fell together. I have seen it. Well now, she's dead. Eh? The dead lizard is the sign. So, when they destroy people with black magic, well, they do that. (hmm) They bring that lizard and stab it, and place it there, and cover it with a sleeping mat, or go and bury it.

P   When they stab it there? <points to chest>
K   Eh, stab it there . . . with a coconut palm stem.
P   In its chest?
K   Eh. And then it dies and they go and bury it or place it near a person's mat. (uh huh) If, when the lizard is stabbed, and buried or hidden under the mat, then three days later the person will die. Well, this I say, it's because they have placed a lizard under the mat by the woman.

Well, now, Ḷamawūno has come to cover the woman, the younger sister there—
He comes to cover her with three leaves of the Rubiaceae tree [utilomar].
And then, he covers her up. (hmm)
Now, the man he promises, he says, "When you hear,

<low raspy hum> **MMMMMM**

Don't move because you will not have yet arrived on the earth.
When you hear it say,

<low raspy growl> **OOOOOO**

Well, you can then open your blanket there."

Then, the man sends her to the earth.
Now, the young woman obeys.
Then, it says,

<low raspy hum> **MMMMMM**

She doesn't move.

<low raspy growl> **OOOOOO**

She opens the blanket.
Then, when she opens it, she enters into the house of her old mothers.
She stays on and on for a while mmmm, then two coconuts fall.
And she says,"Mmm my happiness is great."
The old women ask, "What is going on?"
"Oh, my older sister is pregnant."
Then, she stays on and on and sees a coconut seed.
Then, it falls and turns to her. (uh huh)
Then, she is happy . . . she's as happy as if it were her own child.

See?

Her old mothers ask, "What's that?"
"MY OLDER SIBLING HAS MANY CHILDREN." <laughs, coughs>

These are the signs which Lino had given to her.

Then, she stays on and on and one day, it passes.
There is a dead lizard under her sleeping mat.
Then, she cries, lays down and just cries.
And, her old mothers ask,"What are you doing?"
She says, "She's dead, my older sister is dead."

But you know they say she's dead, because she is only permanently gone.
Eh? It's just that she can't return again. The older sister can't really die since
she is in the sky, she can't really die. She's somewhat like a spirit and she
stays in the sky, see? <laughs> She's seems dead because

She can't return back to this earth.
The younger woman returned, but the older one cannot return.
Then, because it is like this, she says her sister is dead.

In the customs of these islands, you see, they speak about a *ṇoonniep*. (uh huh) If you go to be with those *ṇoonniep*, and you say that you have been with them, and then you go to look for them, you will not see them again. But if you never speak about them, you will remain with them. Just remain with them, and then you will not return again to your family. Well now, the family will say you have died, but you really remain alive. Because you can't return, they say you are dead . . . (uh huh) Well, thus it is. *Jiribinoọñ.* <laughs>

P   *Jiribinoọñ?*
K   The end of the tale. <he laughs hard>

This dialogue and the embedded myth come in three episodes. First, we have the episode of the origin of the banana tree (motifs A2611.0.1, A2681, A2687.5) from the man Joṛukwōd and his daughters meeting their ogress mothers who argue over eating them. Then we have the escape of Joṛukwōd's daughters from the crowd and their fooling the cannibal demons by throwing out the bananas and peels. Last, there is the separation of the sisters, the signs of pregnancy and death, and Kometo's contextualization of these signs in his own life. The mythic origin of the banana tree is common enough in the Marshall Islands.[10] At least five other versions have been recorded. The key variation in each of them is the location of the narrated event. Three place it at Arṇo atoll (Tobin 2002; Tanner 2008), another at Aelōñḷapḷap (Downing et al. 1992), and the other at Namḍik (Kelin 2003), the same location where Kometo situates the event of his telling. Interestingly, Kometo acknowledges the alternative version from Arṇo and explains that each of the island chains has its own localized version.

The other versions more or less follow Kometo's performance with the father (Joṛukwōd) giving instructions to his daughters for how to bury him, informing them about his sisters, the growing of the banana plant from the father's grave, the ogress sisters arguing over whether they should eat the children, and the revelation of the sisters' identity through their song. Kometo enjoys taking on the voices of the ogress sisters as they argue, enacted through reported speech. However, all the other versions end at the manifestation of the new food staple, whereas Kometo enters a second episode in which we find out a little more about why the banana is significant in the first place. Kometo even states at the conclusion of this part of the story, "Now, with those islanders this is the end of their knowing. The story you will hear takes it to the end." He lets me in on something he believes most others do not know. I will shortly come to this inside knowledge manifest through several cultural tropes, but first, Kometo presents an interesting narrative theme that poses a significant issue within riM̧ajeļ conceptualizations of both magic and the mythological past, and this will bring us back to the significance of the banana.

The birth of the two young sisters from the boil of their father, Joṛukwōd, represents an asexual realization of being and echoes other myths about the origin of the gods. Birth from a boil is in one part metaphoric, but it also represents a principle of contagion as parent and children will retain a special relationship through the original contact. In some versions, Letao and his brother are born from the boil (*wōt*) of Wullep (Erdland 1914), which stands for a recurring motif in much of the riM̧ajeļ mythology. When Kometo introduces this motif at the beginning of the story, he quickly breaks away into metanarration to inform me that this man, a being of long ago, also possesses a certain kind of power. Whenever he would do this, he wanted me to understand that the character belongs among those primordial beings that were seen to operate in a different way than contemporary humans. They possessed abilities and powers that no longer remain with people. In the context of the myth, we see that, from this man, emerges key things: in life, his daughters spring from the metonymic boil, who will assist in bringing important magical knowledge; in death, the banana plant will emerge, which will not only serve as an important staple for the riM̧ajeļ, but also becomes a metaphor of humans themselves based on a principle of similarity. I will get to this shortly.

The presence of the ogress sisters also represents a recurring motif (G10) in much riM̧ajeļ storytelling, even though there are no records or stories about them practicing ritual cannibalism. Stories of cannibalism are numerous and widespread throughout all of Oceania (see Kirtley 1953, 1971). In actual practice, anthropophagy was rare, and contrary to fanciful representations that the act formed part of the native diet (see Edmond 1997), the ceremonial practice was to take into one's self another's *mana,* or spiritual potency. For the riM̧ajeļ, this spiritual power is contained within the *an,* or soul of an individual, and sometimes referred to as *abōn.* So, in this myth, these primordial females who eat children (referred to as *mejenkwaad*)[11] imitate a familiar pattern (Knight 1980; Tobin 2004). Two things stand out about these women: first, they represent "uncivilized" cannibals (cf. Tobin 2002). There is no greater asocial behavior, both in the precontact and Christian periods. In the chant-like song, the reference is made to "spell of the bush," which Kometo later explained substitutes for the word "demons." Thus, these ogress women are demons, something understood as dark (*marok*) and dangerous in precolonial tradition, and later counterposed to Christian sensibilities described as "the coming of light" (*itok eo an meram*). Here, again, as with the myth of Kikiao, just at the moment before the young sisters are to be dispatched (in this case, eaten) their true identity is revealed through chant-like song.

A second feature that stands out here is how Kometo and other storytellers accentuate the debate between the two sisters whether to eat the young women. They do not debate over the propriety of cannibalism, but over whether the young sisters are their children (classificatory daughters). If they prove other than kin, they would be candidates for ingesting. On the other hand, if they prove relatives, a different kind of reception will be offered altogether. Here a fundamental matter of stranger versus kin is at stake. Strangers present a threat, and people are always vulnerable to their potential violence. The word for stranger (*ruwamāejet*) means "those others who come in the canoe"; in other words, those arriving from the outside. In contrast, relatives are *nukwi*, metaphorically relating to those of the same cloth, or as members of a matriline (*bwij*) or matriclan (*jowi*) sharing the same umbilicus, or patriline (*bōtōktōk*), those sharing the same "blood" (in this case, blood is a euphemism for sperm).[12] Also, relatives epitomize vital people with whom one is obligated to share food. The ogresses arguing over whether to eat the young women foregrounds the uncertainty around how to identify someone, and this can either lead to a great act of sociability and care, or to death and a most unsociable act. The equation of the children to be cooked and eaten like a pig is a familiar metaphor in deep history. Out of this mythological world Kometo will narrate other magical powers that remain, and which he will integrate into his own personal practice of riM̧ajeļ tradition with a Christian worldview.

Kometo begins the young women's chanted song and then immediately breaks to an aside to offer comparative commentary on ancient riM̧ajeļ singing with American and Japanese songs. He admires them all, and in a way makes a disclaimer about the nature of riM̧ajeļ chant-like song; they often proceed slowly. By this he means not only the pacing of the chanted song, but also how one slurs and registers the voice in a low to raising tone. At the end of a chanted song, the riM̧ajeļ chanter/singer will also emphasize the last words of the last lines. But once Kometo connects the song to the narrative event and my presence as an American, he immediately shifts back into the story, locates the main character, and completes the chanted song. Again, as explained in the previous chapter, this chanted song seems a bit aborted and incomplete,[13] a fragment of the past voices Kometo offers me. In paralleling the chant, he even alters the wording. He then returns to the song again as the ogress sisters listen. The chanted song genre represents a discourse of revelation; it brings forth the truth. The chanted song is an enduring signpost to the past, and in the context of this narrative, it provides the means whereby the true identity is revealed. While the chanted song serves this purpose of revealing the truth, so too does the dialogue between the ogress mothers and the young sisters. Narrated dialogue brings forth the truth through interrogatives that will lead to the union of these two sets of sisters. In our conversations, if I ask the right questions, we also generate a union—at least I was always hoping so. Kometo demonstrates through the performance of this myth a model for relationship making.

After the narrated conversations among the characters, Kometo shifts abruptly into another episode, one which I never heard from another storyteller or found in other narrative collections. He narrates other people coming for the younger sisters to take them to a character named Ḷamawūno to become his wives. This shift seems to take the narrated event in a different direction, but it will eventually make complete sense as a subsequent episode to the first. Those who come for the young sisters come in three waves, representing three stages of life. First, they come as children, then as youthful adults, and then as the elderly. This recapitulation of the human life cycle is somewhat obscure, but we can surmise it represents the full range of society (albeit demon beings) that has converged on this important scene with the two young women. Their arrival is threatening, and the ogress aunties become defensive. Those who come arrive singing on behalf of Ḷamawūno. They sing to "Lino," who is the eldest of the young sisters.[14] The emissaries sing that Ḷamawūno sends gifts to her. The old ogress sisters speak on her behalf and ask about what they bring (as a standard kind of gift tribute). The visitors then count out a variety of trees that provide key staples. The women call back that this is nothing more than what they already have as their possessions. Kometo later explains how this teasing and sarcasm would cause embarrassment. This routine is repeated three times with each of the different visiting age groups.

Then the crowd pushes in upon the house. Kometo quickly returns to the narrative event to explain their motives, that these people are also cannibal demons. He then, just as quickly, returns to the narrated event. The sisters escape from these demon cannibals by eating bananas and throwing out the skins, which the cannibals take to be human flesh (by smell) and devour them, thus permitting the sisters to escape. The gift from their father, that which comes of his body, the banana (and foreshadowed by the chant that they should eat their father), provides the means for their escape again from demon cannibals. Here, the banana, once a metonymic link to their father, now serves as a metaphorical substitute for human flesh, and even in some way is equivalent to human scent.

I never really queried Kometo about this homeopathic equivalence between humans and bananas, but the idea is certainly suggestive, that lying under the skin is a "fruit," its origin that of the father demigod. Now, instead of humans, the banana provides the sacrifice to appease the cannibal demons. Their appetite for human flesh is great, but the substitute offering fools them, and they become satisfied with a food suitable for human consumption. In an enigmatic convoluted fashion, the two young sisters, by eating the banana, a symbol whose phallic appearance is underscored by its association with the flesh of the father, eat their progenitor, and are thus cannibals, too.[15] There is no evidence that the riM̧ajeḷ ever practiced ritual cannibalism, although there are some legendary stories of anthropophagus to stave off starvation in accidental canoe drifting. Nevertheless, their mythological narratives of cannibal figures abound,[16] providing an image used as the antithesis to human propriety, and for modern riM̧ajeḷ, their Christian respectabilities. Nonetheless, this lowest condition of humanity symbolized by cannibalism will eventually be substituted by the symbolic sacramental ingestion of the Christian God. Just like the two sisters who are given life and rescued through the transformed flesh of their father in the riM̧ajeḷ myth, the Christian God's body will become an emblem of life and salvation. This integration of the Indigenous and Christian mythological worlds provides the subcontext for Kometo the storyteller to explore his syncretic beliefs with me in a narrative event.

Here now we come to the third episodic shift in Kometo's presentation of the myth. Once the sisters escape, they arrive at Ḷamawūno's house in the sky (motif R49.3). They find safety with the man who has sent the cannibal messengers. Perhaps this was his ploy, or perhaps we are dealing with something else entirely, but the sisters going to stay with Ḷamawūno is significant. Who is this being and in what way will he be part of Kometo's juxtaposition of precontact magic beliefs with Christianity? We get a little hint about him when Kometo narrates how he has sent the messengers to retrieve the young women to become his wives. This comes as no surprise to a riM̧ajeḷ audience, as they are all very familiar with the polygyny of former chiefs and demigods. But it also epitomizes something they recognize as a practice discarded and forbidden by the Christian missionaries. At this point, Kometo also slides something else into his commentary; he refers to him as "eel man" (*mam̧m̧an m̧aj*). He then makes an aside to explain how men have always been this way, today and in long times past.

The riM̧ajeḷ metaphorically characterize the male proclivity as either "eel man" or "earthworm man" (*m̧ajkadāl*) because, as Kometo explained, "both seek to enter any hole they can find." Here, Kometo jokes about Ḷamawūno as being highly sexed. He submits here more than just a commentary on a mythological god and by implication past chiefs who took any liberty they desired; he imparts a statement about males in general. All the same, this male behavior, seen as the normal course, is also something preached against by the Christian missionaries. So here again, Kometo sets up Indigenous conceptualizations to contrast them with the Christian present. He has identified cannibalism and promiscuity as those things from the past antithetical to Christian values. Moreover, other than his promiscuity and possible cannibalism, Ḷamawūno's "darkness" is embedded in his name, which means "Man of Medicine." But this is not just any kind of medicine, as we will see. Sometime later after the performance of the myth, we resumed a discussion about its meaning.

P Why did you share this story after the two of us talked about the eel man?

K *<laughs>* Because, the reason I shared it—to attend to the person in the sky who was also an eel man. <I chuckle> Eh? They say his name is, "Ḷamawūno."

P What is Ḷamawūno's medicine?

K The medicine of death.

P The medicine of death?

K If you were to compare it to the Bible, who would it be? Whose medicine is it?

P I don't know.

K Possibly also like Lucifer. Is it clear? (uh huh) <chuckles> And he is proud. (mmm) His work is, earthworm man! <laughs hard>

P That's the work of Lucifer?

K Correct? Eh, because, really examine it, who gave the eel man? <pause, we laugh> Well. <Long pause> Eh?

P You tell me.

K Look please, ah, the two of us are talking-story about the eel, it's not just the riM̧ajeḷ who have the eel.

P Mmm, all men.

K All men. I saw it in those films.

A man—there are many American men.
They have it.
And a man goes from his house to a club with many young men.
And then afterward, he goes with the woman. <chuckles>
{Dance, dance, dance} "Oh, the two of us go to bed and lay down." <laughs hard>

Well, what is that? An eel! <we laugh> If you talk-story with the Americans about this, they won't really understand. <I chuckle> Eh? They can't understand. Now, you could say, "Freshwater eel" <chuckles>

P   "Freshwater eel?

K   *Toŋ* is the thing, it's called in English, "*Snake*"

P   Snake? <he laughs> Freshwater eel man in America.
     <we laugh hard; he shakes with laughter; pause>

K   <Whispering with a gleam in his eye> What is that freshwater eel man?
     <chuckling> The snake man, Letao is also a snake man. <we chuckle> Eh,
     perhaps. Because these things we two are talking about are the qualities
     that really belong to him. <pause> This word, "eel," it's a little word, but it
     has big meaning. So, in our lives it's about the eel man. <we laugh> This is
     its meaning. It's about the flesh.

P   The flesh? Oh, LaKometo.

K   <chuckling low> Oh, LaPhillip. <laughs low but hard>

Well, the reason the two of us are sharing this story is because the eel man
comes from him, from the man, Ḷamawūno.

P   So, what is the significance of the women in the story? They bring the
     medicine?

K   They bring the medicine. The two of them revealed the medicine. <long
     pause> If the women had not been with Ḷamawūno, they could not have
     known about the medicine.

P   What did he teach them?

K   When he showed it to them, the one woman says, "That medicine there
     reveals power!" If the coconut will fall . . . and they see the coconut, see?
     It is a sign. The coconut seed is another sign. The dead lizard is another
     sign.

P   So, is Ḷamawūno in the skies?

K   He is in skies.

P   And . . . the younger woman came down to earth?

K   She came down to earth. And showed it to the people of the earth . . .

P   Why did those women bring the medicine of destruction to these islands? Is
     it a blessing or misfortune or what?

K   <chuckles> Thus is the medicine okay, they brought it and said, Ḷamawūno
     gave this power to them. <pause, laughing> Well, this thing is hard. Eh? (uh
     huh) People don't always see it. In the Bible it says, "Lucifer," but in this
     story of long ago, they say, "Ḷamawūno." <we chuckle>

At the beginning of this follow-up dialogue, I seek to understand how he
connected our discussion of the promiscuity of males to a myth about cannibalism, magic, and reading signs, as he never used the word for medicine (*wūno*) during the exchange except embedded in the name of the god,

Ḷamawūno. He explicates how this divine male being was also like an "eel men," or sexually promiscuous. I then want to know more about the medicine Ḷamawūno provides, and Kometo calls it the "medicine of death." Suddenly, the morbid picture of the myth about cannibalism and the signs of death come into focus. It is not just any medicine with its magical efficacy, but that which signals or causes death. Consequently, the link back to Christianity lies in how Lucifer tricks Adam and Eve to partake of the forbidden fruit that leads to the inevitability of their death. This myth of death in the Judeo-Christian canon serves as a subtext for Kometo's narrative telling and dialogue with me. He even asks me to compare the story and character to that of the Bible. Such a comparison is not unlike other riM̧ajeḷ as they work out the Christian metaphysic and its epistemologies with Indigenous mythology. He invites me to view the intertextual connection with him. Kometo offers that the work of this being, Ḷamawūno, is the equivalent of Lucifer. They are both earthworm (or eel) men; in other words, they represent promiscuity while also death.

In the next segment of this interchange, Kometo begins to ask me a series of questions about from whom this male quality derives. The "eel man" connotes more than something only belonging to the riM̧ajeḷ, but to all men, and most certainly American men. Through his own comparison of having watched American films, he cleverly identifies the same kind of script in American male behavior. This analogy creates intense mutual laughter, and then he tells me that Americans may not know the metaphorical reference to eel man, but they nonetheless participate in the reality. By metonymically linking the riM̧ajeḷ mythological and Christianity traditions, he again establishes a common ground through his intertextual work (the Bible and American films with riM̧ajeḷ myths). Similarity is achieved through a metaphor that establishes equivalence. Yet he also emphasizes our shared Christianity and Mormon morals; both our traditions speak back to this inclination, which our currently held values identify as something to avoid. He continues to grow the comparative link; whereas Americans may not understand the metaphor of the eel man, they will certainly understand it if we substitute it for another phallic metaphor, a fresh water snake. Here, he shows his understanding of lexical differences (freshwater eel vs. freshwater snake) linked to their respective environments, to reveal a common reality among the males of the two cultures. Then, altering the form of his speech, Kometo links the "snake man" to Letao. The trickster has arrived, or really just finally unveiled himself, having all the while hung around. He implies that unbridled male sexual desire itself represents a form of trickery, deception, and hiding. And that in addition to Letao and his libido, Ḷamawūno, the equivalent of Lucifer (the serpent in the Garden of Eden), bestows this universal male proclivity.

When he sums up the meaning of all this, that it all comes down to our carnal nature (the flesh), I am fascinated by his cleverness and the circuitous work of a trickster storyteller. For this purpose, I exclaim, "Oh Lakometo," or "Oh Man-Kometo." He rejoins, "Oh LaPhillip," or "Oh Man-Phillip," again making me part of this game. This mutual recognition, that we are male with all the potential vicissitudes of men, leads to laughter. For the remainder of the dialogue, we can then explore the specific content of the myth. I learn about the link of this death medicine to the eel man, and how the younger sister is the one who brings it to earth, having received it from Ḷamawūno via her sister. As I seek to understand the value of such a medicine to destroy people, Kometo waffles, and in doing so he reconfirms Ḷamawūno as the substitute for Lucifer, and thus the metonymic link between Indigenous riM̧ajeḷ magic and Christianity. Lucifer brought death and exploits desire, so too did Ḷamawūno. The coupling of sexuality with death is most intriguing and reconfirms the precarious margin between life and death; each underscores the other. Lurking behind all this is Letao, and Kometo sneaks him in at the right juncture to remind me of the kind of play on meaning we are exploring.

Now to return to the narrative, the older sister Lino remains with Ḷamawūno as the younger sister returns to earth with her new knowledge about the medicine or death magic. He then narrates how the older sibling provides the signs that will identify her pregnancy and eventual death, again coupling life with death. The falling of the two coconuts represents the sign of pregnancy, whereas the appearance of the dead lizard under the sleeping mat indexes death. The symbolism of the two coconuts reflects the mother and child (a coconut shell has the facial appearance of a person), and the lizard form serves as an iconic sign of a human. Here, Kometo breaks from the narrative to substantiate these signs; he himself has witnessed them, and then enters into a memorate about his sister.[17] This insertion of his personal testimony creates a tightening between Indigenous riM̧ajeḷ beliefs about magic and Christianity. The magical powers that are recounted in the myth about the primordial past are confirmed through the personal experience in the Christian present. In this context the past/present, myth/personal story, Indigenous magical belief/Christian belief, interpenetrate. There is no divide between these poles; the story may prove fictional, but the magical practice is real. The practice can be "confirmed" in the personal accounts of others. He simply shares the myth that recounts the origin of these magical routines. The modern Mormon Christian is a witness and participant in these Indigenous magic practices.

Kometo adds to his memorate a description of how black magic works when used to destroy someone. In a kind of voodoo doll practice, but using a lizard, someone with malicious intents stabs it with the coconut palm stem, and then places it under the mat by the person they wish to destroy. This act combines the law of similarity with that of contagion; the act of stabbing the lizard is homeopathic, and placing it near the desired victim contagious (motif D2061.2.2). This aside continues his discussion on how magic really works. The story that he relates elicits these connections and foregrounds again the juxtaposition of magic with a Christian metaphysic. These practices of the past as registered in the narrated event continue to prevail in the present. Back into the narrated event, he is at his most dramatic as a storyteller. Through a range of reported speech acts, he relates how Ḷamawūno provides magical instructions to the younger sister for her return to earth (imitating a kind of death and resurrection). If she hears, "*MMMMMM*" she is not to move, and then when she hears, "*OOOOOO*" she is to open her leaf blanket. She follows the instructions with exactness, and in doing so is able to enter the home of her two old ogress mothers. Kometo's vocalizations of these sounds are haunting. They offer recontextualizations of primordial sounds, not those of human beings. Similar evocative vocalizations used in creation were noted by Davenport (1953), and the riMạajeḷ still listen for such sounds in the night to detect malevolent or dangerous presences from the beneficial and benevolent. Kometo is very animated when performing these sounds, and coming off his discussion about potent magic (*kkōpāl*) all levity or laughter is removed from the dialogue, and joining with others who have gathered to listen in on his storytelling, we become apprehensive and anxious.

The warnings given about the signs prior to the younger sister's descent are then realized in the outcome of the narrated event; her sister gives birth and she celebrates, then her sister dies, and she mourns. The older sister will not be able to return to earth; she is now dead to the younger. The young sister learning the signs foreshadows the outcome. No surprise comes with this result and the medicine of death (motif D2060) has been revealed to people on earth. After completing the story, Kometo again abruptly shifts to conclude the dialogue. This idea, of not being able to return and assumed dead, parallels the riMạajeḷ belief tradition about the *ṇoonniep,* little humanlike people who live below the earth. A person may remain with a *ṇoonniep* and never return again, and thus, others will conclude they have died. In drawing the parallel between the idea of absence with death and the *ṇoonniep,* Kometo makes an intertextual reference to another story cycle to corroborate his point.

Before exiting the somber ending to the story of cannibalism and the medicine of death, Kometo throws in a twist to reframe the whole myth. He concludes,

"Well thus it is," making it seem like, "here is the truth," but then uses the formula *jiribinoñ*, meaning, "the end of the tale." This signals that we have just experienced an *inoñ*, or those stories identified as fiction. He laughs at this. I repeat the formula to ensure I heard right and he laughs even harder. In listening to Kometo tell stories over two years, this was the first time I had ever heard him use this concluding formula. It signals the end of a story for the *inoñ* genre (note the root word), a fiction or folktale, or a term sometime interchangeable with a falsehood or "lie." I had read about this formula (Davenport 1953, 224) prior to my fieldwork, but I had only heard it a few times by a couple other elderly storytellers, and I had begun to believe it characterized a faded stylistic device that once framed the narrative and its truth status. I took the relative absence of the formula to mean that riM̧ajeḷ generic boundaries were shifting as a result of alternative modern discourses, and that tales of magic now blur into a larger corpus of mythological renderings. But here, in one of our very last conversations, perhaps the last narrative he would ever recount to me, Kometo slips this formula in at the end. During the performance of the story, he affirms the seriousness of the narrated event, that dangerous medicine is not something to trifle with. And then, after all that, he throws the whole story into doubt. Had he only been telling me a magic tale, a folktale, and that this was perhaps all a lie? Has he played the trickster as a teller of tales one last time? Indeed, in the follow-up meeting, the resulting conversation ensued.

K   Look please. The power of medicine, it comes from that man. The man's name is Ḷamawūno!
P   Ḷamawūno
K   Eh. <laughs>
P   And the banana tree grows from the father of the young women?
K   From their father.
P   Why do they appear from a boil?
K   <chuckles, pause> Well, what now? <chuckles> The people of Arṇo say it happened on Ḷōñar. The islet furthest east on Arṇo. <chuckles> Well, the tale is just a lie. <laughs> It's . . . a story about our riM̧ajeḷ you see, and you are really judging it.

So, they say, "The tale is just a lie." <we laugh> But what is the truth? See? Because perhaps they made the stories to teach the children and the people a way of life in the Marshalls. <laughs> If we judge it, why? Well, we may say it's true, but they then say it's a lie. <chuckles, long pause> Well, what now?

In our interchange, I kept pressing for the specifics of the mythological story and pushing for details about the riM̧aję Indigenous belief and its underlying epistemology, not to question its rationality, but to unpack any symbolism I felt I was missing. With my final question about the boil, he chuckles and pauses; then in a kind of exasperated way, asks rhetorically, "What now?" I think he means, "Haven't you learned anything yet? Will you keep asking such questions?" He then reveals his folkloristic knowledge again about this myth's distribution and suggests that I should see them all as just versions of the same story. Narratives have lives of their own. He, as a storyteller, seems to possess as much sensitivity to this as I, the trained folklorist. This story is just a story among many of the riM̧aję. Of note and lost in translation, he calls them "our riM̧aję," using the inclusive possessive form (*adro*), meaning both his and mine. He asserts that I am trying to judge it in terms of its truth status. Now, actually, that is not what I was trying to do, but rather to simply understand the details of the story. In any case, I come across as picking it apart to question things about magic and a plot that do not make rational sense. And for him, why should I do this as he has already knowingly communicated that this was just storytelling? He even offers an explanation for the pedagogical virtue of such "untrue" stories; fictional truth is good for children and serves as a carrier of culture. Why should we "judge it" in terms of its rational sense or historicity? It is just a magic tale, not with the intent to do harm through deception, but to uncover other kinds of understanding. For Kometo, while the ontology of the narrated event may prove suspect, the veracity of magic remains, and so does the reality of the deeply held belief structure. Have I been naive? Have I not learned anything? He laughs at both the complex interplay of these possibilities and signals that I need to take all this differently than he thinks I am taking it.

This explanation would all be fine and good if only he had not added the last two sentences. "Well, we may say it's true, but they then say it is a lie?" Who is the "we?" He has again used a plural inclusive pronoun (*kōjro*) that includes me. How is it that "we" say it is true? Does the "we" of the riM̧aję now include me? Or is it that we two see the truth in it that others fail to detect and will write off as nonhistorical fiction? And who are the "they?" Is it anyone who would listen in? Or are the outsider Americans "they," those who would bring such Indigenous meanings and epistemologies about death and magic into question? Is the "they" the other Christians or Mormons? I do not know. But then he asks again, "What now"? or "Where do we go from here?" Is there really anything else to say? Is he simply teaching me another iteration for how the hidden becomes manifest? Can our dialogues reveal anything more about this complex relationship of Indigenous belief about death magic and its entanglement with Christianity?

Is this just Kometo's subtle, and perhaps decolonizing way of containing his Mormonism and Christianity by sifting it through Indigenous epistemologies, sensibilities, and beliefs about magical power? Are we two just tricksters playing on the margins of belief and powerful forces, cultural tropes, and an intercultural relationship? Is there really much sympathetic difference between Indigenous myths about the past and Christian stories in the present, between magic and reality, between the two of us? Are they simply metaphors and metonyms of each other?

CHAPTER 6

Dirty and Dangerous Tricks
Taking Dialogic Risks

Tricksters frequently involve themselves in dirty and dangerous matters. Dirt itself can be threatening; it is matter out of place (Douglas 1966), upsetting boundaries and cultural categories. And yet, paradoxically, the "character who can freely play with dirt" may also prove a culture hero and bring about "fundamental change" (Hyde 1998, 189). The ethnographic dialogue is, from the outset, a bit messy as the respective cultural categories and boundaries brought to the encounter must be transgressed in order to achieve understanding. We grant this disarray to a degree because of mutual ignorance about each participant's categories. The danger in such moments may be to give offense and disrupt the dialogue entirely. Such dialogues seem to always teeter on the brink of disaster, and still, the conversations may continue with their hazards and possibilities. They oblige interlocutors to take some risks to maintain the dialogue, and accordingly, they provide a salient location for trickster work.

Along the Margins of the Sacred and Profane

Tricksters like Letao achieve a double task; they at once violate and mark boundaries (Hyde 1998). The risks taken that may violate intercultural boundaries can also bring them to view, making clearer the cultural differences. Kometo approached several hazards with potentially sullied content. Because of our shared background in a religious community, such risk-taking posed a potential challenge to the "looking good principle" (Ochs and Capps 2001, 47) in communication. Kometo sometimes resisted assuming a persona of piety and decorum, whether based on the standards of riM̧ajeḷ tradition or modern religion. In consequence, this further eroded the cultural distance between us; it created mutual insiders to Letao's indecorous secrets, and more appreciably, accentuated our mutual liminality. Social tricksters like Kometo do not always play the role of the clown or act in a subversive manner, oftentimes they participate in standard protocols, living quite normally without drawing attention to themselves. What makes social tricksters unlike others is the possibility that they may slip into one of their antics at any moment, even in the middle of a most discreet setting. Because of this ever-present possibility, we keep an eye on them. In the context of our intercultural dialogue, wherein we share common beliefs and models of moral behavior, we would not expect dirty and dangerous disruptions. But because many of our discussions centered around Letao, and because Kometo was himself a clever trickster, over time we developed a joking relationship in which we could slide back and forth between the most serious and jovial. The occasional profane (*ttoon*)[1] dialogues and stories characteristically marked and accentuated a shared sense of the sacred (*kkwōjarjar*). Letao the trickster illuminates the potency of the sacred and often facilitates bringing about the numinous, paradoxically through the vulgar and profane. At this point in riM̧ajeļ history, any attempt to disentangle Indigenous sensibilities of the sacred and profane from Christianity will not only prove futile, but also ignores how our dialogues took shape in the interplay of the pure and venerable with the dangerous and forbidden (cf. Douglas 1966).

In the last decade and half of his life, Kometo was a devout Mormon. He served as an "Elder" in the church and occupied positions of leadership in the local congregation. Even though the membership knew about his "trickster ways" and anticipated that he would often assume the role of a clown in public performances, they also knew that he was a gifted orator, knowledgeable about theology, and sincere in his devotion. When Kometo humbly displayed his sentiments in "bearing testimony," the congregation was sympathetically moved. Our lives were intimately intertwined in this context. We had become bonded friends years before during my voluntary missionary service, not long after his religious conversion. We took some risks then, but not many, as my structural role in the community expected a different kind of decorum. In any event, we found a connection through our joking and mutual effort to create positive camaraderie.

Even with the overlap of our religious commitments, to the end of our conversations Kometo continued to take risks to explore the possibilities that come with considering a little dirt. I sensed that he recognized that the sacred requires the profane for definition. That perhaps the greatest danger is not a little dirtiness here and there, but the denial of it, which would lead to ignorance and possibly leave one in the most vulnerable position without any ability for discernment. Kometo did not celebrate the profane for its own sake, and anybody who proved perpetually irreverent annoyed him. He saw them as culturally, intellectually, and religiously shallow. But conversely, he did not appreciate religious arrogance, and always called people on their dogmatism and hypocrisy, usually through a joke. In my company, trickster myths and cunning discourses represented the primary forms that structured our interactions. Such forms seemed most appropriate to the ambiguity of our ethnographic friendship. They allowed us to explore the uncertain margins along the sacred and profane. And still, this required some risk as wedding these things often proved precarious and obliged us to enter into some impudent and audacious topics. We brought "together what is normally separate" to "disrupt systems of classification that underlie the social order" and to "turn the social and cosmological order upside down, eliciting all the emotions of humor" (Stoeltje 2014, 106). In this chapter, I will present moments when we took some dialogic risks that were "saturated with potential for the unexpected; for combinations of the incongruous … risk, reversal, and sometimes danger" (Stoeltje 2014, 106). Speaking about such matters heightened a sense of liminality as it clouded the boundaries between insider and outsider, indigeneity and Christianity, appearance and reality, the sacred and profane. Because he wished to probe these illusory oppositions, I came to admire even more Kometo's deep sense of spiritual and religious commitment.

Breaching the Bodily Boundaries

Talk and performances about the "lower bodily stratum" typically oppose the serious tone of a religious hierarchy (Bakhtin 1968). Such behaviors fall outside a church and religiosity, and can provide a temporary liberation from its strictures. Breaching the bodily boundaries and laughter at such trespasses simultaneously serves a subversive role as it may also give life to the social body. In riM̧ajeḷ society, Letao provides the license for entertaining the bodily profane, and laughter at his irreverent and sexual antics simultaneously subverts and renews (cf. Carucci 1986). In a world of imperfections (Hyde 1998), tricksters like Letao remind of us of the disorder that lies in the cracks of the social and physical body. They may also provide personal and collective catharsis, and refresh culture with creative new possibilities (Turner 1982). Letao and social tricksters in the Marshall Islands occupy an ambivalent position; they are at once dangerous, while also necessary and advantageous. But within our conversations, the rules of cross-cultural engagement on topics such as the lower bodily stratum become strained as each side seeks to apprehend the norms and boundaries by which the other operates. The riM̧ajeḷ are fully aware that outsiders may read their performances of Letao tricks as totally unbecoming of Christians, as indicated by their quick glances at outsiders to detect their responses, and reflect on themselves being watched and judged. But they have grown used to looks of disdain or confusion, and freely participate anyway in culturally germane contexts that create surprise and pleasure.

The dialogue below with Kometo and M̧ake rehearses a time when Kometo enacted the part of a clown in a church celebration. The Christmas festival (*Kūrijmōj*) in the Marshall Islands involves a two- to three-month preparation of songs and dances (*al* and *biit*) to be performed on Christmas day accompanied by a great feast. This celebration lasts the whole of Christmas day. During the preparation period, "competing" groups (*jebta*) conduct surprise attacks (*iaboñ*) on each other in which they "duel" with songs and gifts of food. During these "raids," performers take liberties to mock and tease each other, often with innuendo and romantic taunts. This play may include dousing high-ranking individuals with powder to make them appear old or, conversely, baby-like, and with perfume to make them romantically enticing. The whole celebration of social structural inversions may seem out of place with a reserved Christianity, yet Laurence Carucci (1988, 1997a) has shown how this festival draws upon the Indigenous fertility deity (Jebro) embodied in the constellation Pleiades, which corresponds with the Christmas season and Christ, the god who overcomes death and represents the giver of life. During one of the surprise attacks coordinated to take place in the social hall at the church building between two of its congregations, Kometo assumed the role of the clown whom several younger women "attacked," mocked, and taunted as a "desirable lover," including many of his taboo (*mo̧*) relatives.[2] At these events, called the *kam̧ōļo* (to make cool, or happy), customary prohibitions are temporarily suspended and liberties taken that in any other context would be seriously condemned. Here we rehearse what happened to Kometo.[3]

M   If you then act falsely at the *kam̧ōļo* during Christmas time, it's ignored. <laughs>

P   So, at the *kam̧ōļo* time, people can cause mischief?

M   <chuckling> Yes.

P   I remember a *kam̧ōļo* at the Mormon Church. <K chuckles> They really, what's it called? Covered that old man (referring to K) with perfume. /

M   /Yes, yes. Oh, that man? Yes, yes. <I'm laughing> It's a riM̧ajeļ custom now.

P   They spray perfume in his face and eyes, and he is really blind. <K laughs> And hug and kiss him.

M   Yes.

P   And, the women danced (*eb*) around him, flirted (*katoojoj*) with him, and lifted <I laugh, can hardly speak, all laugh hard> his trousers, high to here <point to above knee> . . . anoint his legs with coconut oil. <lots of chuckles> Do you remember? <K waves me off, hard laughter at K's gesture> He doesn't forget . . . <all laughing> I took a picture of this.

K   <laughs in intense high pitch> You took a picture? Oh jeez, that's just awful!
P   It will be in my book about Letao. <all laughing really hard> It will appear—
      to all the Americans. <all still laughing> They will see the face of Letao
      <can hardly be heard with all the laughter> and also the sexy leg of Letao.
      <hard laughter continues>
M   <laughing> You took a picture so that they understand, good.
K   Oh jeez! <laughter by all>

Here we recall when Kometo performed the clown and even "desirable lover" in the celebration at the church, and we all joke about his role and how I will expose him as the trickster in my own book with the photos I took. I never imagined I would actually write a book about Letao, but this joking felt right in the moment as we teased him. The community well recognized his role as trickster and clown.

In addition to performing the role of the trickster clown, Kometo would take discursive risks. The grotesque of the lower bodily stratum can also break frame when employed in everyday discourse. In the following dialogue, Kometo completely upended the frame to create an awkward moment for the others participating with us.[4] The risk he takes to talk about something "dirty" generates a great deal of intercultural reflexivity, as much for those listening in as for the two of us. The conversation took place at M̧ake's one-room house and included Kometo, M̧ake, and Neibōj,[5] his wife, working on handicrafts on the other side of the room. She acts as if she is not listening, but at certain junctures she makes a comment or laughs. I had asked these elders some serious questions about kinship and matrilines when I suddenly sneezed. (N designates Neibōj in the dialogue)

P   <sneeze> Excuse me. My manners are really bad. <they all chuckle>
K   Why? Since when we do it, it makes health?
P   *Gesundheit,* a word from the Germans.
M   Mmm.
P   I don't know the meaning of the German word.
K   <laughs> Well, is that kind of thing prohibited?
M   Sneeze, cough, and . . . you see in the times of gathering you don't do this
      kind of thing—make this kind of thing.
K   Why is that man?
P   <chuckles> If people sneeze, another will say, [in English] *"God bless you."*
M   Mmm.
P   [translate to Kajin M̧ajeļ] *"Anij en kajeraam̧m̧an eok."*

M   Yes.

K   <laughs> If he sneezes we say, "God bless you"?

P   A custom from long, long ago. People don't know the reason.

K   <laughing> Oh jeez.

P   And it's true what M̧ake says, if in a gathering, it's inappropriate to sneeze and cough in front of people without covering your nose and mouth.

K   What is the reason for this? Because it was from his mouth? So, a fart is good?

P   What is good?

K   A fart is good? <all laugh hard, especially N>

P   Worst of all. <all laugh>

K   <laughs hard to cough> If one farts in front of others does it really break the American custom?

P   Also farting. <all laugh hard> Also with the riM̧ajeḷ?

K   <laughing> Well, the riM̧ajeḷ are really the kind of—<tapers off laughing>

P   I heard a story, from maybe Ānewetak. A chief farted in front of people/

M   /Mmm. /

P   /and he kills himself because he was really embarrassed.

M   This story is also in Epoon.

P   <K still laughing, N laughing hard> What is the word for the thing when a person, "eegh," from there? <points to throat> Remind me the word in Kajin M̧ajeḷ?

M   *M̧aje.* [sneeze]

N   No, *wūlik* [burp].

K   Burp.

M   Yes. Yes.

P   Is a burp also bad?

N   A burp is also bad./

M   /It's also bad.

K   It's not. Eh, all things that give life are good. <everyone laughs intensely, high pitch from N and K>

P   You are really being mischievous? <K sustains wheezing laugh>

M   The man is really bad.

K   If I meet with my family, see? If I want to cough, I cough. If I want to burp, I burp.

P   So coughing and sneezing, they are not bad with the riM̧ajeḷ, yea?

M   They are not bad. /

K   /They are not bad.

P   So, to say, "excuse me" is not important?

K   If I want to fart, I fart. <all laugh hard, N in shrill tone>

M   There you go, just he alone is bad. <we all continue to laugh> He grew up in
       Epoon. <keeps laughing>
P   <laughing> He wasn't a mischievous person then?
M   He is a really mischievous man.
K   <still laughing hardest> No, but—<laughs>
P   Is he being Etao?
M   Eh. The man is like Letao. <all laughing hard, K coughs, M chuckling
       hard>
K   It itches. Why . . . what is the reason it's prohibited? These things give life to
       my body.
P   <laughing> It's not bad, but it's bad in front of people.
M   Yes. Yes. It's bad in front of people. <N laughs>
P   Only by yourself is it good. <K still laughing>
M   You know it's a bad custom with the riM̧ajeḷ. It's really bad. <K still laugh-
       ing> You know the story about the man of Epoon?

Long ago.
They are meeting, the lineage heads and chiefs.
And a chief, he feeds all of them.
And, the man brought food together and distributed the food. (mmm)
And, he distributes it, "there is your food there, your food there, and your
food there."
He goes on and on, and the man turns and he farts. <K laughs>
He stops distributing the food and goes ocean-ward, hurries to the middle of
the islet.
Goes—

And you see the coconut, you can hold it, the husk? After nearly a month
followed by another month, it becomes really dry and hard. Its skin is hard.
The name of that thing is *bweo.* It's like a sharp coconut husk. But the front
of the coconut husk that you hold, it is not sharp, see?

The woman says, "You have done a wrong.
You don't know the custom.
For what reason did you say 'iririri'?" <K chuckling>
All of them there tear at him with the bweo and all his intestines . . .
<signals falling from stomach>

P   His stomach is cut open and falls out? He dies?
M   And all of his stomach . . . eh. <I chuckle, M laughs, speaks to K> I say to
       you, you don't know. <speaks to me> He doesn't know the custom.

K   <laughs, chuckles, chokes, we all laugh with him> The thing is good, but you say, "Excuse me." I say, "What is the reason to excuse me man?"

P   The Americans say, "Excuse me."

K   Yes, but the thing is good since it gives life. <chuckles> If there is a sneeze, now life is good. Well, what is the reason to excuse me when it brings life? <quiet pause, then he laughs> That it's bad? That point is mistaken.

P   I don't know the reason a fart is bad. <K laughs hard> It smells bad? <they all laugh hard> Perhaps coughing and sneezing are not really that bad.

K   They are not; they are really good.

P   But farting is bad. <K laughs hard> It destroys the air. <we laugh>

M   Kometo says, "It's good."

K   Well, my stomach is lighter, my sickness runs away. <much laughter by all>

P   It's not fragrant. <we laugh hard, M laughs to a mumble> It's not like a flower. <we continue laughing>

M   Is that thing running? <everyone looks at tape recorder>

P   Yes. <everyone including N laugh to point of crying>

M   Ah, man.

P   <laughing> Perhaps only I am to listen? <we laugh hard> No, I will give this tape to a chief. <we all continue laughing hard, K to the point of coughing>

M   Eh, eh.

K   <stops laughing> In these islands, it's also good for a chief to do the same.

P   If I listen to it in America, I will laugh.

M   Yes. <K chuckles> The Americans will really laugh over there. When you explain it, you just say Letao is over there in the Marshalls. <we all laugh>

In this hilarious interchange, Kometo exploits the bodily functions, especially those of the lower stratum, to create a message that celebrates life by subverting riMajeļ and American manners and the very nature of dialogue itself. This little scene represents a "social drama," (Turner 1982) but one with very little consequence other than managing our *personas* within the interaction. I made what I thought was a social breach; that is, I sneezed in the company of others and promptly drew upon my own tradition to excuse myself. Such social interactions, and certainly where there is a breach in relations, no matter how mundane, represent an intertextual link to previous social performances. I drew from my stock formula an appropriate ritual phrase to "redress" the breach and translated it into Kajin Majeļ. This gesture, however, provides Kometo with the opportunity to bring the cultural resource into question, undermine my attempts at redressive action, and then maintain the "crisis" by furthering the social breach himself through his teasing antics about bodily functions. In part, he directs this subversive trickster work toward me, my protocols, traditions, and sense of social propriety. It represents a risk in that he brings forth some abject talk about flatulence, a taboo subject not only among most congregants, but also the riM̧ajeḷ generally. But this scene represents more of a performance with me for the others present, M̧ake and Neibōj. He shows them how far he and I have come as intercultural jokers, and that the risks we take with each other reveal the contour of our relationship. This recognition is a highly reflexive double performance; he is aware of himself being watched performing for me, much like a play within the play. And I watch him perform for me to the others. With this awareness, I collude with him in risk-taking. M̧ake and Neibōj also play their parts well; M̧ake represents the decorum of both the riM̧ajeḷ and American manners, and Neibōj provides the gauge through her laughter for true subversion as she sits in pretend aloofness. Still, M̧ake cannot help but laugh while deploying perfunctory criticisms of Kometo's behavior.

After I excuse myself, Kometo brings this gesture into question and inserts the theme about health and life, which will guide his mischievous game through the remainder of the dialogue. His challenge of my redressive action accentuates the social crisis. Even though the crisis corresponds to a small social breach in an ongoing conversation, it nonetheless generates the ritual action of a microdrama. But the trickster will not let the drama unfold in its anticipated structural pattern, he challenges the structure itself by manipulating the efficaciousness of the ritual and by dismissing the expectations of social manners. He insists that M̧ake and Neibōj participate in this game, and that we all assume a degree of intercultural accountability by revealing our respective traditions.

Once Kometo questions the merits of excusing oneself for sneezing, I enter into an explanation of colloquial sayings, rationalizing my actions in terms of a broader Western tradition. M̧ake intimates that he knows my tradition while Kometo seeks to question it. Kometo's interrogatives do not seek to gain understanding—he actually understands the tradition—but rather undermine it, detecting an inconsistency. First, he asks me if my tradition prohibits sneezing, using the same Kajin M̧ajeḷ word (*mo̧*) as would be used to indicate prohibitions around a chief or to avoid incest. M̧ake supports me by substantiating his own understanding of the customary practice, that in a public gathering such manners are inappropriate without gestures to cover one's nose or mouth. Kometo asks again why. I do not answer his question, but instead provide the response to the excuser, "God bless you," the polite response. Again, M̧ake emphatically concurs, but Kometo will have none of it. Why should God bless us for a sneeze? I want to just chalk it up to tradition, something the riM̧ajeḷ will do when a custom cannot be explained: they will claim, "Thus it is according to custom"

(*Āindein ekkar ñan m̧anit*). He challenges this as absurd with "Oh, Jeez." His tone becomes clearly sardonic. I support M̧ake's description of the custom and use him as a prop. But then Kometo takes it to the next level. If something coming out of the mouth is bad for the Americans, then something coming out of the rear-end could be conversely good. Of course, he is being sarcastic here to create the inversion.

With this, the building social breach reaches its peak. Up to this point, he simply challenges the custom's merit, but once he elicits the word for "fart" (*jiñ*) we all laugh intensely, and especially Neibōj. We give jokers license to make such breaches, but still, in doing so, they bring to view the cultural architecture of social decorum. Up to this point, Neibōj has remained silent. But when Kometo speaks of flatulation as something good, she can contain herself no longer. To utter such words in a mixed-gender context seriously breaks a riM̧ajeļ prohibition. He has crossed the line. By moving from the upper bodily stratum orifice (mouth) to the lower stratum (anus), he has reduced custom to the most coarse and profane. We meet this inversion with great laughter, partly because we cannot believe he has said this, and partly because he has opened up indecent things for overt consideration. Now this could prove a dangerous social move, yet Kometo manages his *persona* as an old man and trickster by claiming certain privileges to talk of such debase things.

Through his next rhetorical question about American custom, he foregrounds my tradition and juxtaposes it to the riM̧aje ļ. I think he intends to make the case that the riM̧aje ļ do not have such scruples about farting in public. But I challenge him by referencing a story I had heard on another atoll in which a chief takes his own life after he humiliates himself by flatulating in public. When I argue that the riM̧aje ļ tradition also prohibits such behavior, M̧ake picks up on this thread to connect it with a story that he knows from their shared atoll, Epoon. At this point, Kometo and Neibōj continue to laugh together. Her laughter at once acknowledges Kometo's words as a significant breach, and serves the implicit role of encouraging him to carry on with the social disruption. I ask about burps, as I had momentarily forgotten the word, to see what they will say about it in terms of manners. M̧ake concurs that it too is "bad" or offensive, and Neibōj corrects for the accurate Kajin M̧aje ļ term and confirms its inappropriateness. This is one of the only two times she speaks in this segment of the dialogue.

Kometo disagrees with the three of us. He continues to argue that anything that brings life is good. The very intense mutual laughter of the deepest and most visceral kind becomes the apex of the hilarity and physical intensity. Life and laughter mutually generate each other. Kometo uses something profane and dirty—risky to the social setting—to bring forth the principle of renewal, a trick-ster's trick. Bodies are good. That which comes from bodies sustains life. Cultural prohibitions keep all these ruptures in check and prohibit life. I know he is bait-ing us and call him "mischievous," the same term applied to Letao and anyone who causes mischief like him. M̧ake concurs. This censure characterizes less a grand declarative about Kometo as a person and more a statement that acknowl-edges his Letao-like actions, and ironically eggs him on. He next creates a hypo-thetical situation among family where he can do such things if he likes. I then seek to understand the range and limits of the bodily boundaries and orifices, and find that sneezing and coughing are not really bad. So, when I seek to sub-stantiate that I need not say, "excuse me" (jo̧ļo̧k aō bōd, which literally means "throw away my wrong"), Kometo disrupts my objection to carry on with his list of things he can do if he wants to, including flatulation. Again, we cannot con-tain our laughter and Neibōj laughs in a shrill fashion, near the point of a scream.

By this point, Kometo has established himself outside all tradition; both the action of public flatulation and talking about it places him outside the margins of social propriety. In doing so, he forces us to face our traditions and recognize the possibility that customs are more contingent than necessary. M̧ake and Neibōj appear sensitive to how I will take all of Kometo's play. Neibōj laughs out of embarrassment and M̧ake laughs to acknowledge Kometo as a troublemaking trickster. He tries to rescue us from this low point by breaking into a story from Epoon. This narrative provides a parallel reference I made to the chief flatulating earlier and it provides the intertext that elicits M̧ake's story. He does not develop the narrative very far. The man he describes also farts, apparently during the formal distribution of foods at a ceremonial event. We may infer from this that he was also a high-ranking person performing ceremonial distribution for a chief. This would be a significant social breach in public, so by using this narra-tive, M̧ake simultaneously makes a commentary on the violation and the discus-sion we are having with Kometo. The man in the story runs off to the middle of the islet. M̧ake makes an aside to describe for me the instrument from the coco-nut husk that will be used to impale the custom breaker. He then returns to his narrative through the reported speech of a woman, likely the female chief and perhaps even the sister that challenges the man's impropriety. This verbal exchange is followed by a violent killing by disembowelment. The harshness and violence of this story, which leads to death, is strangely juxtaposed to Kometo's claim that the same action, an offense to others, actually enhances life. After his story, M̧ake challenges Kometo on his knowledge of appropriate customs, and then turns to me seeking to confirm his point and reestablish the merits of tradition.

At this point Kometo cannot quit. The hilarity has continued after the somber story, and in fact, now the story seems a bit excessive and kind of comical. When I seek to rationalize custom again, he brings forth the matter of renewing life. Why would we ever need an excuse for life? By reinvoking the life principle directly, he challenges the death allusion created in M̧ake's story and reaffirms how renewal may come by dismantling tradition. As M̧ake seeks to show the complementariness between American and riM̧ajeļ customs, Kometo seeks to disentangle the superficial comparison between cultures to establish a human commonality rooted in body. In this setting, Kometo takes a risk to joke about profane things in front of M̧ake and Neibōj. They are somewhat embarrassed, especially due to my presence, both in terms of their riM̧ajeļ protocols as well as those they accept through Protestantism. As they watch me watch him to see what my response will be, Kometo challenges culture on all fronts and opens the door for a different kind of communion.

I must have sensed Kometo seeking for me to collude with him in challenging social strictures because I then become a joker myself good-humoredly suggesting that flatulation is bad because of the smell and how it "destroys the air." The others, and especially Kometo, enjoy this and laugh hard. I am now a trickster, too, which undermines all of M̧ake's efforts. Kometo and I then play off each other, doing a one-upmanship with our jokes. The others cannot help but join with laughter, but M̧ake remains uneasy; he asks if my tape recorder is running. When I say yes, everyone laughs as intensely as ever. Some of this laughter comes with the unease that we may not be able to manage the impressions of others. We will be exposed for our participation with the trickster regarding profane things. This realization marks a profoundly reflexive moment in the dialogue; we are now aware of ourselves as performers, and in our own little social drama, we may be accountable to future audiences not even present.

When Kometo performs to me for the others, and then I perform with him to them, the layers of audience become acute. But when we anticipate that we will be scrutinized and judged by future audiences, we are forced as a group to recognize our mutual performance. Are we comfortable with the accountability we have assumed? I briefly promise to keep it to myself, but quickly turn this into my own subversive joke, that I will expose Kometo to a chief. He enjoys this immensely and laughs at himself and at us. But so what? The chiefs, he contends, are just like us, they too live in bodies. The realities of bodies levels social power. When I talk about listening to the recording in America, M̧ake anxiously submits that the Americans will laugh at them. He recommends I tell the Americans how Kometo is behind all this as he seeks to distance himself from the trickster. In Victor Turner's social dramaturgical model, once the rituals of redressive actions are made to remedy the crisis generated through the breach, we either come to social reintegration or schism. Kometo's relationship to me did not come apart with this little conversational game of dirty talk, nor do I think his relationship with M̧ake and Neibōj changed. If anything, their impressions of me may have been altered. Instead, Kometo achieves not so much a reintegration as a lasting integration of the two of us. We came together as liminal figures exploiting the ambiguities of our ethnographic encounter, reconfirmed our mutual humanity, and through tainted talk, established a trust to consider such sensitive things. We had performed together, and played with possibilities about bodies and life. We pushed the margins of pious acceptability, yes, but by extending the trickster's metaphor of celebrating the body, we minimized cultural difference.

Incest and the Trickster's Libido

Letao's enormous libido is axiomatic. Like all tricksters, in addition to his hunger, his unbridled appetites and hyper-sexuality drive his wandering and creative work (Radin 1958; Hyde 1998). His lasciviousness violates boundaries, and in the process defines that order. This "tolerated margin of mess" (Babcock 1975) presented in story and dramatic ritual actually serves to bring the social order into existence; only when the rule is violated does one understand its structure, much like the biblical Adam and Eve (Eco 1976). These violations of the order usually lie within the narrated event of the text or are enacted through ritual or dramatic performance. My interest here, however, is in how the violation and messiness expressed in the narrated event may trespass role expectations in the intercultural narrative event. To recontextualize a "dirty" narrative into our conversations, Kometo had to take some risks in terms of the management of his *persona,* both as a riM̧ajeļ elder and practicing Mormon. All friendships require some risk-taking to develop beyond superficial social familiarities. Yet Kometo also recognized the complexity of impression management in this kind of social theater (Goffman 1959). To discuss Letao's role in sexuality requires some risk, not only because of his culturally subversive actions, but also because it draws attention to culture itself and the possibility of embarrassment to one's own traditions. Sometimes we may hesitate, and withhold stories in a cross-cultural setting, to avoid potentially offending or giving an unfavorable impression. Much interpersonal, and especially intercultural talk, entails working out the slippage between appearance and reality. When our discussions turned to Letao's sexual exploits, Kometo would hedge about their truth, and in doing so reveal the ambiguity between what is and what is said (Barnes 1994).

The following dialogue, in which Kometo embedded a mythic narrative about Letao's profane behavior, required risk-taking by both of us, certainly more so for him than for me. Yet telling such "lies" requires collusion; each of us contributes by drawing upon our discursive resources (Bauman 1986). I had heard about Letao committing incest (*kōpa*)[6] with his mother from others who would not, either out of limited knowledge or social propriety, provide the full myth. My purpose for asking was to round out my understanding of Letao's primordial actions. Because tricksters are often identified as the harbingers of human sexuality, I wanted to unpack Letao's role in riM̧ajeḷ procreative mythic origins. riM̧ajeḷ abhorrence of incest is clearly marked in everyday discourse and behavior, yet here in this story, like so often, sexuality and procreation begin through an incestuous union. I thought no one better than Kometo could shed some light on this for me. I did not expect, but I should have, that he would invoke the salacious myth to generate hilarity and uncertainty in the ethnographic dialogue.[7] The identification of the "toy" is a reference to the vagina.

P   I heard about a story when Letao committed incest with his mother.[8]
K   <pause> I don't know if it is true, but thus they told the story. <I chuckle, he chuckles> It says before—<clears throat>

There is nothing there with a woman. (oh)

Before there was nothing.

Then, Letao has a toy, a particular kind of plaything.

P   A toy of Letao?
K   Mmm, the toy object. An instrument he can use. <chuckles>

They say this kind of thing is just like those butterflies.

You know that butterfly, it flies and . . . it pleases children. It is about that long <thumb and finger three inches apart> and it likes to fly.
P   Butterfly, hmm.

K   *He places it in the upper story of his hut.*

<notes confusion in my face> The upper story (*po*). Just like up there above in a house. <points toward rafters> Because in the days long ago, see? Those

men do not sleep on the ground. Their mothers sleep below on the ground.
Only those men sleep in the upper story.

P   Oh, ok it's clear. I saw pictures of this.

K   *The toy thing of the man is in the upper story.*
Now, he goes and—
He goes and just plays with it oooo and keeps coming back.
He uses his plaything.
He says,"Kakkabiebojāje." [nonsense syllables]<laughs hard>
It is up above.
Really a lot of times.
He comes again.
Then, he exits, he leaves again.

His mother says, "What, what is the reason Letao goes there every time he comes home?
He does not eat, but just goes straight over there."
His mother then goes to the thing, she sees it, she sees the toy.
Then, she takes it.
Takes it and places it on her head, and the thing touches her head.
Then, they say, "The reason that there is so much head hair is because of that thing."
<pause>

P   Why to the head?
K   Well, since his mother did not have head hair.
P   There was none?
K   Thus, is this story. I don't know if it's true! <laughs>
P   Oh, ok. I just want to understand the story. It's clear now.

K   *Then—Now, there is much hair on the head of people.*
Then, she sees Letao coming.
She says, "Where will I put it?"
She places it under her arm. (oh) <laughs briefly>
After that there is hair under the arms of people. <laughs>
After placing it in her armpit, she looks, and sees him still coming.
She says, "Mmm, Letao will see it."
Then, she says, "Ah, where can I put it?"
She just hides it inside of there. <points to crotch>[9]
Hides it in there . . . and covers it with her clothing.

Now, because she hid it there, that thing has really black hair. <brief chuckle>
(hmm)

Letao then comes and climbs up to get the plaything.
When he reaches for it, it's gone. <laughs>
He says, "MOTHER OOOO.
WHERE IS MY TOY?" <laughs>
"WHAT MY CHILD?
"WHERE IS IT?"
I DON'T KNOW." <laughs hard, I do too>
She has stolen it. <we laugh hard>

A story, I don't know, is it true?

P   I don't know.

K   <small laugh> *Then, he looks for it, he says, "Well, it is with my mother."*
Then, on another day.
He says, "MOTHER COME HERE!"
He comes and piles up the sticks—

You see?

He rubs them and makes fire.
"Come and warm up so that we two can make our fire."
Then, his mother comes over by him and he rubs the sticks.
<rubs hands back and forth>
His mother sits on the sticks for the fire.
They say, "It makes fire."
He rubs, rubs the sticks to make fire. <pauses, smiling at me>

P   Okay. I get it.

K   *Letao was just {gone a long time, he comes} again and just smells it.*
Now, men have beards. <laughs, pauses, I laugh hard with him>

P   Now, why do men have beards?

K   *Because Letao just* <sniffs> *it there.* <points to crotch>
Just kisses it.

P   Oh! <we laugh hard> Oh Letao.
K   Thus they say, but I think it's a lie, but thus they spoke.
P   Oh yes. Well, then what?
K   Then, this is the reason a lot of beards have come to men, it's from the but-
     terfly. <he laughs>
P   Becasue he kisses the butterfly?
K   <laughing hard> He kisses it. <we laugh>

Now, he comes—he wants to use his tight plaything.
But his mother has taken it and possesses it. <chuckles>
He says, "Ok I'll await for my mother to sleep."
<long pause>
Oh, his mother is working husking coconuts.

Long ago there was no clothing there underneath, there were only two
pieces of matting. One in front and one in back. (uh huh)

His mother stands, but aways off.
His earthworm, <about to laugh> he pokes it down under the ground.
And he makes it longer. <K laughs>
He makes it longer.
Mmm, makes it longer over to his mother.

P   Where is his mother?

K   *She stands outside husking coconuts.*
     And, as the thing does it to her . . . his mother, now, she really—
     His mother then starts to really move about.

     <laughing> Like what?

     His mother dances—<we laugh>

P   Now, how is that?
K   You know, she likes it, we say—<rubs hands, we laugh hard>

     She's pleased. <high pitch laughter>
     His thing goes and enters her . . .
     <can barely talk with laughter>*That butterfly there with her.*

He digs down under the earth.
It reaches over to her and does that with his mother.

P   And his thing appeared out of the ground?
K   Eh, to that toy Etao created. <we laugh hard>
P   It's clear now. <more hard laughter> This story is really comical.
     <we keep laughing hard>
K   <he can hardly talk> Don't you laugh since you wanted me to repeat this
     story! <we keep laughing>

His mother is really—<breaks off laughing> She just stands and dances.

     See? <hard laugh> And you see long ago? It was prophibited for a woman to
     do such.
P   Move like that?
K   Yes. It is prohibited for the woman to move like that and just dance if there
     are several sons outside. These days, the children of today, and women of
     today, they dance anywhere.
P   Oh, so the movements of Letao's mother is like dancing?
K   Like dancing.
P   What is the name of the dance?
K   <chuckles> I don't know the name of the dance, well, I don't know its name.
P   Oh well.
K   I only know when Letao dug his earthworm down under the ground and
     made it appear under his mother and he did it with her.
P   But where was Letao when he dug?/
K   /He was inside the house.
P   So, the earthworm was really long?
K   <u>Long</u>. <we laugh again>
P   Then what happened?
K   Well, that is it.

They say, "He committed incest with his mother." (mmm)

     Here is the reason, because his mother stole his plaything.
P   Mmm. Letao acquired his toy from where?
K   Maybe he made it.
P   Well, if there is nothing there with a woman before, how was Letao born
     from his mother?

K   I don't know, since I asked the same thing? Then, they say, "Thus, is the
      story." It's a lie. <we laugh>

Before discussing this performance within the dialogic narrative event, some
points about the manifest content of the story need elucidation. The narrated
event is clearly situated in the primordial beginnings before the world as we
know it today, at the time the orders of existence were still emerging. Such an
incestuous relation will become utterly prohibited afterward in riMṃajeḷ society
(cf. Radin 1965; Benedict 1934). "The trickster's actions . . . have social value simply because they would be placed against social values as they exist outside the
narrative" (Scheub 2012, 11). In this mythic time, Letao creates the vagina (*kōd*),
referred to as his "toy," and it appears like a butterfly (*babbūb*). The similarity of
a butterfly shape to female genitalia in appearance is evident, and that it also
serves as his "plaything" intimates a sense of male sexual entitlement. When in
the narrated event Letao refers to the "plaything" in reported speech, he uses the
first-person singular possessive. This signals that he is the possessor of the butterfly and suggests that he is "entitled" to his toy. This sense of male possession in
the myth, however, contrasts with actual gender conceptualizations in riMṃajeḷ
society; that is, men do not "possess" women. In fact, it is men who are expend-
able, they simply provide the sperm (*pek*) and their strength (*kajoor*) to the
matriline, who then takes possession of it.

Then curious about why Letao spends so much time with his toy, his mother
retrieves it from its hiding place in his absence. About to be caught with it upon
his return, she tries to hide it, first on her head, then under her arm, then eventually between her legs. Letao seeks to expose her deception (trying to trick a trickster may prove dangerous) for his own gratification. While she works outside, he
commits incest with her by extending his penis (*wōl*) down under the ground to
reach her. This Indigenous myth explains the origin of vaginas and body hair
(head, armpit, pubic, facial), and initiates sexual relations. Up to this point in the
cosmogonic mythology, primordial beings have been asexually generated. It also
alludes to an important dance movement. Because his mother took pleasure in
this activity, she responds by performing the movement called *jibadbad,* which
comprises "a slight spreading of the legs and a forward movement of the pelvis to
expose the genital area" (Carucci 1986, 169). This copulative gesturing is encoded
in some Indigenous riMṃajeḷ dances. Despite early missionary efforts to prohibit
them, these gestures are still used in several kinds of performances, especially
those in which Letao actions become manifest in mockery and buffoonery, such
as the time described previously when Kometo was teased at the *kamṃōlo* celebration. Kometo does not elaborate on the actual gesture and cannot give its name

(I wondered if he would corroborate the term Carucci identified), but he does clearly articulate that the gesture is risqué because of the prohibition of performing it before male relatives. In any event, by committing incest with his mother, Letao does not so much break taboo (*mọ*), as establish it, and his mother's movements comprise the gestures that subsequently are wholly inappropriate among mothers and sons and cross-sex siblings. Through this myth, the prohibited behavior is presented first, which then marks off appropriate social behavior to be followed.

This narrative exhibits an important intertextual link to another Indigenous mythic story about how the trickster's deception and indulgent libido introduces sexuality to humans (Erdland 1914). After creating the vagina, Letao initiates conjugal relations by outwitting an ignorant man who looks up his wife's skirt as she climbs a pandanus tree only to see her red labia and believe she has been severely cut. When she comes down, she too finds for the first time her "damage." Letao advises the man to go far across the atoll to obtain medicine to heal his wife. While he is away, Letao has sexual intercourse with the woman, who consequently can now introduce it to humankind.[10] Until Kometo shared with me the mythic narrative of Letao's incest with his mother, I had only heard passing references to this story and the one about the duped husband. Clearly, the stories are known, but they comprise something guarded by the social propriety of intergender relations among relatives. And due to Christian sensibilities and scruples about public discourses on sexuality, these narratives cannot be found in contemporary collections and education resources. Nevertheless, Kometo not only presents the incest narrative, but using this myth he also turns our dialogue into a game that heightens the enigma of truth and lies as well as the boundary along the margins of the sacred and profane.

Within the dialogic moment of the narrative event, after I reference the myth, Kometo immediately makes a disclaimer about the story's truth status; he does not know if it is true. As a result, from the beginning he has framed the narrated event in terms of doubt and displaces its status, "thus they told the story," the "they" referring to the ancestors. As explicated in chapter 2, attributing the myth to the ancestors is less a means of substantiating the truth than a method to reduce the commitment the narrator must take toward it. "This is what they say," but "we don't know." It also provides a rhetorical tool to distance his Christian/Mormon beliefs from a non-Christian past, which sets up the frame for the dialogue to come, with its embedded narrative. Kometo then takes a moment to clear his throat, perhaps a reflexive gesture that registers his apprehension about entering such a story. His first narrative line is descriptive (note the present tense) about the absence of female genitalia. He does not use the Kajin M̧ajeļ word for vagina (or for penis either) and will not do so through the remainder of the dialogue and narrative. He will only indirectly reference it, thus avoiding the use of the culturally vulgar term.[11] Even though he will take the risk to present an irreverent narrative, he continues to check himself to be discreet to some extent, and to keep his reference ambiguous. He can acknowledge profanity without himself being overly profane.

He just barely launches into the myth when I pull him out to ask about the word "toy." He uses the Kajin M̧ajel̦ word *nājiū,* which more literally means "my toy (belonging to me)," and is also the same way to express "my child." Only by context can one determine whether it is a child or toy, and in many respects both of them connote things that play or are played with. So, from the outset, Letao's toy corresponds to something that brings satisfaction. He clarifies its use and then describes the toy as being like a butterfly. This creature too is a plaything that children enjoy and presents something colorful and thus desirable. As a metaphor for the vagina, this pleasing object also possesses curves similar to a woman's labia. This description is communicated through natural references without mentioning the culturally prohibited term directly.

After returning to the story, he quickly pauses to clarify a new term for me, a word used to designate the upper story of the traditional riM̧ajel̦ thatch hut. Kometo has clearly placed the story in the past, when such architecture prevailed, which gives him an opportunity to offer an explanation about this historical artifact. Such architecture can no longer be found on the island landscape, but Kometo would have known it from his childhood. The thatch houses constructed today do not have the upper-story loft. Kometo's description provides more than a simple reference to traditional home building; it designates how men and women once slept separately, men above and women below. In riM̧ajel̦ spatial semantics, men are associated with above, they climb trees to harvest and erect thatch buildings, while women are rooted in the ground below, they cook in earth-ovens and provide the connection to the matriline's lands. This arrangement is less a hierarchical reference than an identification of engendered space and the division of labor. Letao places his "toy" in this upper/male space to be away from his mother's space. For her to retrieve the "toy," she must crossover into the male domain. This may prove a misstep equal to the actual theft of the toy.

Once I acknowledge understanding the architecture and engendered spaces, he reenters the narrated event. Letao enjoys his toy, using it for the sensual pleasure that it can provide. Kometo's reported speech, actually nonsense sounds of gratification, makes him laugh hard. This indulgence is something the trickster does "a lot of times." His mother is curious about Letao's intent because he "goes straight over there," skipping his meals. The toy consumes the trickster; he is obsessed with the pleasure it brings. While away, his mother locates the toy, crossing over into the male space. Once in her possession, she places it on her head. From Kometo's narration, this incident seems to lack motivation. I suppose he simply wants to begin showing the series of positions at which the mother places the toy and thus, by the principle of contagion, signal the origin of hair at each respective bodily location. Kometo attributes the explanation of this origin to the "they," the ancestors who told this story. Confused by the stimulus to place it on her head, I ask him, and he boldly disclaims the truth of the myth and communicates his own doubts. He tells me not to try to make rational sense out of this. It is just a story—let it be, and perhaps we will find something out by the end. His laughter at this association accentuates his doubt, or at least reaffirms the ambivalent position he takes toward it. After my apologetic justification, I seek to return us to the story. He picks up where he left off.

The mother again sees Letao coming, and wishing not to be detected she speaks to herself, proposing hiding places and then questioning her own ideas. Kometo's use of reported speech to move this part of the narrated event permits lively action as we witness the actions of the mother. A simple narrated description would not reveal any more clearly the mother's emotional state and motivations. Kometo's use of reported speech proves again one of his greatest performance qualities. Here, once more, he alters his tone in order to communicate a change of speaker, gender, and emotional state. These dialogues within the story come in rapid fire and push the flow of action in the narrated event along quickly. It also reveals an economy of discourse; action and character motivation can be quickly achieved through reported speech. So here, Kometo has the mother place the toy under her armpit, doubt the move, question herself, and then hurriedly seek the last alternative: her crotch. And still, Kometo continues to avoid the profane terminology by indirect reference ("it"), locatives ("inside of there"), and indexical gestures (points to crotch).

Placing the toy at her crotch provides the explanatory origin for pubic hair. That the toy is contagious in terms of hair suggests again how it leaves a residue on anything it touches. The series of hair placements presents the sexualization of hair through association and contiguity. Pubic hair is contiguous to genitals, pubic hair resembles head hair, and head hair identifies gender and refers back to genitalia. In riM̧ajeḷ culture, a woman's head hair constitutes a primary location for communicating desirability. Much attention is directed to the length, texture and grooming of hair as well as to scenting and oiling it to create just the right smell and shine. Such adorning and beautifying of hair indexes sexual attraction most markedly expressed at festival occasions such as the hybridized Christmas

(Kūrijm̧ōj) celebration of renewal and during dance performances (see Carucci 1997, 1986).

Letao then returns home, looks for his toy, finds it missing, and suspects his mother. Kometo performs another series of dialogues through reported speech. When Letao asks for it, his mother claims ignorance. He performs the voices of this exchange in an animated fashion. Our laughter also punctuates this conversation between characters. The idea of Letao looking for his toy is certainly funny, but as I have explored in previous chapters, finding something hidden presents a way to achieve social power over another. Such a detection humiliates the loser and always receives laughter. Letao realizes his mother has taken his toy. We both laugh at this realization, and also at the awareness that we are talking about something profane. This awareness makes Kometo reflexive again and he disclaims for the third time, expressing doubt about the truth status of the myth. The dialogues within the narrated event lead to a reflexive consideration of the conversation we are having in the narrative event. These two events come to bear on each other. The narrated event is assessed within the narrative event, and the narrative event is shaping how he will perform the narrated event. The narrative, especially the portion presented in reported speech, constructs the event as true, whereas the laughter and metanarration in the narrative event question its veracity. Within this discursive friction lies the tension between appearance and reality.

Letao determines his mother has taken the toy—we are let in on this understanding through the reported speech to himself. On "another day," he orders his mother to come to him. Having time transpire suggests that he has been planning. Ordering his mother itself stands as a social breach for the riM̧ajeļ; men do not speak to their mothers in such a commanding fashion. This behavior also foreshadows other offensive acts: he will break all the rules of cross-gender kinship relations. The dialogue and story at this point enter into a scene of rubbing sticks to make fire. The imagery is unmistakably suggestive and the riM̧ajeļ will often (similar to other cultures in the Oceania) refer to sexual intercourse as fire-making. The double entendre in Letao's invitation to warm up and make fire foreshadows the conjugal act, and then his mother intensifies this imagery by sitting on the sticks.

Once I understand the connection created in the narrated event, Kometo narrates Letao smelling the toy on his mother's person. As he tries to enter into this most salacious scene, Kometo hedges a bit, adjusting the tenses between something completed and removed, to something uncompleted and very present. Placing his face contiguous to the genitalia transfers hair from the toy (which has now become very female) to the male. At this point, by intimating oral sex, the story has arrived at a most prurient level. It epitomizes the extent to which the narrator trickster can go. He checks my response to see if I get it, taunting me with pauses to determine whether I follow him, and inviting me to catch the joke. The intense laughter at this point communicates multiple messages: one, a shared recognition of the profane action; two, it references the nervousness we share in arriving at this point in the story. In the midst of this ambivalent yet intense laughter, Kometo disclaims for the fourth time, distancing the content from himself and attributing it to the ancestors ("Thus they say" and "thus they spoke"), but for the first time he moves beyond a doubtful position to a declarative stance about its truth status ("I think it's a lie). In doing so, he disrupts the narrative to minimize its profanity and to absolve himself from its content. He now simply identifies the profane and, despite appearances, he knows what is real. Now, with the "toy" securely part of the trickster's mother, we allude to the metaphors of butterflies and cunnilingus, still avoiding direct reference to any culturally vulgar term.

Letao continues to desire his pleasurable toy, but now that his mother possesses it, he must devise a plan to get to it. He first considers waiting until his mother sleeps (which he corrects after a pause), and then chooses to rape her when she works husking coconuts.[12] To perform this kind of labor, she would have been using the *doon,* a sharp stick forced into the ground. The phallic overtones are clear, and having it come out of the ground provides additional foreshadowing. Kometo breaks away before continuing the story to explain how the pending act will be possible. He briefly describes the traditional matted clothing for women (*ed*),[13] which covered the front and the back with the bottom open. Then he returns to the narrative. His mother stands at a distance and Letao pokes his "earthworm" into the ground and extends it over to her. Kometo continues to use the term "earthworm" to maintain the avoidance of a prohibited term. The reference to the "earthworm" or "eel man" presents an intertextual link to previous conversations (see chapter 5) and he knows I know the reference—that it provides commentary on male desire, and that its source is Letao.

Then, through a sing-song pattern of story and metanarration, Kometo narrates the elongation of Letao's penis down into the earth to come out under his mother, the penetration, and her dance of pleasure. We shift in and out of the narrative as I seek to ensure I understand the actions, and then for the fifth time, Kometo disclaims through a reflexive check returning us to our ethnographic dialogue. My own laughter at this subversive upside-down story brings to his attention that we are mutually involved in this profane scene, and when he tells me not to laugh, and then essentially blames me for getting us into this because I wanted to know the story, he displaces some of the accountability of the telling onto me. Because he has established this mythic narrative as a lie, then I am the one who wants to hear the lie, and I need to be accountable as well. Here, the roles of accountability, that of the performer and audience, turn in on each other so that the narrative and dialogic accomplishment results from a mutual collusion. The narrated event and the narrative event are both farcical and full of uncomfortable topics and images. By calling it a lie, we do not need to accept such profanity as it does not represent reality, we only collaborate in unveiling appearances. We do interactionally what the myth does thematically—reveal the consequences of unchecked male desire.

We spend the remainder of the dialogue trying to cast the myth into some kind of sociological explanation. Kometo first explains and details some about the prohibitions of women dancing in front of male relatives. I seek to corroborate the term for the mother's dance gestures. He cannot supply one. He rehearses the outline of the myth in the past tense (we are fully out of the narrative at this point) by claiming this corresponds to all he knows about it. We joke a little about Letao's ability for phallic shape-shifting. This reconfirms the trickster's sexual prowess and male fantasies about personal endowment projected onto the trickster. Kometo concludes that the mother's theft has led to this unpardonable act. In blaming the woman for the theft, the story faults the woman for male untoward behavior, and by extension, men desire women because what they want was stolen by women. Now that the toy is attached and belongs to the woman, men must go to women to "play." On the surface, these actions cast a negative image upon women, that a male figure created their anatomy and when she obtains it through theft, she becomes the target of male sexual aggression and even rape. But the riM̧ajeļ do not look upon the image of woman negatively, what is more she occupies all the ranked positions of the males, and the men of the lineage will defer to their mothers and sisters. An oft-repeated truism by the riM̧ajeļ, "Women have greater value than men" (*Eļapło̧k an tokjan kōrā jen m̧m̧aan*), identifies how women as mothers are the starting point from which the islanders think about kinship and social relations. Concomitantly, the birth of a girl is celebrated with the proverbial phrase, *iep jāltok* (the woven basket faces toward us, or the blessings are coming our way), whereas when a boy is born it is said, *iep jeļļok* (the woven basket faces away from us, or the blessings are moving away). This expression means that the girl will ultimately provide labor and procreate the matriline, whereas a boy will take both his labor and procreative contribution to his wife's matriline. Female sexuality is also not controlled, and in truth the islanders view it most positively as it regenerates the matriline. Any unwanted male advances are met with strong responses, sometimes violent, by the matrilineal relatives toward the aggressive suitor. This myth, then, appears as an inversion of the riM̧ajel̡ social life as lived (cf. Benedict 1934). To be sure, Letao's conduct is more reproachable; his incestuous actions, rape, and public display epitomize negative social disruptions in terms of both Indigenous tradition and today's Christian proprieties. The key here is that romantic trysts result from deception and trickery, and that even its continuation characterizes a game of hide-and-seek, something I will come to shortly. In this dialogue, Kometo risks more than just telling me a dirty story, but the danger of me not getting it—that the profane has its origin in deception.

We end this interchange with my question about the origin of Letao's toy. I simply want to fill in my understanding. Kometo speculates that perhaps Letao made it himself. At this point, I ask a logical question about the chronology of events—if Letao functions as the source of female genitals, then how could he have been born from his mother? Such a question typifies a Western perspective challenging the mythic with a rational question and looking for epistemological consistency in how the Indigenous myth explains things. I do not believe I was seeking to be overly rationalistic in the moment, but was really attempting a trick on Kometo to see how he would respond. Kometo reveals his own rational modern self with his answer, that he himself had asked the same question of none other than the ancestors. Their answer informs Kometo's answer, "thus is the story," take it as such, it is what it is. And what it is, is a lie, an untruth. With this realization, we laugh in part in relief, in part in agreement, and in part, because after all this, we can only conclude that it signifies a deception. That Kometo defers the truth status of the story onto the ancestors allows him to get out of any obligation to justify it and then side with me. He assumes we agree, and by agreeing that the story is a lie, and a dirty one at that, we need not be attached to anything so profane. He has simply been reporting what the ancestors have said.

And yet, what Kometo means by the story proving a lie may not be so transparent. He exploits two ways to tell a falsehood. First, he embodies enough of a modernist man to challenge the ontology of the event with a rational argument, and he embodies enough of a Christian man to suspect it in terms of religious history. It characterizes a lie in this first sense because it does not square with modern assumptions. But additionally, it also denotes a falsehood in a riM̧ajel̡ cultural and sociological sense; namely, it is a lie not so much because of its false explanation, but because what it dramatizes appears to lie (cf. Toelken 2003). It characterizes a lie in this second sense because the behaviors of the trickster and his mother are false; they act contrary to appropriate social conventions. Their behavior is laughable because of the rules they break; they invert the norm. The social reality, not an ontological reality or the truth of history, is inverted in this myth. Kometo's risk was to tell a story that dramatized the inversion of his society's mores through deception as well as perform in such a way as to overturn our social and religious expectations of each other. Talking of such things was interpersonally dangerous, but the risk unveiled much about his culture and how the prohibitions on intergender relations work among relatives, while it also created a sense of intercultural *communitas* through liminal chance taking and laughter. The paradox here is peculiar; by inverting a shared set of religious expectations, the accompanying values come into greater focus. By revealing how incest and male sexual aggression present a lie, because they relate to acts of deception and socially dangerous outcomes, he has craftily reconfirmed a shared sense of the sacred.

Dalliance, Disease, and Drunkenness

The riMajeļ recognize the dissonance between Indigenous assumptions about sexual practice and modern Christian ones. Sexual dalliance within traditional social life attested a lie, not because it was something conceived of as an "evil" sin (*jeroҳwiwi*) in Christian terms, but because it may often result from an intent to deceive. Kometo and many others described for me how sexual liaisons were and continue to be like a game of hide-and-seek, which carries all the cultural significance of the practice of hiding and personal empowerment described in previous chapters. Hiding and deception to engage in such trysts indicate a capacity to succeed as a Letao figure. If one were to be revealed or caught in their hiding game, it may or may not lead to a social drama. Indeed, the cuckold husband cannot overreact or he will lose face. More often, the wife or girlfriend will create a public scene if her paramour has proven unfaithful. The expectation that such clandestine activities take place is in part rooted in sociological principles of riMajeļ matriliny. As the following dialogic excerpt reveals, "sleeping around" does not undermine the traditional social order, in effect it is enabled by the order itself. This conversation between us conveys a rather matter-of-fact quality as he taught me an Indigenous sociological principle. With minimal humor, the content seems less profane and simply more descriptive. We had been talking about the role of women in relation to the matrilineal family unit and how its structure implicates a different attitude about their sexual behavior. I asked him about a term I had heard many using: "wander/roam around" (*m̦m̦ōkadkad*).[14]

K   I say, the reason there is power with the woman, eh, is because a woman can give birth to a child. But her children are not the children of just one man. She can have children from three or four men.

P   Uh huh. So, all her children will come from many men.

K   Yes, yes.

P   According to riM̧ajȩl custom this behavior is basically acceptable.

K   She can sleep with many men. You know the woman just stays at the house and the two of them sleep with each other there. See? (uh huh) Now the man goes and makes a child over there. <points in one direction> See? (uh huh) After making it, another child also appears over there at a different place. Then another child appears. <points in another direction> See? He has gone from that woman and has children over at those places with the others. Just where is the real parent? <long pause> With their mother. With their mother. Because their fathers have also fathered children over there at the other locations. <chuckles> Well, thus it is. Thus, are the riM̧ajȩl. Like I said to you before, "There is not just one father for all the riM̧ajȩl children." And so, the woman will remain in the land.

Now there was a child over there, of the Raarn̥o clan, see? (uh huh). His father was of the M̧ōkauleej matriclan. He has fathered over there with the Raarn̥o clan. So, who does the child belong to here? It belongs to the Raarn̥o.

Here, Kometo explains how riM̧ajȩl women (and, by implication, men) can have multiple partners without any social stigma. This arises from the matrilineal principle: no matter who fathers the child it will belong to the matriline. Consequently, no child is illegitimate and falls without this social order, and paternity becomes less relevant. As Kometo concludes this interchange, he emphasizes that a man will be of one clan and his offspring another as they belong to their mother's clan. Also important in this exchange is Kometo's description of how a woman "stays at the house" (meaning a matrilineal land tract) and the man roams about. This behavior takes us into some nuanced cultural semantics, something Kometo wanted me to understand.

In the narrative about Letao committing incest with his mother, Kometo calls the trickster's phallus his "earthworm." This creature penetrates the ground in order to eventually arrive at his mother, who possesses the butterfly toy. If the earthworm (or eel) signifies the male phallus, then what it penetrates, the ground (*bwidej*), serves as the symbol for woman. The riM̧ajȩl will overtly compare the similarity between the woman impregnated with the metaphorical seed (*ine*), to be like the earth into which a seed is implanted. And they will also extend the metaphor: within the womb a mother nourishes the child so that it may grow, similar to a seed in the soil of the land, which primarily belongs to the woman and the matriline.[15] This widely distributed metaphor takes on added meaning in the Marshall Islands because of how it connects with the totalizing concept of matrilines and the semantics of gender.

A man brings from his domain those things that are raw (*ukood*) such as fish and fruits, or also described as those things that are *jañin mat* (literally, "not yet cooked/finished/complete"). He brings these uncompleted foodstuffs into the woman's domain where she cooks them. The Kajin M̧ajel̦ word for "cook" is *kōmat* (literally, "to finish, complete, or make done"). Also, when food is cooked, they will say *emat* (literally, "it is complete/done") and a person who is full from eating will say *imat* (I am finished/full/complete). In the process of cooking, then, the woman completes what is unfinished or raw (cf. Lévi-Strauss 1969). Through eating, one is made "complete" and given the strength (*kajoor*) that food provides. Traditional cooking involves fire pits (*wūpaaj*) and earth-ovens (*um̧*). Thus, it is in the earth (symbol of woman) from which a person eats and is made complete. When men engage in sexual intercourse with women they bring their strength contained in the sperm (*pek*), which is partial and incomplete (raw), and the woman receives it and completes it by feeding the child in the womb through the umbilicus (*bwijen*) and by nursing (*ninnin*) after birth, thus making it "*mat*" or complete. Because chiefs too are linked to the land and the food that comes from it, mothers and chiefs become complementary images. This paired association is compounded by the fact that the chief (*irooj*) has received the land by which he feeds his people through his mother. It is also often described that his people (*kajoor ro*) will nurse (*ninnin*) from him, creating an additional metaphor back to woman and mother.

These metaphors correlate with the islanders' view of male and female behaviors, especially with regard to sexuality. As previously presented, riM̧ajel̦ describe men as either "small eel man" (*m̧m̧aan m̧aj*) or "earthworm man" (*m̧ajkadāl*). Men perform like the *m̧aj* and *kadāl* because they enter the reef or earth, the symbol of woman. These metaphors often accompany the description of men as *m̧m̧ōkadkad*. The word literally means "wander and roam about," but in this context it refers to how men go around seeking partners. These behaviors are also encoded in the male and female domains: men actively move about and women remain connected to place. In riM̧ajel̦ sexual protocol, the man will make advances on the woman. A woman described as *m̧m̧ōkadkad* is frowned upon, not because of her sexual activity, but because she would be behaving like a man. Kometo repeated often the following familiar proverb: "Our mother forever, our father the father of others." Because men "wander and roam about," siblings will likely have different fathers.[16] Nonetheless, they all share one mother, which binds them together. These siblings are also described as sharing "only one clothing mat" (*juōn wōt nieded*), the mat (*nieded*) being the symbol of their mother. Kometo described this arrangement as follows: "The clothing mat, like their mother, is shared by her children, see? (uh huh) And she is rooted in the land <points to and pounds ground> that will go to her children. Because sharing the clothing mat is like sharing the land." These proverbial sayings register clearly the idealized matrilineal practice and clarify sexual behaviors rooted in an Indigenous sociological principle with deep epistemological and historical roots, which corresponds to the general application of the matrilocal principle as well. When couples cohabit, the male will typically go to live on his female companion's land, although this matrilocal practice has always been flexible. Even so, seeking partners must be done discreetly in a hidden fashion, to avoid appearances of sensual activity before prohibited relatives or lose at the game of deception.

If such sexual liberty makes sense within the sociology of riM̧ajeļ matriliny, it nonetheless conflicts with Christian standards and its patriarchal assumptions, and Kometo and the riM̧ajeļ are well aware of this fact. The tension between the sociology of riM̧ajeļ sex and Christian morality is always present. Sexual immorality in the religious community denotes a form of dishonesty and disloyalty, and thus it is an immoral lie. In riM̧ajeļ tradition, the lie is granted social valiance and tolerated, but with the new religious morality, the lie represents a serious social breach with significant spiritual outcomes attributed. For this reason, Kometo, while risking a sensitive subject, wished to separate explanations of the Indigenous sociology of sex from a modern Christian one. Also, if Letao supplies the source of sexual play, that prohibited by the new religious morality, then we can easily see how his image gets folded into conceptualizations of the "devil."

Kometo often called Letao, Lucifer (*Lujibur*). Driven by appetite, highly sexed, devious, and a great liar, the trickster corresponds to the Judeo-Christian source of temptation and desire. But now herein lies the strangeness of how Letao serves multiple functions; he is at once a disruptive figure in both the modern Christian world and traditional social life. His sexual behavior, although it brought procreative power to earth, can be used in such a way as to disrupt the social order. Being highly sexed is not the problem, but his misapplication or misuse of it is; he commits incest and rape, which is profoundly socially disruptive and confuses relationships. The sexual drive must now always be guarded to avoid Letao's kind of social sin, and many sociological checks and prohibitions (*mo̧ ko*) have been put in place to ensure it. Consequently, the public display of sexuality is intensely prohibited, and in an unanticipated fashion, modern religions and riM̧ajeļ ways, although out of different motivations, become complementary. As a result, Letao stories curiously affirm both the new religion and Indigenous traditions by making commentary on lying and unseemly behavior. For this reason, I do believe Kometo felt he could take the risk to discuss such profane matters with me.

The riM̧ajeļ "way" significantly contrasts with the broader American tradition of public displays of affection and body, which engender a great deal of negative discussion by older riM̧ajeļ. As we recall, Letao traveled to America taking all his proclivities with him, and so it comes as no surprise that the Americans behave like Letao. And a new danger comes with them, not just the atomic bombs, but sexual risks as well, as the next short interchange reveals. We had been rehearsing the history of Western diseases coming to the Marshall Islands and their effect on the population.[17]

K   The beginning of bad illnesses for the riM̧ajeļ people—the foreigners brought them.
P   Before the coming of the foreigner there was no serious sickness?
K   None.
P   So, they really lived a long time.
K   They really lived a long time. True. The foreigners brought the sickness. You see the sickness that happens to men—mucous? (uh huh), the riM̧ajeļ call it, "*Mādke.*"
P   *Mādke?*
K   *Mādke.*
P   What does this mean?
K   *America!* <with strong accent>
P   America? <we laugh> The sickness?
K   Eh. Mucous appears . . . like it spits there, white appears (mmm) like it's hard and yellow. See? Sometimes a little green may appear from a man. (huh) Then, after appearing with the man, he later gives it to the woman. The woman also gets it. (uh huh) So, when the two join together this makes what is called an infested sore. Now, we say, "*Mādke.*" <we laugh>

So, Letao and the Americans not only brought destructive bombs, they also imported venereal disease. One of the Kajin M̧ajeļ terms for the disease, *mādke,*[18] derives from a transliteration of the word for America itself. Thus, America stands for dalliance and a sexual disease. America is again seen as dangerous, and yet the source of their danger originates with Letao, the highly sexed trickster. Consequently, not only has Letao returned in the guise of US military power and imperialism, but his (dangerous) libido has returned as well.

In the thinking of many riM̧ajeļ, including Kometo, my culture provides the contradictory source of both irresponsible sexual relations (that brings disease) and the moral standards from Christianity. For Kometo, these two contradictory trajectories actually identify a return to a deep historical origin because it was Letao who brought the Americans. Most contemporary troubles emanate from America. Violent warfare and bombing, sexual dalliance and disease, even drunkenness, all these qualities identify an indulgent trickster. But again, as with the trickster, contradictory qualities merge into one image. The Americans also brought food (in chiefly abundance), modern comforts, and Christian morality. If the Americans seem contradictory, that is because they truly are, combining a range of antithetical qualities. Kometo often seemed to want me to know that all of it, the good and the bad, comes from my culture, and often took risks to ensure I knew it. Once in the company of M̧ake, we talked about how alcohol has accompanied male violence, suicide, and alienation within the family. This dialogue ensued.[19]

M   The Americans came and taught the riM̧ajeļ about drinking.
P   But there was a drink to get drunk/
K   /Ah there is none.
P   /before the Americans. /
K   /There is none. /
M   /There is none. /
P   From palm toddy?
M   They only make it now. /
K   /They make it after the Americans brought alcoholic drinks.
P   There is no coconut toddy before the Americans?
K   There is none. /
M   /There is none.
P   I didn't know this. <K chuckles>
M   We just have it now, but in the past, there was none.
K   You see it comes with the Americans. (Eh)

The Americans [sailors] come here and stay, on and on, and then many companies appear.
Now, they bring alcoholic drinks.
And they, the Americans get drunk.
They make a club at Jebwad.[20]
Now, all the sailors of the ships, they come to drink in the club.

P   Yes, but I thought that coconut toddy is a thing from long ago.
K   Only after they know about the alcoholic drinks to get drunk.
P   It's not a riM̧ajeḷ drink?

K   *The drink is brought from the people of Kiribati.*
     They make coconut toddy.

It belongs to the people of Kiribati, <chuckling> it's not a riM̧ajeḷ thing.

They made it.
The people of Kiribati make coconut toddy and make it sour.
And, after drinking it, they become drunk.
They say, "Oh here's another kind of drink." <we laugh>

Both Kometo and M̧ake place the arrival and problems of drinking on the Americans. I am surprised as I had seen and heard much about coconut palm toddy (*jekaro*), a mild alcoholic drink created through the fermentation of the toddy as it slowly drips into bottles on the carefully cut and prepared young coconut trees. This beverage, they both claim, comes after the Americans brought alcoholic drinks. Drinking corresponds to a postcontact reality, and the coconut toddy itself identifies something that comes from outside the Marshall Islands, from Kiribati to the south. After learning from the American sailors to apparently desire strong drink, the riM̧ajeḷ also adapt the preparation of the toddy. Again, my culture introduces a real social problem, and by implication, their own drunken trickster supplies the original source.

Kometo's stories of Letao's sexual exploits and incest, and about contemporary dalliance, disease, and drunkenness, involved some risk in terms of impression management, and challenged the standards of decorum created by Christianity and his new religious faith. Yet, like any trickster, he found ways to interweave the subversive into the most socially restricted topics. My interest in this chapter has been less with the meanings of tricksters, although I have explored these also, and more with how the performance of the riM̧ajeḷ trickster is enacted and transacted (Basso 1987) in an intercultural dialogue that provides a satire (Radin 1956) on both the immediate setting and a larger social history in which both Indigenous and Christian ideologies about the sacred and profane become entangled. Kometo used these dirty and dangerous moments to comment on social proprieties, and to dramatize his modern decolonizing world, one that blurs an Indigenous mythological past and traditions with the present, stories of a primal trickster god with Christianity, the American presence with traditional forms of intersex relations, and our own relationship within the ethnographic moment. The trickster is still doing his work, not just that captured in stories, but in the manner he is enacted by a contemporary storyteller.

To close this chapter, I wish to provide one last short segment that shows how our dialogues became moments of intercultural risk-taking. This time, many of Kometo's relatives were present, including several of his grandchildren. One of his teenage granddaughters keenly listened in on our interchange. riMajeļ grandparents and grandchildren, unlike parents and children, may engage in joking and suggestive conversations and actions without prohibition (c.f. Radcliffe-Brown 1940). Tellingly, the root Kajin Ṃajeļ term for both grandmother and grandchild is the same (*jibwi-*), suggesting a sense of equality and openness between the two alternate generations. Whereas with parents and children strict prohibitions prevail on talking about anything of a sexual nature, grandparents and grandchildren may enter into joking relationships. At the time of this dialogue, the grandchildren were very attentive as Kometo described Limejo̧kdād's (Letao's mother) power and that she had two sons, one a chief and the other a trickster. Other adults including his daughter listened in from a distance, but maintained the pretense of not attending to such talk as it would be inappropriate.[21] (GD is the teenage granddaughter.)

K   One is a chief. One is a mischievous person. One is like Phillip.
     <K and grandchildren laugh hard>
P   Everything, I know you taught me. <long laughter by all> I'm the student of
     Letao. <more hard laughter> It's not me. <more laughter>
K   Mmm.
P   So, this story of Letao, what does it teach people? <we chuckle>
K   Mischief.
P   Mischief?
K   And he is really bad and . . . <pause> the reason riMajeļ girls are so bad is it
     comes from Letao, he taught them. <granddaughter laughs, he then laughs
     hard>
GD   My grandfather, you really lie! <hard laughter by all>
K   Oh *kuuk* (expletive), it's true! <much laughter>

Through a willingness to take some risks, Kometo brings me into the Letao myth directly. When describing the trickster as mischievous, he identifies me by association. The grandchildren listening laugh at their grandfather turning his American and fellow church member into a trickster. They know their grandfather is one, and most certainly his ambiguous foreigner friend could be likewise.

I join with lighthearted banter, thus confirming my marginal status as a neophyte student to the mature trickster. My colluding performance seems to work, and they laugh. Seeking to set Kometo up to give a moral to narratives about Letao (anxious about their suitability for children), he takes this up as an opportunity to tease his teenage granddaughter, insinuating the sexual looseness of riM̧ajeḷ girls. His granddaughter laughs, and to defend herself, boldly claims that he is a liar. Calling him such generates much laughter, not only with the liberty she takes, which is acceptable, but also that she throws it back at him—that here before us is the trickster who says such things. Kometo provides closure when he juxtaposes the lies of the libidinal trickster to the truth. We are left wondering about the truth, especially when it comes to such dirty matters. We again confront the ambiguity between appearance and reality. The profane has identified the sacred and vice versa.

CHAPTER 7

Portending Death
Life-Affirming Laughter and the Telltale Sign of the Trickster

P   My friend.[1]
K   Eh.
P   Can I come again Wednesday?
K   It's good.
P   Wednesday and Friday?
K   Yes.
P   To learn from you? Ask for knowledge?
K   <chuckles> It's good. Anytime you want to come, you can. <tape ends>

How do we end a dialogue? The last two weeks before I left the Marshall Islands at the conclusion of the first two years of fieldwork, I had a hard time closing my conversations with Kometo. As revealed in the short exchange above, I clearly wanted more, and he did too. Both of us anticipated my departure, and both of us were preparing for that certain event. Part of my motivation to perpetuate the dialogue was a matter of ethnographic quantity; I had an underlying anxiety that I had just not procured enough good material from Kometo and other riM̧ajeļ people. I continued believing that I could elicit another story, another cultural explanation, another wise insight, if I kept pressing to the very end. All the same, I knew that in many ways our conversations had become redundant; we were not talking about anything really new, he had exhausted much of what he wanted to tell me and I had become quite uninsightful with the questions I asked, and I was getting more conventional ethnographic data from others. Our primary motive, at least mine, was to keep the conversation going until the very last opportunity—to savor the relationship. I was having a hard time letting go. And as for Kometo, I sensed he wanted me around too. We both knew that my impending departure signaled more than the end to our recurring dialogues; it evoked strong feelings about a more permanent closure—his death. The only narrative left to unfold after our dialogues would be the event of his demise.

Much of the text-making we engaged in through the course of our conversations placed the narrated event recounted antecedent to the telling or narrative event. Not all narratives and dialogues, however, look back and report the past, some look forward to the future; they anticipate future performances and events (cf. Bauman 2004; Sawin 2004). To perform a text that anticipates a subsequent event predicts the future by reasonable consideration of the past. Knowing that death is inevitable, Kometo and I could both foresee its arrival. But a detailed text that forecasts an unknown future also epitomizes the stuff of prophecy (*kanaan*)[2] and divination (*bubu*); the future will more or less resemble the text rendered in the present. Sometimes the prophecy may prove self-fulfilling, but at other times it casts a much larger vision. Much prophetic discourse is framed as a warning, and it may also outline a script that either will (independent of our wishes) or should be realized. Prophecy can be either predictive or prescriptive. Conversations about the future lend themselves to ample prognostication and confident talk about how things will unfold. Sometimes this conversational portending draws upon personal experiences framed as narratives, or from the larger repertoire of cultural narratives. Kometo also drew from a range of textual resources to script his own forthcoming death and to presage, what he saw, as a bleak future for his culture. Up to our last conversation, he continued to cultivate stories to be realized subsequent to our dialogues, and to make commentary on what he anticipated as an inexorable future. It may appear that he characterized a pessimist, yet the trickster has a way of casting death as something to laugh at and as something life-affirming.

Even though Kometo narrated his own death and lamented the precarious future of his culture, his discourses were less tragedy in the classical Greek sense and leaned toward the capacity of satire for reconciliation. Some may perceive Kometo's position as resignation rather than reconciliation, but I offer that his method is better acknowledged as "anti-tragedy," an attempt to scorn death and mock any finality through discursive play and laughter. While his textual productions anticipated ensuing events, finality should not be taken too seriously, and the end of dialogue is always provisional; texts and voices will continue to speak back and forth to each other, and into and out of a variety of contexts. It seemed as if Kometo anticipated that he would continue to speak "from the dust" because he foresaw my text-making and that I would give him life through the narratives I would write. He had crafted me into the teller of his tale. So now how do I write about the end of this raconteur of trickster myths? How do I bring closure to this moment of dialogic creation? Kometo's mythology about death will provide the exit.

A Power in the North

riM̧ajeḷ conceptualizations of death and burial practices exhibit, as with most customs situated in a modern decolonizing present, a rich synthesis of the old and the new—Indigenous religion and Christianity. Unlike some contemporary riM̧ajeḷ Christians, as has become clear, Kometo showed no discomfort in creating hybrids by recalling Indigenous mythologies, deities, and past traditions, and forging links to contemporary Christian practices. As with all of his personal perspectives, Kometo showed variance with other extant texts in how he organized the cultural meanings of the past concerning death. Nonetheless, by placing his discourses in conversation with other textual renderings we can again see, one, how he constituted his eclectic vision on the margins of tradition and modernity, two, the quality of his intertextual work, and, three, how our dialogic encounter continued to move seamlessly along the boundaries of the past, present, and, ultimately, the future.

The early ethnological accounts corroborate that the riM̧ajeḷ believed in an idea of the human soul (*an*) that departs the body at death.[3] This concept may imply the influence of Christianity, nonetheless many of the accounts by early ethnographers put forward that this belief predates missionization. That the old ethnological accounts make this consistent claim does not mean it was so. Nonetheless, the oral histories I collected from riM̧ajeḷ indicate that this idea represents an enduring belief and forms an Indigenous epistemology of the world and spirits (cf. Meyer 2013). From the descriptions of the German ethnologists Erdland (worked in islands 1900) and Kramer and Nevermann (worked in islands 1908–1910), the riM̧ajeḷ articulated a clear concept of both a variety of spirits (*jetōb*) embedded in bushes, trees, reefs, rocks, and places as well as human spirits that transition out from the dead body. These "souls" or spirits, however, need not occupy a person to sustain life, and often make journeys to other locations, especially at night. Consequently, a human does not need a soul to be animated, nonetheless, the soul is individuated and displays continuity beyond the death of the physical person. These accounts, supported by the mid-century work of the anthropologist Jack Tobin (worked in islands 1950–1957, 1967–1974) and my own ethnographic inquiries, identify a strong practice of ancestor veneration and the presentation of offerings (*menin aje*) to the deceased and sacrifices (*katok*) to divinity. All of these descriptions of the afterlife and burial practices present a relatively consistent picture. The earliest accounts by the German ethnologists and Tobin record how spirits depart from the body upon death and travel to Ņadikdik,[4] a small secondary atoll a short distance off the southeastern side of Mile atoll. This atoll appears like a detached appendage. This so-called place or staging ground of the dead not only forms part of Kometo's home atoll, but is also a place where he possessed matrilineal inheritance rights in addition to the neighboring islet, Ḷukwōnwōd. He described on several occasions how he traveled to Ņadikdik by sailing canoe both as a youth and during

World War II when he eluded Japanese soldiers by hiding under some mats with his sailing partners. Kometo was very familiar with this part of Mile and Ṇadikdik, and it loomed large in many of his discussions and stories. He possessed a keen awareness, and some pride, that in the general riṂajeḷ belief his inheritance lands served as the location of the dead. He knew these locations intimately and was well acquainted with the myths and legends centered there.

Descriptions of Ṇadikdik as the place of the departed spirits also present how the deity, Ḷajbwinām̧ōṇ, stands by to judge the fate of each soul. In the riṂajeḷ cosmogony, Ḷajbwinām̧ōṇ "resides" in the north and represents one of the four gods of the cardinal directions. In Kometo's conceptualization, these gods were the offspring of Ḷewōj and Ḷaneej. In the cosmogonies recorded by Erdland, Kramer/Nevermann, and Tobin, these beings represented the four posts of heaven that propped up the sky (motif A625.2). Consistent with these accounts, Kometo identified Ḷajbwinām̧ōṇ as the god of the north who presides over the dead and even holds power over death itself.[5] Invocation of his name can assure that the topic will center on death. Some of the early reports record that corpses were placed in the grave for six days and six nights during which time severe prohibitions were enforced on making noise, eating, sexual relations, and certain words, especially when the deceased was a chief. They also explain that after this waiting period the spirits will depart to meet Ḷajbwinām̧ōṇ. The portrayals of burial practices and Ḷajbwinām̧ōṇ's role are reliable across the reports (I add clarifying points in brackets). "The direction of the grave (is) north–south; north to the djidob ladje beneman [jetōb Ḷajbwinām̧ōṇ]; south, lerik [Ḷōrōk, the god of the south]. . . . The belief is that the spirit boat takes the dead to the heavens.[6] After burial a small sailing canoe replica is launched and is told to 'go away,' (this) means that the soul should now sail to Ngadikdik" (Kramer/Nevermann 1938, 370). Meanwhile the body is prepared and buried in a grave. This same account describes how the spirit of the dead rises early in the morning and walks to the salt water to go to Ṇadikdik. "From the shore, the southern point, the soul wanders to the spirit Ladjbuineamen [Ḷajbwinām̧ōṇ], who lives on the large land in the north and who is on Ngadikdik and devours the soul of the deceased if he did not live properly" (372).

To live properly as they describe is not a matter of sin in the Christian sense, but whether one has been loyal and respectful to chiefs and their kin group. They continue, "Good people . . . return and live in the space below the sky, in the metadodo [mejatoto, or air]. Leuit and Lanidj [Ḷewōj and Ḷaneej] live in the sky itself. From what I heard this is on Mille" (372). It is unclear from this description if Ḷajbwinām̧ōṇ's land lies north of all the Marshall Islands (most accounts align with this) or on the north side of Ṇadikdik, but clearly, they connect him to the island, and he performs the role of judging the souls of the deceased. Similar to their predecessor, Erdland, Kramer, and Nevermann place Ļewōj and Ļaneej in the heavens and describe them as the gods of the sky.[7] For this reason, it is not hard to see why, when we account for Kometo's Christian sensibilities, that he identified these gods of the sky with the "Father in Heaven" of the Bible, and because they are situated near Mile, his home atoll, his attention to this divinity comes into relief.

I too heard several other riM̧ajeļ reference Ṇadikdik as the place of the spirits of the dead and of Ļajbwināmṃōṇ's role.[8] Tobin's descriptions also show that, at midcentury, many islanders continued to identify this island as the place of judgment and the dead. These identifications may point toward a collapsing of the Christian worldview into Indigenous beliefs. When discussing Ṇadikdik, Tobin (2002) claims, "It is believed to be the place where spirits of the departed went before going to Jibuinemōn [Ļajbwināmṃōṇ] in the land of the dead. A qualifying test had to be passed first to determine whether or not the spirit could continue its journey. The spirit leaps across a channel in the reef in which a horrible monster lurks. If the spirit has sinned in life it will fall, to be devoured by the monster" (138). Additionally, he related that the riM̧ajeļ "believed Nadikdik to be the final destination of the spirits of the deceased. They had to jump across a channel in the reef as a test of their worthiness to enter the other world Eb [Ep]" (195).

That the worthy will enter the world of "Ep" is significant, as the mythologies identify it as the homeland of the gods that lies in an unspecified location in the west. I also recorded this qualifying test from others, and Tobin links this deity to the burial practices outlined by the German ethnologists, and as told by one of his storytellers:[9] "When they die, you bury them. Do it with the top of their heads pointing toward Ļajbwināmṃōṇ . . . The reason for this is if they die in sin and are resurrected, he will eat them. But if they keep the words of teaching of the woman Jined ilo Kōbo when they die, Ļajbwināmṃōṇ will give them freedom" (22). Last, when describing how Ļajbwināmṃōṇ was among the posts of heaven who keep the sky from falling, Tobin's storyteller relates how "Ļajbwināmṃōṇ was against the others . . . He killed people, caused sin, and so forth (like Satan)" (48).[10]

These descriptions intimate a collapse along the margins of precontact beliefs about death and burial into the new Christian religion. In addition to Tobin's storyteller connecting Ļajbwināmṃōṇ to Satan, the description is overlaid with Christian conceptualizations of resurrection, the god of heaven, spirit and body, sin and worthiness, and a final judgment. Moreover, the riM̧ajeļ continue to bury their dead with the cardinal directions in mind, but instead of a north–south axis (head pointing north), the preferred direction is east–west, corresponding to notions of a resurrection eastward toward the rising sun. They also continue to practice a six-day ceremony waiting for the soul to rise and depart toward the lagoon. The strict prohibitions have faded, although the mobilization of kin, food, and resources continues during this period (*ilomej*) with feasting, gift giving, and speech making. At the end of this period, marked by a preacher's final prayer, small white coral stones delivered in woven baskets are spread (*eoreak*) around the grave site (*lōb*) and adjacent graves. This practice is consistent with those described by Erdland and others. If the imposition of Christian beliefs and practices seems evident, riM̧ajeḷ beliefs about burial (*kallib*), the spirit (*jetōb*), Ņadikdik, and Ḷajbwinām̧ōņ provided ready-made reference points for the riM̧ajeḷ to make sense of and assimilate Christianity to their Indigenous conceptualizations.

Kometo never told me that Ḷajbwinām̧ōņ performed the role of judge, but he did clearly identify him as the one who retains power over death, and he, too, rehearsed how Ņadikdik provided a destination for the disembodied spirits. And although reluctant to claim that Ņadikdik was equivalent to heaven and hell, he did speak of it with a degree of reverence and respect, and acknowledged the presence of spirits there. For Kometo, Ņadikdik could not represent a final destination as he believed in the Christian ideology of heaven as above the earth and a variation from his Mormon faith regarding three degrees of heaven. For this reason, Ḷewōj and Ḷaneej, as the god of the sky, assumed the most important role. Ḷajbwinām̧ōņ is simply among those beings that this god placed throughout the atolls in the beginning.

Kometo also claimed that before the arrival of Christianity it was Ḷajbwinām̧ōņ who caused death and destruction. And he also linked this god to the power of sorcery. After recounting an anecdote about how a promiscuous wife destroyed her husband on Arņo atoll by using sorcery, he said, "Now in these days they do sorcery. Oh see, when sorcery is used to do good, well it's clear, they ask of Ḷewōj and Ḷaneej. If she does sorcery to destroy people, eh? She asks Ḷajbwinām̧ōņ." For Kometo, the gods of sky, equivalent to the Christian god, can only be used for positive actions, whereas he attributes the negative to Ḷajbwinām̧ōņ. Even though he did not directly identify the god of the north with Lucifer, this Indigenous deity clearly supplies the source of darkness (*marok*) or evil (*nana*) and possesses power over death.

K   There is a power in the north. He is called Ḷajbwinām̧ōņ.[11]
P   The child of whom?
K   The child of Ḷewōj and Ḷaneej.
P   What is his power?

K   Ah, it is power to hold life. He can take the life of a person.

P   Oh. Do you know a story about the man?

K   Ḷajbwinām̗ōṇ? (Eh) He is the one who attends to the life of people. See? (uh huh)

A man's wife on Mile dies.
Then, when he realizes it . . . he loads his wife's body [on a canoe].
Loads her and sails with her to Mājeej [island].
Then, upon arriving at Mājeej, the chief Ḷajbwinām̗ōṇ says, "What is the purpose for you sailing here?"
He says, "I have come to retrieve my woman."
"Where is she?"
"You have taken her spirit.
Would you release her to me?"
The chief says, "Kindly go and find her with those women over there."
When he goes, he sees her.
Then, he says, "THERE SHE IS."
Then, the chief says, "Go grab her."
He goes and grabs her.
When he holds her, the woman comes to life on the canoe. (uh huh)
She again opens her eyes and breathes. (hmm)

Well. <long pause> Thus is the story. <laughs>

P   Finished?

K   <laughing> Eh.

P   That is a really short story.

K   <laughs> Well this story, we will say,

"The power of Ḷajbwinām̗ōṇ is this—the man asked for life and he gave it."

P   Does he live on to this day?

K   Who? Ḷajbwinām̗ōṇ? Yes, He just remains to now. They tell stories about him.

P   It's his decision if a person dies?

K   They say Ḷajbwinām̗ōṇ takes life. But in these days, eh? People say, if a person dies, according to the Bible—<chuckles> They say, "Ḷewōj and Ḷaneej has taken him."

P   So, he is the child of Ḷewōj and Ḷaneej?

K   The child of Ḷewōj and Ḷaneej.

P   Okay.

K   This is the hardest thing for people—if you should ask any other person, "Who is the father of these people?" "Where do these powers come from?"
P   Uh huh, what will they say? /
K   /Well, it's hard, it's hard.
P   Why?
K   They don't know!

P   Oh. So, what is the reason they point the dead toward the north?
K   As I say, they lie down and give way to Ḷajbwinām̗ōṇ. If I die, and M̗ake lives? (mmm) He will say, "Well, lay him down, hold him tight, and point him towards the lagoon." <north from our location> (hmm) All the old people, they know the reason that the pointing is to go towards Ḷajbwinām̗ōṇ.
P   Nonetheless, the Christians, they point toward the east.
K   Well, now/
P   /They rise to the east? /
K   /they rise eastward.
P   When did this custom begin?
K   With the [first] missionaries. The missionaries and . . . those governments. Sure, we know the Bible, so we just do it this way now.

The opening of this dialogue recasts what has already been presented: Ḷajbwinām̗ōṇ represents the power of the north, his divine genealogy goes through Ḷewōj and Ḷaneej, and he possesses power over death. I then ask him if he knows a story about this god and he responds with a short narrative, seemingly only a fragment of a larger myth. I even respond that it is a really short story and he can only recapitulate its central point. I will return to this short mythic narrative momentarily, but at present I wish to show how this mini-narrative further contextualizes our dialogue about death. Kometo acknowledges that Ḷajbwinām̗ōṇ continues to this day, and he recognizes that in the past the riM̗ajeḷ attributed death to Ḷajbwinām̗ōṇ, but that now with Biblical understanding he attributes it to Ḷewōj and Ḷaneej. Because we know he calibrates these two names with the Christian god, it becomes clear why he explains that people of today do not know the genealogy of these beings, and consequently do not recognize their link to the Christian cosmogony. Kometo sees himself as privileged in this understanding. He reveals his adeptness at identifying variation when he clarifies for me the contrast of the body orientation in burials, and that the shift in cardinal directions comes with Christianization.

Kometo dismisses the short mythic narrative by saying, "thus is the story"; that is, there is really little to it. His dialogue lacks any clarifying information to facilitate understanding the plot line, and even Kometo's method for moving action ahead with reported speech helps us very little. He presents an unidentified man from Mile whose wife has died and he knows Ḷajbwinām,ōṇ has taken her soul. He goes to Mājeej, a small coral island in the northern Ratak chain, and through a short rendering of reported speech, the man requests his wife's soul from Ḷajbwinām,ōṇ himself. He is granted his wish. That is it, a simple mythic plot that recognizes this deity's power over life and death.

It is not apparent from this performance why Ḷajbwinām,ōṇ acquiesces to the man's request by simply asking. The only thing that makes the man stand out is his effort to track her soul down at the location of the god. This story has a clear intertextual resonance with a myth recorded in 1900 by Erdland on Jālooj atoll. In this rendering Iroojrālik ("Lord of the west"), identified as one of the four posts or gods that hold up the sky, invites his cousins to bring gifts to a festival at which time his daughter will choose who she will love among these gods. She selects Ḷōrōk, the handsome god of the south. As they prepare to leave "Ḷajbwinām,ōṇ stretches out his hand and scratches the girl's soul, and hides it." None of the other gods see this. "When they reach Ḷōrōk's island, the maid dies, for Ḷajbwinām,ōṇ has stolen her soul." Ḷōrōk then sails off to look for her and finally arrives at Ḷajbwinām,ōṇ's island, where the maid's soul comes out to greet his canoe. He asks Ḷajbwinām,ōṇ why he has taken her. After Ḷōrōk chants, he overturns the tortoise shell, and the woman in the canoe comes to life again. Erdland described how "overturning the magic shell often brings about resurrection or it provides protection" (154).

Here we can clearly identify a variant on Kometo's abbreviated story. It relates how Ḷajbwinām,ōṇ kills a woman and takes away her soul, her god husband seeks and finds her at the island of the god of the north, requests her, and then she returns to life. The difference from Kometo's version is how the man represents one of Ḷajbwinām,ōṇ's cousin gods and not a man from Mile, and, additionally, specifies that the woman is a daughter of the god. In Erdland's account, Ḷajbwinām,ōṇ brings death upon the "maid" by scratching her and taking her soul. Chanting ultimately counters this death touch and reference to the magic of the tortoise shell brings her to life. In many ways, Kometo's version characterizes a fragmented localization of the same story. The older version provides an intriguing implicit association with Letao, and offers an alternative to Kometo's genealogy of the trickster. The use of the tortoise magic is linked to Letao, since according to some collected accounts,[12] the trickster's mother was the tortoise woman of Pikaar who bestowed her powerful magic upon him instead of his brother because he willingly drank a slimy concoction. Because his mother placed the tortoise shell pendent upon Letao, he acquired "magical power over life and death" (Kramer and Nevermann 1938, 353). After this bestowal, the brothers travel to Mājro, where Kometo locates their birthplace and mother Limejo̧kdād. The Kramer and Nevermann version identifies Limejo̧kdād as their ogress aunt (likely classificatory mother) who gave birth to the annoying creatures and was a dirty thief.[13] But although Kometo recognized these variants on Letao's genealogy, he puts forward an alternative cosmological pedigree to remain consistent with his primordial geographical placement of each deity by Ļewōj and Ļaneej. This may in part be due to his idiosyncratic telling and where he learned his stories in the southern Ratak chain. The problem of variants with Letao's genealogy is less the issue than how the trickster is granted power over life and death in a different way than Ļajbwinām̧ōņ. Whereas Letao can certainly leave death and destruction in his wake, he will ultimately bring life back through his libidinal drive and creative energy. Death and life become a complementary image embedded in the trickster. The intriguing factor here is that no matter the variant, intertextual threads re-invoke the trickster at every turn, and in a serious discussion of death and even his own death, Kometo will continue to mediate his Christian/Mormon modernity with Indigenous mythological understanding.

Buried under the Sea

On one occasion, I discussed with Kometo and his two friends M̧ake and Jojej the riM̧ajeļ preference for where a person should be buried. They explained that, formerly, the ideal was to be buried on one's matrilineal inheritance lands (*kapijukunen*).[14] To do so today presents a logistic challenge as most islanders have emigrated either to the urban centers of Mājro and Epjā (Ebeye) island at Kuwajleen or over-seas, and the cost as well as time required to transport a body to its home atoll and islet discourages strict adherence to this ideal. As was often the case, Kometo dominated the responses to my questions even though I was trying to elicit reactions from all three. My sincere question about his anticipated burial led to a joking dialogue.[15] (Jojej is identified by [J].)

P   Where do you want to be buried?
K   Under the sea.

Raise a boat . . . Raise a boat. (ok)
And wrap me with cloth.
And tie a rope over here. <gestures to neck>

P   Your neck?
K   My neck.

And, tie a large stone. <others chuckling, he and I start to laugh>
YOU! You do it. <they chuckle>

P   Me?
K   Yes.
P   It's my responsibility?
K   It's your responsibility.
P   It's clear. *<all laugh>*
M   It's clear. *<chuckles>*
P   Just carry on.

K   *And take me in a motor boat and {go on and on} until you only see a little of*
     those trees,

See?

the coconut and breadfruit trees.
Until you see only a little of them.

P   Oh, when I look back to the island?
K   Eh. (oh)

Look back to the island, and when you see only a little of the coconut trees . . .
Well, now, just release me <J chuckling> so that I'm upside down, having
tied me there, upside down, so that my legs are above, <starts laughing> but
my head is down.

M   *You shall say, "He is finished by the sharks."*
K   *Well, so that the sharks can eat me. /*
M   */The sharks will eat him and he is finished. <chuckles>*

P   So, what is the reason you want that I wait until I only see a little of the
     trees? /
K   /Because then the people won't know to be angry when they eat me with
     their meal of fish. <all laugh>

P   Oh, Letao.
K   <laughing hard> There you go man, Letao.
P   You are just joking with me.
K   No. It's really my wish. I want that it to be thus.
P   Why?
K   Thus is my desire.
J   <laughs> His desire.
P   Do you want to be shark food?
K   Yes.
J   <laughing> He wants to be shark food. /
K   /I want to choke a shark from inside. <we all laugh hard>
P   Letao will make a shark suffer. <we all laugh, especially J>
     <pause> Don't you really want to be buried in Mile?
K   <u>No</u>. And stay at Mile? If I am taken there—then to the sea and
     released—<long pause, J laughs and we join>
P   You are joking much with me. <more laughter>
K   Why do you say that?
P   Did people long ago do likewise? They didn't?
K   They did.
P   They didn't bury under the ground?
K   They didn't, it was likewise.

Here in this dialogue, Kometo returns to his funny tricks when considering his demise and burial. In this interchange, we do not entertain a past event. Instead, he speaks almost in imperatives, anticipating the event of his death and what I will be required to do. Command forms may be considered part of the future tense as they anticipate action that will come subsequent to the speaking. Most all our previous dialogues were either set in the present tense of our interaction, the present tense of the narrated event frame, or the past tense of recounting antecedent events or practices. Only occasionally would we enter into a future tense when discussing what may become of riṂajeḷ culture. Nevertheless, here in this dialogue, we anticipate his death, and he renders a narrated event that will yet come. Such a narration affords a script for future action. I am to follow it so that what will happen will mirror what is spoken. Perhaps most prophecy represents simply a command more than a description of the future. In any case, the future narrated event (this seems like contradiction, to have that which is narrated unrealized) that Kometo articulates provides a satirical comment on his own death, which will ultimately place him in a seemingly subversive social structural position.

At the beginning of this dialogue, Kometo responds to my question about his anticipated burial, stating that he would like to be buried under the sea. His description of raising the boat means to prepare a launch and he begins the narrative about the future. Then he instructs me how to prepare his body, wrap him in cloth, tie a rope around his neck, and then attach a stone so that, we must assume, he will sink. This receives some nervous chuckles from all present. Then he clarifies that it will be my responsibility. After making clear my accountability in the dialogue, he continues to narrate my task; I am to take him in a motor boat out until, when I look back, I can only faintly make out the coconut and breadfruit trees (for low-lying atolls this is only about four to seven miles out, depending on the tide). Then I am to dump him into the sea headfirst with a stone tied around his neck.

This narrative anticipates a macabre event and the way Kometo tells it minimizes himself to convey a sense of his worthlessness. Ṃake directs this somewhat troubling request toward greater levity when he instructs me twice to announce that Kometo will be finished off by sharks, and by this, he contributes an additional narrative voice to the unfolding story. Kometo immediately picks this up to concur that the sharks will eat him. I seek to return to my orders and ask why I should wait until I see a little bit of the trees. This, Kometo explains, is so that people will not know that he will become fish food, and because, ultimately, they will eat the fish, they will also be eating him. If they knew this, they would be angry. Here, Kometo continues to humorously abase himself. I announce that Letao has appeared again, and laughing hard Kometo agrees with my identification. The trickster is exposed, and I think he is pleased that I recognize this discourse for what it is, and we are colluding to see if the others will detect it as well. When I ask about his motivations for a sea burial, Jojej begins to laugh more. With Letao now referenced, I suggest that Kometo is simply joking with me, and he verifies that he really desires to be buried at sea, and Jojej echoes with laughter. Perhaps not lost on the others, I do not know, but there is a potentially furtive subtext to this final resting place, as Kometo's name literally means "run away" or "escape" [ko] to the "sea" [meto].

So now how do we take this? Is this something Kometo really expects me to do for him? Or is he making it hard for all of us to ascertain his designs on the occasion? I decide to have fun by asking if he really wants to be shark food. He does, and Jojej again laughs and comments on this. Is he now laughing with or at Kometo? If he laughs at him, he does not get Kometo's subversive spoof and he thus laughs naively. But if he laughs with him then he knows my friend is playing the trickster. Then Kometo delivers his funniest line yet: he wants to choke the shark. All of us erupt into laughter. Even in death he will cause trouble, even for the shark. The animal that evokes the deepest fright will be agitated by the trick-ster. I pick up on how Kometo the trickster will make the shark suffer. All enjoy this image, and we continue to laugh viscerally. After Jojej laughs, I seek to return to some form of seriousness, assuming that with our moment of levity complete, I really do wish to know where he wants to be buried, if not at his home atoll of Mile. Kometo responds that if we take his body there then it still needs to be released to the sea. There is a long pregnant pause; we find it hard to determine how to take Kometo's feigned seriousness. Then Jojej cannot bear the charged sarcasm any longer and he laughs, and we all join him.

At this point, I claim he is joking, and everyone laughs. Kometo asks for what reason would he want to joke, and I am not sure, so I ask if this was ever done in the past and he confirms that the riM̧ajeļ originally did not bury bodies under the ground but cast them out to sea. Now this represented the first time I had heard such a thing, and I took it as one of Kometo's peculiar ways of envisioning the past. This claim about sea burials seems out of character with the descrip-tions of burials I presented previously, except the little-documented idea about a spirit canoe. So, I was pleasantly rewarded when I reread some of the old ethno-logical accounts. Only through this intertextual work did I realize the adroit extent of his subversion in our dialogue with the others that day. When Kramer and Nevermann (1938, 370) cite Erdland's work about riM̧ajeļ burials, they describe the shallowness of graves and their orientation to the north, and then they concur with his description that chiefly burials were of a different kind. Sure enough, when I scoured Erdland's work (1914) again I found that he described sea burials in two locations in his monograph. The first came in a footnote in a section on "Religious Myths: Spirit Myths": "In former times few corpses were buried. For the most part subjects who died were wrapped in mats and left to drift away (kobelok), whereas the chiefs were weighted to sink (kodonlik). Big stones were wrapped in the mats at the head and feet of the corpse" (180). Later, in a section on "The Soul in Life and After Death," he wrote: "Common natives are buried without ceremony. They, as well as chiefs, were formerly buried at sea, the only difference being that the corpse of the common subject was simply put into the water, while that of the distinguished person was submerged. Once his body had been put into the water, the canoe immediately sailed away, and no one was allowed to look back" (251).

With these corroborating references, we can see how Kometo clearly reached back into a past tradition that predates European contact and the practice of ground burials. His command to do for him the same thing places him, the trickster, and concomitantly me, in alliance with the more ancient burial prac-tices. Like those in the deep past, I am to wrap him up (in cloth rather than the mats of old) and put him out to sea. But most telling about his instructions is that I am to weigh him down with a stone so that he sinks. In Erdland's descriptions, only the "chiefs" or "distinguished person(s)" received this treatment, not the "common person." By giving me these clear instructions, Kometo not only resituates our anticipated activity within the deep historic past, but also cleverly identifies himself as someone of significance, a chief. This meaning runs counter to how he frames the anticipated narrated event when he creates an image of himself as so insignificant that once dead I can cast him into the sea to become the food (and tormentor) of sharks.

In narrating his own sea burial, he appears self-effacing, minimizing his significance. Yet when carefully attending to how I am to perform this act, and with additional knowledge about the deeper past, we see how he grants himself a burial "fit for a king." The contradiction in this discourse, stylistic self-minimization juxtaposed with narrative self-aggrandizement, creates a curious tension and reveals Kometo at his most circuitous and crafty. He subverts riM̧ajeḷ hierarchies that place him in a subordinate position within the larger social context in which this anticipated narrated event is situated. And just as important, he subverts Jojej's laughter at him in the narrative event, and perhaps the laughter of the rest of us as well; what we took to be joking self-degradation actually reversed social positions. Thinking I was purposefully collaborating with him in his tomfoolery, I failed to see just how much Letao informed this game of reversals. I had become party to and even a resource to his trick. And why me? Why did his anticipated narrated event have me perform this act of regal burial? I believe Kometo wished to make a point to me and about me to the others. For one, he clearly wanted me to know that we had become bonded enough for him to assign me this significant task. This was not just any task, but one in which he, through his death, would continue to draw me into deep histories. He also signaled that we would be collaborating again in subversive behavior, two tricksters, one from within and one from without, challenging social power both in the moment of the narrative event and in the larger social and historical contexts in which we dialogued. And two, I cannot help but think, that despite the socially subversive jesting about his burial, he is again, like a good trickster, undermining any power-driven ego. That is, even though we can be buried like a chief, in the end, all of us, no matter our station, will become no more than shark fodder. In death, all are equal.

The Sign of Death

One day Kometo and I were exploring the different kinds of navigational signs used to determine island locations. Because I had heard that he sailed much as a young man, I asked him what he knew about waves (*ŋo*) or currents (*aet*), a knowledge for which the riM̧ajeḷ are so famously identified. The complex understanding of currents and wave action are rendered in their multiple sophisticated stick charts.[16] I seriously queried if he knew about this technology as most living understand very little about it and the majority of travel between atolls today is by motorized boats rather than sailing canoes, although there has been a renaissance since the 1990s to bring back the technology for which their ancestors are so celebrated. Kometo immediately disclaimed any ability in this area and maintained that he would only drift away, unable to arrive at his destination. Such a scenario was always fraught with anxiety because drifting often led to starvation or encounters with hostile others. After joking that if he sailed he would drift away only to be eaten by cannibals, he became contemplative about reading celestial and oceanic signs. He connected this facility to the riM̧ajeḷ cosmogony, and outlined again the four deities that correspond to the cardinal directions. While he refers to them as chiefs, they are understood to be god chiefs of the original cosmogony. At one point, he began speaking of another kind of sign, not about sailing, but death.[17]

K   The sign is called *aao*. When you are close to dying it appears. (uh huh) Me, I will say, "Mmmm, go and speak to those relatives of mine." (uh huh) Say that "Your younger brother—I sense why he shows his aao." It's like he's different, they will say he is different, see? (uh huh) Well, they don't say different, but they say his *aao* shows.

P   Hmm. And *aao* is what, it is—?/

K   /One of those powers. If that person shows the *aao*—if he is dying no one will be able to hold him back. See?

P   Hold him back from dying?

K   <chuckles> Yes.

P   So, it's different from a spirit, how?

K   It is different from a spirit. See? It means we can look and see it.

P   Have you presented to me a story about the *aao*?

K   Mmm/

P   /I don't remember. Is there one?

K   There is.

P   What is it?

K   The *aao*, it is just linked to that person, Lāwūnpikaar.

There is a chief of the Rālik chain. (hmm)
In the life of the riM̧ajeḷ, there are many chiefs. (uh huh)

One is in the south. (uh huh)
One is in the west.
One is in the north.
One in the east.

He then describes how the god-chief Lawullep, provides the most senior starting point of a matrilineal genealogy. This represents an alternative name to Iroojrālik that other accounts record as the god/chief of the west, a name Kometo himself had provided me as well.

K   <pointing, poking the ground> *Well, the name of this chief is Lawullep.*
The chief of the north, that man is called Ļajbwināmọ̄ṇ.

See?

The man takes life; he makes death.
He is there, and if he says, "Come."
No one will say, "No."
Nonetheless, these people,

See? (uh huh)

they are all the children of Ļewōj and Ļaneej. (oh)
Well, <chuckles> *the chief of the west he knows, he knows about—*

Eh . . . what's his name? <pause> Eh . . . the one who had many birds . . . and turtles? Lāwūnpikaar.

But now, the chief of the west tells his strongest warrior next to him, to go and retrieve from Lāwūnpikaar, the aao. (hmm)
He embarks to retrieve the aao. (uh huh)
Now, the warrior goes.
He walks through the ocean, but the water is at this level. <points to shoulders>
But when Lāwūnpikaar walks in the water, it is at this level. <points to knees>
<chuckles, I join>

P   He is really tall./

K   */He is really tall.*
He is very strong. (ah ha)
Then, the chief says, "Go."
The warrior goes on and on and on, and then meets up with Lāwūnpikaar—
He [Lāwūnpikaar] says, "What are you doing?"
The warrior says, "Ooh greetings to you." Mmmm
"Greetings to you."
"What are you doing?"
He says, "Ooh well, not much."
Now, Lāwūnpikaar says, "Then you Should Eat."
He [the warrior] eats.

Well those two then depart.
The two of them sail northward from Pikaar to Bokak.
The atoll in the north is Bokak.
The thing that is over there is the aao. (hmm)
He grabs the leg of the warrior. <chuckles>
Lāwūnpikaar grabs his leg. (uh huh)
And lifts him. <waves arm about as if holding the leg>
And thus, he does this on the sea.
He baits the eel. (hmm)
The eel shows her teeth and comes to bite the warrior.
Like this. <imitates biting teeth>
Lāwūnpikaar sometimes wishes to feed his pet eel.
He can take along people as food. (uh huh)
But he takes along any kind of food.
He baits; the eel appears.
The eel comes to bite, and he reaches out his hand and scratches.
He scratches the drool from off of her tongue.
The thing is white on her tongue.
He scrapes it and takes it.
The two of them return to Pikaar and he gives some to the warrior.
Then, Lāwūnpikaar keeps some.
After returning, all his companions come.
As they arrive he initially gives it to the first bird that comes—

You will see a white bird, (uh huh) it's called

Mejo̧.
He comes fast. (uh huh)

He comes and dives inside the aao.
The frigate bird comes.
Lāwūnpikaar scrapes a little aao and paints his chest.
Another bird comes—

What's his name?

It is Pejwak; a smaller bird.
He scrapes what little is left and places the aao there on his head. (uh huh)
<chuckles>*Thus it is.*
He says, "Well, the birds come fast to get <chuckles> their aao."

A sign, it's like a sign. But the *aao*, the meaning of the *aao*, it is like, what could we say about it, man? See, it's about the way we die. (mmm) If one is ready to die, that sign appears. <laughs>

P   I don't really understand what the eel did in the story?
K   The *aao* is in the eel. Inside her mouth.
P   And the eel these days, does it have that stuff inside it?
K   It has, that stuff is inside its mouth, it's like spit.
P   Spit?
K   Mmm. Just like <coughs purposefully to bring up mucus>. (oh) It is inside the mouth of the eel. (mmm) Well, it was obtained over there. Lāwūnpikaar took it from her at Bokak. <tape ends>

In the beginning of this dialogue, Kometo explains how the *aao* provides an indexical sign of someone's approaching death. As one nears death, their appearance changes; once that shift occurs, he explains, there is no holding them back from dying. It is not a manifestation of the spirit, but something else. The Kajin Ṃajeḷ dictionary defines the *aao* as a halo, and also that which appears as a "white spot on the head of a toddy" bird (Abo et al. 1976, 18). That it identifies a marker on a bird comes clear in Kometo's story and I will address this shortly. I am unsure whether translating it as halo characterizes an independent riṂajeḷ identification or the influence of Christianity. In this context and from Kometo's perspective, it certainly does not carry any suggestion of sanctity or saintliness, but simply provides a sign of a pending death. So that I may get some clarity on this sign, I ask Kometo for a story. He brings forth the name Lāwūnpikaar, and situates him in relation to the gods of the cardinal directions.

When Kometo links Lawullep to Lāwūnpikaar—after explaining how he represents the beginning of a genealogy—he speaks again of Ḷajbwināmọọṇ. He repeats how he has power over death and through an abbreviated interchange he substantiates again that no one can resist his call. That Kometo identifies L̦ajbwinām̦ọṇ by name in particular, leaving the other cardinal direction gods except Lawullep unnamed, suggests an important link to the discussion we are having about death. This deity provides a logical context to elaborate on a myth that explains from whence the sign of death comes. Also important at this juncture is how Kometo identifies both Lawullep and L̦ajbwinām̦ọṇ as the children of L̦ewōj and L̦aneej, reaffirming his particular articulation of the genealogical link among these deities all of whom exhibit significant social and metaphysical power.

In the next segment of the dialogue, Kometo reminds himself that he wants to tell a story about Lāwūnpikaar. The root word of this god's name (*pikaar*) triggers his memory as it corresponds to the name for one of the uninhabited atolls of the northern Ratak chain, known for its abundance of birds and turtles. The resources of this atoll, along with Bokak, another uninhabited atoll, continue to be strictly controlled by the chiefs of the northern Ratak chain. Framing the mythic setting by rehearsing genealogies and locational details before entering into the stories was in part specific to our ethnographic dialogue due to my numerous questions. But it is also similar to other storytelling sessions I witnessed in which riM̦ajel̦ participants engage in questioning dialogues about genealogies and locations that draw out a narrative, followed by more questions and explanatory considerations. Accordingly, with this contextual frame set, Kometo begins the narrative.

The storyline presents a little challenge to follow. He begins with the chief of the west, whom we know from the dialogue is the deity Lawullep, a descendant of the god(s) L̦ewōj and L̦aneej. This god sends his strongest warrior to retrieve the *aao*. He likens him to a giant—when the warrior walks through the ocean the water comes up to his shoulders. This colossal size however, pales in comparison to Lāwūnpikaar; when he stands in the ocean, the waters only reach his knees. Kometo signals these depths of water through paralinguistic or nonverbal gestures, and he chuckles at the content of this motif, signaling a little incredulity. After some quick interchanges about his height and strength, he describes the warrior meeting Lāwūnpikaar. The interchanges between Lāwūnpikaar and the warrior demonstrate greetings and questions that appear to hedge and conceal their respective motives. Lāwūnpikaar appears to discern the warriors unstated motives to acquire the *aao*. In a gesture of goodwill, Lāwūnpikaar invites the man to eat. Then they travel together north from Pikaar to Bokak to obtain the *aao*. Upon arriving, Lāwūnpikaar grabs hold of the leg of the warrior and lifts him up. Kometo enacts how he swings the man around by his leg and in this way baits the eel at Bokak. The eel appears, shows her teeth, and then comes to bite the warrior giant. Kometo strengthens this image by gesturally imitating a biting eel. The "pet" eel can be fed with any kind of food, even giant humanlike beings. At this point in the story, the tension mounts and it appears that perhaps the warrior will be fed to the eel. But just as the eel opens her mouth ready to bite, Lāwūnpikaar reaches out his hand and scratches the drool (the *aao*) from her tongue. He scrapes off the white substance and takes it. Quickly, Kometo narrates the return of Lāwūnpikaar and the warrior to Pikaar atoll. Some of the *aao* he gives to the warrior, who we can assume will return it to Lawullep.

The link between the *aao* and birds becomes clear when Lāwūnpikaar's "companions" come, that is, the birds who nest on Pikaar. The first is the white tern (*mejo*)[18] who arrives quickly. He dives inside the *aao* and thus covers his whole plumage with it (the *mejo* is an all-white bird). Then when the frigate bird (*ak*)[19] arrives, he scrapes a little and paints it onto the bird's chest. This giant of all sea birds is identified by the white spot on its chest. The third bird Kometo identifies is smaller, the brown toddy (*pejwak*),[20] and he places what little is remaining on his head. The story concludes with a description of how these birds speedily obtain their *aao*. Consequently, the markings on the birds are the same as the sign that identifies a pending death. Kometo does not explain why these bird markings share the same source as the index of death,[21] he simply identifies how Lāwūnpikaar provides the *aao* from his pet eel that is located in the far north. Without explaining it directly, but having set up the link in the framing dialogue and opening to the story, this sign of death is acquired from the direction of the Ḷajbwināmōṇ, the god of death. After he concludes the story, I seek to ensure that I understand that the god-chief procured the *aao* from the eel, and we determine that it remains still in the mouth of an eel. Kometo compares it to spit or mucous. And he concludes this portion of our dialogue by reaffirming that it was Lāwūnpikaar who took it from the eel's mouth.

Traveling north toward Ḷajbwināmōṇ is clear enough, both the direction and the god establish an association with death. But what of the eel (*dāp*)? These creatures are respected by the riM̧ajeḷ; they are at once dangerous and aggressive, and often are referred to as divine-like or powerful spirits. Through much of Oceania and in Micronesia particularly, the eel is sometimes identified as a protective god that secures a sacred location (e.g., Pohnpei's Nan Modal, Dobbin 2011). The smaller eel (*m̧aj*) also serves as a phallic symbol, as indicated by how men are often described as *m̧m̧aan m̧aj* (see chapter 5), but in this case the eel is female. I should have asked Kometo why the sign of death would come from an eel, but in the moment, it did not occur to me. He presented this as just a matter of fact. In a way, the myth does not achieve what I expected it to: explain how the *aao* works as a sign of death, which was the question that elicited the story.

Kometo presents how it was obtained, but I get no more clarity about how to link its appearance to a person's countenance prior to death. I come to understand how one can now identify various birds by their white plumage, but I am left guessing why bird markings have any association with the sign of death. I am also left wondering how the sign moves from the possession of these primordial deities to human beings.

There seems to be a missing piece that either Kometo avoids telling me, struggles remembering, or just does not know. He identifies the sign, explains its origin, and links it to bird markings, but he does not tie it all up. Are birds somehow linked to humans and the dead as with the Melanesians? There is no indication that this is so in the riMajeļ myths or genealogies. Are the birds somehow a symbol of death? Again, no association can be found in extant texts, and I never heard any riMajeļ identify a relationship of this kind, although the birds sometimes serve as mediators between the gods and humans (see chapter 5). The only correlation comes from positioning the *aao* in the north or domain of Ļajbwinām̧ōņ, the god who controls power over death. And this is achieved indirectly from our dialogue and the opening of the story. But most certainly Kometo saw the link between the story, death, and its sign, and perhaps in his mind the symbolic glue between the myth and sign is not that complicated. The *aao* is a sign of death, obtained by a god from a primordial eel, and given to a giant warrior to be passed on to the god/chief of the west.

Others have documented versions of this story. Erdland (1914, 153–154) presented two versions. One identified the man who sought to take life back from Ļajbwinām̧ōņ as the same chief who sends the giants warrior off to Lāwūnpikaar to retrieve the *aao*, or sign of death. This account is abbreviated but calibrates nicely with Kometo's version. Erdland's second version identifies Lawullep as the chief who fetches the *aao*. It is this chiefly god (also referred to as Iroojrālik) who comes from the west, the direction of the ancestral homeland of Ep. That this character, in both versions, comes from the western homeland is important with regard to the link of the *aao* to death.

One more telling version comes from a collection of "legends" produced by the historical preservation office (Downing et al. 1992). These texts were not from actual recordings but drawn from other collections made by previous scholars and collectors. They are also adapted to contemporary English and prose. The "Story of Aao" in this collection is long and elaborate, with several episodes. It follows Kometo's shorter oral version in general terms, but also departs from it in several ways. Some of the differences are inconsequential, such as a different list of birds who receive the *aao*, but both identify the *pejwak*, the smaller and slower bird, as the one who receives the least amount by being last to arrive. Otherwise, the key differences from Kometo's version includes how the story unfolds in the context of a father (Iroojrālik, just another name for Wullep) at the island of Ep who wishes to give his favorite son (the *pejwak*) something to make him handsome, clever, lucky, and last forever. So he devises the retrieval of the *aao* that unfolds just like Kometo's version of the myth, but with much more flare, drama, and plot development (it is a written version!). Once obtained, the *aao* is brought back to Ep. But key here is that, through a trick, the faster bird is able to procure most of the *aao* to leave very little for the *pejwak*. Nonetheless, the *pejwak* remains his father's favorite, which explains how the appearance of this bird provides the sign for an abundance of food in the coming year, and concomitantly signals the time to begin a festival season.[22]

The Downing version gives greater detail about the characters, the events, and the motivations behind the actions. It also emphasizes more the etymological significance of the myth and how it explains an ongoing condition in nature. But what Kometo does add, completely absent from the Downing version, is the link between the *aao* and death rather than good looks and good fortune. The Downing version lacks any morbidity, and on the face of it so does Kometo's. But when situated within a narrative event of the dialogic encounter, Kometo uses the story to explain the origin of the sign of death that will appear in a person's countenance. The most significant contrast between the two versions centers on what the *aao* represents. In one, it serves to identify positive qualities (good looks, luck, and cleverness) and in the other an unwelcome signal of an approaching death. Kometo's contextualization of the myth is morbid, whereas the other version makes an optimistic statement about human virtues appropriate for a children's school reader. Nonetheless, both versions suggest other understandings that are not necessarily obvious.

In the Downing version, while the sneaky little bird obtains the *aao*, thus making him handsome and lucky, he is still not favored by his father. Instead, the *pejwak*, who appears to be the loser, retains his privileged position and becomes the indexical sign of life and fecundity linked to the first fruits festival (first documented by Lay and Hussy 1828). The quick sneaky one obtains more of the *aao*, yes, but he does not supersede his brother in significance. As a result, while Kometo's version only rudimentarily links the *aao* to intrigue among the birds, within the context of the dialogue he seeks to emphasize, one, a genealogy of those characters involved in the procurement of the *aao*, and two, that the *aao* is a sign of death, and it belongs most abundantly to the first bird to arrive, who pulls a trick on the other birds and the god. Kometo foregrounds the genealogy of Lāwūnpikaar and the location of the events in order to register that the sign of death is obtained adjacent to the world of Ḷajbwināmọọṇ. Any sense that the *pejwak* is associated with life is absent, but he does narrate the *aao* moving from

the northern Ratak to Lawullep (god of the west), the direction of both the setting sun and ancestral homeland, or another location of the dead. Perhaps he did
not know about the *pejwak*'s historical significance in relation to the festivals
long disbanded in the islands. He may have also assumed that I knew well the
three birds he identified and anticipated that I would understand why the first
bird to receive the *aao* (*mejọ*) would receive the most, and then lesser amounts to
the subsequent birds. So the first bird to arrive, the most decorated with the *aao*,
is the fastest and most clever, and displays some Letao-like qualities. But still,
what is the link here between the birds, the *aao*, death, and our dialogic encounter? This connection will unfold with subsequent dialogues about death.

The Telltale Sign of a Trickster

About two and half months after his performance of the story of the *aao*, we were
again speaking about the sign of death. For a segment of the interchange, I teased
him a little about his ability to joke with everyone, an ability he adamantly
denied possessing, and then I asked him about his past.[23]

K   <coughs> Yes. When I was younger and growing up, I was very bad.
P   Mmm. In what way were you bad?
K   I caused mischief.
P   You caused mischief?
K   Eh. <laughs>
P   Did you get drunk?
K   <laughs> Eh, now I'm an adult and have shed the things of a child.
     <we laugh hard>

     <long pause>

     <laughing> Do you see it here; it is my *aao*?
P   I have not yet seen it. I don't really recognize all those things. Me, I only see
     laughter. <he laughs> If your *aao* appears like a smile, well . . .
K   <laughing> It's not long before I die, yea?
P   You can't.
K   <laughing> "You can't!" According to your thought there—you will not
     release me. But ah, my body is weak now. <softly> Uuuuh.

It becomes clear in this short segment that any serious conversation between
us often became decorated with laughter. When Kometo refers to how he was

"bad" in the past, it was because of his "mischief," the same descriptor applied to Letao the trickster. When I ask about his drunken youth, he claims that as an adult he has shed childish things. We both laugh intensely, not because he does not tell the truth about how he has set aside his inebriated past, but because he continues to be a man of mischief so that any clear distinction between adulthood and childhood becomes somewhat blurred. After the laughter subsides, he pauses as if to contemplate the past and his trickster ways, and then, out of nowhere, asks if I can see his *aao* while laughing. He knows he taught me that the *aao* signifies death. Not wanting to become complicit in any declaration that proclaims his impending death, I deny having seen it. I try to joke clumsily, how I only see laughter in his face, and nothing like the *aao,* unless it corresponds to a smile. He enjoys this connection drawn between the *aao* and a smile (he always seemed to have a permanent grin on his face anyway, even when speaking of serious things) and while laughing he speaks of the brief time left before he dies and asks me to concur. Meekly, I assert he can't die, and laughing he quotes me with a sarcastic tone. I speak as if I have authority to prevent his death, and he concludes that such a gesture exists only in my thoughts, not reality. I have no power over his life, and in fact he grows weaker. His soft sounds at the end signal his resignation to the inevitable.

Two things stand out in this short exchange. One, a discussion about his mischievous past and joking brings forth the principle of the *aao* and his impending death. Two, and most startling, in the middle of a discussion about his death, he continues to laugh. This is not nervous laughter, but the laughter of a trickster at death itself. Perhaps laughter at once challenges the power of death and accepts it. Conjoining trickster jokes with the appearance of the sign of death is not as arbitrary as it may first appear. And here the etymology of words and Kometo's performance as a trickster take on new salience, something I did not understand at the time, but discovered through my own intertextual work. In one of his footnotes Erdland (1914) makes an astonishing connection. He too had heard the story of the *aao.* The material in brackets includes my clarifications of his description. "Edao [Etao], or better, Ladao: aad, 'eyebrow,' ao, white forehead spot of the bird bijuak [pejwak]" (235). Here, Erdland clarifies the etymology of the trickster's name, that it literally means the "white spotted eyebrow." This meaning is embedded in the trickster's name: *et* (or *āt*) for eyebrow and *ao* (*aao*) for white spotted as well as the sign of death (the "l" phoneme designates a masculine gender in this case). Accordingly, the riM̧ajeļ trickster possesses the *aao* markings, just like the birds in the story. And, if this is true, the trickster always contains in his appearance the sign of death. This then, reveals why Kometo highlights a connection between joking and the trickster ways with a discussion of the *aao*. After considering alternative etymologies Erdland continues:

> This etymology is connected with a legend from Jemo. Some froth was taken from the mouth of a terrible eel called Literao and smeared on the forehead of the tern by Iroojrilik, which made this bird a beauty, thanks to the white flecks on its forehead. The froth, however, was at the same time the eel's strength; therefore the head fleck, ao, also signifies "power" and in metaphorical speech even today a chief or chief's favor is called ao. The meaning of the word Ladao [Letao] would thus be: "The one with the white eyebrow, the powerful, the crafty, the favored one." This meaning also fits the character Edao. (235)

This instructive reference speaks across time to illuminate tricksters, their power, Kometo's self-identification as a trickster, and death. Placing the narrative at Jāmo̧ corresponds to the Downing version, but contrasts with Pikaar and Bokak in Kometo's versions. The alternative locations indicate Kometo's method, I believe, in attempting to provide a genealogy of "death" to the primordial characters (Ḷajbwināṃo̧ṇ and Lāwūnpikaar) at their chronotopic, or cosmological time-space locations (cf. Bakhtin 1981), and to the origin of the telltale sign of the trickster. Erdland's account is similar to the Downing version (from which I think the latter is derived) in the manner in which it relates to how the *aao* is taken from the mouth of the eel and applied to the birds. Iroojrālik (another name for Lawullep) is also accounted for, but here he is the one who applies it to the birds and there is no mention of how he obtained it. Notably, Erdland provides the name of the eel, "Literao," which we have yet to see in the other versions. Clearly, the name contains the root stem *aao* (just as with Letao),[24] and thus with a feminine prefix the eel's name identifies a female who possesses and is the source of the sign of the trickster.

The most striking part of this account, however, explains how the froth, which is the *aao*, supplies strength to the eel, and that the sign of the *aao* identifies power, including that of the white-eyebrowed trickster who is both favored and crafty. As a result, this etymological thread ties together my friend, the trickster, and his death. When Kometo claims that his *aao* now appears, and that he even laughs about it, it becomes the final way in which he associates himself obliquely to Letao. The story of the *aao* forges a link to the trickster and all his power because the clever one possesses it. The sign that forecasts an impending death also identifies the trickster, and when Kometo announces the appearance of his *aao*, he makes his final collusion with the image of Letao. And thus, the strange ambivalence, to laugh while talking of his own death, takes on new salience. What I thought was a displaced and idiosyncratic version of a myth now comes more clearly into focus, and only through textual calibration among his stories, his play on words, and the texts of others, can we see how this crafty trickster anchored his discourse out, portending death while affirming life through laughter. Only after some time did I realize Kometo was asking me to peer into a hole, the reality of his death, and in doing so come to understand how mythological texts and their meanings interweave into a larger cultural whole, and cast into relief something very human. Through the telltale sign of the trickster that signals his death, I begin to see faintly a contextual whole both beyond me, and that includes me.

Epilogue

Ethnographic Exit

Kometo died after I left the islands. The thing is, while my friend passed away, I realized that the trickster never really dies. Our ethnographic friendship constituted two years of dialogic conversations in which I pressed for riM̧ajeļ epistemologies and cultural knowledge, stories and their meanings, and he offered them. In the last few minutes of our last conversation together, just days before I would depart with my family from the Marshall Islands, the following poignant dialogues occurred. We had talked about a variety of things, including the great changes to social life that had come upon the Marshall Islands, and of course, Letao; he again teasingly followed the trickster on his travels all the way to Idaho and then even to Scotland, where he knew many of my ancestors were from. Several times I attempted a summation of our dialogues. Here is one.[1]

P   Is there anything you really want to explain to me before the two of us end this tape?

K   <laughing> What will it be, man?

P   Anything. What is the significance of all your teachings? I have asked for knowledge from you over these past two years. <he chuckles> Two years have passed with us just talking-story.

K   There is none. Now what else is there to think of? <chuckling> I tell you, don't say it's me, because people will make fun of you. <I laugh, he joins>

They will ask, "Where did you get it?" (oh)
The people will say, "McArthur got it from a foolish man."

P   Who will know?

K   Not the Americans?

P   The Americans don't know you. How would this be significant anyway? <he is chuckling> Like I said to you before,

The Americans will say, "Wow, that man is really smart."

K   <chuckling> *Well, the riM̧ajeḷ will say, "IT'S NONSENSE!"*
     They will really make fun.

P   But who will see much of these things?
K   Why not? Many riM̧ajeḷ know you are making a book. They will see the
     book. Many of them know English.

P   I will really respect your name in my writings. <K laughs>.
K   But it doesn't matter, they will still say,

     "You! You are a fool."
     "You got it from another foolish man." <laughs>

P   Then I will place at the front of the book, "Knowledge of fools."
K   <laughing> <u>Well</u>, Good! <hard laughter by both of us>

P   Truthfully, is there a way I can harm your name if I write a book?
K   There is none.
P   I just wish to thank you very much. If not for you my work in these islands
     would be of little significance. <he chuckles softly> Most of all, you really
     helped me understand riM̧ajeḷ stories and culture.
K   Well, thus it is.

In this segment of our last dialogue, we both anticipate a future audience to
whom I will write. I attempt to get him to give me one last good word and sum up
our time together. He jokingly tells me I should not give his name otherwise
people will make fun of me. We then enter into a playful exchange, going back
and forth. He asserts that others will say I obtained my knowledge from a foolish
man, and I counter that the Americans will recognize his intelligence. The real
audience he anticipates, however, will be other riM̧ajeḷ, who will be disgusted
("IT'S NONSENSE!"), and that even though I will write in English, many will be
able to read it and claim that I too am foolish since I got it from another foolish
man. This anticipation of the possible future readership evokes a riM̧ajeḷ sensibility in Kometo—avoid taking any credit. And yet, looking to a future text and
creating imagined references to it continues to be playfully explored through a
joking relationship. Imagining the future is funny, and when I explain that I will
put a disclaimer at the front of my book about the "Knowledge of fools," he acts
pleased, and we laugh intensely. Perhaps the joke will be on those who will read
this. In a way, it will be our last and ultimate trick we perform together. Even

when I come back around to thank him for his significant contribution to my research, he continues to chuckle, not at me (I don't think), but at the possibilities of the text yet to be made. On more than one occasion, Kometo told me that he hoped he would be dead before I published anything about him, and even instructed me not to until that time. So, my accountability to create a text about him has honored this commitment.

In the last few minutes of our dialogue, we try to create a summation of the valuable epistemologies that the riM̧ajeḷ still retain and his claim that this knowledge progressively becomes lost through modernization, American imperialism, and what he portends to be the end of his homeland and culture due to climate change.

P   So, won't you be sad if the riM̧ajeḷ customs disappear?
K   Well, since I will be sad where? I'm under the sea. <we laugh>
P   If you were to live on would you be sad?
K   Eh, I would be sad, but only because I know that <chuckles> in fifty years these islands will sink <laughing> below the sea. <laughing> The Americans have said so.
P   Perhaps.

At the beginning of these lines, I ask if he will not be sad to see the loss of riM̧ajeḷ customs. He responds with a quick intertextual joke. By that time, he will be gone himself, and where will that be? "Under the sea." This refers back to our dialogues even a year before when he instructed me to bury him in the sea. I get his reference and we laugh together. Even while groping toward something new and insightful to end our conversations, we continue to generate meaning through intertextual work, words we have already spoken. Then Kometo registers his fatalism again with a prophetic portent. Even if he were to live fifty years from that time, it would not only be him under the sea but also all the Marshall Islands. This, he argues, is because the Americans have said so, and I suspect he refers to global warming (the islanders have long been aware of the precipitous rise of sea levels and the risk to their low-lying atolls). As a result, not only the social trickster will be buried in the sea, but the final trick of the Americans, those who also brought such environmental transformations with the bomb made possible from the knowledge of Letao, will also bury everyone in the sea. Kometo's joke about himself, and a dark one at that, is also a trickster's joke on all the riM̧ajeḷ. His American friend will bury the trickster, and the tricky Americans will bury the culture and islands, currently through cultural imperialism, and ultimately with water. He sardonically entertains how the eventual death of the islands, its culture, and its people, is foreshadowed by the death of the trickster himself.

As we move toward a dialogic exit, the following brief exchange provides a concluding statement for both the ambivalence and poignancy of our text-making practice, and the depth of the ethnographically situated friendship we generated.

P   Why are you so kind to share all this knowledge and stories <he chuckles> over the past two years?

K   Those things are knowledge? I don't have real knowledge. The stories are like just making jokes. <he chuckles, long pause, looks directly at me with grin> Or?

As a familiar refrain, Kometo rejects that what he has given is knowledge; rather it is "just making jokes." Could it be that all that he has offered me, all that he has explained, all the stories he has told, represented simply one long, extended trick? He may simply have been seeking to minimize accountability to everything he told me. But Kometo was much more discerning than that. I do think he was in one part disclaiming, but from all our dialogues it became clear that salient sociological insights were made manifest through joking and narrative tricks. It was these things that shed light on riM̧ajeļ culture and even the human condition we shared. That is why, once he claims that the riM̧ajeļ stories are just joking, he chuckles and then after a long pause he grins at me and asks, "Or?" Are the jokes something more and do you get it Ḷakūbwe?

We then rehearse how talking-story with me has brought him happiness, and we commiserate a bit about the changes in the Marshall Island and its implication for those of the next generation whom he thinks are imitating American customs too much.

P   What is the significance of you teaching your grandchildren the customs?

K   <clears throat> So, that they know the customs. And that they don't injure the heart of other people. <pause> So, they don't injure the heart of people. <long pause>

P   That's true. To not injure the heart of people. <long pause> Well, my friend, I really want to thank you. <he chuckles> I know there are many more things I could have learned from you. Learn about with you. But our time is done.

K   Well, ah.

P   Thus it is.

K   Thus it is. But . . . The person of peace will give you peace.
P   Who?
K   <chuckles> Ļewōj and Ļaneej will help you. <chuckles>
P   And you also.
K   Well, I'm finished. When you end, it's done. But I say, "You shall be blessed.
     Ļewōj and Ļaneej will help you." <I chuckle softly; he joins chuckle, pause,
     and I turn off the recorder>

In the end of this dialogue, I grope for a way to extract his last pearl of wisdom. I ask about the significance of him teaching his grandchildren, as this was something he often talked about as important. He replies that he just wants them to know the riM̧ajeļ customs and to "not injure the heart of people."[2] To not "injure" (ko̧kkure) another's heart means for the riM̧ajeļ to ensure that we avoid hurting or angering one another, and to accept accountability for others. Impressed with his concluding testament about riM̧ajeļ culture, I then begin to wrap things up, even using one of his culture's ways to accept the reality of things, "thus it is" (āindein).[3] He echoes me in agreement (have I learned well and he acknowledges this?) and then declares I will receive peace from "the person of peace." I am not sure who he is talking about, and he answers, Ļewōj and Ļaneej, the riM̧ajeļ god/s of the sky.

This last great intertextual link folds the riM̧ajeļ cosmological tradition into his Christian and Mormon modernity. He does not just appeal to the biblical god to help me, but rather, he reminds me of the riM̧ajeļ cosmogony that we have explored together, and that despite the apparent differences, the gods of the respective traditions fold into one image. He at once invokes both riM̧ajeļ and Christian mythologies, and then offers them to me. I reciprocate this good will. With his final words declaring he is finished, and that when I end at that moment (turn off my recorder), he invokes a blessing and reiterates how the god/s will assist me, perhaps even in writing this work. This invocation collapses the riM̧ajeļ and Christian gods, and grants his approval for what I may do, and more importantly for me personally, he acknowledges that I understand his point that others perhaps would not. Here, in his last words of dialogue, he fuses the Indigenous mythological past, riM̧ajeļ culture and its entanglement with modern religion, the decolonizing present and my presence, our respective cultural epistemologies, himself and me. The texts among our worlds have been wholly calibrated and blurred into one. The trickster has done his work; cultures and personal lives have been altogether mediated. I can only chuckle sympathetically, and he joins me one last time as we both realize its significance.

And, thus, our dialogues ended, at least for a season. I would visit the islands again and reunite with him a couple times before he died, such as the last meeting presented at the beginning of this book. But I would never again bring forth a tape recorder and structure questions to elicit stories and commentary. I would just sit with him and chat, reflecting and laughing about our times together, and catching up on family. But in a way my dialogue with Kometo continues all these years later as I work through the recordings, the texts, and my memories about him. And now this dialogue extends outward to engage other texts, including all those that the readers bring to this book. While dialoguing with this enchanting trickster, he took me into some ambiguous holes along the margins of myth and ethnography. And, in the intimacy of an ethnographic friendship, I followed and participated with him as he traced a faint outline of the elusive whole, a more integrated envisioning of large-scale histories and enduring mythologies with all their Indigenous meanings, epistemologies, and ideologies of social power. Such a vision and the methods of the trickster may offer unanticipated Indigenous resources for decolonization.

Dennis Tedlock's claim (1995, 284) that "dialogue does not so much end as reach a moment of adjournment" seems most appropriate here. Dialogues with Kometo can only be temporarily on hold. Kometo's anticipation of his own death offered a creative accomplishment through a textual working that would go beyond even this inevitable event. Death forms part of a trickster's work, but just as with Letao, we can trust that Kometo's words may also bring us back to life.

Notes

Prologue

1. riM̧ajeļ is the term used by the Marshall Islanders to refer to themselves as a people. Previous spelling was riMajōl. It literally means "people of the Marshalls." To support recent decolonization efforts, I use this term in lieu of "Marshallese."

2. The term the islanders use for their own language. Previous spelling: Kajin Majōl.

3. The spelling for the name of the mythological trickster figure may either be rendered as *Etao* or *Letao*. The earliest ethnographic literature renders the spelling as Edao (Krammer and Nevermann 1938) confusing the [d] for a [t], and sometimes Lādao recognizing the [l] phoneme as an occasional prefix (Erdland 1914). Laurence Carucci (1997a) identifies the trickster as Etao using the correct [t] phoneme. In his comprehensive story collection, Jack Tobin (2002) acknowledges that some of his storytellers pronounced the name as Etao, and others Le-Etao. The addition of the [l] (like Erdland) and [e] phonemes in a prefix ensures identification of the masculine gender. All subsequent collections of stories simply identify the trickster as Letao. Kometo more often used the pronunciation Letao. But because he sometimes used the pronunciations interchangeably, I will render the spelling accordingly.

4. I join a limited, though noteworthy group of scholars who have gone beyond anthologies and collections to address folklore traditions within the context of specific cultures in Oceania. This includes the multiple contributors to Kaeppler and Nimmo (1976) and Finnegan and Orbell (1995). See also multiple references in McArthur (2012).

Chapter 1: In the Grip of a Trickster

1. Most collections of riM̧ajeļ oral traditions include a section on Letao stories. See Davenport (1953); Mitchell (1973); Downing et al. (1992); Kelin (2003).

2. I use this term to avoid the negative connotations of the term "prehistory," which suggests that, prior to Western contact, the islanders of Oceania were without ways of rendering the past. In Oceania, this term captures the precontact history represented in mythologies, cosmogonies, genealogies, oral histories, linguistics, and archaeology, and it resonates with the sensibilities in a region where the "deep" waters are articulated in myth and cosmology. See Dixon ([1916] 2008); Dening (2004); Kaʻili (2017); and references to motifs (A920), (A952), (A952.1), and (A955.8) in Kirtley (1971).

3. Recorded March 4, 1992.

4. Both M̧aļoeļap and Likiep are atolls in the northern Ratak chain.

5. Variants are recorded in Davenport (1953, 230–231), and Downing et al. (1992, 111).

6. The trickster as the harbinger of fire cross culturally (Motif A1414) is noted in Hyde (1998) and Scheub (2013). See also culturally specific versions of Letao as the origin of fire in

Downing et al. (1992, 95–96); Kelin (2003, 109–110); and the riṂajeḷ eco-poet Jetñil-Kijiner's rendering in Keown (2018, 597).

7. Pan-Pacific motifs about deception (K730), (K800), (K1200). See motif references in Kirtley (1955, 1971).

8. Cable television was introduced in the 1970s and VCRs in the 1980s and 1990s at the capital Mājro atoll and Epjā islet at Kuwajleen atoll. With difficulty following the English dialogue, many islanders took most to war movies, ghost stories, and action dramas often referred to as "murder movies" (*pija in uror/mȯrȯ*).

9. Bauman and Briggs (1990, 72–78) identify this as a process of "entextualization," or "rendering discourse extractable" to make a text, and then recontextualizing or resituating it into other social and performance contexts.

10. An initial crucial step toward challenging the "objective" authority of the ethnographer was articulated by James Clifford (1983) and his use of earlier experiments by Dwyer (1979) to record literal exchanges between ethnographer and subject, and the rejection of the separation of the "interpreting self from a textualized other" (Crapanzano 1980, 134).

11. I use decolonize instead of postcolonial because, as Linda Tuhiwai Smith has maintained, the idea that colonialism is "finished business" is inaccurate, and postcolonial discourse "still leaves out indigenous people," and their "ways of knowing and current . . . concerns" (2012, 25). Postcolonialism too often represents a "convenient invention of Western intellectuals which reinscribes their power to define the world" (2012, 14). The riṂajeḷ still face the daunting project to decolonize themselves from American power and controls.

12. See LaBriola (2019, 184) for a good example of the application of Hauʻofa's method that highlights the strategies the riṂajeḷ used to manage and make sense of their historical encounters with outsiders.

13. See Keown's discussion (2018, 595) for how Jetñil-Kijiner uses the oral tradition about *mejenkwaad*, a female demon that engulfs women to return them to her own body, as a metaphor for grieving women who have experienced the negative radiation effects of atomic bomb tests such as miscarriages, birth defects, etc.

14. For examples of using traditional oral resources in contemporary Oceanic contexts, see Siikala and Siikala (2005); Finnegan and Orbell (1995); Māhina (1999); Hezel (2013); Hermann (2011).

15. Indeed, long before literary criticism found the concept of intertextuality (e.g., Kristeva 1980) useful, folklorists developed quite sophisticated methodologies to address "the instability in the folklore text" and textual relationships (Titon 2003, 73). A text suggesting an identity with other texts simply meant "variants."

16. Linguistic dialects correspond with the respective Rālik and Ratak island chains as well as with distinct chiefly histories. The sea between these two chains is referred to as *laḷeḷapḷap*. While riṂajeḷ navigators and sailors traveled between the two chains, the currents and winds were most favorable for sailing along the atolls of each respective chain.

17. There are sixty-six named matriclans (*jowi*) distributed across the Marshall Islands.

18. See Walsh (2003) on the chief's divine authority and political power, and LaBriola (2019) on how this has played out in historical events.

19. LaBriola (2013) has shown how land transactions in Likiep involved chiefs forging alliances and making sales to outsiders.

20. See Kotzebue (1821, 1830).

21. Those dropped on Hiroshima and Nagasaki were less than thirteen kilotons.

22. See Carucci (2004) for a nuanced discussion on how identity formation, rooted in a place, changed as the Ānewetak Islanders were forced to relocate to Wūjlañ for atomic bomb testing.

23. Now named Ronald Reagan Ballistic Missile Defense Test Site.

24. US interests have been more imperial than colonial. The actual occupation of the islands with settlers as an outpost for political, economic, and missionization interests has not been the US strategy, except notably in Kuwajleen with its "militourism" (Teaiwa 1999). But the military interests, control, exploitation, and subjugation of the islanders as well as the discursive practices that ensure dependency and domination characterize the islanders' long history with the United States (Smith-Norris 2012, 22).

25. Tobin (2002, 137) also recounts the history of the castaways from Kiribati and the origin of Kometo's matriclan, Ripit.

26. In 2006, this mission was divided from the rest of Micronesia when the Marshalls and Kiribati became linked in their own independent mission. See McArthur (2023).

27. For anthropological discussions on the local complexities of conversion, see Ramstad (2003); Robbins (2004); and Engelke and Tomlinson (2006).

Chapter 2: Narrative Tricks

1. Ethnopoetics is a method of transcribing cultural narratives and oral poetry to retain the poetic features of performance that would be lost in a single prose rendering.

2. Recorded October 23, 1992.

3. See Bender (1963, 95–103); Downing et al. (1992, 100–102); Kelin (2003, 222–224); and Tanner (2008 as told by Hersha Laneab) for additional versions of the fake canoe made from ironwood (*kōñe*).

4. See Bender (1963, 95–103); Downing et al. (1992, 103–106); and Tanner (2008) for additional versions of the earth-oven trick in Kiribati.

5. The single term *aḷeḷe* can only be translated with multiple words. It identifies both a fishing instrument and a method by which many men use a coconut-leaf-chain to scare a school of fish into a tighter area. Then they spear or club the fish.

6. Key motifs of deception in this myth: (K11), (K100), (K320), (K500). See references in Kirtley (1955, 1971).

7. As with English, the Kajin M̧ajeḷ word *babu*, which literally means to "lie down," provides a euphemism for sexual relations. The word is used to avoid terms prohibited in the presence of cross-sex kin. In other versions of the tale (e.g., Downing et al. 1992, 106), the sexual relations are made explicit.

8. Hersha Laneab, recorded by Tanner (2008), narrates this trick taking place on Roñroñ islet before leaving Mājro.

9. Stephen Colbert first used the term on the *Colbert Report*, October 17, 2005. See also Thompson and Schrempp's (2020) use of the term with mythology and the oral genres.

10. In Kajin M̧ajeḷ, the tense aspect is attached to the subject rather than the verb. For example, the second person pronoun *kwe* with the verb *etal* (go) will take on a variety of tense markers: *kwōj etal* (you are going), *kwaar etal* (you went), *kwōnaaj etal* (you will go), and so forth. To make the English translation, I have attached the tense to the verb.

11. The word *ōrrōr* provides a slang interjection that can mean "oh heck," "oh darn," "ugh," "oh jeez," or "oh my"; also, a vulgar expression of sexual pleasure.

12. Words that specify spatial or temporal location from the perspective of one or more participants in an act of speech.

13. Boundaries between *wāto* are marked by plants, notches on coconut trees, rocks, and other natural formations. Residents on every atoll are very familiar with these boundaries, the names of all the land tracts, who has rights to them, and to which chief they belong (except on the densely populated urban settings of Mājro and Epjā islet of Kuwajleen). Some *wāto* serve as residences while others are worked by those who have land rights to them. The width of a land tract varies from ten to several hundred meters. Extending the *wāto* from lagoon to ocean allows kin groups to exploit the varying land resources across the atoll.

14. This is similar to Hansen's (2002, 22) concept of "genre-variance," or how the "same story can be found at one place and time as a myth and at another place and time as a legend or folktale."

15. Bronislaw Malinowski (1926) was among the earliest to provide definitions for the three folklore forms through his work in the Trobriand Islands.

16. Most scholars continue to primarily delineate the narrative categories of myth, legend, and folktale by the identification of a story's truth status and placement in time. See Thompson and Schrempp (2020).

17. Bascom in turn used this label to correspond with his definition of legend.

18. This framing device and the concluding formula are rarely used by storytellers today.

19. August Erdland (1914) worked in the islands in 1900; Kramer and Nevermann (1938) worked in the islands from 1908 to 1910; and Tobin (1967, 2002) worked in the islands from 1950 to 1957 and 1967 to 1974.

20. My approach here is "focused on a close analysis of myth in specific, situated sociohistorical contexts" (Schrempp 2002, 8) rather than unpacking the universal meanings of the text.

21. Schrempp (2002, 1–15) notes how the analysis of myth by scholars moves between the literal (that the myth represents a factual description of the past for the people who tell it) and the symbolic (that myth represents a figurative expression).

22. We certainly cannot know how those in the deep past conceived of these stories in terms of fiction, fact, the sacred, and not-sacred, or even if such conceptualizations were meaningful designations.

23. The term *etto* means the ancient past, whereas *raan kein,* the term for the present, literally means "these days (proximate at hand to those in dialogue)."

24. My use of the term sensibility resonates with Ka'ili's (2017, 5) definition of indigeneity to include ancient systems of thinking and behaving, and Meyer's (2013, 98–99) consideration of the meaning of Indigenous as a synonym for "older ways to view the world" or an epistemology. See also Hezel (2013) on Indigenous logics in Micronesia.

25. At the *m̧am̧a* festival, people made offerings to the god Jebro at the onset of the breadfruit season.

26. Paying tribute and deference to a chief is also communicated in the proverb "*Kwōn jab ālkwōj pein ak,*" or "Don't bend the wing of the frigate bird." The *Ak,* or frigate bird, is the largest bird in the Marshall Islands, flies higher than any other, and serves as the symbol of the chief. Equivalent Western proverb: "Don't bite the hand that feeds you."

27. This is formally signified through *badikdik,* to gesture as if to keep one's head lower than the chief's while in their presence.

28. Like great warriors, some refer to the Americans as tough and bold (*kijoñ*). This term can also suggest being immoral.

29. See Carucci (2019) for the flexible and expansive meaning of the concept of friendship among the riM̧ajeļ.

30. Carucci (1989) characterizes this as "The Source of the Force."

31. On Runit islet of Ānewetak, the cement dome that covers the radioactive waste repository is weathering and compromised, and is leaking high levels of radioactivity. See reports by Gerrard (2014) and Willacy (2017).

Chapter 3: Dialogic Riddling

1. Letao's perpetual travel resonates with the idea of the Pacific islander as a traveling, mobile explorer, always expanding boundaries and frontiers. See Hau'ofa (2008) and Ka'ili (2017).

2. For several examples of riM̧ajeļ riddles, see Davenport (1952b, 265–266).

3. Recorded March 4, 1993.

4. Versions of Letao sailing to America on his own accord are also found in Bender (1978); Carucci (1997a); Tobin (2002); Kelin (2003); Tanner (2008).

5. The storyteller Jelibōr Jam (Tobin 2002, 227) also indicates that Letao can sometimes prove subversive and at other times benevolent as suits him.

6. riM̧ajeļ mythology and cosmology offer suggestive parallels to the comparative grid proposed by Thompson and Schrempp (2020) that include time, space, quality, quantity, and relation.

7. Kapilōñ is the Kajin M̧ajeļ word for "western sky," and also a reference to the Micronesia area west of the Marshall Islands.

8. The term *menmenbwij* is also used to designate a matrilineal genealogy only.

9. The storyteller Iban Edwin, identifies Ep as a kingdom below the sea. This can also be understood as beyond the western horizon. See Kelin (2003, 237).

10. Motif A625.2 is among the most common cosmological motifs in Oceania. See Kirtley (1955, 1971).

11. See Abo et al. (1976) and Tobin (2002) for how the riM̧ajeļ elders and scholars refer often to an ancient version (*kajin etto*) of Kajin M̧ajeļ. Some of this language is retained in chant and the names of mythological gods. Only a few of the elders understand the obscure references in the chants. While in this myth the storyteller identifies Ļakam̧ as the coconut son of Jineer ilo Kōbo, the umbrella term used for all varieties of the coconut is "*ni*," and similar forms of this word are found in most Austronesian languages in the Oceania. See Blust (2009).

12. Carucci (1989, 85) also identifies these two gods as the "primal first rulers of earth."

13. To increase through division and multiplication of the gods, and their creation work at their respective locations and spheres, represents a familiar pattern in Oceania. See Schrempp (1992) and Thompson and Schrempp (2020).

14. All mother's sisters and all father's sisters will be identified as *jine-*, or mother. All father's brothers will be identified as *jemā-*, or father. Mother's brothers receive a different term, *wūllepa-* or *rūkorea-* (depending on dialect) to mark their significance within the *bwij*, or matriline. Title inheritance will pass from the maternal uncle to the maternal nephew, or *mañde-*.

15. Other variant spellings of her name include Liktanur (Downing et al., 1992) and Lōktañūr (Abo et al. 1976; Carucci 1997a; Tobin 2002). The second is more typically accepted.

I have cross-checked the spelling I use here with the pronunciation of this goddess's name by several male and female elders from Aelōñḷapḷap, the atoll identified as her home as recounted in the mythologies. This spelling makes a salient link to her primordial action when she descended from the skies or heaven above (lōñ) to visit her sons on Aelōñḷapḷap.

16. Recorded February 10, 1992.

17. Motif T554.0.2. Woman as mother of all animals.

18. Rat (*kijdik*), gecko (*korap*), green lizard (*mānnueal*), black lizard (*aop*) ant (*ḷoñ*), fly (*ḷọñ*), mosquito (*ŋam*), spider (*kauḷaḷo*), cockroach (*kuḷuḷ*), dog (*kidu*), cat (*kuuj*).

19. A green variety of a lizard (*Dasia smaragdina*).

20. A black variety of a lizard (*Dasia smaragdina*).

21. See Thompson and Schrempp (2020, 126–132) on the elaboration of "quality" or kind in mythology.

22. The matriline is like the *kōñejubar,* the ironwood plant that takes root in the hard and stable coral, in contrast to the patriline that is like the *lutitbok,* a plant that takes root in the unstable and shifting sandbar.

23. For the riMajeḷ, tracing kinship through both the matriline and patriline remains important for their ambilineal identities, but most especially, to avoid incest. The spiritual power and sometimes literal land inheritance that flows through the patriline is seen to weaken (*mōjṇoḷok*) through the generations. Since a chief's title is received through his mother and her matriline, his patrilineal descendants are identified with less and less royalty (unless he mates with a royal *lerooj* rather than a commoner). A paramount high chief's (*irooj ḷapḷap*) children are referred to as *bwidak* and his grandchildren *ḷajjibjib,* after which no specific term is applied and royalty no longer recognized.

24. See Walsh (2003) for additional description of the intersection among land, matrilineal kinship, commoners, and divine authority. See also Carucci (1997b).

25. The high chief Jortōkā of Likiep sold the atoll to the Portuguese traders A. Capelle and Jose Anton debrum in 1877. After these European men married local riMajeḷ women, the inheritance pattern on Likiep atoll shifted to patrilineally ascribed lands within these families. See LaBriola (2013). Ānewetak also presents adaptations and variations that tend toward a patrilineal emphasis. This is in part due to its close proximity to other islands in *kapilōñ* (Micronesia), and because of disruptions brought about by forced migration and dislocation of these islanders to Wūjlañ Island for atomic bomb testing. See Carucci (1997a).

26. In everyday speech, this word serves the linguistic function of signaling a possessive, meaning "belonging to he, she, or it." But at the same time, it encodes an individual's spiritual will or soul.

27. This principle is captured in the proverb (*jabōnkōnnaan*), "*Kandikdik in io̧kwe,*" literally, "a little bit of food (is) of love." This means even if one only has a small portion of food, they distribute it to others to show love, especially to matrilineal kin. See Stone et al. (2000). See also Pollock's (1974) discussion on how matrilineages come together to cooperate and act as the primary social group.

28. See the earliest contact descriptions in Lay and Hussey (1828), and in Paulding (1831).

29. Recorded March 6, 1992.

30. Kometo described for me on many occasions how terrified the riMajeḷ were when the US military launched the attacks in 1943 with aircraft bombing runs, mortar from ships, Marine landings, and fierce battles on land. Falgout et al. (2008) offer poignant descriptions by

the Indigenous peoples of Micronesia, including the Marshall Islands, of the shock, hardships, and suffering during the war.

31. These handicrafts today are presented as gifts (*tōptōp*) at major life cycle events such as the first-year ceremonies for an infant (*keemem*), marriages (*pālele*), graduations (*diwōjḷọk*), wakes (*ilomej*) and funerals (*kallib*), and provide an important exchange in the tourist economy. See Taafaki and Fowler (2019).

32. Recorded April 1, 1992.

33. The United States administered the Trust Territory of the Pacific Islands from 1947–1978. The headquarters for Micronesia was placed on Saipan, Marianas Islands.

34. In 1983, the Republic of the Marshall Islands entered into a "Compact of Free Association" with the United States. In 1987, the nation was granted complete independence, and still with a negotiated compact. Independence was not recognized by the United Nations until 1991, when it was admitted as a full member.

35. See LaBriola (2013) for a notable exception on Likiep atoll.

36. Recorded December 18, 1992.

37. In order to vote in the Marshall Islands elections, one must demonstrate they have *jowi* (a matriclan) and land rights. Because every individual has land rights in multiple atolls they may choose to vote from any of them (whether in residence or not), and from one election to the next an individual may identify different atolls to which they will cast a vote.

38. Recorded November 6, 1992.

39. This royal court included at least one of the following: diviner (*ribubu*), sorcerer (*rianijnij* or *rijọubwe*), magician (*rikkōpāl*), medicine specialist (*riwūno*), genealogist (*rimenmenbwij* for matriline, *rikadkad* general), storyteller (*ribwebwenato*), navigator (*rimeto*), weather prognosticator (*rikatu*), fishing master (*rieọñōd*), steward (*rikōmoñā*), and lead warrior (*riḷakkūk*).

Chapter 4: Hide-and-Seek

1. Recorded October 23, 1992.

2. Erdland spells the name "Edao." He heard a voiced alveolar stop instead of the hard, voiceless phoneme [t]. The [d] phoneme in Kajin M̧ajeḷ is actually a light retroflex trill. The name "Etao" combines two morphemes *āt* (eyebrow) and *aao* (halo or sign of death). In the spelling, the [ā] sound (low front vowel) is stretched to an [e] (mid front vowel). The [l] phoneme with the accompany [e] vowel designates male gender.

3. Tobin (2002) also identifies a form of divination called *boḷā*, when beach pebbles (*lā*) are counted out in a series to determine an auspicious time to build a canoe.

4. Recorded March 4, 1992.

5. *Kaju* in the Ratak dialect and *kiju* in the Rālik dialect.

6. That gods possess two names is clearly presented in the mythology. For instance, in addition to the Ororao and Lojenmile pairing, Iroojrālik is equivalent to Wullep, and Jebro, the obedient son of Lōñtañūr, is often also referred to as Lōjelañ. See Carucci (1997a); Tobin (2002).

7. While these beings occupy an important place in mythic stories, they continue to appear in contemporary legends and memorates. Kometo and his friend M̧ake both recounted how they knew a man on Kuwajleen who was the son of a *ņoonniep*. Stories of the *ņoonniep* recount how they brought food, a fragrant oil (*kiōp*), the brimmed hat worn by women, and the *jebwa*, a spectacular, complicated, and exuberant stick dance accompanied by chanting.

8. The *waḷap* was a large deepwater outrigger sailing canoe, reaching up to thirty meters in length and able to carry up to fifty people with food supplies. It was used mainly for inter-island voyaging. The *tipñōl* is a smaller sailing canoe used to cross lagoons or sail just outside the reefs on ocean-side. The *kōrkōr* is a paddling canoe used only within lagoons.

9. All the Marshall Islands are low-lying coral atolls or raised islands, never more than 4.5 meters in elevation. Travel to volcanic high-islands was rare historically. However, as mentioned to me by a few elders and recorded by Tobin (2002), some chants refer to ancient travel to Nan Madol of Pohnpei Island in the central Caroline Islands. There are also accounts of travels to Kosrae (a high-island) by ABCFM (1859), Tobin (2002), and my recording of Kometo (November 9, 1992).

10. The majority of early Protestant missionaries were Hawaiian. See Hezel (1983); Walsh and Heine (2012).

11. It is tempting, though unsupported, to find resonance in this island-fishing motif with the "earth diver" (motif A811) through native North America and elsewhere.

12. Recorded February 10, 1992.

13. *Waini* is the dried meat or kernel of the coconut. Coconut oil (*pinneep*) is extracted from copra.

14. Kometo identifies it as the first matriclan, whereas Amata Kabua (1993) identifies it as the clan that controlled the northwestern atolls of the Rālik chain (except Ānewetak), while the Errepa clan controlled the southern Rālik chain.

15. Amata Kabua (1993) identified only eight original clans. From the Errepa came the first *irooj pweio*, or offspring of both a chief father (*irooj*) and chief mother (*lerooj*). See also Mason (1986).

16. LaBriola (2019) also identifies Liwātuonmour and Lidepdepju as sacred female ancestors and the mothers of the chiefly clans (*jowi* or *jou*) in the Rālik and Ratak islands, respectively.

17. Animals are referred to as *menninmour,* which literally means "this living thing." Humans are referred to as *armej,* which can be interpreted to mean "of those that die," or "it is our lot to die."

Chapter 5: A Trickster's Tropes

1. Recorded December 13, 1991.

2. See Downing et al. (1992, 121–127); Knight (1982, 25–31); Tanner (2008, as told by Bia Jabeo) for additional versions of the boy who drifts off at Aelōñḷapḷap.

3. See references in Kirtley (1953, 1971).

4. The root morpheme *bwij* is the same term used for "matriline."

5. First president of the Republic of the Marshall Islands. Lived 1928–1996. Served 1979–1996, five consecutive terms.

6. The Protestant missionaries of the ABCFM first arrived in 1857, followed by the Catholics in 1891, then the Baptists and Assembly of God in the early part of the twentieth century, followed by sects such as the Mormons and others in the latter part of the century. See ABCFM (1891); Hezel (1983, 1995); Walsh and Heine (2012); McArthur (2023).

7. See Taafaki et al. (2006).

8. Recorded June 12, 1993.

9. In the traditional riMajeḷ thatched hut (*em̧*), the windows, covered by a firm woven panel, were placed at the bottom of the structure. They could be opened and supported by an

extended stick to allow air flow and breezes across those lying on woven mats (*jaki*), or closed during rain and heavy winds.

10. See Downing et al. (1992, 39–42).

11. Like Letao, the *mejenkwaad* may also shape-shift by stretching their necks for miles to capture their victims. See Tobin (2002).

12. The word *bōtōktōk* or literally "blood," to designate the patriline, serves as a veiled term for *pek* or "sperm," a word not to be used in mixed-gender company or among cross-sex kin. Consequently, kinship in riM̧ajeļ society is reckoned either through navel lines or sperm lines.

13. An alternative chant of Kikiao is provided by the storyteller La bedbedin in Knight (1982, 27).

14. One of the primal demigoddesses in the cosmogonic genealogy for the Ratak chain.

15. The male-centric patriarchal emphasis in Freud's model runs contrary to riM̧ajeļ society of matrilineal descent. There is no oedipal complex here with the two young female protagonists. The relational strain is not between father and sons in riM̧ajeļ society, but rather between the maternal uncle or mother's brother (*wūllepan* or *rūkorean*) and nephew, or sister's son (*mañden*), similar to what Bronislaw Malinowski raised years ago. In this matrilineal society, a story of daughters eating their father who offered himself as a sacrificial substitute challenges, to a degree, the idea of oedipal patricide.

16. See Knight (1980); Kowata et al. (1999); Tobin (2002); Kelin et al. (2003).

17. A memorate is a narrative told in first person that rehearses a personal encounter with the supernatural, magical, or numinous.

Chapter 6: Dirty and Dangerous Tricks

1. The word *ttoon* can mean "dirty," "profane," "obscene," or "vulgar." Sometimes the word *kōtrae* may also be employed to suggest the profane, to desecrate, or break taboo. It is linked to the idea of infringing upon the sacred lands of the chief.

2. These would be women in his matriline, matriclan, and patriline, including classificatory sisters (parallel-cousins), daughters, and mothers. Even though he was older, some of the women occupied a senior position in the previous generation of his extended matriline and patriline.

3. Recorded April 1, 1992.

4. Recorded February 26, 1992.

5. This is a pseudonym as I do not recall her actual name.

6. Incest for the riM̧ajeļ includes sexual relations with all classificatory relatives except cross-cousins as they would belong to other matrilines and patrilines, and in fact they are often highly desirable unions to keep royal blood lines connected.

7. Recorded February 21, 1992.

8. Motif T412, mother-son incest.

9. Motif 1313.2.2. Origin of female sex organs.

10. See references to motif A1352 (origin of sexual intercourse) in Kirtley (1955, 1971). Letao was associated with the "sex school" for young women in former days on Lōñar islet of Arņo atoll. See Tobin (2003, 310).

11. These Kajin M̧ajeļ terms are considered vulgar and strict prohibitions are in place to avoid using them, especially in mixed-gender company and among relatives. They are only used by same-gender agemates, and then only in certain contexts given to playful banter.

12. Motif T471. See references in Kirtley (1953, 1971).

13. The term for the male loincloth, *in,* was made from coconut leaves and hibiscus fiber. Men also wore the *kaḷ,* made of finely plaited pandanus leaves. The women's *ed* was made of finely plaited pandanus matting. Today many will also refer to the women's loincloth as *in.* See Taafaki and Fowler (2019).

14. Recorded February 21, 1992.

15. See Peterson (2009) for the adaptive advantages of matriliny in the resource vulnerable atolls.

16. Kajin Ṃajeḷ: *Jinaad ilo kobo, jemād im jemān ro jet.* See also Stone et al. (2000).

17. Recorded October 30, 1992.

18. *Jeplej* is the historical term for venereal disease. But *mādke* is more commonly used.

19. Recorded April 6, 1992.

20. Main islet and district government center on Jālooj atoll.

21. Recorded October 23, 1992.

Chapter 7: Portending Death

1. Recorded June 14, 1993.

2. Prophecy in Kajin Ṃajeḷ is referred to as *kanaan,* or literally "to make a word happen," and the prophet is *riKanaan,* "person who makes a word happen."

3. Historically, the Kajin Ṃajeḷ terms for "soul" (*an* for his/her soul, *aṃ* for your soul, *aō* for my soul, *aer* for their soul, etc.) was distinguished from *jetōb,* which identified nonhuman spirits. But today, likely due to the influence of missionization and how the concepts were translated into the Bible, the terms are often used interchangeably. A human is now seen to possess either the *an* or a *jetōb.*

4. Knox Island on old maps.

5. Motif 1315, origin of death. See multiple references in Kirtley (1955, 1971) for a god's role and power over death.

6. According to Indigenous riṂajeḷ historian James Milne, the sky was once only believed to be the place of the gods and their power, not a final destination for the dead. The association of people rising to heaven comes with Christianity. See Kowata et al. (1999, 69).

7. Carucci (1997a) also describes how the Ānewetak Islanders ascertain Ḷewōj and Ḷaneej as the sky gods.

8. See also Kowata et al. (1999, 68–69) for a similar account by Indigenous historian James Milne.

9. Jelibōr Jam.

10. Litarjikūt Kabua.

11. Recorded April 6, 1992.

12. See Kramer and Nevermann (1938); Grey (1951); Downing et al. (1992); Kelin (2003).

13. That this woman is dirty and gave birth to the animals is first cited in Erdland (1914, 147).

14. The term *ḷāmoran* is most often applied to patrilineal land inheritance. Many today will use the term *ḷāmoran* for *kapijukunen* (matrilineal land inheritance), or as a cover term for all inherited lands, much to the dismay of many chiefs and traditionalists.

15. Recorded December 7, 1992.

16. The riṂajeḷ navigators used the stars to plot their position as well as cloud formations and the appearance of certain birds that signaled particular atolls close by. They also interpreted

the intricate mixing of wave (*ṇo*) and current patterns (*ae*) that interweave in predictable patterns. These waves and currents, when encountering atolls, bend and refract so consistently that they serve as signatures for the location of each atoll. This accumulated wisdom was recorded in oral narratives and sophisticated stick charts that served as instructional aides. One of the important charts, the *wapepe*, literally means "canoe decision," that is, the chart helps the navigator make the important decisions about where to point the canoe to arrive safely at the desired destination. See Erdland (1914); Kramer and Nevermann (1938); Spennemann (1993).

17. Recorded March 4, 1992.

18. Gygis alba.

19. Frigate birds (*Fregata minor*) are prevalent through all tropical zones and loom large in the mythology and cultures of Oceania as a representation of chiefly or divine authority. See Dixon (2008).

20. *Anous stolidus.*

21. Motif 2411.2, Origin of color of bird. See references in Kirtley (1953, 1971).

22. This would likely have been the *akeo̧,* a harvest of the first fruits of coconut (*ni*) or pandanus (*bōb*), or the *ṃaṃa* harvest for breadfruit (*mā*); or, *añōneañ* (the winter with strong winds out of the northeast), a harvest time for arrowroot (*ṃaṃōk*).

23. Recorded May 21, 1992.

24. When the word *aao* is attached to the full name of the trickster, the first low back unrounded vowel, [a], is dropped. This is typical in many compound Kajin Ṃajeḷ words when the double vowel follows a consonant.

Epilogue

1. Recorded June 18, 1993.
2. Kajin Ṃajeḷ: *Jab ko̧kkure būruon armej.*
3. *Āindein* can also mean "so it is."

REFERENCES

Abo, Takaji, Byron W. Bender, Alfred Capelle, and Tony DeBrum. 1976. *Marshallese-English Dictionary*. Honolulu: University of Hawai'i Press.

Abrahams, Roger, and Alan Dundes. 1972. "Riddles." In *Folklore and Folklife: An Introduction*, edited by Richard Dorson, pp. 129–143. Chicago: University of Chicago Press.

Alexander, William. 1978. "Wage Labor, Urbanization and Culture Change in the Marshall Islands." PhD diss., New School of Social Research.

American Board of Commissioners for Foreign Missions (ABCFM). 1859. Letters and Papers of the American Board of Commissioners for Foreign Missions: Mission to Micronesia, 1852–1909. 19 vols. 19.4–19.6, Harvard University. Houghton Library, Cambridge, MA.

Appadurai, Arjun. 1996. *Modernity at Large: Cultural Dimensions of Globalization*. Minneapolis: University of Minnesota Press.

Arvin, Maile. 2019. *Possessing Polynesians: The Science of Settler Colonial Whiteness in Hawai'i and Oceania*. Durham, NC: Duke University Press.

Babcock, Barbara. 1975. "A Tolerated Margin of Mess: A Trickster and His Tales Reconsidered." *Journal of the Folklore Institute* 11, no. 3:147–186.

———. 1978. Introduction to *The Reversible World: Symbolic Inversion in Art and Society*, edited by Barbara Babcock, pp. 13–36. Ithaca, NY: Cornell University Press.

Bakhtin, Mikhail M. (1968) 1984. *Rabelais and His World*, translated by Hèléne Iswolsky. Bloomington: Indiana University Press.

———. 1981. *The Dialogic Imagination*, edited by Michael Holquist, translated by Caryl Emerson and Michael Holquist. Austin: University of Texas Press.

———. 1986. *Speech Genres and Other Late Essays*, translated by Vern W. McGee. Austin: University of Texas Press.

Barclay, Robert. 2002. *Melal: A Novel of the Pacific*. Honolulu: University of Hawai'i Press.

Barker, Holly M. 2004. *Bravo for the Marshallese: Regaining Control of a Post-nuclear, Post-colonial World*. Belmont, CA: Thomson and Wadsworth.

Barnes, J. A. 1994. *A Pack of Lies: Towards a Sociology of Lying*. Cambridge: Cambridge University Press.

Bascom, William. 1965. "The Forms of Folklore: Prose Narratives." *Journal of American Folklore* 78, no. 307:3–20.

Basso, Ellen B. 1987. *In Favor of Deceit: A Study of Tricksters in an Amazonian Society*. Tucson: University of Arizona Press.

Bauman, Richard. 1977. *Verbal Art as Performance.* Prospect Heights, IL: Waveland Press.

———. 1986. *Story, Performance, and Event: Contextual Studies in Oral Narrative.* Cambridge: Cambridge University Press.

———. 1989. "American Folklore Studies and Social Transformation: A Performance-Centered Perspective." *Text and Performance Quarterly* 9, no. 3:175–184.

———. 1992. "Contextualization, Tradition, and the Dialogue of Genres: Icelandic Legends of the Kraftaskald." In *Rethinking Context: Language as an Interactive Phenomenon,* edited by Allesandro Duranti and Charles Goodwin, pp. 125–145. Cambridge: Cambridge University Press.

———. 2004. *A World of Others' Words: Cross-Cultural Perspectives on Intertextuality.* Oxford: Blackwell.

———. 2016. "The Philology of the Vernacular." In *Grand Theory in Folkloristics,* edited by Lee Haring, pp. 63–70. Bloomington: Indiana University Press.

Bauman, Richard, and Charles L. Briggs. 1990. "Poetics and Performance as Critical Perspective on Language and Social Life." *Annual Review of Anthropology* 19:59–88.

———. 2003. *Voices of Modernity: Language Ideologies and the Politics of Inequality.* Cambridge: Cambridge University Press.

Beckwith, Martha. (1940) 1970. *Hawaiian Mythology.* Honolulu: University of Hawai'i Press.

Ben-Amos, Dan. 1976. "Analytical Categories and Ethnic Genres." In *Folklore Genres,* edited by Dan Ben-Amos, pp. 215–242. Austin: University of Texas Press.

Bender, Byron W. 1963. "A Linguistic Analysis of the Place-Names of the Marshall Islands." PhD diss., Indiana University.

———. 1978. *Spoken Marshallese: An Intensive Course with Grammatical Notes and Glossary.* Honolulu: University Press of Hawai'i.

Bendix, Regina. 1997. *In Search of Authenticity: The Formation of Folklore Studies.* Madison: University of Wisconsin Press.

Benedict, Ruth. (1934) 1959. *Patterns of Culture.* Boston: Houghton Mifflin.

Berman, Elise. 2019. *Talking Like Children: Language and the Production of Age in the Marshall Islands.* Oxford: Oxford University Press.

Blust, Robert. 2009. *The Austronesian Languages.* Canberra: Research School of Pacific and Asian Studies, The Australia National University.

Brenneis, Donald. 1996. "Telling Troubles: Narrative, Conflict, and Experience." In *Disorderly Discourse: Narrative, Conflict, and Inequality,* edited by Charles L. Briggs, pp. 41–52. Oxford: Oxford University Press.

Briggs, Charles L. 1996. Introduction to *Disorderly Discourse: Narrative, Conflict, and Inequality,* edited by Charles L. Briggs, pp. 3–40. Oxford: Oxford University Press.

Briggs, Charles L., and Richard Bauman. 1992. "Genre, Intertextuality, and Social Power." *Journal of Linguistic Anthropology* 2, no. 2:131–172.

Buckingham, H. W. 1949. Collection of Marshallese Legends: Told by Lokrap, Ebon. Transcript. Kwajalein, Marshall Islands.

Burke, Kenneth. 1941. *The Philosophy of Literary Form: Studies in Symbolic Action.* Baton Rouge: Louisiana State University Press.

Carucci, Laurence Marshall. 1986. "Sly Moves: Ritual Movements in Marshallese Culture." *Semiotica* 62, nos. 1–2:165–77.

———. 1988. "Small Fish in a Big Sea: Geographical Dispersion and Sociopolitical Centralization in the Marshall Islands." In *State and Society: The Emergence and Development of Social Hierarchy and Political Centralization,* edited by J. Gledhill, B. Bender, and M. T. Larsen, pp. 33–42. London: Unwin Hyman.

———. 1989. "The Source of the Force in Marshallese Cosmology." In *The Pacific Theater: Island Representations of WWII,* edited by Geoffrey M. White and Lamont Lindstrom, pp. 73–96. Honolulu: University of Hawai'i Press.

———. 1997a. *Nuclear Nativity: Rituals of Renewal and Empowerment in the Marshall Islands.* Dekalb: Northern Illinois University Press.

———. 1997b. "Irooj Ro Ad: Measures of Chiefly Ideology and Practice in the Marshall Islands." In *Chiefs Today: Traditional Pacific Leadership and the Postcolonial State,* edited by Geoffrey M. White and Lamont Lindstrom, pp. 197–210. Palo Alto, CA: Stanford University Press.

———. 2004. "The Transformation of Person and Place on Enewetak and Ujelang Atolls." In *Globalization and Culture Change in the Pacific Islands,* edited by Victoria S. Lockwood, pp. 414–438. Upper Saddle River, NJ: Pearson and Prentice Hall.

———. 2019. "Friends in the Making: The Contextual Framing of Jerā-Relationships among Marshall Islanders." *Pacific Studies* 42, no. 3:139–167.

Cashman, Ray. 2016. *Packy Jim: Folklore and Worldview on the Irish Border.* Madison: University of Wisconsin Press.

Chambers, Keith. 1969. *A Preliminary Collection and Study of Marshallese Folklore.* Unpublished manuscript. Honolulu: University of Hawai'i.

———. 1972. "Tale Traditions of Eastern Micronesia: A Comparative Study of Marshallese, Gilbertese, and Nauruan Folk Narrative." MA thesis, University of California, Berkeley.

Clifford, James. 1983. "On Ethnographic Authority." *Representations* 2:118–146.

Clifford, James, and George E. Marcus, eds. 1986. *Writing Culture: The Poetics and Politics of Ethnography.* Berkeley: University of California Press.

Crapanzano, Vincent. 1980. *Tuhami: Portrait of a Moroccan.* Chicago: University of Chicago Press.

Cruikshank, Julie. 1998. *The Social Life of Stories: Narrative and Knowledge in the Yukon Territory.* Vancouver: University of British Columbia Press.

Cummins, Tom. 1984. "Kinshape: The Design of the Hawaiian Feather Cloak." *Art History* 7, no. 1:1–20.

Davenport, William H. 1952a. Popular Sayings and Tales of the Marshallese. Typescript. Honolulu: University of Hawai'i.

———. 1952b. "Fourteen Marshallese Riddles." *Journal of American Folklore* 65, no. 257:265–266.

———. 1953. "Marshallese Folklore Types." *Journal of American Folklore* 66, no. 261:221–230.

Dégh, Linda. 1969 *Folktales and Society: Story-Telling in a Hungarian Peasant Community,* translated by Emily M. Schossberger. Bloomington: Indiana University Press.

Dening, Greg. 2004. *Beach Crossings: Voyaging across Times, Cultures, and Self.* Philadelphia: University of Pennsylvania Press.

Diaz, Vincente M. 1993. "Pious Sites: Chamorro Culture between Spanish Catholicism and American Liberal Individualism." In *Cultures of United States Imperialism,* edited by Amy Kaplan and Donald E. Pease, pp. 218–252. Cambridge: Cambridge University Press.

———. 2010. *Repositioning the Missionary: Rewriting the Histories of Colonialism, Native Catholicism, and Indigeneity in Guam.* Honolulu: University of Hawai'i Press.

Dixon, Roland B. (1916) 2008. *Oceanic Mythology.* Charleston, SC: BiblioBazaar.

Dobbin, Jay. 2011. *Summoning the Powers Beyond: Traditional Religions in Micronesia.* Honolulu: University of Hawai'i Press.

Dorst, John D. 1983. "Neck-Riddle as a Dialogue of Genres: Applying Bakhtin's Genre Theory." *Journal of American Folklore* 96, no. 382:413–433.

Douglas, Mary. 1966. *Purity and Danger: An Analysis of the Concepts of Pollution and Taboo.* London: Ark Paperbacks.

———. 1975. "Jokes." In *Implicit Meanings: Essays in Anthropology,* pp. 90–116. London: Routledge and Kegan Paul.

Dowell, Jenny. 1988. "The Nuclear Pacific: An Interview with Patrick Flanagan." *Monthly Review* 39, no. 8:26.

Downing, Jane. 2003. *The Trickster.* Canberra: Pandanus Books.

Downing, Jane, Dirk H. R. Spennemann, and Margaret Bennett, eds. 1992. *Bwebwenatoon Etto: A Collection of Marshallese Legends and Traditions.* Majuro: Ministry of Internal Affairs and Historic Preservation Office.

Dundes, Alan. 1975. "Structural Typology in North American Indian Folktales." In *Analytical Essays in Folklore,* pp. 73–79. The Hague: Mouton.

Dvorak, Greg. 2018. *Coral and Concrete: Remembering Kwajalein Atoll between Japan, America and the Marshall Islands.* Honolulu: University of Hawai'i Press.

Dwyer, Kevin. 1979. "The Dialogic of Ethnography." *Dialectical Anthropology* 4, no. 3:205–224.

Dye, Tom, ed. 1987. *Marshall Islands Archaeology.* Honolulu: Bishop Museum Press.

Eco, Umberto. 1976. *A Theory of Semiotics.* Bloomington: Indiana University Press.

Edmond, Rod. 1997. *Representing the South Pacific: Colonial Discourse from Cook to Gauguin.* Cambridge: Cambridge University Press.

Engelke, Matthew, and Matt Tomlinson. 2006. *The Limits of Meaning: Case Studies in the Anthropology of Christianity.* New York: Berghahn Books.

Erdland, August. 1914. *Die Marshall-Insulaner: Leben und Sitte, Sinn und Religion eines Südseevolkes.* Münster: Anthropos Bibliothek.

Evers, Larry, and Barre Toelken, eds. 2001. *Native American Oral Traditions: Collaboration and Interpretation.* Logan: Utah State University Press.

Fabian, Johannes. 1994. "Ethnographic Objectivity Revisited: From Rigor to Vigor." In *Rethinking Objectivity,* edited by Allan Megill, pp. 81–108. Durham, NC: Duke University Press.

Falgout, Suzanne, Lin Poyer, and Laurence M. Carucci. 2008. *Memories of War: Micronesians in the Pacific War.* Honolulu: University of Hawai'i Press.

Finnegan, Ruth, and Margaret Orbell, eds. 1995. *South Pacific Oral Traditions.* Bloomington: Indiana University Press.

Flood, Bo, Beret E. Strong, and William Flood. 2002. *Micronesian Legends.* Honolulu: Bess Press.

Frank, Arthur W. 2010. *Letting Stories Breathe: A Socio-Narratology.* Chicago: University of Chicago Press.

Frazer, Sir James George. 1922. *The Golden Bough: A Study of Magic and Religion.* New York: Macmillan Company.

Gerrard, Michael B. 2014. "A Pacific Isle, Radioactive and Forgotten," Op-ed, *New York Times,* December 3, 2014.

Glassie, Henry. 2010. *Prince Twins Seven-Seven: His Art, His Life, His Exile in America.* Bloomington: Indiana University Press.

Goffman, Erving. 1959. *The Presentation of Self in Everyday Life.* New York: Anchor Books, Doubleday.

Goldman, L. R. and C. Ballard, eds. 1998. *Fluid Ontologies: Myth, Ritual and Philosophy in the Highlands of Papua New Guinea.* Westport, CT: Bergen & Garvey.

Goldsmith, Michael. 2000. "On Not Knowing One's Place." In *Ethnographic Artifacts: Challenges to a Reflexive Anthropology,* edited by Sjoerd R. Jaarsma and Marta A. Rohatynskyj, pp. 43–60. Honolulu: University of Hawai'i Press.

Goldstein, Diane E. 2021. "Unfinished Stories: Problematizing Narrative Completion." *Journal of American Folklore* 134, no. 532:137–146.

Grey, Eve. 1951. *Legends of Micronesia,* 2 vols. Honolulu: Department of Education, Trust Territory of the Pacific Islands.

Hansen, William. 2002. "Meanings and Boundaries: Reflections on Thompson's 'Myth and Fairytale.'" In *Myth: A New Symposium,* edited by Gregory Schrempp and William Hansen, pp. 19–28. Bloomington: Indiana University Press.

Harris-Lopez, Trudier. 2003. "Genre." In *Eight Words for the Study of Expressive Culture,* edited by Burt Feintuch, pp. 99–120. Urbana: University of Illinois Press.

Hau'ofa, Epeli. 1993. "Our Sea of Islands." In *A New Oceania: Rediscovering our Sea of Islands,* edited by Eric Waddell, Vijay Naidu, and Epeli Hau'ofa, pp. 2–16. Suva: School of Social and Economic Development, University of the South Pacific.

———. 2008. *We Are the Ocean: Selected Works.* Honolulu: University of Hawai'i Press.

Heffernan, Thomas Farel. 2002. *Mutiny on the Globe: The Fatal Voyage of Samuel Comstock.* New York: W. W. Norton and Company.

Heim, Otto. 2017. "Island Logic and the Decolonization of the Pacific." *Interventions* 19, no. 7:914–929.

Heine, Carl. 1974. *Micronesia at the Crossroads: A Reappraisal of the Micronesian Political Dilemma.* Honolulu: University Press of Hawai'i.

Helu, 'I. F. 1999a. *Critical Essays: Cultural Perspectives from the South Seas.* Canberra: Journal of Pacific History.

———. 1999b. "South Pacific Mythology." In *Voyages and Beaches: Pacific Encounters, 1769–1840,* edited by Alex Calder, Jonathan Lamb, and Bridget Orr, pp. 45–54. Honolulu: University of Hawai'i Press.

Hermann, Elfriede, ed. 2011. *Changing Contexts, Shifting Meanings: Transformation of Cultural Traditions in Oceania.* Honolulu: University of Hawai'i Press.

Hess, Jim. 2004. "Wave and Reflection: Charting Marshallese Participation in Globalizing Processes." In *Globalization and Culture Change in the Pacific Islands,* edited by Victoria S. Lockwood, pp. 182–99. Upper Saddle River, NJ: Pearson and Prentice Hall.

Hezel, Francis X., S.J. 1983. *The First Taint of Civilization: A History of the Caroline and Marshall Islands in Pre-colonial Days, 1521–1885.* Honolulu: University of Hawai'i Press.

———. 1995. *Strangers in Their Own Land: A Century of Colonial Rule in the Caroline and Marshall Islands.* Honolulu: University of Hawai'i Press.

———. 2001. *The New Shape of Old Cultures: A Half Century of Social Change in Micronesia.* Honolulu: University of Hawai'i Press.

———. 2013. *Making Sense of Micronesia: The Logic of Pacific Island Culture.* Honolulu: University of Hawai'i Press.

Hill, Jonathan D. 2002. "'Made from Bone': Trickster Myths, Musicality, and Social Construction of History in the Venezuelan Amazon." In *Myth: A New Symposium,* edited by Gregory Schrempp and William Hansen, pp. 72–88. Bloomington: Indiana University Press.

Huntsman, Judith. 1995. "Fiction, Fact, and Imagination: A Tokelau Narrative." In *South Pacific Oral Traditions,* edited by Ruth Finnegan and Margaret Orbell, pp. 124–160. Bloomington: Indiana University Press.

Hyde, Lewis. 1998. *Trickster Makes This World: Mischief, Myth, Art.* New York: North Point Press.

Hymes, Dell H. 1975. "Breakthrough into Performance." In *Folklore: Performance and Communication,* edited by Dan Ben-Amos and Kenneth Goldstein, pp. 11–74. The Hague: Mouton.

Irwin, Geoffrey. 1992. *The Prehistoric Exploration and Colonisation of the Pacific.* Cambridge: Cambridge University Press.

Jakobson, Roman. 1960. "Closing Statement: Linguistics and Poetics." In *Style in Language,* edited by Thomas A. Sebeok, pp. 350–377. Cambridge, MA: MIT Press.

Jetñil-Kijiner, Kathy. 2017. *Iāp Jeltok: Poems from a Marshallese Daughter.* Tucson: University of Arizona Press.

Kabua, Amata. 1993. *Customary Titles and Inheritance Rights: A General Guideline in Brief.* Mājro.

Kaeppler, Adrienne L., and H. Arlo Nimmo, eds. 1976. *Directions in Pacific Traditional Literature: Essays in Honor of Katherine Luomala.* Honolulu: Bishop Museum Press.

Ka'ili, Tēvita O. 2017. *Marking Indigeneity: The Tongan Art of Sociospatial Relations.* Tucson: University of Arizona Press.

Ka'ili, Tēvita, 'Ōkusitino Māhina (Hūfanga), and Ping-Ann Addo. 2017. "Introduction: TĀ-VĀ (Time-Space): The Birth of an Indigenous Moana Theory." Special issue, *Pacific Studies* Tā-Vā (Time-Space) Theory of Reality 40, nos. 1/2:1–17.

Keju-Johnson, Darlene. 1987. "Ebeye, Marshall Islands." In *Pacific Women Speak,* edited by Women Working for a Nuclear-Free and Independent Pacific, pp. 6–10. Oxford: Green Line.

Kelin, Daniel A. H., II. 2003. *Marshall Islands Legends and Stories.* Honolulu: Bess Press.

———. 2013. *Future Adventures of the Great One.* CreateSpace Independent Publishing Platform.

Keown, Michelle. 2017. "Children of Israel: US Military Imperialism and Marshallese Migration in the Poetry of Kathy Jetñil-Kijiner." *Interventions* 19, no. 7:930–947.

———. 2018. "Waves of Destruction: Nuclear Imperialism and Anti-nuclear Protest in the Indigenous Literatures of the Pacific." *Journal of Postcolonial Writing* 54, no. 5:585–600.

Kirch, Patrick Vinton. 2000. "Micronesia: in the 'Sea of Islands.'" In *On the Road of the Winds: An Archaeological History of the Pacific Islands before European Contact,* pp. 150–183. Berkeley: University of California Press.

———. 2012. *A Shark Going Inland Is My Chief: The Island Civilization of Ancient Hawai'i.* Berkeley: University of California Press.

Kirtley, Bacil F. 1955. "A Motif Index of Polynesian, Micronesian, and Melanesian Folktales." PhD diss., Indiana University.

———. 1971. *A Motif-Index of Traditional Polynesian Narratives.* Honolulu: University of Hawai'i Press.

Kiste, Robert C. 1974. *The Bikinians: A Study of Forced Migration.* Menlo Park, CA: Cummings.

Knauft, Bruce M. 2002. *Critically Modern: Alternatives, Alterities, Anthropologies.* Bloomington: Indiana University Press.

Knight, Gerald. 1980. *Man This Reef.* Majuro: Micronitor News and Printing Company.

Kotzebue, Otto Von. 1821. *A Voyage of Discovery into the South Sea and Bearing's Straits . . . in the Years 1815–1818.* 3 vols. London: Longman and Brown.

———. 1830. *A New Voyage around the World in the Years 1823, 24, 25, 26.* 2 vols. London: Colburn and Bentley.

Kowata, Kinuko, Terry Mote, Donna K. Stone, and Bernice Joash. 1999. *Inoñ in Majōl: Marshallese Folktales.* Majuro: Alele Museum, Libraries, and National Archives.

Krämer, Augustin, and Hans Nevermann. 1938. *Ralik-Ratak (Marshall-Inseln),* edited by G. Thilenius. Ergebnisse der Südsee Expedition, 1908–1910. Hamburg: Friederichsen and De Gruyter (Esse, II, B. XI).

Kristeva, Julia. 1980. *Desire in Language,* translated by Leon S. Roudiez. New York: Colombia University Press.

LaBriola, Monica C. 2013. "Likiep Kapin Iep: Land, Power, and History on a Marshallese Atoll." PhD diss., University of Hawai'i at Manoa.

———. 2019. "Planting Islands: Marshall Islanders Shaping Land, Power, and History." *Journal of Pacific History* 54, no. 2:182–198.

Lawless, Elaine. 1993. *Holy Women, Wholly Women: Sharing Ministries through Life Stories and Reciprocal Ethnography.* Philadelphia: University of Pennsylvania Press.

Lawson, Stephanie. 2010. "'The Pacific Way' as Postcolonial Discourse: Towards and Reassessment." *Journal of Pacific History* 45, no. 3:297–314.

Lay, William, and Cyrus M. Hussey. 1828. *A Narrative of the Mutiny on Board the Ship Globe of Nantucket in the Pacific Ocean, Jan. 1824, and the Journal of Residence of*

Two Years on the Mulgrave Islands; with Observation on the Manners and Customs of the Inhabitants. New London: Facsimile Publishing.

Leach, Edmund. 1964. "Myth as Justification for Faction and Social Change." In *Political Systems of Highland Burma: A Study of Kachin Social Structure,* pp. 264–278. London: London School of Economics and Political Science.

Lessa, William A. 1961. *Tales from Ulithi Atoll: A Comparative Study in Oceanic Folklore.* Folklore Studies 13. Berkeley: University of California Press.

Lévi-Strauss, Claude. 1969. *The Raw and the Cooked: Introduction to a Science of Mythology,* vol. 1. Chicago: University of Chicago Press.

Māhina, ʻŌkusitino. 1999. "Myth and History." In *Voyages and Beaches: Pacific Encounters, 1769–1840,* edited by A. Calder, J. Lamb, and Bridget Orr, pp. 61–88. Honolulu: University of Hawaiʻi Press.

———. 2010 "Tā, Vā, and Moana: Temporality, Spatiality, and Indigeneity." *Pacific Studies* 33, nos. 2/3:168–202.

Malinowski, Bronislaw. 1926. *Myth in Primitive Psychology.* London: Kegan Paul.

Mannheim, Bruce, and Dennis Tedlock. 1995. Introduction to *The Dialogic Emergence of Culture,* edited by Dennis Tedlock and Bruce Mannheim, pp. 1–32. Urbana: University of Illinois Press.

Marcus, George E. 1989. "Chieftainship." In *Developments in Polynesian Ethnology,* edited by Alan Howard and Robert Borofsky, pp. 175–209. Honolulu: University of Hawaiʻi Press.

———. 1998. *Ethnography through Thick and Thin.* Princeton, NJ: Princeton University Press.

Marcus, George E., and Michael M. J. Fischer. 1986. *Anthropology as Cultural Critique: An Experimental Moment in the Human Sciences.* Chicago: University of Chicago Press.

Mason, Leonard E. 1947. "The Economic Organization of the Marshall Islands." Vol. 9 of US Commercial Company Report on Economic Survey of Micronesia. Library of Congress, Washington, DC.

———. 1986. "Land Right and Title Succession in the Rālik Chain." UH-Manoa Archives, file—box 12, folder: 5, manuscript Poo061.

McArthur, Phillip H. 1995. "The Social Life of Narrative: Marshall Islands." PhD diss., Indiana University.

———. 2000. "Narrating to the Center of Power in the Marshall Islands." In *We Are a People: Narrative and Multiplicity in Constructing Ethnic Identity,* edited by Paul Spickard and W. Jeffery Burroughs, pp. 85–97. Philadelphia: Temple University Press.

———. 2004. "Narrative, Cosmos, and Nation: Intertextuality and Power in the Marshall Islands." *Journal of American Folklore* 117, no. 463:55–80.

———. 2008. "Ambivalent Fantasies: Local Prehistories and Global Dramas in the Marshall Islands." *Journal of Folklore Research* 45, no. 3:263–298.

———. 2012. "Oceania." In *A Companion to Folklore,* edited by Regina F. Bendix and Galit Hasan-Rokem, pp. 248–264. Oxford: Wiley-Blackwell.

———. 2023. "The Church in the Marshall Islands: A Cultural History." In *Battle Grounds to Temple Grounds: Latter-Day Saints in Guam and Micronesia,* edited by R. Devan

Jensen and Rosalind Meno Ram, pp. 71–104. Provo, UT: Religious Studies Center, Brigham Young University.

McDowell, John H. 2011. "Customizing Myth: The Personal in the Public." In *The Individual and Tradition: Folkloristic Perspectives,* edited by Ray Cashman, Tom Mould, and Pravina Shukla, pp. 323–342. Bloomington: Indiana University Press.

Meyer, Manulani A. 1998. *Native Hawaiian Epistemology: Exploring Hawaiian Views of Knowledge.* Cambridge, MA: Cultural Survival.

———. 2013. "Holographic Epistemology: Native Common Sense." *China Media Research* 9, no. 2:94–101.

Mitchell, Roger E. 1973. *Micronesian Folktales.* Nagoya: Asian Folklore Institute.

Narayan, Kirin. 1989. *Storytellers, Saints, and Scoundrels: Folk Narrative in Hindu Religious Teaching.* Philadelphia: University of Pennsylvania Press.

Niedenthal, Jack. 2001. *"For the Good of Mankind": A History of the People of Bikini and Their Islands.* Majuro: Bravo.

Noyes, Dorothy. 2003. "Group." In *Eight Words for the Study of Expressive Culture,* edited by Burt Feintuch, pp. 7–41. Urbana: University of Illinois Press.

———. 2016. *Humble Theory: Folklore's Grasp on Social Life.* Bloomington: Indiana University Press.

Nunn, Patrick D. 2004. "Fished Up or Thrown Down: The Geography of Pacific Island Origin Myths." *Annals of the Association of American Geographers* 93, no. 2:350–364.

Ochs, Elinor, and Lisa Capps. 2001. *Living Narrative: Creating Lives in Everyday Storytelling.* Cambridge, MA: Harvard University Press.

Ogden, Michael R. 1994. "MIRAB and the Republic of the Marshall Islands." *ISLA: Journal of Micronesian Studies* 2, no. 2:237–272.

Otero, Solimar, and Mintzi Auanda Martinez-Rivera. 2021. "Introduction: How Does Folklore Find Its Voice in the Twenty-First Century? An Offering/Invitation from the Margins." In *Theorizing Folklore from the Margins: Critical and Ethical Approaches,* edited by Solimar Otero and Mintzi Auana Martinez-Rivera, pp. 3–21. Bloomington: Indiana University Press.

Paulding, Lieutenant Hiram. (1831) 1970. *Journal of the Cruise of the United States Schooner Dolphin among the Islands of the Pacific Ocean and a Visit to the Mulgrave Islands, In Pursuit of the Mutineers of the Whale Ship Globe.* Honolulu: University of Hawai'i Press.

Petersen, Glenn. 2009. *Traditional Micronesian Societies: Adaptation, Integration, and Political Organization.* Honolulu: University of Hawai'i Press.

Pollock, Nancy J. 1974. "Landholding on Namu Atoll, Marshall Islands." In *Land Tenure in Oceania,* edited by H. P. Lundsgaarde, pp. 100–129. Honolulu: University of Hawai'i Press.

———. 1976. "The Origin of Clans on Namu, Marshall Islands." In *Directions in Pacific Traditional Literature: Essays in Honor of Katharine Luomala,* edited by Adrienne L. Kaeppler and H. Arlo Nimmo, pp. 83–100. Honolulu: Bishop Museum Press.

Radcliffe-Brown, A. R. 1940. "On Joking Relationships." *Africa* 13, no. 3:195–210.

Radin, Paul. (1958) 1972. *The Trickster: A Study in American Indian Mythology.* New York: Schocken.

Rainbird, Paul. 2004. "Fluid Boundaries: Horizons of the Local, Colonial, and Disciplinary." In *The Archaeology of Micronesia*, pp. 7–69. Cambridge: Cambridge University Press.

Ramstad, Mette. 2003. *Conversion in the Pacific: Eastern Polynesian Latter-day Saints' Conversion Accounts and Their Development of a LDS Identity.* Kristiansand: Høyskoleforlaget Norwegian Academic Press.

Riesenberg, S. H. 1965. "Table of Voyages Affecting Micronesian Islands." *Oceania* 36, no. 2:155–170.

Robbins, Joel. 2004. *Becoming Sinners: Christianity and Moral Torment in a Papua New Guinea Society.* Berkeley: University of California Press.

Rohatynskyj, Marta A., and Sjoerd R. Jaarsma. 2000. Introduction to *Ethnographic Artifacts: Challenges to a Reflexive Anthropology,* edited by Sjoerd Jaarsma and Marta A. Rohatynskyj, pp. 1–17. Honolulu: University of Hawai'i Press.

Rosaldo, Renato. 1989. *Culture and Truth: The Remaking of Social Analysis.* Boston: Beacon Press.

Rudiak-Gould, Peter. 2010. "Being Marshallese and Christian: A Case of Multiple Identities and Contradictory Beliefs." *Culture and Religion* 11, no. 1:69–87.

Sacks, Harvey. 1992. *Lectures on Conversations.* Vols. 1 and 2, edited by Gail Jefferson. Oxford, UK: Blackwell.

Sahlins, Marshall. 1985. *Islands of History.* Chicago: University of Chicago Press.

Sawin, Patricia. 2004. *Listening for a Life: A Dialogic Ethnography of Bessie Eldreth through Her Songs and Stories.* Logan: Utah State University Press.

Scanlon, Emma, and Janet Wilson. 2018. "Pacific Waves: Reverberations from Oceania." *Journal of Postcolonial Writing* 54, no. 5:577–584.

Scheub, Harold. 2012. *Trickster and Hero: Two Characters in the Oral and Written Traditions of the World.* Madison: University of Wisconsin Press.

Schrempp, Gregory. 1992. *Magical Arrows: The Maori, The Greeks, and the Folklore of the Universe.* Madison: University of Wisconsin Press.

———. 2002. Introduction to *Myth: A New Symposium,* edited by Greggory Schrempp and William Hansen, pp. 1–55. Bloomington: Indiana University Press.

Schrempp, Gregory, and William Hansen, eds. 2002. *Myth: A New Symposium.* Bloomington: Indiana University Press.

Scott, James C. 1985. *Weapons of the Weak: Everyday Forms of Peasant Resistance.* New Haven, CT: Yale University Press.

Shami, Seteney. 2001. "Prehistories of Globalization: Circassian Identity in Motion." In *Globalization,* edited by Arjun Appadurai, pp. 220–50. Durham, NC: Duke University Press.

Shuman, Amy. 2005. *Other People's Stories: Entitlement Claims and the Critique of Empathy.* Champaign: University of Illinois Press.

Siikala, Anna-Leena, and Jukka Siikala. 2005. *Return to Culture: Oral Tradition and Society in the Southern Cook Islands,* No. 287. Helsinki: Suomalainen Tiedeakatemia Academia Scientiarum Fennica.

Smith-Norris, Martha. 2016. *Domination and Resistance: The United States and the Marshall Islands during the Cold War.* Honolulu: University of Hawai'i Press.

Spennemann, Dirk H. R. 1993. *Ennaanin Etto: A Collection of Essays on the Marshallese Past*. Majuro: Historic Preservation Office, Republic of the Marshall Islands.

Spoehr, Alexander. 1949. "Majuro: A Village in the Marshall Islands." *Fieldiana Anthropology*, vol. 39. Chicago: Chicago Natural History Museum.

Stoeltje, Beverly. 1988. "Gender Representations in Performance." *Journal of Folklore Research* 25, no. 3:219–241.

———. 2014. "Carnival and Festival." In *Encyclopedia of Humor Studies*, vol. 1, edited by Salvatore Attardo. pp. 105–109. Thousand Oaks, CA: Sage.

Stoeltje, Beverly, and Richard Bauman. 1989. "Community Festival and the Enactment of Modernity." In *The Old Traditional Way of Life: Essays in Honor of Warren E. Roberts*, edited by Robert E. Walls and George H. Schoemaker, pp. 159–171. Bloomington: Trickster Press.

Stone, Donna K., Kinuko Kowata, and Bernice Joash. 2000. *Jabōnkōnnaan in M̧ajel̗— Wisdom of the Past: A Collection of Marshallese Proverbs, Wise Sayings and Beliefs*. Majuro: Alele Museum, National Archives.

Taafaki, Irene J., Maria Kabua Fowler, and Randolph R. Thaman. 2006. *Traditional Medicine of the Marshall Islands: The Women, the Plants, the Treatments*. Suva: IPS Publications, University of the South Pacific.

Taafaki, Irene J., and Maria Kabua Fowler. 2019. *Clothing Mats of the Marshall Islands: The History, the Culture, and the Weavers*. Self-published.

Tanner, Ron. 2008. *Marshall Islands Story Project*. Majuro: Historic Preservation Office, Republic of the Marshall Islands.

Tedlock, Dennis. 1995. "Interpretation, Participation, and the Role of Narrative in Dialogical Anthropology." In *The Dialogic Emergence of Culture*, edited by Dennis Tedlock and Bruce Mannheim, pp. 253–287. Urbana: University of Illinois Press.

Teaiwa, Teresia. 1999. "Reading Paul Gauguin's *Noa Noa* with Epeli Hauʻofa's *Kisses of the Nederends*: Militourism, Feminism, and the 'Polynesian' Body." In *Inside Out: Literature, Cultural Politics, and Identity in the New Pacific*, edited by Vilsoni Hereniko and Rob Wilson, pp. 249–263. Lanham, MD: Rowan and Littlefield.

———. 2008 "Globalizing and Gendered Forces: The Contemporary Militarization of Pacific/Oceania." In *Gender and Globalization in Asia and the Pacific*, edited by Kathy E. Ferguson and Monique Mironesco, pp. 318–332. Honolulu: University of Hawaiʻi Press.

Tengan, Ty Kāwika. 2001. "Reclaiming Space for an Indigenous Anthropology: Some Notes from Social Science Building 345." *Public Anthropology: The Graduate Journal*. Honolulu: University of Hawaiʻi at Manoa.

Tengan, Ty Kāwika, Tēvita O. Kaʻili, and Rochelle Fonoti. 2010. "Genealogies: Articulating Indigenous Anthropology in/of Oceania." *Pacific Studies* 33, nos. 2/3:139–167.

Thompson, Tok, and Gregory Schrempp. 2020. *The Truth of Myth: World Mythology in Theory and Everyday Life*. Oxford: Oxford University Press.

Titon, Jeff Todd. 2003. "Text." In *Eight Words for the Study of Expressive Culture*, edited by Burt Feintuch. Champaign: University of Illinois Press.

Tobin, Jack. 1967. "The Resettlement of Enewetak People: A Study of a Displaced Community in the Marshall Islands." PhD diss., University of California, Berkeley.

———. 2002. *Stories from the Marshall Islands.* Honolulu: University of Hawai'i Press.

Toelken, Barre. 2002. "Native American Reassessment and Reinterpretation of Myths." In *Myth: A New Symposium,* edited by Greggory Schrempp and William Hansen, pp. 89–103. Bloomington: Indiana University Press.

———. 2003. *The Anguish of Snails: Native American Folklore in the West.* Logan: Utah State University Press.

Trask, Haunani-Kay. 2000. "Natives and Anthropologists: The Colonial Struggle." In *Voyaging the Contemporary Pacific,* edited by David Hanlon and Geoffrey M. White, pp. 255–263. New York: Rowan and Littlefield.

Tuhiwai Smith, Linda 2012. *Decolonizing Methodologies: Research and Indigenous Peoples.* London: Zed Books.

Turner, Victor. 1967. "Betwixt and Between: The Liminal Period in Rites-of-Passage." In *Forest of Symbols,* pp. 93–111. Ithaca, NY: Cornell University Press.

———. 1982. "Social Dramas and Stories about Them." In *From Ritual to Theater: The Human Seriousness of Play,* pp. 61–88. New York: PAJ.

Vaai, Upolu Lumā, and Aisake Casimira. 2017. *Relational Hermeneutics: Decolonising the Mindset and the Pacific Itulagi.* Suva: University of the South Pacific and The Pacific Theological College.

Van Gennep, Arnold. 1960. *The Rites of Passage.* Chicago: University of Chicago Press.

Von Sydow, Carl Wilhelm. 1948. *Selected Papers on Folklore.* Copenhagen: Rosenkilde and Bagger.

Walsh, Julie. 2003. "Imagining the Marshalls: Chiefs, Tradition, and the State on the Fringes of United States Empire." PhD diss., University of Hawai'i at Manoa.

Walsh, Julie, and Hilda Heine. 2012. *Etto Ñan Raan Kein: A Marshall Islands History.* Honolulu: Bess Press.

Weisgall, Jonathan. 1994. *Operation Crossroads: The Atomic Tests at Bikini Atoll.* Annapolis, MD: Naval Institute Press.

Wheelwright, Philip. 1965. "The Semantic Approach to Myth." In *Myth: A Symposium,* edited by Thomas A. Sebeok, pp. 154–168. Bloomington: Indiana University Press.

White, Geoffrey M., and Lamont Lindstrom, eds. 2009. *Chiefs Today: Traditional Pacific Leadership and the Postcolonial State.* Honolulu: East-West Center.

White, Geoffrey M., and Ty Kāwika Tengan. 2001. "Disappearing Worlds: Anthropology and Cultural Studies in Hawai'i and the Pacific." *Contemporary Pacific* 13, no. 2:381–416.

Willacy, Mark. 2017. "A Poison in Our Island." *ABC* (Australia), November 28, 2017.

Index

Note: Page numbers in **boldface** refer to illustrative matter.

Aelōñḷapḷap (Ailinglaplap) atoll, **24**, 91, 92, 95, 144, 153–155, 260n15, 262n2
Amata Kabua, 105, 107, 160, 163, 262n14
ambiguity, 13–16, 38–40, 61–64, 81, 100, 221
ambivalent analogies, 41–42, 68–77
American Board of Commissioners for Foreign Missions (ABCFM), 26, 262n6
Ānenkio (Wake Island), 88
Ānewetak (Enewetak) atoll, **24**, 28, 100, 259n31, 260n25, 264n7
Arṇo (Arno) atoll, **24**, 112, 174
atomic bomb testing, 6, 27–29, 72, 75, 104, 256n21, 257n22, 260n25
Aur atoll, **24**, 91, 146
authenticity, 17, 36, 89
author's positionality, 3–5, 17, 18

Bakhtin, Mikhail, 16, 17
Bauman, Richard, 256n9
bodily boundaries, 189–199
Bokak atoll, **24**, 88, 239–241, 247
breadfruit (*mā*), 47, 53, 128, 234, 258n25, 265n2; for canoe, 44; story about, 169–170
Briggs, Charles, 256n9
burial practices, 231–236; funeral (*kallib*), 227, 261n31; spread stones (*eoreak*) at grave (*lōb*), 227; wake (*ilomej*), 261n31. *See also* death

cannibalism, 175–179
Carucci, Laurence, 163, 190, 255n3 (prologue), 257n22, 259nn29–30, 259n12, 264n7

chief (*irooj*), 23, 98–99, 146, 163, 165, 260n23, 262n15; Americans as, 71–72, 100–114, 138; bow head before (*badikdik*), 258n27; chief analogous to mother, 101–102; distributes resources (*ajej*), 23, 25, 70, 101; female chief (*lerooj*), 98, 99, 260n23, 262n15; as fierce warrior (*lāj, rūttarinae*), 25, 71, 101; as frigate bird (*ak*), 258n26; as kind (*jouj*), 70–71, 101; nurse (*ninnin*) from mother and chiefs, 101, 105, 108, 215; receives tribute (*ekkan*), 23, 70, 101, 109; spiritual power of (*ao, an*), 101, 260n23; title (*laajrak*), 23
Christianity, 32, 89, 126, 151, 164–166, 181–182, 218–219, 264n6
Christian missionaries, 4, 26, 34–36, 164–165, 178–179, 262n10
Commoners (*kajoor ro*), 23, 101, 109, 163; as analogy for strength (*kajoor*), 70, 111, 215. *See also* chief
Compact of Free Association, 26, 75–76, 261n34
cosmology, 70, 78–79, 87–100, 255n2 (chap. 2), 259n6
cross-cousin (*riliki-*), 91, 99, 263n6

death (*mej*), 73–74, 91–92, 133–134; sign of (*aao*), 236–246; sign of trickster (*aao*), 248, 254, 261n2. *See also* burial practices
death magic, 164–186
death mythology, 223–231
deception (*m̧oṇ*), 11, 13–15, 31–33, 86, 256n7, 257n6; forms of, 86, 115–116, 145, 149,

164; hidden below the surface, 127–140; laughter at, 61–63; sex as, 181, 205–206, 212–213, 257n7, 263n10 (chap. 6). *See also* trickster stories

decolonizing methodologies, 3–6, 20–21, 25, 255n1 (prologue), 256n11; by riṂajeḷ, 6, 40, 88, 113, 165, 253–254

deep past (*etto*), 10, 66, 255n2 (chap. 1), 258nn22–23

deictics, 58–61

demons (*tiṃoṇ, mejenkwaad*), 165, 171, 174, 175–178, 256n13. *See also* death magic

dialogic ethnography, 16–22, 79–87, 115. *See also* ethnographic writing

dialogic riddling, 79–87

Diaz, Vincente, 40

diseases, 217–218, 264n18

divination (*bubu*), 27, 92, 96, 129, 133–134, 139, 146–149; with pandanus leaves (*bwe en*), 125; with pebbles (*boḷā*), 261n3; revelation by, 85, 115–116, 120–122, 126–127, 136–137, 163–164. *See also* magic

earth-oven (*uṃ*), 53–54, 57–58, 64, 70, 73, 215, 257n4; story about, 46–49

eel (*dāp*), 169, 178–182, 214–215, 239–243, 247

epistemology (*jeḷāḷọkjen*), 19, 65, 224, 258n24; epistemological holes, 11–16, 40; epistemologies, 9, 17, 29, 69, 181, 253–254; riṂajeḷ epistemologies, 6, 20, 40, 68, 113, 186, 224

Epjā (Ebeye) Island, 231, 256n8, 258n13

Epoon (Ebon) atoll, **24**, 26, 34–35, 92; story at, 192–193

Ep (Yap) Island, 88, 91–92, 146, 161, 226, 243–244, 259n9

Erdland, August, **93**, 224, 230, 235–236, 246, 247, 261n2

ethnographic writing, 8–10; dialogics of, 16–22; liminality and, 38–40

ethnopoetics, 42, 137, 257n1

fairy tale (*inoñ*), 11, 13, 66–68; concluding formula (*jiribinoñ*), 184; framing device (*kiriwatne*), 66

father (jemā-), 177–178, 214–215, 244, 259n14, 262n15, 260n23; story of, 153–160

fire (*kijeek*), 11, 14, 209, 255n6

food (*mōñā*), 45, 70, 100, 109, 197, 215, 244, 260n27; Americans sharing, 102–103; pandanus paste (*jāākun*), 44–45, 53; sharing of, 70, 101, 176; story about, 44–52, 127–132, 135–138, 193; story about banana, 167–171

Frazer, James, 152

genres, 56, 120, 122, 136–137, 257n9; blurred, 42, 53, 64–68

German administration, 26–27, 70, 101, 103, 109

gods (*anij*): demigods (*anij ran*), 75, 85, 160; genealogy of (*kadkad*), 90, 93–94; general, 66, 85, 132

Hauʻofa, Epeli, 18, 256n12

Hawaiʻi, 88, 102, 139

hide-and-seek game (*kūttiliekek*), 12, 14, 115, 116–126, 135, 164, 212–213. *See also* trickster stories

human soul (*an*), 101, 260n26

Ijjidik clan, 144, 145, 146–147, 149

incest (*kōpa*), 216, 219, 263n6; story about, 199–214

intelligence/smart (*mālōtlōt*); Americans as, 54, 72, 74, 85–87, 100; Letao as, 30, 32, 87, 98; Letao making Americans smart, 42, 52, 83–84

intertextuality, 17, 21, 64, 67, 96, 181, 235, 256n15; intertextual links, 76, 136, 138, 194, 206, 210, 231, 253

Iroojrālik, 91, 92, **94**, 230, 238, 244, 247, 261n6

Jālooj (Jaluit) atoll, **24**, 70, 264n20

Japanese occupation, 27, 33–34

Jebro, 70, 71, 92, **94**, 96, 190, 258n25, 261n6; as Lōjelañ, 261n6

Jemāluut, 53, 56, 63, 122, 125, 125; kinship of, 91, 92, **93–94**, 95, 96–98; stories about, 45–50, 118–120

Jetñil-Kijiner, Kathy, 19
Jineer ilo Kōbo, 92, **93**, 95, 101, 259n11
Jojej, 234–235
Ḷorukwōd, 166, 168, 174

Kajin Ṃajeḷ, 4, 5, 26, 55–61, 255n2
   (prologue), 259n11
Kijdik, 141, 147, 149, 260n18
Kikiao, 158–159, 161–163, 176, 263n13
kinship: adoption (*kaajiriri*), 99, 160–161,
   163; ancestors/elders (*rūtto*); of author,
   5–6, 38; commoner (*kajoor*), 23, 70, 109,
   111, 163, 260n23; established on
   kindness (*jouj*), 70–71, 101; lineage head
   (*aḷab*), 23, 98, 99; matriliny (*bwij, jowi*),
   23–25, 34, 140, 213, 214–216, 259n14,
   260n27, 264n15 (chap. 6); metaphors of
   basket (*iep jāltok, iep jeḷḷok*), 211;
   metaphors of canoe (*wa*), 148; patriliny
   (*bōtōktōk*), 25, 95, 99, 146, 176, 260nn22–
   23, 263n12; of power, 100–109;
   terminologies, 98–100, 122, 135, 259n14,
   263n15, 260n23; titles (*laajrak*), 23. *See
   also* cosmology; riṂajeḷ culture and
   society
Kiribati, 34, 35, 52, 67, 73, 138; story about,
   46–50, 129, 219, 257nn25–26
Kometo Albōt, **3**; on America, 102–109;
   cosmogony by, 87–88, 89, 90–92, **94**;
   death of, 1–2, 222, 248, 249, 254;
   decolonizing method of, 6, 18–19, 36, 65,
   149, 186, 219; description of, 1–2, 7, 89;
   last dialogue with, 1–3, 222, 249–254;
   matriline and patriline of, 34; meeting
   the author, 4–5; poetics of storytelling
   by, 56–65; as social trickster, 33–38;
   storytelling by, 4–6, 19–20, 22, 30, 113,
   153, 183, 185. *See also* Letao; trickster
   stories
Kramer, Augustin, **93**, 145, 224, 235
Kuwajleen (Kwajalein) atoll, 28–29, 72–73,
   104, 257n24
Kwajalein Missile Range, 28–29

Ḷajbwinām̧ōņ, 91–92, **93–94**, 225–231, 238,
   240–244

Ḷakam̧, 92, **93**
Ḷakōm̧raan, 91, **93–94**
Ḷakūbwe, as name, 1, 98, 99, 252
Ḷamawūno, 169–172, 177–180, 181–184
land, power of, 109–114
land tenure system: house (*m̧weiō*) as
   metaphor for land tract, 111, 168; land
   tract (*wāto*), 23, 60, 111, 258n13;
   matrilineal lands (*kapijukunen*), 231;
   patrilineal lands (*ḷamoran*), 264n14
   (chap. 7); rooted in earth (*bwidej*), 70,
   101, 214
Lañinperan, **94**, 119–120, 121–122, 125,
   127–140
laughter, 4–7, 15–16, 61–65, 183, 189,
   209–210, 248
Lawullep (Wullep), **93**, 95, 238, 240–245,
   247, 261n6
Lāwūnpikaar, 237–244, 247
Letao, 29–31, **93–94**; American qualities
   and, 52, 54, 68–77, 86; author as friend
   of, 38–39; deception of, 116–126;
   departure from Marshall Islands
   narrative, 42–53; genealogy of, **93–94**,
   90–98; imperial violence and, 25–29;
   incest and libido of, 199–213; names of,
   133, 255n3 (prologue). *See also* Kometo
   Albōt; riṂajeḷ mythic narrative;
   trickster stories
Lewa (Ḷowa), 88, 91, 92, **93–94**
Ḷewōj and Laneej, 91, 92, **93–94**, 95, 226;
   story about, 127–133, 227–229, 238–241,
   253, 264n7
libido, 30, 199–217, 181
Lidepdepju, 91, 262n16
Lijenenbwe, 92, **94**, 96, 117, 122, 146–147;
   story about, 118–120, 127–132
Likiep atoll, **24**, 11, 256n19, 260n25
Limejo̧kdād, 92, **94**, 117, 231, 264n13
   (chap. 7); offspring of, 95–98
liminality, 30, 33, 38, 63, 187, 199, 213
Lino, **93**, 166, 169–173, 177, 182, 263n14
Liwātuonmour, 91, 146, 262n16
loincloth (*kaḷ*), 83–86, 106, 108, 264n13
   (chap. 6)
Ḷōm̧tal, 88, 92, **93**

Lōñtañūr, 88, 92, **94**, 96, 117, 259n15, 261n6
Ḷōrōk, 91, **93–94**, 128, 134, 137, 225, 230
Lucifer, 179–182, 216
Ḷukwōnwōd islet, 51–52, 224
lying (*riab*), 13, 14, 32, 61, 69, 73, 116

magic (*kkōpāl*), 25, 34, 124, 126, 134, 148,
    151–153; of death, 164–186; of political
    power, 153–164. *See also* divination
Mājeej Island, **24**, 228, 230
Mājro atoll, 1, 11, **24**, **43**, 70–71, 95; Mājro
    islet, 42, 45, 53
Ṃake, 11–16, 35, 102–106, 190–199, 218–219,
    231, 261n7
Malinowski, Bronislaw, 258n15, 263n15
Maḷoeḷap atoll, **24**, 11, 71, 255n4 (chap. 1)
Marshallese. *See* riṂajeḷ, as term
"Marshallese Folklore Types" (Davenport),
    66–68
Marshall Islands, overview, 22–29, 88, 262n9
    (chap. 4)
maternal nephew (*mañde-*), 134, 135,
    259n14, 263n15
maternal uncle (*wūllep-*), 133, 135, 259n14,
    263n15
matriclan (*jowi*), 23, 34, 95, 149–150, 176,
    256n17, 262n14; story of first, 140–144.
    See also kinship; matriliny
matrilineage (*bwij*), 23, 100–101, 140,
    260n27. *See also* kinship; matriliny
matriliny (*bwij, jowi*), 95–101, 135, 148, 161,
    231, 260nn22–24; brother speaks on
    behalf of (*ṃṃaan maroñroñ*), 99;
    genealogy (*menmenbwij*), 259n8. *See also*
    kinship
medicine (*wūno*), 165, 180; medicine of
    death, 179, 183; story about death
    medicine, 169–177
metaphors of sex: dance movement
    (*jibadbad*), 205; finding romance
    (*ṃṃōkadkad*), 213, 215; making fire
    (*kijeek*), 202, 209; male as earthworm/eel
    (*ṃṃaan ṃaj/ṃajkadāl*), 178–179, 215,
    242; woman as butterfly (*babbūb*), 200,
    203, 205, 207, 214; woman as earth
    (*bwidej*), 201, 214–215

metanarration, 14, 55, 57, 60, 122–123, 209
Mile (Mili) atoll, 1, 5, **24**, 26, 34, 35,
    224–226; story at, 50–52, 127–139
mischievous (*kakūtōtō*), 37, 74, 95, 192–193,
    220
Mormons, 4, 35–36, 188, 227
mother (*jine-*): logic of, 99–111, 211, 215–216,
    259n14, 260n17; story about, 96–98,
    127–132, 140–144, 153–160, 166–174,
    200–205, 262n16. *See also* matriliny
movies and television, 13, 15, 256n8
myth (*bwebwenato in etto*) defined, 53–56,
    65–68
mythic narrative. *See* riṂajeḷ mythic
    narrative

Ṇabubu islet, 141–142, 147
Ṇadikdik island, **24**, 52, 60, 224–227
Naṃdik (Namorik) atoll, **24**, 26, 166–167,
    174
Naṃo (Namu) atoll, **24**, 91–92, 96, 145–146;
    story at, 118–120, 127–132, 140–144
Nevermann, Hans, **93**, 145
Nitijelā, 112, 113, 125, 261n39
ṇoonniep, 134, 165, 174, 183, 261n7

ontology, 31, 32, 56, 67, 121, 185
Ororao, 127–135, 139, 261n6

patriliny (*bōtōktōk*). *See* kinship
pejwak, 240, 242, 243–245, 246
philology, defined, 87
Pikaar (Bikar) atoll, **24**, 88, 239
Pikinni (Bikini) atoll, **24**, 28
poetic devices, 42, 56–65
power (*kajoor*): author's positionality and,
    17–21; kinship of, 100–109; Kometo's
    storytelling on, 30, 37; of land, 109–114;
    magic of political, 153–164; riṂajeḷ
    social, 133–150
profane (*ttoon*), 5, 15, 67, 188, 200, 210, 212,
    263n1. *See also* sacred and profane
prophecy (*kanaan*), 223, 233, 264n2

Rālik and Ratak, 93, 153, 155, 162–163,
    262n16; dialects of, 34, 256n16, 259n14,

261n5; Rālik Islands (chain), 22, 27, **93**, 146, 262n14; Ratak Islands (chain), 22, 34, **93**, 146, 230, 241, 263n14; story at, 129, 153–160, 237–240

reported speech, 31, 57–59, 62, 106–107, 122, 136, 183, 208

riddling (*lōñña*), 79–87

riM̧ajeļ, as term, 255n1 (prologue)

riM̧ajeļ culture and society, 23–25, 100–109, 133–150; breadfruit festival (*m̧am̧a*), 258n25, 265n22; celebration (*kam̧ōļo*), 190; first fruits harvest (*akeo̧*); fishing technique (*aļeļe*). *See also* kinship

riM̧ajeļ cosmogony, 89–100

riM̧ajeļ mythic narrative (*bwebwenato in etto*), 8–10, 56, 66–67, 75, 89–100, 166. *See also* Letao; riM̧ajeļ storytelling; trickster stories

riM̧ajeļ storytelling, 1–2, 4, 22, 31, 32, 53, 116; through dialogic riddling, 79–87; genres labels in, 65–68; poetic devices in, 55–65. *See also* Kometo Albōt

Roñeļap (Rongelap) atoll, **24**, 28

sacred (*kkwōjarjar*), 62, 66–68, 188, 213, 258n22, 263n1; chief as, 23, 25, 70, 132, 163, 165. *See also* sacred and profane

sacred and profane, 67, 206, 219, 221; margins of, 187–189. *See also* profane; sacred

sailing canoe (*waļap*), 23, 135, 262n8 (chap. 4); anchor rope (*kōm̧n̄ur*), 130–131; small house on (*bo̧tōk*), 129, 135

Sawin, Patricia, 16, 17

sensibilities, 3, 9, 19, 69, 255n2 (chap. 1); Christian, 36, 176, 186, 188, 206, 226; indigenous, 42, 68–77, 100, 108, 151–152, 165, 250, 258n24

shape-shifting, 14, 30, 71, 121

sibling/parallel cousin (*jei-*), 98, 99–100, 122, 146, 161, 263n2; of gods, 91, 93–94, 118, 130, 230; of Letao, 95, 96–98; oldest (*utm̧aan*), 99; story of, 166–174, 215

sign of death, halo (*aao*), 133, 237–247, 261n2, 265n24. *See also* Letao

spirits (*jetōb*), 165, 224, 227, 264n3

Smith, Linda Tuhiwai, 18, 256n11

sorcery (*anijnij*), 25, 91, 124, 165, 227; cast a spell (*kko̧o̧l*), 162

stick charts (e.g. *wapepe*), 23, 237, 265n16

storytelling (*bwebwenato*). *See* riM̧ajeļ storytelling

subversion, 15, 41, 61–62, 73, 74, 98–99, 113, 235. *See also* trickster stories

Tedlock, Dennis, 16, 254

Teļap islet, 4, 11, 42, **43**, 46, 96, 127

tense, as poetic device, 56–57

time, as poetic device, 56–57

Tobin, Jack, 92, **93**, 137–138, 224, 226, 255n3 (prologue), 257n25, 261n3

trickster stories, 115; breaching the bodily boundaries in, 189–199; as decolonizing method, 6; diseases in, 217–218; on divination, 116–126; drunkenness in, 218–221; hidden below the surface, 127–140; on holes, 11–16; incest and trickster's libido in, 199–213; of magic, 151–153; between sacred and profane, 187–189; sexual dalliance in, 213–217; telltale signs in, 245–248. *See also* hide-and-seek game; Kometo Albōt; Letao; riM̧ajeļ mythic narrative

truth (*m̧o̧ol*), 13, 14, 32, 61, 69, 70, 73, 116

truthiness, 42, 56, 61, 64, 67, 76, 257n9

Tūm̧ur, 70, **94**

Turner, Victor, 198

United States: Compact of Free Association with, 26, 75–76, 261n34; invasion of Marshall Islands by, 28–29, 33–34, 257n24; Kometo and M̧ake on, 102–109; Letao and qualities of, 68–77, 78–79, 100; Letao's travels to, 52, 54, 68, 78; warfare and weaponry of, 28, 71–72

unmasking social difference, 140–150

Vandenberg Air Force Base, California, 28–29

veiling (*n̄n̄ooj*), 32, 33, 38, 115, 121–125, 133, 164, 211

venereal disease (*jeplej, mādke*), 217–218, 264n18
violence, 17, 19, 72, 76, 176, 218; imperial, 23, 25–29, 114, 257n24. *See also* power
Wōja islet, 153
World War II, 1, 26, 28, 35, 72, 106, 225, 260n30
Wōtto (Wotho) atoll, **24**, 88

About the Author

Phillip H. McArthur is Professor of Anthropology and Cultural Sustainability, Integrated Humanities, and Affiliated Faculty of History and Pacific Studies at Brigham Young University Hawai‘i. He has authored publications on Marshall Island mythology, folklore, cosmology, performance, epistemologies, and social power. He served for many years as editor of the journal *Pacific Studies* and is the editor-in-chief for the Jonathan Napela Center for Hawaiian and Pacific Studies Publications.